Bhagavad Gita, Hereafter, a

C000115625

With references to:

The Bhagavad Gita (Hindu Scripture—translation by Hari Patel. Available at Amazon.com)

The Bible (Christian Scripture—New King James Version [NKJV])

The Wheel of Life and Death (a book about Buddhism)

Shri Guru Granth Sahib (Sikh Scripture—Khalsa Consensus translation)

Koran/Qur'an (Islamic Scripture)

--- Copyright ©2023, Hari Patel

ISBN: 9798865657521

--------- ৭৷------

Author's note:

Things in spiritual realms are often challenging to describe and often have no earthly terms to convey them. To overcome this problem, I have used standard worldly terms such as days, months, doors, courtyards, medals of honour, etc., to convey concepts outside the dimensions of time and space.

I was given a second chance in life. I have woven the knowledge I gained in the hereafter into story form.

These are my personal views. I grew up in East Africa (Kenya), where my Hindu parents taught me the *Bhagavad Gita* from age four. I started reading the Bible and the Koran when I was ten and twelve. There were no Christians around us. I spent many years with the Lord on my own. I came to the UK when I was eighteen and joined a church when I was twenty-three.

The Lord God is the author of the Bible, the *Bhagavad Gita*, and all the Holy Scriptures that carry the divine message "of a loving God and our duty to love God and one another".

Please ask Him to open your eyes and mind to see the wondrous things in the Lord's books and His creation.

The Bible states in Matthew 18:16 that *'Every word may be established by the mouth of two or three witnesses'*. Therefore, God also needed to confirm His message through several Holy Books.

God has revealed his purpose and intention for the creation and how He will fulfil them in various Holy Books. (In the Gita, Chapter 11. In the Bible, 2 Timothy 1:9 and Isaiah 11:6-7).

Let God's Spirit *(Atman)* show you from His words your inheritance in God's Kingdom. Ask yourself what God is trying to convey through the Scriptures. Fly on the wings of the eagle (of the Holy Spirit, or your liberated Atman) into the past, present, and future, if possible, beyond your imagination. You cannot do it alone, but God can, and He will confirm your visions with foreknowledge of events occurring on Earth.

I hope my book will promote a more compassionate world for humanity and all living things. I pray that all will work together to give our children and grandchildren a better future.

Hari Patel.

You can contact me at harxpatel@gmail.com

Part 1 Bhagavad Gita

Bhagavad Gita

Contents

Gita Glossary

Atman: Divine consciousness. Each person receives it at conception. It is also called 'the life-giving breath of God.'

Brahman: Supreme existence, or absolute reality in the Upanishads (Indian sacred writings), is the eternal, conscious, infinite, omnipresent spiritual core of the Universe. Nonetheless, *Gita* needs to give a clearer picture. We obtain more light on Brahman in the **Bible[1],** but it is controversial even there. Brahman also manifests to many Hindus as Lord Vishnu and Christians as Jesus Christ (the Messiah/the Word of God). A divine being who comes to Earth (as a person or in visions) to relieve oppression and restore righteousness.

Dharma: The law of duty that maintains the unity of creation. Dharma means righteousness, justice, goodness, and purpose rather than chance. The highest Dharma is Ahimsa: nonviolence and universal love for all living creatures. Every kind of violence violates Dharma, the fundamental law of duty that maintains the unity of creation and life.

Hinduism: A major world religion originating in the Indian sub-continent, comprising several philosophies, beliefs, and Ritual systems in India and Nepal and followed by a large population outside the subcontinent and has over 900 million adherents worldwide.

Karma: The web of cause and effect. It encourages us to contribute to life and the welfare of all rather than pursue selfish interests at the expense of others.

-------- ૐ------

*Bible. John 1:1-4. In the beginning was the **Word (Brahman)**, and the Word was with God, and the Word was God. He was in the beginning with God. All things were made through Him; without Him, nothing was made. In Him was life, and the life was the light of men. (1:10) He was in the world; the world was made through Him, and the world did not know Him.* ----

Kly-son Ability: A unique Spiritual ability to hear and see events happening in a distant place or access another person's past life and telepathically project it back into their mind. It is often experienced at extreme moments of trauma and described as 'seeing your life flash before your eyes.'

Krishna: Supreme Lord of the Universe to the Hindus.

Moksha: The spiritual liberation that is life's supreme goal.

Renunciation (sannyasa): Withdrawing from work and the family's everyday affairs to pursue a contemplative life as a Sadhu (ascetic holy man, monk).

Samadhi: A state where all the senses and emotions are controlled, and the spirit is free (Mukta).

Spirit: The duality of Atman and the soul is referred to as a person's spirit.

Soul: A person or animal's moral, emotional, and intellectual nature.

Gita Elaboration-Testimony A1 - J4 Based on the Author's own experience.

---------๛------

Bhagavad – Gita Prelude

The *Bhagavad Gita*, often called the *Gita*, is a 700-verse Hindu Scripture, part of the epic *Mahabharata* (Chapters 23–40), written around the second and third centuries BCE.

The Mahabharata is one of the two major Sanskrit epics poems of ancient India, the other being the Ramayana, which tells the story **of** a struggle for the throne of Kuru Kingdom, around 1000BCE, Northern India (capital Hastinapura), between two groups of cousins, the Kauravas and the Pandavas princes. Their Legal grandfather was King Vichitravirya.

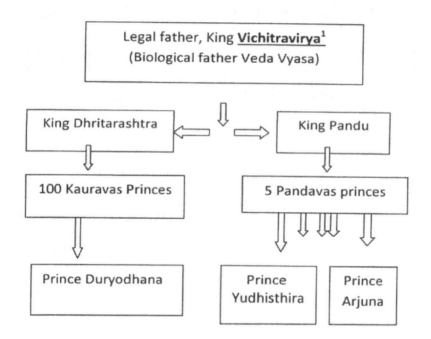

[1] **King Vichitravirya** was married to Ambalika and Ambika, the beautiful daughters of the king of Kashi. After seven years, Vichitravirya falls ill and dies childless. Subsequently, his half-brother Sage Veda Vyasa and Vichitravirya's wives, through a **Niyoga*** relationship, give birth to two children: Pandu (mother Ambalika), and Dhritarashtra born blind (mother Ambika).

*Niyoga (Sanskrit: नियोग) was an ancient Hindu practice. It permitted either the husband or the wife who had no child by their spouse to procreate a child with another man or a woman.

Prince Pandu inherited the Kuru kingdom but later handed it to his half-brother Dhritarashtra. His action resulted in a succession crisis in Hastinapura.

It also resulted in a rivalry between the children of King Pandu, the Pandavas princes, and blind King Dhritarashtra's children, the Kauravas princes. Duryodhana, the eldest of the Kauravas, is consumed by envy, anger, and hatred towards his cousins, the Pandavas, and these emotions ultimately lead to a devastating war.

The Bhagavad Gita is challenging to access, partly because its teaching is obscured by the ancient Sanskrit words and the context of a very different culture and time. It contains philosophical and devotional material on duty and responsibility, morality, wisdom, and the consequences of envy, greed, selfishness, and ambition.

Modern translations often need to unlock the spirit behind these ancient words. In His mercy, The Lord has given me wisdom that can be trusted. Hence, I share it with you by adding it to the *Gita* verses in italics as (*Gita Elaboration-Testimony A1-J4)*, thereby unlocking the spirit behind the Scriptures.

The *Bhagavad Gita*, or *The Song of The Lord*, was revealed by Lord Krishna to Arjuna as the epic war of Mahabharata was about to commence on the battlefield of Kurukshetra, North India, around 500–1100 BCE.

Dhritarashtra, a blind king ruling the Kuru Jangala kingdom, and his one hundred sons, known as the Kauravas, headed by Duryodhana, are at war with Pandu's five sons, known as the Pandavas, headed by Yudhisthira. Among the Pandavas, Yudhisthira's younger brother, Arjuna, was the most fearless warrior, a great archer, and their hero.

In a game of dice, the Kauravas, by treachery, won the Pandavas' share of land and kingdom. After winning the game, the Kauravas humiliated the Pandavas by disrobing Arjuna's wife in public view.

Then, the Kauravas sent the Pandavas into exile to the forest, imposing stringent conditions on them if they wanted to regain their share of the kingdom. After spending years in exile, the Pandavas fulfilled these conditions, but the Kauravas refused to return to the Pandavas' their land and kingdom.

A war between them became inevitable. Consequently, Pandu's five sons, headed by Yudhisthira, and Dhritarashtra's one hundred sons, led by Duryodhana, were facing each other with their armies on the battlefield.

Most kings who ruled the Indian subcontinent participated in this war, siding with one of these two warring groups.

Both armies wanted Lord Krishna's support. Krishna offered his entire army to one side and his physical and moral support, without taking up arms, to the other side. He asked them to choose.

Duryodhana was happy to receive Krishna's large army for his side. Arjuna, on behalf of the Pandavas, chose Krishna's physical and moral support, and Lord Krishna offered to be the charioteer for Arjuna.

Gita then traces Pandu's son Arjuna's ascent from fear, ignorance, lamentation, and confusion to love and compassion for all beings and creatures.

A detailed account of the reasons that led to such a destructive war is given in the section 'The Setting of the *Bhagavad Gita*' towards the end of the book.

Nonetheless, this book is about fighting the adversaries within us and unlocking the full potential of the divine love available to us. Earth is the best arena in the Universe for achieving this goal.

--------- ௭------

Chapter 1 – Bhagavad – Gita

The Divine Song of God

The first chapter begins with a dialogue between King Dhritarashtra and his minister, Sanjay. The blind King Dhritarashtra could not leave his palace in Hastinapur but was eager to know what was happening on the battlefield.

Sanjay was a disciple of Sage Ved Vyas, the author of the epic *Mahabharata* and several other Hindu Scriptures. Sanjay possessed a mystical ability *(Kly-son: A unique Spiritual ability)* to see and hear events occurring in distant places, having learnt this ability from Sage Vyas. Thus, he could see and listen to what transpired on the battleground of Kurukshetra and gave a first-hand account to King Dhritarashtra in his palace.

On the Battlefield of Kurukshetra, the Supreme Lord instructs Prince Arjuna to defend his family's claim to the throne as he is about to go into battle against his cousins.

Like Arjuna, we face daily battles within and outside ourselves. External conflict confronts us with the aspects of ourselves that we are least conscious of and least wish to recognise. In that sense, we are always on the Battlefield of Kurukshetra, the field of action; it can be turbulent and unpredictable, with sudden and unexpected changes in fortunes.

(Gita 6:5. The mind can be our enemy or friend.) The Pandava Army represents the mind that allows us our higher potential. The Kaurava Army represents the self-destructive mind.   --- ➤ ---

Battlefield of Kurukshetra and the Consequences of War

The Mystic Sanjaya recounts the Battlefield of Kurukshetra to the blind King Dhritarashtra.

Chapter 1:1. The old blind King Dhritarashtra, father of the Kauravas, said to his minister Sanjaya: My son Duryodhana and the sons of Pandu are arranged against each other with their armies for battle. They are in the holy fields of Kurukshetra, the place of pilgrimage. Sanjaya, what is happening?

The king's conscience was troubled. The king had said nothing about all the evil his sons had plotted against their cousins, the Pandavas. His sons had stolen their cousins' kingdom and ordered his guards to strip Arjuna's wife naked in public. Furthermore, the king knew that his son Duryodhana's hatred of Pandavas clouded his son's judgement. Nor had his sons made any effort to reason with the Pandavas when Prince Arjuna attempted to settle the matter peacefully. Now, the armies of the two cousins were arranged against each other.

1:2. The Supreme Lord has granted Sanjaya incredible spiritual power (Kly-Son ability) to see and hear what was happening on the battlefield. Sanjaya reports to the king: Your son Duryodhana analyses the forces opposing him and finds them more formidable than he had anticipated. He is alarmed and runs to his old archery teacher, Drona, perhaps because he lacks confidence and seeks guidance.

1:3. Sanjaya continues: Your son Duryodhana is annoyed at his teacher Drona and rebukes him for teaching his enemy Prince Arjuna the art of military leadership.

1:4-6. Your son is naming all the mighty commanders in Arjuna's army (who were Drona's former students). Your son says, 'These are mighty warriors you taught, and now they are my enemies. Look at what you have done.'

1:7-8. Now, your son is quoting the names and calibre of his commanders, almost to reassure himself. He puts the names of General Bhisma and Karna at the top.

1:9-10. Your son says that many heroic warriors are ready to lay down their lives for him. His words lack confidence, as though he is worried. He emphasises his army's strength and says that the formidable General Bhisma is on his side. Yet, his voice betrays a lack of confidence.

1:11. Your son orders his commanders to take their positions and protect General Bhisma.

Summoning the warriors to battle

1:12. Sanjaya continues with his report: I now see General Bhisma, the great guardian of the Kuru dynasty, blowing his war horn with all his might, summoning the warriors to battle, giving Duryodhana and his brothers joy.

1:13. All the warriors standing behind him are getting into military formation, ready to charge the enemy. There is a great sound of war drums and trumpets.

The opposition

1:14-15. On the other side, I see Lord Krishna and Arjuna standing on a glorious chariot drawn by white horses, blowing their war horns. Their opponent, the formidable General Bhīma, joins in and blows his horn, alerting his armies to prepare to charge.

1:16-18. King Yudhiṣṭhira (Head of the Pandavas army) blows his trumpet, and other commanders follow his example.

1:19. There is a tremendous amount of noise, like thunder. The great noise unnerves Duryodhana and his brothers (the Kauravas). Both sides claim to be fighting for the right cause.

Prince Arjuna views the battlefield

1:20. Prince Arjuna, the son of Pandu, seated in his chariot, now takes up his bow and prepares to fire his arrows. He hesitates as he sees his cousins drawn in military formation against him and turns to Lord Krishna.

1:21-22. **Arjuna** says: Sire, please drive my chariot between the two armies so that I may see those who desire to fight with me and those who oppose me.

1:23. I want to see those who have come here to fight and die on behalf of the evil-minded sons of King Dhritarashtra.

Both sides assess each other's warriors

1:24. Both sides watch as Lord Krishna draws up the fine chariot between the two armies.

1:25. **Lord Krishna,** facing Bhisma, Drona, and all the other chieftains of the land, said to Arjuna: Behold, all those assembled here.

1:26-27. Arjuna surveys the two sides. He is overwhelmed with sadness, compassion, and confusion. His family members, grandfathers, uncles, cousins, teachers, and friends are on both sides.

Prince Arjuna hesitates; he is overwhelmed with sadness and sorrow

1:28. **Arjuna** says: Lord Krishna, I see my friends and relatives on both sides ready to fight and die, and, suddenly, I am overwhelmed with sadness and sorrow.

1:29. My whole body is trembling, my mouth is dry, and my hair stands on end. My bow, Gandiva, has slipped from my hand, and my skin feels like it is burning.

1:30. I am unable to stand. I can hardly hold my bow. What is happening to me?

1:31. I see no good in killing my kin in this battle. Causing death and destruction is not how I want to be victorious and win back my kingdom.

1:32-35. What good is a kingdom or even life when all those on whose behalf we fight face each other on this battlefield? When my people, teachers, fathers, sons, and neighbours, on whose behalf I would gladly die, are standing against me? Why should I wish to kill them, even though they oppose me? It is wrong to gain a kingdom on Earth or Heaven this way. What pleasure will we derive from killing my cousins, the sons of Dhritarashtra?

1:36. Killing my kin would make us as evil as them. Therefore, it is not proper for us to kill the sons of Dhritarashtra or our friends.

1:37-38. O Lord, although these men are my relatives, they are overpowered by greed. They see no evil in destroying families or quarrelling with friends. I cannot be like them. I know their consciences are blurred, but killing them is wrong.

Consequences of war

1:39. Spiritual wisdom is lost in battle with the family elders' premature deaths, and those remaining will gradually descend into ungodliness.

1:40-41. When families break up, widows and orphans are left lonely and vulnerable to corruption. The unity of the family declines, and the country plunges into chaos.

1:42. Social upheaval is hell for families, society, and those who destroy families. It eliminates the spiritual foundation laid down by our ancestors.

1:43. Thus, unity, the spiritual foundation for families, and society's morals are degraded.

1:44. How strange that we are caught in this evil for the sake of an earthly kingdom.

1:45. Knowing this, how can I, in good conscience, kill my relatives to gain a kingdom?

1:46. It would be better for all if I were to die unarmed and unresisting on the battlefield at the hands of my enemy than if I were to participate in this evil.

1:47. Sanjaya relays this conversation to the king and ends his commentary by saying that Arjuna is overcome with anguish, casts aside his bow and arrows, and sits on the chariot. His mind is overwhelmed with grief.   ---------৸৸------

> **Further light on Gita 1:26-46 Arjuna's Dilemma on the battlefield. (*Elaboration* A1-J4 and** Gita Reference are based on the Author's insight).

Gita 1:26-46 / Elaboration-Testimony A1-23.

A1. As Arjuna views the battlefield, his heart is heavy. Sorrow and sadness overwhelm him. He weighs the consequences of war—sons and fathers dead, wives and children are deprived of husbands and fathers. Widows and orphans are reduced to poverty and misery, scraping a living. The seeds of hatred, anger, resentment, and retribution are sowed and would grow and thrive from generation to generation. Decades and centuries later, the stories of victory or defeat would still be told, and another generation would grow up hating their neighbours. (Based on Gita Ch 10:1. 9:20).

A2. He regarded himself as more than a prince. This role was temporary. He and many other selected people were set apart as warrior priests of the Supreme Lord of the Universe to serve Him and humanity for eternity and to seek and promote everyone's welfare. He looks at all those gathered on the battlefield, good, decent people on both sides mingled among the evil, amoral leaders. How could he, a warrior priest with good conscience, engage in this destruction? (Gita 2:3. 3:1-2. 16:9).

A3. If he survived the carnage of war, he would need to devote his life to reconstructing both sides. The role of healing, reconciling, restoring, and making restitution for all the victims of war, friends and foes, would fall on his kind. (Gita 4:33. 10:11-18).

A4. A child with a matchbox could burn down a village, or a power-hungry leader with a loose tongue could set a country at war with its neighbour and undo generations of work. All are brought to ruin by a single word, a matchstick, or a bomb. However, the cost of the war would be trivial compared to the cost of restoring the country and the effort to make everyone whole again. (Without Divine help, the loss of loved ones and broken hearts would be impossible to heal and make whole. (Gita 3:30 & 43).

A5. These are the Earthly consequences of war—pain, suffering, injustice, cruelty, and destruction, but its fruit reverberates to the Heavens. When people die, they take no worldly possessions to Heaven, but only goodness, hate, anger, or malice, and the Saints and the Elders of the Universe are left to clear the mess. (Gita 5:16-20).

A6. The spirit of The Lord in Arjuna reveals that even in Heaven, the work of counselling, healing, reconciliation, restoration, restitution, and making each whole has to continue if there is going to be eternal peace. That would require the special abilities, time, and effort of godly eternal warrior priests like him to help heal and restore until all are made whole and the evildoers are brought to justice. The daunting task ahead and hereafter demoralises him and subdues his spirit (Gita 11:1-31). (Made whole: restored to a sound, healthy, physical, mental, and spiritual state.)

A7. Armed with Kly-son's ability, Arjuna sees himself standing before the heavenly cloud of saints and sinners on 'The Day of The Lord' (Judgement, Evaluation Day). He has no fear of this day, for his conscience is clear. All his days, he had harboured no ill or malice towards anyone. He had worked tirelessly to bring about peace, justice, and goodness, making fourfold restitution to all he had hurt. (Gita 10:11-31. **Kly-son Ability:** A unique spiritual ability to hear and see events happening in a distant place.)

A8. Conversely, he sees the power-hungry politicians, leaders, criminals, and thieves who have instigated so much misery shiver as their day of reckoning approaches. Moreover, behind them stood a multitude of camp followers who had carried out the wishes of these evil people. A few would be treated leniently, with compassion, for they were compelled to carry out the orders. Others who had willingly joined, supported, and conspired with their leaders would be dealt with harshly. (Gita 11:32. 14:2 14:26).

A9. Arjuna's mind wandered to the beginning when he was just a thought in The Lord's mind before anything came into being. Even in this period, when he was just a thought, he was aware of his being. Arjuna mumbles, 'My Essence (Atman) has always been with The Lord and will always be with Him. My roots are from this beginning.' (Gita 11:1-31. 11:47-48).

A10. As Arjuna ponders over his dilemma on the battlefield, a sombre atmosphere pervades the Universe and Earth. Angels stand stunned as they witness the inhumanity and barbarism displayed all over the Earth in a dog-eat-dog world. Everything on Earth is struggling for dominance and survival at all costs, and in the middle of this pandemic, Arjuna finds himself. (Gita 11:1-31).

A11. In a different time and place, when Arjuna was just an essence in The Lord's mind, he had perceived creation as a beautiful plan. The Universe teeming with many plants, happy people, and animals. His essence had rejoiced at the very idea of God's creation. (Gita 7:2. 11:15-16).

A12. He had looked forward to it. The earlier rejoicing had turned to profound, *deep despair in his spirit. Now, he is in the reality of life, and the repercussions of creation, pain, sorrow, and suffering are felt all over the Universe. (Gita 11:8-16).*

A13. 'Lord,' Arjuna says, 'in my essence, in my naivety, I did not foresee this coming,' as tears rolled down his face. He questions himself. Is all this pain and suffering worth the little joy we see on Earth? Doubts about creation, God, and life cloud his mind as he gazes into the future for inspiration. (Gita 11:47-48).

A14. As sorrow and doubts overwhelm Arjuna in the middle of the battlefields; he hears a voice from the very depth of himself, where The Lord had placed his Atman. It cries, 'All the evil you see is not God's making. This is humanity's making. Just as the darkest hour appears before dawn, so is your current journey in this valley of death. You see tears and doom before you, but your work has only started. (Gita 11:52-55).

A15. 'The Lord has anointed you, O Mighty warrior, but your enemies are not flesh and blood but darkness, ignorance, selfishness, greed, apathy, injustice, and spiritual darkness that pervades the Universe and dwells within you. Moreover, that which lurks within is your greatest opponent. So, fight the good fight. Have faith in Me and follow My guidance. In My Sanctuaries, My saints and I will make everything whole. In 'The Fullness of Time' (a period between now and 'The Day of The Lord'), We will wipe away all tears. (Gita 11:16. 14:5-10).

A16. Your spirit lacks love, compassion, knowledge, wisdom, and ability. Nonetheless, you have the willingness to empty the ocean of darkness within and around you with the palm of your hand. Knowledge, wisdom, and respect are earned while toiling under freezing cold and boiling sun, paid with tears, sweat, and blood, or else it will be treated lightly. (Gita 14:10-11 & 13).

A17. 'My (adopted) son, though you walk through the valley of death, I am with you. No being is worthy to sit in My council unless they have proven with My help that they have the will and determination to empty the ocean of despair, ignorance, and darkness with the palm of their hand, which is being perfected and refined in you in this fire of My creation. (Gita 3:4. 4:10 & 38. 5:19. 7:3. 16:23).

A18. 'My son, this Eternal struggle is much more demanding than picking up your sword or dying for a good cause. To engage in this Eternal struggle, you will need a new (re-invigorated) heart and spirit for the journey ahead. (Gita

18:5-12).

A19. As a lotus plant grows undefiled in muddy waters, so shall you walk beside Me, undefiled by sin. Bear no evil thought, malice, or hate for your opponents. With My aid, fight ignorance, evil, and injustice with a warm heart and a clear conscience. Then, the clarity of 'Who and what you are' in God's kingdom will be apparent to you. (Gita 5:10. 16:1-3).

A20. 'With My assistance, make all who cross your path, friend and foe, whole, and claim your inheritance as My joint heir and My (adopted) son.' (Gita 18:55-58).

A21. Arjuna reflects on those few words as his spirit awakens to the formidable task ahead, with God's help reconciling the world atom by atom, thought by thought, until all worthy of The Lord's grace and mercy are made whole. (Gita 6:10-14. 11:47-48).

A22. 'How could I or any man contemplate such a formidable task?' he asks. (Gita 18:55-57).

A23. 'Not by your strength but by My Spirit (Atman I gave you). All things are possible to those willing to empty the ocean of misery with the palm of their hand,' says The Lord. (Gita 18:63-65).

A24 Loyal eternal priest

Three qualities distinguish these Heavenly anointed saints from others.

1.   They are empowered to foresee, interpret, and implement God's eternal plan.
2.   They have access to God's creative power. With The Lord's help, they display a unique ability to account for every thought and deed. Furthermore, they can potentially restore all things, atom by atom, and make all things/beings whole.
3.   They have a steel resolve and the ability to empty the ocean with the palm of their hand.
These qualities are achievable and are perfected by God among his children. This unique gift of God is available to those willing to surrender their lives, thoughts, and time and bravely seek Him with all their heart, mind, and strength. --------- ↔------

Chapter 2 – Knowledge

In this chapter, Arjuna confronts questions regarding life and death. What is the human soul/spirit? Is there a life hereafter? How do intelligent people control their senses and feelings? How does one learn to control the mind, body, and senses?

We learn Arjuna falls into a debilitating personal crisis. He refuses to participate in the battle and requests Lord Krishna to guide him on the proper path of action. In despair, he even questions remaining alive. He tells Lord Krishna that he cannot engage in this forthcoming battle, where he may end up killing his elders and teachers.

The Supreme Lord begins by imparting divine knowledge to Arjuna, starting with the nature of the human spirit, which is imperishable. He states that death only destroys the physical body, but the spirit continues its journey. Just as a person discards his old clothes and adorns himself with new ones, the spirit acquires a new body after death.

The Lord then reminds Arjuna that he must fight for justice and righteousness. He explains that performing one's social duty is virtuous, while dereliction only leads to shame and humiliation.

He then explains to Arjuna how to carry out his duty by performing his task without attachment to its fruits. This path of duty without a desire for rewards is called the *intellect's yoga* (*buddhi-yoga).* Here, the indwelling Atman guides the mind, senses, and body. With such intent, one can attain spiritual freedom in heavenly realms.

On the other hand, Arjuna is curious to know more about those situated in divine consciousness. Lord Krishna states that people who have attained spiritual awareness learn to keep their minds absorbed in God and overcome attachment to fear and anger. In addition, with their senses subdued, they overcome greed, lust, selfishness, etc.   ---- ➤ ----

Dharma

Sanjaya's commentary utilising his Kly-son ability

2:1. Sanjaya relays to blind King Dhritarashtra the battlefield scene that unfolds before him and the dialogue between Lord Krishna and Arjuna. He reports that Arjuna is overcome with compassion and depression, with tears in his eyes.

2:2. **The Supreme** Lord turns to Arjuna and says: My dear friend, where does all this despair and confusion come from? You are an honourable man called to live a life of Dharma (duty), sacrifice, and righteousness. This lack of weakness and clarity in a crisis is not worthy of you.

2:3. Do not yield to this impotence. This display of weakness is not befitting a great warrior. Cast off this weakness of heart and stand firm.

2:4. **Arjuna** replies: Lord Krishna, how can I battle with men like Bhisma, who has been like a grandfather to me, and Drona, my former teacher? These are people I look up to and respect. Engaging in a fight with my elders is dishonourable behaviour.

2:5. Surely it would be more honourable to live in this world as a beggar than to strike at my elders, even though they are wrong. If I kill them, I lose my dignity and self-respect, and their blood will taint everything I stand to gain.

2:6. If I let my evil cousin win this battle, then evil will prevail, and I will have failed to do my duty to protect society and our kingdom. How could I live with a clear conscience if I engaged in this battle and killed family members? Either way, I lose.

2:7. I am confused. Both options before me are dishonourable. I need your wisdom, your divine guidance. I am your disciple, and I kneel before you.

2:8. My Lord, I am overcome with grief, and my resolve is draining. My senses tell me this battle should not be about achieving a kingdom, but what is in the people's best interest, and I have no insight. What good are victory and a kingdom gained dishonourably?

2:9. Viewing this from afar, Sanjaya continues to relay the scene to the king: Arjuna has informed Lord Krishna that he will not fight and now falls silent.

2:10. Lord Krishna smiles and addresses the grief-stricken Arjuna as they stand between the two armies.

Those who are wise can see the whole picture

2:11. **Lord Krishna** says: My friend, your words may feel wise, but those spiritually in tune with Me can see the whole picture through the windows of past, present, future, and eternity. Grieve neither for the living nor for the dead.

2:12. Your Atman and that of these kings and soldiers have always existed and will continue to live hereafter. Their physical bodies may cease to live, but their spirits (Atman and the soul) will continue to live. On the 'Day of The Lord' (Judgement Day), the Atman will be your friend or foe, depending on how you have lived. It will be your counsellor or prosecutor on that day, so do not neglect its counsel.

2:13. The Atman dwells in a body for a while in each being. It experiences the body through childhood, youth, and old age. Just as a caterpillar casts off its cocoon and attains another body, the spirit reaches another body at death. These changes do not delude the wise. Flaws taint all who leave the Earth; none is complete or wholesome.

Do not neglect the permanent for the sake of the temporary

2:14. A person's senses coming into contact with objects create sensations of heat, cold, smells, tastes, visions, and happiness or distress. Still, these are temporary, like winter and summer; they come and go. Do not neglect the permanent for the sake of a brief life on Earth.

A mature spiritual person's priorities lie in the eternal

2:15. A mature spiritual person knows where his priorities and values lie, and worldly feelings and sensations do not sway him.

2:16. A spiritual person's priorities lie in the eternal, not the temporary, physical world. Those who acknowledge this truth have attained helpful insights and knowledge, affirmed by signs and miracles from The Lord. Thus, such evidence establishes reality in their spiritual walk and inspires them to walk beside Him as He guides, corrects, and prepares them for eternity.

The Immortal Atman

2:17. That which encompasses the body, the *Atman, is immortal but not the human spirit.

---

*Atman Commentary.

Gita 2:17 / Elaboration-Testimony B1-4.

B1. Think of the Atman as a garment of gold from God that encompasses the body. As the body grows, the garment conforms to fit the body. In death, the physical body is discarded. However, the gold cloth, the Atman (immortal), still encompasses the soul (mortal), and they attain a spiritual body. (Gita 15:7-9. 2:12-13. 2:30. 7:21. 8:2-3. 12:6-7. 13:20 & 28. 13:32).

B2. In 'The Fullness of Time', the soul, and the new body may pass away at some future stage called 'The **Second Death**[1]'. Then, the gold cloth, the indestructible Atman, returns to its rightful owner, God. That which came from God, the Atman, never perishes. It was, and will be his gift to all living entities for the duration of their journey. Only God is immortal. (Gita 2:18 & 20-25. 5:14. 13:24).

B3. Like the Sun, the soul (mortal) seems eternal, but it is not. Only God is eternal. However, the soul and Atman's long journey in the hereafter, 'Until the Day of The Lord', seems like an eternity from the human viewpoint. For example, the Sun appears eternal, but one day, it will fade and die, be swallowed by a black hole, and disappear in time. (Gita 2:20-25 & 29. 9:19. 13:3 & 23. 15:7).

B4. On the other hand, the Atman is immortal and will eventually return to its original owner, God. (Gita 8:27. 15:7).

Spirit: The duality of the Soul and Atman is referred to as a person's spirit. (Gita 15:7).

In the **Second Death**[1], the Human spirit = Atman (immortal part returns to God), but the Soul (mortal) perishes. (Gita 11:26-32)

2:18. **Lord Krishna**: Your body is temporary and may perish in this conflict.

Your Spirit (soul and Atman) will continue its journey until the 'Day of The Lord' (Judgement, Evaluation Day) and perhaps beyond. Therefore, I call upon you to fight.

2:19. You talk about killing or being killed, and you say one person is a killer, and the other is his victim. A knowledgeable person knows that at stake is something of far greater importance. Matters of Eternal values should override the temporal.

2:20. This Atman (the breath of God, the vessel of gold) was never born, nor will it die. When the body is dead, the spirit, the true self within, remains alive. They do not die.

2:21. This concept is hard to grasp, but the true self has an infinite lifespan. It does not kill or be destroyed until 'The Day of The Lord'.

After death, there is a new birth

2:22. As a person abandons worn-out clothes and acquires new ones, the spirit develops a new spiritual body when the material body is dead.

2:23-24. Human spirits are not damaged or destroyed by the material world, such as weapons, fire, wind, and water. They remain indestructible.

2:25. Spirits are invisible and have no form, no scent, nor can they be touched. It is not easy to fathom this mysterious concept of the true self. Yet, knowing this, you should not grieve for the body.

If there is no life hereafter

2:26. However, if you believe that a person dies forever at death, you have no reason to grieve. Once gone, you will have no memory.

All born will die at some stage

2:27. All born will die at some stage, and there is a new birth after death. So, why grieve over your duty?

2:28. In the beginning, there was no life. At conception, life becomes visible, and the material body returns to its lifeless form at death. So, what need is there to grieve over temporary things in the context of eternity?

2:29. Some look at the life-giving Atman as unique; some describe it as wondrous; and others cannot comprehend it.

2:30. O mighty warrior, all those gathered here, friend and foe, have indestructible spirits. Therefore, you need not grieve if they should fall in the battle.

Engaging in a fight against evil is a spiritual warrior's duty.

2:31. You are from a warrior clan. For a spiritual warrior, nothing is higher than a war against evil. A spiritual warrior must fight against corruption, greed, cruelty, ignorance, hate, poverty, and injustice.

2:32. A warrior confronted with such a war against unrighteousness and evil should be pleased, for it comes as an opportunity that opens the door to My divine assistance and grace. So, be happy and rejoice at this opportunity.

2:33. If you do not participate in this battle of good over evil to protect society, you will incur My displeasure. You will violate your duty and honour as a warrior for the oppressed.

2:34. People will always speak of you as a dishonourable person—a warrior who fled from the conflict. For a person in a high position of trust, dishonour is worse than death.

2:35. Your family, leaders, and people who respect and depend on you will feel you have let them down. They will believe their warrior leader is afraid and treat you with disdain.

2:36. Your enemies will laugh at you and call you a coward. What could be more painful than this?

2:37. My dear Arjuna, you face two outcomes: fight to the death, attain Heaven or conquer your enemies and gain a kingdom on Earth as My steward.

2:38. Consider yourself alike in pain and pleasure, victory and defeat. By doing so, you will be free from My displeasure.

Karma Yoga: Union with God through Action

2:39. **Lord Krishna** continues: I have described the intellectual explanation. Let Me show you how to live a spiritual life and render service to others without incurring sin.

2:40. This path is called Karma Yoga: the oneness of mind with Me through Action. Even a little spiritual advancement on this path will protect you from your greatest fear.

2:41. Those who desire to serve Me, humanity, and creation (all life forms) will attain a singular purpose with great resolve. For those who lack resolution, life's decisions will divert them from Me to material things.

Selfishness and ignorance

2:42-43. Some people take solace in the Scriptures' flowery words yet lack their true meaning. Their hearts are full of selfish desires. Their perception of Heaven is life's enjoyment based on gratification: wine, women, good food, and material luxury. The aim of all of their activities is pleasure and power. These ignorant people say there is nothing more than this on Earth and Heaven.

Samadhi

2:44. The pursuit of pleasure and power sweeps away their minds. They are incapable of following the supreme goal. They cannot attain **Samadhi*,** the stage of perfection, free from the pull of the material and sensual world. Nor will they be seen as purified, sacrificial, wise, enlightened spirits.

 (***Samadhi** is a state where all the senses and emotions are controlled, and the spirit is free; Mukta).

Be established in the eternal truth

2:45. Hindu Scriptures identify three modes of material nature. I will describe them later. For now, begin by letting go of Earthly pleasures and focus your energies on that which is eternal. Be established in the eternal truth, cultivate self-control, and be free from undue anxiety for gain or comfort.

Duty and a meaningful relationship with the divine

2:46. A meaningful day-to-day relationship with Me transcends the Scriptures.

2:47. Perform your duty honestly and to the best of your abilities, but entrust its results to Me. Nothing happens without My consent. Do not engage in your responsibility purely for reward or long for inaction.

2:48. Perform your duty as a loving service to Me, without selfish self-interest, in success or defeat.

2:49. Keep away from all abominable activities and, in all circumstances, surrender all things unto Me. Perform your duty as a service to Me without anxiety about the result. All sincere actions on My behalf, good or bad, including mistakes, eventually result in a good outcome. Those motivated only to enjoy the fruit of their work are misers.

Fruit of devotional service

2:50. Devotional service frees you from self and attachment to the material world. Second, it lifts you into My presence and enlightens you with My purpose for creation. Third, it instils in you a sense of oneness with all life.

2:51. Thus, engaged in devotional service to Me, you learn to rise above bondage to worldly activities and attain a position above the miseries of life.

Seek eternal values over material values

2:52. When your intelligence has overcome the dense forest of delusion, you will become indifferent to worldly things. You will seek eternal values over material values.

Comprehend your goal in life

2:53. When you have clarity of mind, apprehending your closeness with Me, your consciousness will merge with My will. Then, you will start to comprehend your goal in life.

Conduct of an enlightened person

2:54. **Arjuna** asked: My Lord, tell me about the enlightened people. How do they talk, sit, move, and conduct themselves?

2:55. **Lord Krishna** replied: An enlightened person learns to subjugate his selfish desires and all types of sensual gratification. Having his mind purified of selfish desires, he is satisfied with his true self. He is said to have risen above his natural state.

2:56. An enlightened person does not overreact to either sorrow or happiness. He is free from these three: obsessive attachment to worldly pleasures, fear, and anger. Such is a wise man of a steady mind.

2:57. Having subjugated selfish attachments, such a person is unaffected by whatever good or evil fortune comes his way, always trusting in My providence. He does not overtly rejoice or become depressed by such outcomes. Faith and sound wisdom guide him.

2:58. He has learned to rein in his senses from the world's pull, just as the tortoise draws its limbs within its shell to protect itself. He is firm and calm in all situations.

2:59. As his knowledge of My Divine nature grows, affirmed with signs and miracles from Me, the pleasures of the senses diminish but do not fade away.

The senses' pleasures are intense and treacherous

2:60. The senses' pleasures are intense and treacherous, and even the disciplined sage's mind can draw away from Me.

2:61. Healthy and wise is the person who subdues his senses and keeps his mind ever absorbed in Me.

Uncontrolled desires

2:62-63. When a person keeps thinking about physical objects, attachment develops. Uncontrolled desires give rise to lust, anger, and an unhealthy obsession with acquiring. Lost is the judgement to choose between wise and unwise. Delusion sets in and drags the person into irrational thinking. His intelligence is clouded and drawn to material existence.

The fruit of having the senses under control

2:64-65. However, a person who has his senses under control is free from attachment and aversion. His mind is at peace. The power of material existence has no decisive influence. Instead, intelligence and spiritual wisdom guide him.

2:66. A mind not in tune with Me is far from wise; how can it maintain stability? How can it be at peace? Without inner peace, how can one know real joy or happiness?

2:67. When the mind follows the roaming senses' call, they carry away the person's better judgement, just as a storm drives a ship off its charted course.

2:68. People who restrain their senses from obsessive attachment are wise.

To the spiritually minded, spiritual things are tangible

2:69. Material things take precedence over everything to the worldly-minded person, obscuring their spiritual existence. To the spiritually minded, worldly things are temporary; spiritual things are tangible, visible, and clear as day.

2:70. Many rivers flow into the ocean, but the sea never fills up. Similarly, selfish desires and attachments continuously flow into a person's mind, which remains unsatisfied. However, a wise person asserts control over his mind, never yielding to them. Such a man dwells in peace, which is not so with the person who strives to satisfy his unrestrained desires.

A steward of The Lord

2:71. My devotees are free when they give up selfish material desires and false egos. They hold all proprietorship as My stewards rather than as owners, taking what they need to sustain them. Such devotees attain inner peace and remain calm at the prospect of death.

2:72. Those who live a spiritual and godly life attain calmness and pass peacefully into the Kingdom of God at death.

--- ॐ---

Chapter 3 – Beginning of Creation and Karma-yoga

Lord Krishna explains karma yoga (yoga of action) in this chapter. He recommends that karma yoga be carried out diligently, but one should remain unattached to its result, leaving the outcome in The Lord's hand. Lord Krishna states that all living beings, good and evil, are integral to God's creation and have roles and responsibilities to fulfil. Creation rotates along the axis of sacrifice. The sun sacrifices its heat, the clouds their water, and the plants and trees their fruit to sustain life on Earth. Those living only for the delight of their senses without accepting responsibility in this sacrificial cycle are displeasing to The Lord. They live in vain.

Lord Krishna says that when prescribed duties are performed as an offering to God, humanity and creation, they are considered sacrificial. Therefore, the wise should continue working without any personal motive and set good examples for others. He gives an example of the enlightened King Janaka, who sacrificially and selflessly performed his earthly duties for his subjects as an ideal king and father.

Arjuna then asks Lord Krishna why some people sin, often unwillingly, led by some inner compulsion. Lord Krishna explains that desire and lust are all-devouring enemies; just as a fire is covered by smoke or a mirror covered by dust, selfish desire shrouds one's knowledge and deludes the person.

Finally, Lord Krishna advises Arjuna that by controlling the senses, mind, and spirit, one can slay this enemy called lust and selfish desire, which embodies sin. ---- ➤ ----

Spiritual knowledge and selfless service

Arjuna

3:1. **Arjuna** said: O Lord, why do you want me to engage in this war when you say a life spent pursuing knowledge is better than a life spent in destruction?

3:2. It makes no sense. I am confused. Please show me a way forward that will benefit everyone.

Two Paths of Faith

3:3. **Lord Krishna** (Supreme Lord) replies: From the beginning of time before creation came into being, I laid out two paths of faith. First, to pursue spiritual knowledge for those inclined towards contemplation, and the second path of selfless service for those inclined towards action.

Withdrawing from the world

3:4. A person acquires life experience by participating in the world and contributing to its welfare. By withdrawing from the world, one does not contribute to the world's welfare and thus cannot achieve spiritual perfection.

No person can refrain from doing something

3:5. No person, no creature, can refrain from doing something. Everything and everyone acts' according to their nature.

3:6. A person who refrains from the action while allowing his mind to dwell on sensual pleasure cannot aspire to spiritual wisdom.

All duty-bound to work

3:7. Conversely, the better option is for the mind to learn to control its senses for selfless service for the higher good of all.

3:8. All are duty-bound to work and support their families and themselves. One cannot maintain one's physical body without work.

Selfish action imprisons a person

3:9. Selfish action imprisons a person in the material world. Therefore, always act selflessly, performing your duties as a service to humanity and Me without thinking of personal benefit.

The principle of selfless, sacrificial service from the beginning of time

3:10. **The Supreme** Lord of Creation continued: At the beginning of creation, I blessed creation and set in motion the principle of selfless, sacrificial service to promote the welfare, interest, and happiness of all creation. Thus, through this selfless service, all creation would be prosperous and fruitful, fulfilling its desires.

Collaboration between humanity and creation brings prosperity

3:11. Participate in this sacrificial service to My creation, and you will receive My blessing. Collaboration between humankind and creation brings prosperity to all.

3:12. I will meet all your basic needs during your selfless service to humanity, creation and Me. One who takes from the world without selfless service is a thief.

Free from God's displeasure

3:13. The spiritually-minded are freed from all sin, i.e. My displeasure, because they carry out all life functions selflessly in the spirit of service. Those who carry out all life tasks for selfish enjoyment abide in My displeasure.

Creation depends on selfless service and sacrifice

3:14 The whole of creation depends on selfless service and sacrifice. All living things are nourished and sustained by food provided by the gifts of others. Plants and trees sacrifice their fruit, flowers, and shade without complaining, and if someone cuts them down, they remain free from malice and the desire for revenge. Sun, clouds, and rain work together selflessly to offer warmth and water freely to benefit all. They all provide service without expecting anything in return. The performance of prescribed sacrificial duties sustains all life. One who takes more often than gives is selfish and not sacrificial.

[From the example of Nature, God reminds us of the sacrificial duties expected from all living entities each day. The spiritually sightless, the selfish, and the ungrateful do not see this.]

Brahman, the life-giving breath of God

3:15. All selfless action comes from Brahman (the life-giving breath of God), the Absolute, and the Highest Consciousness. With My blessing, Brahman created everything seen and unseen. Therefore, Brahman is present in every act of service to promote the welfare, interest, and happiness of all, no matter what one's profession.

The Universe rotates on the axle of sacrifice

3:16. The Vedas (Scriptures) state that the Universe rotates on the axle of sacrifice. Brahman and I set this law in motion to train, discipline, and enlighten all in the principle of sacrifice. In Heavenly realms, no adult living entity *(exempting babies and young children)*, not even I, the Supreme Lord, thrive at the expense of another. Those who choose to live only for this world live in vain.

Purpose of life: It is a privilege and a pleasure to serve all

3:17. People who have found their true self and purpose for life in Me are content and happy. Serving humanity, My creation, and Me is a privilege and a pleasure for them.

An enlightened person is self-sufficient

3:18. An enlightened person is not dependent on others to discharge their duty or for their contentment. They are self-sufficient.

3:19. An enlightened person acts as a selfless person to serve others' welfare and leaves the outcome in My hands, whereby they attain the supreme goal of life.

Performing duty with others' welfare in mind

3:20. The great King Janaka found solace and favour in My presence by performing his duty sacrificially and selflessly with others' welfare in mind. Similarly, do your work with the interests of others in mind.

3:21. When great men lead, others follow their examples. Moreover, others will aspire to the standards they set.

I act for the welfare of the world

3:22. Arjuna, listen carefully; no work is prescribed for Me. I am self-contained. I require nothing, nor have I a need for anything. Yet, I continue to act for the welfare of the world.

3:23-24. If I cease to work, all creation will follow My example, and there will be cosmic chaos and the destruction of humanity.

Ignorant people

3:25. Ignorant people perform their duties for their welfare. However, enlightened people work for the interests of all, leading others down the right path.

3:26. Do not neglect the ignorant attached to selfish work, but show them by example that works done with the right spirit can be made sacred to improve the welfare of others.

3:27. An ignorant person under the influence of a false ego thinks of himself as the doer of activities. In fact, the three modes of his material nature, the body's cravings, senses, and the mind, govern his actions.

Enlightened person

3:28. An enlightened person understands how the three modes of material nature (the body's cravings, senses, and the mind) work together. He knows the difference between selfless devotional work influenced by My divine nature and works for self-gratification influenced by material nature.

3:29. The ignorant engage in material activities by yielding to their fundamental nature. Although these duties are of inferior quality stemming from a lack of knowledge, the wise should not refrain them from such action, but set a good example.

Fulfilling God's divine plan is pleasing to God

3:30. Arjuna, fix your mind on Me, and surrender all your works unto Me. Fulfil My divine plan to improve all creatures' welfare, interest, and happiness. Do it without any desire for personal gain.

3:31. Duties performed without complaining as a selfless way of life, with the interests of others in mind and established in the faith, are pleasing to Me. Such people do not have to worry about offending Me. I guide, correct, and refine their activities. I take responsibility for their work. I brought joy, pain, and suffering into the world. In 'The Fullness of Time' *(a period between now and 'The Day of The Lord')*, I will make restitution to all affected and make them whole again, wiping away all tears. There will be no more tears. Therefore, no one in the Universe can say we thrived at his or her expense. *[Gita 3:16. 14:1-4 & 26.]*

Ignoring the Scriptures

3:32. However, those who complain and ignore the Scriptures lack knowledge. They are deluded, spiritually lost, and devoid of hope of enlightenment in life.

People act according to their mode of nature

3:33. Even men of knowledge act according to their nature. All creatures follow their hearts. This is rooted in their thoughts and tendencies. Therefore, if one's nature is so powerful, one might question the value of attempting to live by scriptural injunctions. One could ask: What is the use of repressing one's material nature?

3:34. The answer is not to restrain your nature but to progressively improve it. One's senses can be major stumbling blocks to spiritual attainment. Senses derive their power from one's likes and dislikes. Do not let your likes and dislikes influence you. Otherwise, they can become obstacles.

3:35. It is better to strive for a duty that serves humanity and Me, even if carried out imperfectly, than to engage in something for selfish self-interest.

The force that encourages us to act selfishly

3:36. **Arjuna** said: O Lord, what is this vital force that encourages us to act selfishly even against our will?

Fruit of Selfish desires

3:37. **Lord Krishna** answered: From the mode of passion comes selfish desire and anger. These two are the worst enemies in the world. Furthermore, unfulfilled selfish desires lead to irritation.

3:38. Just as smoke covers a fire, as dust obscures a mirror, selfish desire for sense gratification clouds sound judgement.

3:39. The spirit becomes smothered by the eternal enemy, selfish desires, which are never satisfied and burn like fire.

3:40. Life's purpose is forgotten as selfish desires overcome the body, senses, and mind.

Bringing senses, mind, and intellect under divine supervision

3:41. Therefore, Arjuna, learn to bring your senses, mind, and intellect under My supervision with all your strength. Conquer your worst enemy, selfishness, destroyer of My divine purpose that abides in you.

3:42. Senses are superior to the body, and the mind can rise above the senses. Intelligence can rise above the mind, and the spirit can rise above intelligence.

Power of the indwelling spirit

3:43. Thus, your true self, the indwelling Atman imparting My divine spiritual strength, can guide your intellect, mind, senses, and desires. Therefore, your true self gives you the power to overcome this insatiable enemy, selfishness.

Chapter 4 – Wisdom, Action, and First Man

In this chapter, Lord Krishna reveals the origin of sacred knowledge to strengthen Arjuna's faith.

He says to Arjuna, 'As you are My devotee and a dear friend, I will now disclose this sacred knowledge from the beginning of time that only a few know. This divine knowledge was given to Viviana and many other ancient saints and sages.'

Arjuna wonders how Lord Krishna, standing before him and appearing to be his age, could have existed so many centuries ago. He asks Lord Krishna, 'How could you have given this knowledge to Viviana and the others so many years ago?'

Lord Krishna says that, although God is unborn and eternal, whenever there is a decline in the *Dharma* (the path of righteousness), he descends on this Earth to rekindle it. His earthly appearance and activities are divine and cannot be tainted by material imperfections. Once a devotee knows this secret and engages in devotion with great faith, he attains divine wisdom.

Then, Lord Krishna goes back to *karma yoga,* the subject from the previous chapter. He explains the nature of work and its three principles: action, inaction, and illegal action.

He says the ancient sages performed their work as sacrifices for God's pleasure and society's benefit. They were not influenced by happiness, distress, success, or failure, but were guided by divine knowledge and altruistic intentions and thus were cleansed of all impurities. Even the biggest sinner can cross the ocean of material miseries by renouncing his past and boarding this boat of eternal knowledge. Such knowledge, he says, should be acquired only from him or a genuine spiritual master.

Lord Krishna then instructs Arjuna to remove all doubts in his heart with this sword of divine knowledge and to get up and perform his duty as a warrior.

---- ➤+ ----

Manu, the Father of humanity

Krishna

4:1. **Lord Krishna:** I entrusted this eternal secret to Viviana (ancient sage), who taught Manu, the Father of humanity, who taught Ikshvaku.

4:2. This supreme message passed through a succession of eminent saints and sages. Over time, this succession was broken, and the message was distorted.

His plans for eternity

4:3. To a select few, I revealed My existence and plans for eternity (past, present, and future worlds to come). You are My friend and devotee, and in due time, as you gain My favour, I will **reveal*** these mysteries and explain your role here on Earth, in the spiritual world, and in the far distant future. You and other trusted devotees will build My material and spiritual kingdoms in this world and hereafter and walk beside Me in all My realms. I will guide and teach you all as a Father.

> ### *NOTE: *Reveal.*
>
> *Gita 4:3 / Elaboration-Testimony C1-10.*
>
> *C1. These promises are for all humanity. However, very few will give the Supreme Lord of the Universe the time to plant these mysteries as seeds and water them in their spirits, where these seeds could come to life and bear much fruit. (Gita 7:25-27.)*
>
> *C2. Arjuna, or any devotees, could free themselves from worldly worries if they tried. Once freed from the yoke of Mother Earth, they happily serve their Lord and humanity (all life forms), entering into that sought-after eternal place of rest and inner peace. (Gita 11:38-39. 18:51-53.)*
>
> *C3. Established in this secure position, they aspire to acquire a more profound knowledge of the Supreme Lord. What was it like for the Almighty before creation? What pains and sorrows did he feel? Was loneliness a state of*

despair for him, alone in solitary confinement, without space or time? (Gita 2:59. 3:3. 4:4. 5:16. 6:8. 7:2.)

C4. As difficult as it may be to believe, the question arises: Did the Supreme Lord despair, long for a companion, a family, a friend? (Gita 7:2. 10:12-13. 11:45-48.)

C5. Were the Almighty's tears the first three tears in the Universe? Were these tears, the result of pain and suffering, transformed into love, hope, and joy, giving this living entity that we call God a purpose and meaning to His existence? Why would God want to share this intimate self and His inner longings? (Gita 11:45-48. 11:52-54. 13:13. 13:18-19. 14:1-4. 18:64.)

C6. What kind of love, faith, and hope motivated it to create the Universe? How could it justify the pain and sorrow that would flow from creation? (Gita 8:2. 9:33. 11:15. 12:13-14. 18:6.)

C7. As Arjuna stood before his creator, spiritual knowledge and wisdom confirmed with signs and wonders flowed through him, opening the mystery buried from time immemorial, releasing a flood of joy in the Great Life-giver and the speck of humble dust. (Gita 11:10-12. 11:14. 18:64.)

C8. Arjuna stood firm and cried out, 'I may be a child of humble dust, but I have risen above darkness and ignorance by the grace of my Lord to grapple with the most profound mind in the Universe, to feel its heart (an expression) beating in unison with mine.' (Gita 6:20-23 & 32. 14:26.)

C9. There is no more excellent sound in the Universe, no sound so sweet, so longed for, as 'Om, Tat, Sat, Abba Father' from a speck of dust to the most powerful being in the Universe, who acknowledges it by covering this speck of Earth with a shield and a warm divine blanket. (Gita17:23-27.)

C10. Finally, the Supreme Lord's years of loneliness, isolation, distress, and anguish are over. He has found a person after his own heart. (Gita 4:10. 10:10. 12:13-14 & 16.)

4:4. Arjuna is overwhelmed with knowledge and cannot grasp its spiritual depth and eternal value. It would take many years to take firm root in his life. Meanwhile, he appears confused as he looks at Lord Krishna's human form and asks: Vivasvān was born a very long time before you, so how could you have instructed him?

I have appeared many times in human forms

4:5. **The Supreme Lord** (Krishna) replied: I have often appeared to various generations in human forms. Unaware as you are, I have guided your Atman since your birth.

My real being has no human form

4:6. I am the sovereign Lord. My breath of life resides in all creatures. Although I have an imperishable nature, I make an appearance as a human from time to time. However, My real being has no enduring human form.

Decline in Dharma

4:7-8. Whenever there is a decline in Dharma (devotional duty) and humanity's goal is lost, I (or My Apostles, prophets or Gurus) appear in every age to restore Dharma, re-establish religion, protect civilisation, and destroy evil.

Where I am, My devotees will be

4:9. Those who know My true nature and follow My teachings will take their rightful place in My eternal home upon leaving this material world. Where I am, they will be.

4:10. My followers taking refuge in My abode are free from the slavery of fear and selfish attachment. Their greed, anger, and love are slowly refined, cleansed, purified, and sanctified in My presence.

> *Gita 4:10 / Elaboration-Testimony C11, My devotees forgo food, sleep, comfort, companionship, and family to intercede on behalf of their family, neighbour, and country with tears and deep anguish of spirit. Then, out of their spirit flows worship in spirit and truth that pleases Me. The door to Heaven opens, and the heavenly saints gather around them, joining in the prayers as one family and pleading to The Lord to intervene. Rivers of living waters gush out from the throne, nourishing Heaven and Earth. Specific prayers with day, time, and hour are requested, and the divine being moved by the heavenly gathering yields—sacred love in action. (Gita 11:5-32.)*

4:11. As My followers draw closer to Me, I encourage and reward them with their specific prayers, drawing them ever closer.

People who worship worldly pleasures

4:12. Meanwhile, people who worship worldly pleasures and the gods of materialism will continue to chase temporary, unfulfilling desires.

The four divisions of human society

4:13. The three modes of material nature (the body's cravings, senses, and mind) and the ancient four divisions of human society (priest, administrator, merchant, labourer, and all the associated sub-divisions) originally came from Me, but I am not part of them.

All reap what they sow

4:14. No work affects Me. I am involved in every activity of creation but am not attached to any material activities of the world, nor do I seek any reward. All creatures reap what they sow and are responsible for their actions and results. Those who know Me are not entangled in material rewards.

4:15. All the enlightened ancient sages understood this nature of Mine and acted accordingly. Therefore, you should perform your duties in the same manner as them.

What action (conduct) is acceptable

4:16. Even the great sages are confused by what action (conduct) is acceptable to Me and what is inappropriate. I will explain later what action is proper, freeing you from bewilderment.

4:17. The nature of the action (devotional conduct) is challenging to grasp. You should know what acceptable action is, what inaction is, and what inappropriate activity is.

4:18. The wise see action in inaction, and inaction in action. Sacred Scripture teachings guide their intelligence and activities. Hence, they enjoy happiness in discharging their duties.

Divine wisdom consumes selfish desires

4:19. A wise person is said to be fully knowledgeable when all his undertakings are free from anxiety about the result and devoid of a selfish sense of gratification. The fire of My divine wisdom has consumed all his selfish desires.

Wise person

4:20. An intelligent person acting for the good of creation and in servitude to Me is not anxious about the outcome. He is engaged in all kinds of undertakings on My behalf, leaving the result of his work in My care, knowing everything will eventually work for the best result, even his mistakes.

4:21. The wise person acts with his mind and intelligence perfectly controlled, regarding all his possessions as Mine, and uses only the necessities of life. He serves humanity's interests and Me. Hence, he incurs no sin (displeasure from Me) in his activities.

4:22. The wise person is steady in success and failure and does not compete or compare with others. He is free of envy, content with whatever the outcome, and safe in knowing that all results are under My divine control.

4:23. The wise person, purified in the knowledge of My divine nature and freed from selfish desires, performs his duties in the spirit of sacrifice as an act of devotion and offering.

Brahman's kingdom

4:24. A person who is entirely devoted on My behalf to Brahman and his creation, contributing to Brahman's material and spiritual kingdom, is sure to attain the spiritual realm.

Worship and offering sacrifices

4:25. Some choose to worship and offer sacrifice to Gods (Shiva, Vishnu, Ganesha, Rama) or saints and sages, bearing the ultimate divine being in mind. When performed with true devotion, these offerings may bring spiritual growth. In contrast, others provide selfless, sacrificial services to Brahman's cause, which bears much fruit.

Restraining sense gratification

4:26. Some mature devotees learn to restrain the senses' enjoyment by mental control, and others choose to divert their energies from the gratification of their senses to meditate on My words for higher spiritual experiences.

Achieving spiritual growth

4:27. Others interested in attaining spiritual growth bring the functions of senses and mind under their Atman's control.

4:28. For spiritual growth, many take strict vows to worship Me and offer their wealth and possessions towards My cause. Others perform severe austerity or study the Scriptures, making their knowledge and themselves available to others.

4:29. A few gifted devotees can control the inhalation and exhalation of breath, enter into a spiritual trance (mysticism), and gain insight and wisdom from Me.

Cleansed of sin

4:30. All disciples of Mine who sincerely offer their lives as sacrifices become cleansed of sin. Having tasted the goodness of holy life, they draw closer to Me and My creation.

Sustenance lies in service and sacrifice for the welfare of society

4:31. A disciple's proper nourishment lies in serving humanity and Me. Without it, one can never live happily on this planet or in the afterlife. Those who choose to live only for this world live in vain.

4:32. I (the Supreme Lord) approve all generous offerings and sacrifices offered to Me and used to promote the welfare of society. When practised as a way of life, devotees will find it liberating.

The goal of creation is spiritual advancement and promoting everyone's welfare and happiness.

4:33. The primary purpose of creation is the spiritual advancement of all, and the secondary purpose is sharing My Eternal plan with those who seek it with all their hearts, minds, and strengths. Signs and wonders accompany sacred knowledge and are not revealed to those who place little value on it. Sacrifices made to promote spiritual understanding are better than material offerings. The fruit of spreading spiritual knowledge in the community is love, joy, peace, longsuffering, gentleness, goodness, righteousness, and truth. The fruit of righteousness is sown in peace by those who make peace.

Follow the guidance of a spiritual master

4:34. Follow the guidance of a spiritual master and render service unto him. The spiritual master can instruct you in this wisdom.

All living entities are part of one family

4:35. Having gained spiritual wisdom, you will not be deluded again. You will see that all living entities are part of the divine plan, part of one family, and have the same breath of life from the divine. Hence, as you progress in your spiritual growth, you will regard all life forms as an extension of The Lord and your family. (Original. yena – whereby; bhūtāni – living entities; aśeṣāṇi – all; drakṣyasi – you will see; ātmani – in the Supreme Soul; atha u – or in other words; mayi – in Me).

Spiritual knowledge is liberating

4:36. Spiritual knowledge is liberating. Even if you were once the most sinful sinners, once you board the boat of spiritual experience, you could sail beyond the ocean of your sins.

4:37. As a blazing fire turns firewood to ashes, the fire of spiritual knowledge, affirmed by Me with signs and power, incinerates sinful thoughts and desires.

Spiritual knowledge purifies the soul

4:38. Nothing in this world purifies like spiritual knowledge. Living in conjunction with it is the pinnacle of perfection hoped for by all saints. One who practises this wisdom comes to enjoy inner peace.

Attaining wisdom and peace

4:39. Those who take spiritual knowledge as their highest goal and have it validated by the Supreme Lord, remaining steadfast in the faith, with senses controlled, attain wisdom and peace.

Ignorant and faithless people

4:40. But ignorant and faithless people who doubt the Scriptures waste their lives. They can never achieve lasting happiness in this world or the hereafter.

Freedom and duty

4:41. Those people established in devotional service, having renounced selfishness and overcoming their doubts through spiritual wisdom, live in freedom.

4:42. Therefore, Arjuna uses the sword of spiritual knowledge to remove this doubt from ignorance. Arise, stand firm, and fulfil your duties.

---------- ॐ ------

Chapter 5 – Active Spiritual Life (Theory and Practice)

In this chapter, Lord Krishna compares *karma yoga* (selfless service) with *karma sannyāsa yoga* (the path of the renunciation of actions).

He says that a person can achieve spiritual growth through selfless service. Therefore, *karma yoga* is a more appropriate path for most. The *karma yogis* with purified minds and thoughts perform their worldly duties sacrificially and selflessly without attachment to their fruit. They dedicate all their works and their results to God and His creation.

Endowed with the vision of Heaven, they look upon a learned scholar, an outcast, a cow, an elephant, a dog, and all living entities as part of their and God's extended family. Seated in the Heavenly realms, such wise people acquire divine qualities.

Karma yogis do not pursue worldly pleasures. Instead, they seek and enjoy the bliss of God, which resides inside them. On the other hand, ungodly or spiritually unsound people strive to relish their sense of objects, and do not realise that the pleasures they seek are the source of their misery.

Lord Krishna then describes renunciation (*sannyāsa*) as withdrawing from work and the family's everyday affairs to pursue a contemplative life. Buddha provided the classic example of a prince who gave up a comfortable life to seek a lonely way to self-realisation. He became a wandering monk, attained enlightenment, and rejoined society to teach others. However, Lord Krishna recommends selfless service as a better way than renunciation.

Samadhi: a state where all the senses and emotions are under control and the spirit is free (Mukta).

---- ➤ ----

The Supreme Lord recommends the path of selfless service as a better way than renunciation

5:1. **Arjuna** asks: Lord, you recommend the path of selfless service (without attachment) rather than the practice of sannyasa: withdrawing from the everyday affairs of work and family to pursue a contemplative life. Why?

5:2. **Krishna, the Supreme Lord,** replies: The path of selfless service is better than the course of sannyasa, though both lead to the same goal.

5:3. A person in devotional service to Me can overcome his material nature, whereby he neither hates nor desires personal sense gratification beyond everyday needs. Such a person is singular in purpose, liberated, and free from all paths, so whatever he does, he does for Me. I ensure that all his actions, intentional or not, including his mistakes, will eventually bear good results.

The wise see selfless service and analytical study as the same

5:4-5. Immature people think selfless service and the analytical study of the Scriptures are different devotional service paths. The wise see both as the same. Those established in one course will achieve the results of both. The goals of service and study are the same.

5:6. Withdrawing from worldly activities to pursue a contemplative life without service cannot make one happy. However, the wise engaged in selfless service quickly reach the Supreme Being.

An enlightened person sees the divine in all creatures

5:7. A mature, enlightened person provides selfless services, learns to control his senses and mind, and sees the divine in all creatures. Though engaged in work, he is never entangled in worldly actions and is not disappointed or happy due to the outcome, but leaves the result in My care.

Those walking in the divine presence

5:8-9. Although engaged in all human activities of hearing, touching, eating, sleeping, and so forth, a person walking in the divine presence understands that these are only the actions of their material senses. Their spirit is detached from the material senses.

5:10. Those walking in the divine presence and learning to surrender all selfish attachments to the Supreme Lord are like the leaf of a lotus plant floating clean and dry in muddy water. Similarly, those who surrender all selfish attachments to the Supreme Lord no longer have the desire to sin.

5:11. A mature, enlightened person learns to free himself from selfish attachment to the world. Renouncing their selfish attachment, those who follow the path of service with their bodies, senses, minds, and intelligence do so for self-purification.

Attaining peace and contentment

5:12. A devoted soul learns to submit his life and actions to Me and attains peace. In contrast, a person entangled in selfish self-gratification cannot submit his life to Me.

5:13. Those who have learned to control their sensory, emotional, and mental activities live contentedly in their material body.

The Atman

5:14. The Atman is neither the proprietor nor the controller of the material body. It does not create activities, nor does it induce people to act. It seeks to guide their material nature, but does not control it.

Good or evil deeds

5:15. Lord Krishna: I do not partake in any person's good or evil acts. Ignorant people are bewildered by this because they lack spiritual understanding.

The light of knowledge reveals the Supreme Lord

5:16. When the knowledge of the self is enlightened, ignorance is replaced with understanding. The light of knowledge illuminates My Divine nature, just as the sun lights up everything.

On the path to liberation

5:17. People absorbed in Me have their intelligence, mind, and faith fixed on Me. As they progress, spiritual knowledge cleanses and refines them, liberating them from hate, lust, worldly affairs, and a desire to acquire vast wealth.

Equal regard for all

5:18. My devotees have equal regard for all. They see *(vidya-vinaya-sampanne)* the same self (the breath of God) in a learned scholar, an outcast, a cow, an elephant, and a dog. All are contributing directly or indirectly towards God's kingdom and our salvation. Therefore, they *(panditah)* have a heightened sense of appreciation and a duty to care for and promote everyone's welfare. Hence, as they progress in their spiritual growth, they regard all life forms as part of their and God's extended family. *(They see this as part of God's eternal plan: A Universe where the lion and lamb sit together and eat straw one day, and a child plays with them.)*

5:19. Such people have conquered the fear of life and death. They rest in the perfect Brahman and Me, gradually refined and made flawless.

5:20. They are firmly established in Brahman and Me and are free from delusion. They are not moved by good fortune nor depressed by bad.

5:21. They are not excessively attracted to sensual pleasure or dependent on external stimulation but enjoy the inner joy of spiritual awareness and the divine presence.

Pleasure and misery have a beginning and an end

5:22. Pleasure and misery derived from the senses have a beginning and an end. The wise do not look for happiness in them.

5:23. They overcome the senses' impulses and control their lust and anger. They are well-situated and will remain happy.

5:24. The wise find joy, happiness, purpose, and fulfilment within themselves and attain freedom in Me.

5:25. The wise, freed from the internal conflict of doubts and sin (conduct displeasing to Me) and engaged in all creation's welfare, interest, and happiness, achieve liberation in Me.

5:26. The wise can control their anger and selfish desires. They are self-realised and disciplined. Their mind is under control, and they seek perfection; such find liberation in Me.

5:27-28. Sitting in a comfortable position, closing their eyes, and shutting out all external senses and objects, they steady their breathing. By meditating on the Scriptures, gradually, they bring their reason, mind, and intellect under My guidance. Their selfish desires, fears, and anger are controlled; hence, they acquire a sense of inner peace and freedom.

Freed from the clutches of materialism and selfish desires

5:29. People in full consciousness of My divine nature know I am the beneficiary of all sacrificial works and a friend of humanity and creatures. They are free from materialism and selfish desires and acquire deep joy, fulfilment, inner peace, and contentment.

---------- ᧕ᢣ------

Chapter 6 – Selfishness versus Becoming Whole

In this chapter, Lord Krishna compares *karma yoga* (practising spirituality while performing daily duties) and *karma sanyās* (practising spirituality in a renounced state).

He emphasises that *karma yoga* is a more appropriate path than *karma sanyās* and that when work is done as a selfless act of devotion, it purifies the person.

He encourages the devotees to bring the mind under the influence of the Scriptures through meditation. While a trained mind is the best friend, an untrained mind can be the worst enemy for a spiritual aspirant.

Lord Krishna cautions Arjuna that one cannot progress on the spiritual path by merely engaging in severe austerities. Therefore, moderation must be maintained, even for basic needs such as food, sleep, work, and recreation.

Lord Krishna then explains *yoga sādhanā,* the spiritual practice of uniting with God. He states that keeping the mind steady in meditation is difficult but can be controlled by exercise and detachment. Whenever the mind wanders away, one must focus on God until one experiences divine bliss.

Arjuna asks what happens to those spiritual aspirants who begin their journey but cannot reach their goal due to an unsteady mind. Lord Krishna reassures him that those who strive for God-realisation will not be abandoned.

The Lord then concludes this chapter with a declaration that discipleship is founded on good works, spiritual knowledge, and the practical action of love for creation and Him, which is superior to pursuing knowledge. --
-- ➤ ----

Personal sacrifice and selfless service go together

Krishna

6:1. The Supreme Lord said: Those who learn to control their sensory and emotional feeling to contemplate Me without expecting reward will grow spiritually.

6:2. Personal sacrifice and selfless service go together. To grow spiritually, one must suppress selfish desires and cultivate selfless service.

Climbing the spiritual mountain

6:3. For those who want to climb the mountain of spiritual awareness, the path is selfless devotion to My creation and Me. The Heavenly Saints and Elders of the Universe have set an example for us to follow in their steps. This way leads to serenity and peace for those who reach the summit. *(Gita 10:6, 11:14-17.)*

6:4. Spiritual growth requires freedom from undue attachment to material wealth and sensual gratification, apart from routine needs to maintain a healthy body and spirit.

Renewing the mind

6:5. Those who aspire to grow should transform themselves by renewing their minds and not allowing their minds to degrade them. The [1]**mind** can be a friend or an enemy.

---

[1]*mind. Gita 6:5 / Elaboration-Testimony D1*

D1. The seeds of ignorance, darkness, and hate float through the air. We inhale them effortlessly. They settle freely in our minds and grow, but one must seek, cultivate, and nourish the precious seeds of love, generosity, kindness, knowledge, and wisdom. It takes effort and time. Understanding this is the first step towards developing respect and love for all beings and creatures.

6:6. People who renew their minds by the Scriptures' teachings rather than yielding to sense objects discover that their minds are their best friends. For those who yield to sense objects, the sense objects will remain their worst enemy.

Fruit of a renewed mind

6:7. One whose mind is renewed by the divine Scriptures lives in peace. In servitude to Me, a person's resolve is unmoved by happiness, distress, cold, heat, pain, or pleasure.

Controlling the senses

6:8. People who have acquired spiritual wisdom from Me affirmed with signs and divine power and have their sense of gratification under control eventually climb to the *summit of human consciousness. Academic knowledge without action is like pebbles or stones to such people, while others may see it as gold. (*Gita 11:7 & 16. 14:2 & 26.)

Spiritual people are self-controlled

6:9. Spiritual people learning to control their emotions and senses exercise equal dispositions towards family, friends, or foes. They will rise to a great height of wisdom.

Meditate on The Lord

6:10. People who aspire to grow spiritually should always have their bodies, minds, and selves in servitude to My creation and Me. They should meditate on My words in a secluded place, free from desires and feelings of possessiveness.

6:11-12. People in such a situation should find a quiet place, sit comfortably, and still their thoughts. They should fix their minds on the Scriptures and reflect on their teachings.

6:13-14. Seated comfortably, their wandering mind stilled by meditating on the Scriptures, they wait upon Me for guidance.

Drawing closer to the divine

6:15. By focusing their body, mind, and soul on Me, they learn to glide into My presence.

6:16- 17. Success lies in moderation. Those who sleep, eat, work, and recreate in moderation will succeed. They avert errors and many painful lessons in life.

6:18. With practice and discipline, they can withdraw the mind from selfish cravings and be absorbed in My divine presence.

Fruit of a controlled mind

6:19. As a lamp is steady in a windless place, so is a calm mind able to be steadfast in My divine presence.

6:20-23. In union with Me (Samadhi), the sensory and emotional feelings are subjugated to contemplate the spiritual. They begin to fill up with inner joy and fulfilment. They now walk in truth and are free from all miseries from material contact. Here, they desire only to please Me. The joys or sorrows of life do not govern their life, but My divine influence.

6:24. They meditate on the words of the Scriptures with faith and determination, subjugating all selfish desires. With determination and practice, their mind learns to control the senses.

6:25. Slowly, step by step, with firm conviction and intelligence, their mind becomes still in My presence.

Wandering mind

6:26. They should bring it back into My presence wherever the mind wanders due to its fickle nature.

Inner happiness

6:27. Those who have their minds fixed on Me attain healthy inner happiness. They are beyond the craving for passion and free from the influences of all past deeds as their minds are renewed and purified.

Fruit of union with the divine spirit: showing kindness to all living things.

6:28-29. Those collaborating with My divine spirit are happy and free from material worldly ties. They see My divine nature within and in all creatures and creation.

6:30. I am ever present to those who have realised Me in every creature. Seeing all life as My manifestation, they are never separated from Me.

6:31. Enlightened people worship Me by showing kindness to all living things. Wherever they may live, they abide in Me. Hence, all their actions proceed from Me.

6:32. People who see equality in all beings and creatures have profound empathy for all and respond to their joy, and sorrow as their own. They have attained one of the higher states of spiritual union with Me and My creation. *(Gita 5:18)*

How can one control one's thoughts?

6:33-34. **Arjuna** responds: My Lord, my mind is restless and unsteady. How can one control one's thoughts? The mind is powerful, turbulent, and wild; trying to control it is like restraining the wind.

6:35-36. **Krishna:** It is undoubtedly challenging to control a restless mind. Nonetheless, one can bring a mind under control through discipline, practice, detachment, self-control, and earnest desire.

What happens to those who wander away?

6:37-39 **Arjuna**: What happens to those who have faith but cannot control their thoughts (mind) or become deluded and wander away from spiritual and material paths? Will they lose the support of both worlds (Earth and Heaven)? I am troubled by such thoughts, O Lord.

6:40. **Krishna:** My friend, I will not discard them. Anyone who has accepted Me and acts selflessly, performing their duties as a service to humanity and Me without thinking of personal benefit, becomes My devotee.

Death and Spiritual Realms in the Afterlife

6:41. When people who have accepted Me die, they go to a spiritual realm where the righteous live (reborn, metamorphosed in sanctuaries). Whenever My devotees pass away into the hereafter, they leave behind a legacy of love, kindness, justice, and fairness, having enriched the lives of others.

Gita 6:41 / Elaboration-Testimony D2-3.

> *D2. All humans are tainted with flaws; none is entirely wholesome. Thus, they live in these realms for years until they are ready to move to a higher, purer, and more enlightened level. There, they are further purified, refined, and cleansed of hatred, menace, ignorance, and ill feeling until their hearts overflow with gratitude and goodwill to the river of life that had once chained them to feelings such as hate and anger. Thus, their Atman has finally freed them from their shackles of pain, suffering, ignorance, and hate and replaced them with love, compassion, tolerance, knowledge, and wisdom. (Gita 8:24-26. 5:16. 6:41-45. 16:1-3.)*
>
> *D3. Sacred love, kindness, goodness, sound judgement, insight, perception, knowledge, and wisdom confirmed by signs and miracles from The Lord are some of the crowns they wear. All things work for the good of those who follow Lord Krishna's teachings. (Gita 16:1-2. 10:38. 2:49.)*

Spiritual master

6:42-43. Or they may move (metamorphose) into the realm of a great spiritual master. Such a move is rare. Their divine consciousness is reinvigorated by the great spiritual masters, and with their help, they are encouraged to make further progress.

6:44. Due to their disciplined lives, they will become attracted to the new realm. Inquisitive disciples who contemplate Me rise above those who perform rituals.

6:45. These disciplined people in their new realms progress further as their selfish desires are purified. Moving upwards towards higher realms, they eventually attain the seventh Heaven, the supreme goal of all. (Gita 11:7-12)

Discipleship

6:46. The path of discipleship is founded on good works, growing in spiritual knowledge, and practical action of love for creation and Me. This approach is superior to pursuing knowledge or selfless service.

6:47. A disciple of firm faith who abides in Me, walks beside Me and renders loving service to all creation (building My kingdom on Earth and in Heaven) will be with Me forever. Whenever My devotees pass away into the hereafter, they leave a legacy of love, kindness, justice, and fairness, having enriched the lives of all around them. ------- ᛞᛞ-----

Chapter 7 – Intimate Knowledge of Eternal God (Para-Brahman)

Revelation from The Lord about God's desires, plans, and creation.

In this chapter, Lord Krishna describes the energies in the material and spiritual dimensions as originating from Him and resting in Him. All things exist due to him. The entire Universe is suspended around his neck like a necklace of pearls.

All of creation begins and dissolves into Him. Although it is challenging to comprehend, those who surrender to Him can easily overcome their ignorance with His help.

He then describes the pious people who engage in His devotion and the followers of pleasure and selfish desires.

He says that those devotees who worship and serve Him, humanity, and creation are dearest to Him.

He also states many are led by their material nature and diverted from the truth. They worship their gods of pleasure and selfish desires, and he rarely manifests Himself to them. A veil lies between them. Therefore, the worthiest object of devotion is the Almighty God Himself.

Lord Krishna states that he is the ultimate truth and the highest authority. He possesses attributes such as omnipotence, omnipresence, and omniscience. Thus, devotees who surrender to Him are blessed with the knowledge of the Supreme Lord and the self, and find purpose, fulfilment, and happiness.

--- ➤+ ---

7:1. **Lord Krishna:** Listen to Me, Arjuna, exercise discipline, and focus your mind upon Me. Wait upon Me, and I will dispel all your doubts.

7:2. As you grow spiritually, I will declare unto you, Jnana: the highest kind of spiritual **knowledge**[1], direct revelation from Me. Furthermore, I will declare *Vijnan*: the intimate understanding of **Creation²,** how every subatomic particle is created and is accounted for daily, how the Universe is balanced, and the mindset behind this design, affirmed with signs and miracles. *(¹Gita 11:8-46. ²Creation. Reference at the end of the book, pages 178-188).*

Jnana (Knowledge of Divinity): You will understand the mystery of creation from this. How, why, and what I desire, and how I will bring it to pass. You will begin to comprehend My plan and your purpose on Earth and Heaven *(Gita 14:2)*. No one knows Me as I am, and if anyone has come close, such a person is rare.

Vijnan (Wisdom of Divinity): According to our good pleasure, Brahman and I made atoms and many universes (the visible and the invisible). We gave life to all and brought joy, pain and suffering into the world, and in 'The Fullness of Time,' We shall make all whole: restore, reconcile and make restitution and wipe away all pain and suffering *(Gita 14:26)*. The cost of purification of Saints borne by creation will be redeemed and restitution made. We will purge all the unclear/defiled consciousness that pervades the Universe. All will be accounted for. We shall demonstrate to the Universe that nothing thrives in the Universe at the expense of another.

As you get to know Me intimately, all this knowledge will be available. This knowledge is My gift to you. Follow Me, and claim your birthright in Brahman. When you comprehend this, nothing further will remain for you to know in this life. *(Gita 3:31. 10:6. 11:7-16. 14:2 & 26)*

Purification and Perfection

7:3. Thousands seek purification and perfection, but only a small number achieve it. Within this small group, hardly anyone ever dares to climb the summit, where they can come to know Me in truth as I AM.

7:4. Earth, water, fire, air, ether, mind, intellect, and ego are My eight constituents of earthly energies.

7:5. Beyond this, I have another higher energy (spiritual); it supports the entire Universe and is the source of life in all living entities.

The birth of creation and its destruction rests in My hand

7:6. These two aspects of My nature are the source of all created beings. The birth of Creation and its annihilation rest in My hand.

7:7. All things exist due to Me. The entire Universe is suspended around My neck like a necklace of pearls.

My radiance

7:8. Arjuna, I am like the sun's and the moon's radiance. I am the sacred sound Om in the (Vedic Hindu) Scriptures and poems. I am the giver of courage and ability to all.

I am the architect of the creation

7:9. I am the architect of creation, radiance in the fire, breath of life in all creatures, and the source of inspiration to My followers.

I am the seed of life in every creature

7:10. I am the seed of life in every creature, the giver of intelligence and skills to humanity.

7:11. O mighty prince, I am devoid of passion and selfish attachment. I desire life in harmony with the purpose of life.

Goodness, passion, and ignorance

7:12. All states of life—goodness, passion, and ignorance—come from Me, but they do not govern Me. On the contrary, I control them.

7:13. The world indulges in these three modes (goodness, passion, and ignorance) and fails to look beyond them towards Me.

7:14. The three modes of the material world come from Me and are difficult for humanity to overcome. However, those who take refuge in Me can learn to look beyond these three modes.

A fool

7:15. A fool follows his lowest nature and has no desire to seek Me. Material things absorb his heart and mind.

Pious people

7:16. Four kinds of righteous people seek Me for different reasons: the distressed, those who desire wealth, the curious, and those searching for life's meaning and purpose.

7:17. One in search of life's meaning and purpose, unwavering in devotional service to humanity, creation, and Me, surpasses all the others. They are My joy, and I am their joy.

Seekers of truth

7:18. All seekers of truth are blessed. Nevertheless, those established in Me are sure to attain their highest goal.

7:19. Overcoming many trials and errors, the wise continue to persist and freely follow My ways based on informed choice, realising I encompass everything. Such souls are rare, leaving a legacy of love, care, and goodness wherever they go.

Followers of pleasure and selfish desires

7:20. Others are led by their material nature and diverted from the truth. They worship their gods of pleasure and selfish desires.

Free will

7:21. My breath, Atman, is in every person. Each has the free will to pursue their faith. I permit it.

7:22. I allow each person to unify with their faith and desires.

Those who pursue material ends

7:23. Those who pursue material ends worship material gods and attain temporary satisfaction. However, My devotees come to Me for their needs.

7:24. The materially-minded person, lacking understanding, cannot comprehend My imperishable and supreme nature.

He seldom manifests Himself to the materialistic person

7:25. Few see past the veil of materialism to see Me as without birth and changeless. I seldom manifest to a materialistic person. A veil lies between us.

I am the Alpha and the Omega

7:26. I am the Eternal One. The past, present, and future are known to Me. I know every living entity by its names and deeds and regularly take an inventory of its thoughts, motives, and doings. Hence, I know all there is to know about them; however, no one knows Me thoroughly.

All born in ignorance

7:27. All living things are born in ignorance, bewildered by hate, passion, and desire, in their struggle for survival.

Forgiveness and sin

7:28. I forgive the mistakes and sinful actions of pious people who give up their evil and selfish ways and engage in service to promote the welfare and interest of all. Such people are set free from delusion and are well-established in Me.

Old age and death

7:29. Many take refuge in Me, seeking liberation from old age and death. Having acquired a spiritual life, they begin comprehending Brahman in their inner self. They will be united with Me at death.

7:30. Those knowing and serving Me as their Supreme Lord ruling over the cosmos remain conscious of Me at death.

Chapter 8 – Attaining the Supreme Lord

This chapter emphasises the Atman, the divine consciousness, the breath of God that gives life to all entities. The Atman and the soul are like blank pages at conception; as the foetus progresses, they link up.

At birth, the soul is thrust into the river of life, clinging to a raft of makeshift books that begins with a blank page. A page is added each day, and the person's story begins—marred by fear, ignorance, darkness, lust, desire, greed, cruelty, or enhanced by love, kindness, wisdom, joy, romance, and goodness. No two stories are the same. Identical twins, born and raised in the same house, will write different accounts.

All humans are tainted with flaws in life; none is entirely wholesome. Nonetheless, people leave a legacy of love or misery depending on their earthly path.

Later in this chapter, Lord Krishna briefly describes several significant concepts and terms that the Upanishads expound on in detail.

He then explains what happens after death. By implementing His teachings and remembering Him at death, we will attain Him. Therefore, we must practise thinking of God in all our acts. We can do this by considering His qualities, attributes, and virtues. Our minds will be perfectly absorbed in Him, and we will rise from the material dimension to the spiritual realm with practice.

Lord Krishna then talks about the various abodes in the material realm and the cycle of creation and dissolution. He explains how the multitudes of beings manifest in these abodes, and everything is absorbed back into Him at the time of dissolution.

However, the divine abode of God is untouched by this cycle of creation and dissolution. Those who progress on the path of light finally reach the heavenly home.

Those ungodly souls who tread the path of darkness transmigrate in the cycle of birth, old age, sickness, death, lower spiritual realm, and total annihilation.

[The word 'spirit' describes the union of the Atman and soul as it begins its life journey on this unstable, unreliable raft.]

---- ➤

Brahman, truth, and the Atman

Arjuna

8:1. My Lord, I have many questions. What is the truth? Who is Brahman? What is the true self? What is the nature of action?

8:2. How does your breath of life (Atman) reside in My body? Why is Brahman called the 'Lord of Sacrifice?' What kind of sacrificial, devotional service is one required to offer you? How can those engaged in devotional service proceed to you at death?

Krishna

8:3. In My imperishable nature, Brahman resides in My breath of life in every creature as the highest self, Atman. Brahman

and I are the creators and givers of life.

8:4. I am eternal and unchanging. You are continuously changing physically and spiritually. My breath of life resides in you as the Atman, with inert properties of giving and sacrifice.

At the time of death

8:5. Devotees who remember Me at the time of death will come to Me. This is certain.

8:6. At the point of death, one's spirit travels wherever one's true self belongs.

8:7. Therefore, Arjuna, remember Me in all your prescribed duties and call upon Me at the point of death, and I will guide your spirit to Me.

8:8. In all things in life, bear My words in mind and action, and your spirit will reach Me.

All-knowing, all-wise, Lord of the Universe

8:9-10. Meditate on My words. I am the Supreme Lord of all, one who is all-knowing, all-wise, Lord of the Universe, inconceivable and conceivable, almighty. Remember Me at the time of death, and your spirit will return to Me.

All Holy Scriptures

8:11. I am impartial. All Holy Scriptures reveal that those who worship Me are sacrificial, relinquishing selfishness and materialism. They seek to promote the welfare, interest, and happiness of others and Mine. Such people find salvation and eternal life in Me.

At the time of death

8:12-13. Remember Me at the time of death, detach yourself from all senses, and focus your mind on Me. Call out the syllable 'OM', representing the changeless Brahman, and your spirit will peacefully leave your body and come to My abode (spiritual sanctuary).

8:14. My followers constantly serve humanity, creation, and Me. Hence, they quickly attain Me.

8:15. Those who come to know Me, learn to free themselves from the earthly body's miseries forever.

All are subject to joy, pain, and suffering

8:16. Every person and creature on Earth is subject to pleasure, pain, and suffering. However, those attaining My abode acquire the strength to overcome their pain and suffering.

[Suffering. One can learn to overcome it and harness its energy for good. Suffering can enhance compassion, empathy, and non-attachment or *strengthen self-pity and misery.]*

Creation

8:17. A thousand years are like a day and a night to Brahman.

8:18. At the beginning of Brahman's Day, universes came into being, and life sprang forth from Us. Moreover, as the night falls, the Universe and all life fade away.

8:19. Repeatedly, Brahman's days come and go. The cycle of universes, creation, life, and death comes and goes, just as days and nights come and go.

Beyond this material world

8:20. Beyond this material world lays the invisible spiritual reality that cannot be destroyed. Spiritual reality will remain when this world is gone.

The same Lord yesterday, today, and forever

8:21. Those who realise creation's purpose know I am unchanging, the same yesterday, today, and forever. Those who enter My sacred dwelling place freely choose to remain with Me.

All-pervading, omnipotent, omnipresent

8:22. I, the Supreme Lord, am All-pervading, omnipotent, omnipresent (present everywhere), aware of every atom, every creature, every thought, and every deed, in both the material and spiritual realms. I reach out with love to all.

Two Paths at the Point of Death

8:23. There are two paths at the point of death.

8:24. Those who know Me pass through the northern tunnel that leads towards light, brightness, goodness, and Me, whether their time of death is auspicious or not, leaving behind a legacy of love, kindness, justice, and fairness, having enriched the lives of all around them.

8:25. The selfish and evil follow the southern tunnel that leads towards the path of smoke and night, towards a darker, unpleasant place, leaving behind a legacy of greed, selfishness, and misery.

8:26. One leads to light and liberation, and the other leads to ignorance, hate, and darkness.

8:27. Arjuna, do not be troubled by these two paths. Follow My words and listen to the Atman I have given you, and you will follow the radiant path.

Provide selfless service and live a modest life

8:28. Study the Scriptures, give selfless service to others, live modestly, and give to the poor. This selfless duty to others and devotion to My teachings will guide you to your natural spiritual home, My abode.

----9⟩------

Chapter 9 – The Path of Knowledge

Lord Krishna stands in front of Arjuna in His human form, but those seeing only a human being should not underestimate his powers.

In this chapter, Lord Krishna reveals Himself as the Supreme Being who created the Universe, inspiring reverence, devotion, and awe.

He says that as the mighty winds blow everywhere yet always stay within the sky, all living beings dwell within Him. He is involved in every activity of creation. Among all living entities, He stays impartial and unattached until someone or something implores Him to intervene.

In addition, in this chapter, Krishna resolves the apparent confusion of the many gods and goddesses of the Hindu pantheon. It is Krishna and Krishna alone who is to be worshipped: he is the goal, the support, the only refuge, the one true friend; he is the beginning and the end.

Lord Krishna exalts the superiority of pure bhakti, exercising selfless love towards his creation and Him. Such a devotee lives in complete union with His will, doing everything for Him and offering everything to Him. Their pure devotion helps them attain the mystic union with Him.

Lord Krishna asserts that He is impartial towards all creatures; He neither favours nor rejects anyone. When despicable sinners take refuge in Him and amend their ways, He accepts them willingly and quickly reforms them.

Lord Krishna then says He will not let His devotees perish, as He is sited within them in their Atman. From there, He guides them and provides them with whatever they lack to fulfil their mission in life. Therefore, we should dedicate our minds and bodies to Him, worship Him, always think of Him, and make Him our supreme goal.

---- ➤ ----

Krishna

9:1. My dear Arjuna, I shall now tell you a profound mystery: this knowledge will free you from the miseries of material existence.

9:2. This knowledge leads to the perfection of one's self. When applied to daily life, it is a great cleaner, leads to righteousness, and, in the hereafter, to My abode. Use it joyfully.

Those who reject My Holy Scriptures

9:3. Those who reject the teachings of My Holy Scriptures (*sacred teachings given to various nations, races, and tribes*) are walking away from their place in My eternal spiritual home. They will pass from physical death to the spiritual realm appropriate to their nature and then pass away into their final demise.

Creation: Relationship between The Lord and all creatures

9:4. I uphold the entire Universe. I am everywhere, and everything is in Me. All animals and beings find their existence in Me, yet I am aloof.

9:5. With My blessing, Brahman created the Universe, and all the animals and people in the Universe depend on Us, yet I am independent of creation.

9:6. All creatures and created beings rest in Me, just as the mighty wind moves everywhere and comes to rest in the sky.

9:7. We (Supreme Lord God and Brahman) created the Universe with all the creatures, and in the end, we absorb all and begin a new era.

We bring creation and life into being and annihilate it

9:8. The entire cosmic order is under our control. We bring it into being and annihilate it at our pleasure, repeatedly.

9:9. I am involved in every activity of creation. Cosmoses come, and cosmoses go. Among all living entities, I stay impartial and unattached to anything until someone or something implores Me to intervene.

9:10. This material cosmos is part of My natural laws of physics, and they are created and annihilated repeatedly. Thus, the Universe and life are created and annihilated at My will.

Manifestation in human forms

9:11. Fools deride Us when Brahman, angels, or I manifest in human forms. The ignorant do not look beyond the physical to see that The Lord of all creation instigates it.

The ignorant

9:12. Hence, the ignorant are deluded and attracted to atheistic views. Their lives bear no meaning and are fraught with misery; their works are all in vain.

Saints

9:13-14 Great souls always seek to serve Me as the Supreme Lord of the material and spiritual Universe. They humbly bow down and worship Me in loving devotion.

9:15. Some present offerings to Me, seeking knowledge and spiritual wisdom. Others, in ignorance, bow down and worship aspects of My forms and idols instead of Me.

I am the healer

9:16. I am the ritual, the sacrifice. I am the healer, the offering, and the fire that consumes all the offerings.

I am the Beginning and End, Alpha and Omega. The womb in which all life rests.

9:17. I am the Father, Mother, Friend, and the Universe's Grandfather. 'I am incomprehensible beyond the concept of the human mind. Nonetheless, I reach out to humans and creatures at a level where they can comprehend Me; none is turned away, and in 'The Fullness of Time', all will be reconciled, restored, and made whole—no one thrives in God's Kingdom at the expense of another. I sustain all. I am the sum total of all knowledge, one who purifies and the transcendental sound, 'Om'. I am the giver of sacred Scriptures and the Vedas.

9:18. I am the goal, the sustainer of all life, the inner witness, and the abode of all. A friend and refuge for all. The creator and destroyer. The beginning (Alpha), the middle, and the end (Omega), the one who endures through the ages. The basis for all life. I am the womb in which all life rests.

9:19. I am immortal. I give heat and send forth the rain or hold it back. I am life, and I am death. Both spirit and matter reside in Me.

Study and worship

9:20. Those who study the Holy Books and worship Me free themselves from ignorance, darkness, fear, and evil. They attain a place in the heavenly realms and have access to My wisdom and blessings.

9:21. Some engage in the spiritual matter for a short time, are soon exhausted, and return to rituals and the pleasures of the senses.

9:22. I uphold and provide for all the needs of those fully committed to serving My creation and Me.

Followers of other religions worship Me

9:23. Devoted followers of other religions worship Me, even though their ways of serving and worshipping are different. All are acceptable if they are devoted to My creation and Me.

9:24. I am the only Supreme Lord of the Universe and the ultimate object of worship of all faiths. Those who fail to realise My true nature soon sink into material existence.

Those who honour Me will join Me

9:25. Those who worship idols, spirits, ghosts, or ancestors will go to such realms upon death. Those who honour Me will join Me.

9:26. I accept with joy from a pure heart any devotional offerings, such as a flower, a fruit, or a cup of water.

Whatever you do, do it as an offering to Me.

9:27. Whatever you do, the food you eat, the help you offer others, and the suffering you endure, do it as an offering to Me.

9:28. In this way, you will be free from the bondage to duty and, from its result, both pleasant and painful. With your mind fixed on Me, you liberate yourselves from material existence to serve humanity, creation, and Me.

Rendering loving service to My creation and Me

9:29. I look upon all creatures equally. Nevertheless, whoever renders caring service to My creation and Me is My friend. They live in Me, I in them, and I impart spiritual life to them.

Sinners

9:30. Sinners become holy when they take refuge in My ways and amend their ways.

9:31. When such past sinners amend their ways, their sins are forgiven, and they attain lasting peace. None is ever abandoned.

9:32. Regardless of race, sex, colour, or caste, people who call upon Me will gain My attention.

All are born in this transient world of sacrificial love, pain, and suffering

9:33. Even kings and those of noble birth seek My attention. All are born in this transient world of sacrificial love, pain, suffering, and joy. Therefore, engage in loving service to My creation and Me.

Seek Me with all your heart and mind

9:34. Fill your thoughts with Me. Seek Me, worship Me with all your heart, mind, and strength, and I will reward you.

------- ↬----

Chapter 10 – Divine Grace

The previous chapter was about loving devotion to God. In this chapter, Lord Krishna goes deeper into the revelation of his divine being, revealing Himself as the source of all that exists, and from whom all human qualities arise. He is also the ultimate reality.

Devotees who know this engage in His devotion with great faith, derive immense joy and pleasure by conversing about His glories and help enlighten others.

Lord Krishna then says He dwells in the hearts of devotees whose minds are always united with Him. To encourage them, He bestows His divine knowledge and blessings, by which they draw nearer to Him.

It is from Him that the seven great sages, the four great saints, and the fourteen Manus were born, and all the people of this world descended from them.

Arjuna is amazed and requests Him to describe more of His divine nature. Lord Krishna then discloses that everything that exists manifests His energies, and He is the beginning, middle, and end of all. All beings and things get their splendour from Him, and we see nothing but a tiny spark of His energies in this life.

The rest of the chapter describes His personality, objects, and activities. From verse 25 on, the chapter becomes difficult because of the many unfamiliar names mentioned. Krishna is portrayed as the best, most intense, beautiful, and excellent in each category.

However, His true nature is beyond the reach of thought, and He can be known partially in the state of Samadhi, where knower and known become one.

Since God is the source of all life, and our life rests in His hands, we should make Him the object of our devotion.

---- ➤ ----

Supreme Lord Krishna's Splendour and the Compassionate Warrior

10:1. **Supreme Lord Krishna:** Listen, Arjuna, O mighty warrior. Because you are My friend, I will give you a deeper insight into what I have already explained, confirming them by signs and miracles. Thus, such evidence will establish reality in your spiritual walk and inspire you to walk beside Me as I guide, correct, and prepare you for eternity.

10:2. Neither the demigods (*mythological beings with more power than mortals, but less than a God*) nor the many saints and sages know My origin or splendour. In their ignorance, many people and saints often visualize Me as one of the demigods or an idol.

Krishna has no beginning

10:3. Whoever knows Me as having no beginning and as The Lord of creation is free from illusion and comprehends the truth.

All the qualities of living beings

10:4-5. All the qualities of living beings, control of the senses, charity, non-violence, knowledge, wisdom, understanding, intelligence, freedom, forgiveness, truthfulness, happiness, fear, distress, pleasure, pain, courage, birth, and death come from Me.

The mighty seven sages and the ancestors of all humanity

10:6. The mighty seven sages (archangels, guardians of the Universe), the four great ancestors (elders), and the fourteen Manus (ancestors of all humanity) came from Me—born from My mind. All beings populating the various continents, planets, and universes descend from them.

I, the Supreme Lord, passed unto Brahman the breath of life. From Brahman came the *seven great sages, four great thinkers, Sanka, Sananda, Santana, Sanat-kumara, and fourteen Manus. Together, they form the **twenty-five Elders[1]** of the Universe.

> Note: -
> The Bible, written a few centuries after the Gita, has many of Gita's concepts.
> For example, in the Bible's Book of Revelation 5:8, 'Now when he had taken

> *the scroll, the four living creatures and the **twenty-four Elders** bowed before the **Lamb** (the twenty-fifth **Elder**[1]), each having a harp, and golden bowls full of incense, which are the prayers of the saints.'*

10:7. People who understand My mystic power are engaged in devotional service to My creation and walk beside Me.

Everything emanates from Me (Krishna)

10:8. I am the source of all the material and spiritual worlds. Everything emanates from Me. The wise comprehend this and worship Me with loving devotion.

My devotees

10:9. My devotees' thoughts and lives centre on Me. They derive tremendous satisfaction and happiness from their service to society and Me. Teaching one another and conversing about Me, they enlighten one another.

10:10. My devotees serve Me with love. I give them wisdom and dispel their ignorance.

Gracious, compassionate, and merciful

10:11. I am warm, generous, forgiving, gracious, compassionate, and merciful. I dwell in My devotees' hearts and minds, dispelling the darkness born from ignorance with the light from the lamp of knowledge, affirmed with signs and miracles. Hence, My devotees follow My example.

Supreme Lord, the truth, the light, and the Eternal One

10:12-13. **Arjuna:** You are the supreme Lord of the Universe, the absolute truth, the light of the Universe, the Eternal One. Unborn and infinite. All the great saints confirm this, and now you have declared this knowledge to Me and validated it with signs and wonders.

10:14. O Lord, neither the demigods nor demons know your true nature. I accept all the things you have told Me as truth.

Origin of all life forms

10:15. Indeed, you alone know yourself, O Supreme Lord of the Universe. You are the origin of all life forms and their Lord.

10:16. My Lord, tell Me about your divine nature and how it permeates the Universe.

Constant awareness of The Lord

10:17. You are the supreme mystic. How can I gain constant awareness of you, and how can I know you better? What are the things I need to do?

Your creative power

10:18. You are the destroyer of unbelief and ignorance. Tell Me in detail about your mystic creative power. How does it stir up people's hearts? The more I hear, the more I want to taste the sweetness of your words.

Krishna's power and majesty

10:19. **Krishna:** Arjuna, there is no limit to My powers. 'I am incomprehensible beyond the concept of the human mind (na Asti), yet I reach out to all to the extent (vistarasya) they can comprehend Me.

10:20. I am in the heart of all living entities. My breath of life via Brahman flows through all beings and creatures. I am the beginning, middle, and end of their existence.

10:21-22. To some believers, I am Vishnu; to others, I am Lord Indra, King of Heaven. In all living entities, I am the living force (consciousness).

10:23. To some people, I am the Supreme Lord. To others, I am Lord Siva. (To the Jews and Christians, I am Jehovah/Yahweh. In Sikhism, I am Akal Murati. To the Muslims, I am Allah.)

10:24 Brahman is the eternal **high priest*, Brihaspati.** Among the warriors, I am the chief commander of the righteous. [In the Bible's Book of Hebrews 6:20, 'high priest* (Jesus) forever after the order of Melchizedek'.]

10:25. Among the great sages, Brahman is the High Priest Bhrigu. Among the words, the syllable 'Om' is the sacred sound in the Universe. During the offering of sacrifice, My devotees chant My name.

10:26-30. The entire Universe and everything in it glorifies Me.

I am the guardian of the Universe

10:31. I am the guardian of the Universe. Among some warriors, I have been portrayed as Rama.

I am the beginning, present, and end

10:32. I am the Universe's beginning, present, and end. In science, I am knowledge and logic itself.

Among creation, I am in unison with Brahman, the Creator

10:33. I am time itself, infinite. Among creation, Brahman and I are in unison.

10:34. I am all-devouring death and the energy source of all beings still to be born. I have feminine and masculine characteristics.

10:35. Among the months, I am the first month of the year. Among the seasons, I am spring, which brings forth the flowers.

10:36. I am radiance in all that illuminates. I am the nemesis of the gamblers; I am the giver of victory and strength to the righteous.

Lord Krishna represents My opulence

10:37. The name Lord Krishna represents My divine nature and opulence among many cultures.

Judge of the Universe

10:38. I am The Lord who metes out punishment. I empower public officials to punish criminals. Among the wise, I impart wisdom. I am the holder of all secrets.

Nothing exists without Me

10:39. O Arjuna, I give life to all living entities. Nothing exists without Me.

10:40. There is no limit to My divine power. I have shown you a fraction of My infinite energy in a manner you can comprehend.

10:41. Wherever you find strength, beauty, or power, it all springs from a spark of My essence.

I pervade and support the entire Universe

10:42. But what use is all this knowledge to you, Arjuna? All you need to know is that I pervade and support the Universe.

---------- ॐ ------

Chapter 11 – Cosmic Vision (Insight into spiritual realms)

This is the most profound chapter of the entire Gita. In this chapter, Arjuna asks to see Krishna as He really is and is granted a divine vision of Him as The Lord of the Universe.

Arjuna sees the entire cosmos in the body of Lord Krishna, with unlimited planetary systems, stars, nebulae, galaxies, galactic clusters, black holes, atoms, and molecules. Then, Lord Krishna's body stretches in all directions. His arms, face, and body have no beginning or end and extend in all directions. Arjuna's mind is focused, and a super conscious mode of knowledge and insight (Kly-son ability) comes into play.

The sight dazzles Arjuna, and the hair on the back of his neck stands on end. He witnesses the entire Universe in the body of Krishna from the beginning before anything came into existence up to the end time and gets an insight into the Creator's mind. He witnesses the 'Day of The Lord/Judgement)' and how Earth's people are evaluated, sentenced, or rewarded. Furthermore, he sees the glorious future worlds and his role in each arena.

Sitting in the palm of The Lord, Arjuna is surrounded by several sages from every race and faith, offering prayers and singing hymns exalting God. Then Arjuna sees the light of God on *'The Day of The Lord'*, which becomes a fire that consumes all things. All the ungodly (spiritually blind) and evil people, his cousins among them and their allies, are rushing into the mouth of this formidable Lord, like moths rushing with great speed towards the fire, burning in the universal fire.

He struggles to comprehend his role in God's kingdom, his essence in The Lord's mind predestined before creation, now unveiled to him; his enormous roles in all these realms, from the beginning of time, current, and future spiritual realms, and more, to the End of Times. He has free will and the choice to walk away anytime from it all or continue to stay and grow spiritually.

His unique place in God's kingdom also dawns upon him. As God's love permeates him, the tremendous trust and expectations placed upon his shoulders in this life and the hereafter become apparent to Arjuna. It is simply overwhelming. He becomes despondent. He weighs his puny self against the task ahead, requiring all his strength and more.

It would take him many years to figure it out, but for the moment, he is saturated with that brilliant light of love, acceptance, and oneness with the Universe and God. He starts to drown in this ocean of love.

Overwhelmed, fearful, and confused, Arjuna praises The Lord and offers several salutations to Him. He also begs Lord Krishna's forgiveness for any disrespect he may have previously committed when The Lord had appeared to him as a mere human.

Arjuna then pleads to The Lord to help him comprehend all he has experienced and to have the strength and resolve to fulfil his role. He further requests Lord Krishna to take on His human form.

The Supreme Lord sighs with relief, for this moment has brought him and all the heavenly saints an untold amount of pleasure, having waited an infinite amount of time for this golden moment, the birth of a renewed star. Where Arjuna goes, others follow.

Lord Krishna first manifests into His four-armed form, holding a mace, disc, conch shell, and lotus flower in each hand. Then, He resumes His gentle and loving two-armed human form as Krishna.

He then tells Arjuna that no one has ever perceived God in this cosmic form or comprehended their role in God's Kingdom in such depth. Even those who study the Vedas, do severe penance, give charity, and offer sacrifices still do not get this opportunity. Only with devotion, a clean heart, and a pure mind can one perceive God and get to know Him deeply.

As the reader meditates, these words come to life, and the hair at the back of the neck stands up. Electric current surges through the person, and the dormant words from the scripture and the Atman unite through which the Divine Spirit flows, and the person is renewed (refreshed, born again). A warm blanket envelops the body, permeating the spirit and lifting the person into the very presence of the heavenly throne. A sense of oneness with all and a deep peace encompasses the person.

As the storm settles, a sense of calmness, peace, acceptance, purpose, and love flows through the person. Tears of joy and well-being flow through the person, washing away years of frustration, meaninglessness, anger, hatred, and restlessness, all swept away by the torrent of living waters. A child of God has been transformed (born again) and is no longer at odds with his fellow brothers, creatures or himself.

---- ➤ ----

11:1. Arjuna: My Lord, you have kindly given me insight into the mystery of the spiritual realms, confirming Your words with signs and miracles. My delusions are diminished.

11:2. You have shown me your limitless power and eternal existence in visions and revealed the secret of the beginning and end of all creatures and creation.

How and why you created the Universe

11:3-4. Now, I want to know how and why you made the Universe and how you exercise your rule over it. Moreover, please show me your immortal self if you consider me worthy.

I manifest Myself

11:5. Krishna: I manifest Myself to all living entities in a manner and at a level that they can comprehend Me.

11:6. My dear friend, at a level you can understand, I will now reveal more of My eternal self in a form never seen or heard before—a privilege granted to a few rare beings.

Cosmic Cycle: Mysteries of the Universe

11:7. In My body, you will perceive the entire cosmic cycle passing before your eyes. Whatever you want to see: the past, present, future, **creation** (*refer to the end of the book),* Earth, and spiritual sanctuaries will flash before you. You will find answers to questions regarding the terms 'In the Fullness of Time' and 'The end of all material and spiritual realms' and your purpose on Earth and in the heavenly realms. The mysteries of the Universe are available to all brave enough to seek them. *(Gita 3:31. 7:2. 9:8-9. 10:6.)*

Validating with signs and miracles

11:8. Humans cannot see spiritual things with physical eyes. However, they can receive spiritual insight and vision from Me. I grant such **knowledge** *(Gita 7:2)* and wisdom to spiritually hungry people with the courage and tenacity to wait upon Me and claim them. I give insight, knowledge, and understanding, validating with signs and miracles, establishing reality in their spiritual walk and inspiring them to walk beside Me as I guide, correct, and prepare them for eternity.

The divine plan for creation

11:9. Having spoken these words to Arjuna, The Lord God reveals his exalted form and unveils his divine plan for creation.

Sitting on the palm of The Lord, Arjuna sees a multitude of saints singing hymns and praising The Lord. He hears their intercession to relieve humanity's and the Earth's creatures' suffering.

11:10-12. Before Arjuna flashed the cosmos, multiple universes, life forms, and the revelation of the divine mystery, from nothing appeared Brahman and the power of thought; from the thought came the energy, the first three tears, matter, and antimatter.

Gita 11:5-12 / Elaboration-Testimony F1-14.

F1. One of the Sages/Elders catches his eye and walks up to Arjuna. 'Follow me,' he commands. He follows the sage to a place full of books. The distinguishing-looking Elder picks up eight books and hands them to Arjuna. (Gita 10:6. 11:21.)

F2. He says to Arjuna, 'When you read these books, they will unveil the mystery of the Universe. What was in The Lord's mind, how, when, and why He created the Universe, humanity, the spiritual realms, the end times, and

---

your role in all this. (Gita 4:3-4. 10:6-8. 18:55-56.)

F3. *'Everything you see in the Universe will make sense. Nothing will be hidden from you. All you ever wanted to know or would want to know will be available to you in due course in visions, insight, and wisdom as you walk beside The Lord and us and grow spiritually. The Lord will validate His words with signs and miracles. Thus, such evidence will establish reality in your spiritual walk and inspire you to walk beside The Lord as He guides, corrects, and prepares you for eternity.' (Gita 11:3-5.)*

F4. *Time stops as Arjuna immerses himself in the books. He is astounded when he comes to the eighth book and opens it. He looks at the Elder and says, 'Sire, this book is blank!' (Gita 12:2-4)*

F5. *The Elder answers, 'It is your book of prayer, and whatever you write in this book, it will come to pass' (Gita 18:68-69). You will write names and locations and pray for dates, times, and hours for healing to occur or for the rain to fall, and it will happen. Kings, nations, and dictators will fall from grace at your bidding. Write specific things so the world knows The Lord reigns in your life. (Gita 18:68-69.)*

F6. *'In the hereafter, many people and nations will seek your wisdom. They will come from the four corners of the Earth, people of great learning and the broken-hearted and disillusioned, the product of war, poverty, disease, and man's inhumanity to each other. The Lord will permit 'The sorrow of the world' to engulf you. It will break your heart and your spirit. The saint put his arm on Arjuna's shoulder and looked into his eyes. 'Remember, power corrupts. When divine power is used, it is exercised with great responsibility, accountability, and wisdom.*

'Furthermore, it has to be exercised to undo any unintentional consequences and restore, repay, make restitution and make everything affected whole. We believe the Supreme Lord dispenses power under such terms, which is why we feel that on 'The Day of The Lord', before all are evaluated, He will account for all the works of creation and be seen to have fulfilled His terms as a lesson to all (Gita 9:33-34. 15:19-20. 18:5-7.)

F7. *'Be one with us, and we will be one with you. With the help of The Lord, we and other gifted beings in the hereafter will guide you and other tested and refined devotees to reconcile, restore, and make all worthy people whole. It will take more than great strength of character and spirit and untold years to* undo (atom by atom) all the evil done to them. For that, The Lord has made all the resources of Heaven available to us. Will you join us?' (Gita 11:47-48.)

F8. Arjuna remains quiet. His mind is unable to Fathom the situation. (Gita 2:25.)

F9. The Elder continues, 'All the things that have occurred and will take place in your life are being used to prepare and fit you for this task. When you join us, your abilities will be significantly enhanced to carry out this task. Once you have reread these books, gradually, you will see what you have read manifest before you. It will become part of your life.' (Gita 4:20. 5:3. 7:28)

F10. The Elder continues, 'Arjuna, you chose to take solace in The Lord's palm, a jewel refined in Earth's burning, purifying fire.' (Gita 4:3. 7:23.)

F11. Arjuna reflects on his past, and suddenly, it dawns on him that it was a path he had freely chosen with informed knowledge. He asks the Elder, 'How could I have chosen before I was born?' (Gita 7:26. 11:15-16).

F12. The Elder smiles. 'My dear friend, you chose freely with informed knowledge: knowledge validated by Divine signs and power. You chose the path before you were born.' (Gita 7:26. 4:4.)

F13. 'But how could I?' Arjuna asks. (Gita 4:39 & 42. 5:16-17. 6:8. 7:2.)

F14. The Elder replies, 'Our Lord is time itself, all knowledge, all wisdom. Your Atman is part of Him and you. Thus, you were always with Him and not always with Him. Continue on your path and claim the privilege of gaining the right hand of fellowship from the Elders and sitting in their Council, the highest honour granted to humans. 'My Lord,' Arjuna asks. 'What is this honour?' He replies, 'It is your spiritual inheritance from God.' (Gita 2:12-14. 2:20. 8:27-28.)

(ONE SHOULD ONLY PRAY TO GOD, NOT SAINTS. Only God has the resources and appropriate wisdom to meet our needs).

Arjuna's dilemma

11:13 Arjuna: Lord, you have revealed all this to me, but this plan is vast and beyond my comprehension. You have invited me to share your goals and be part of them. If I choose to go my own way, as some have done, and die in the natural order, I will remember nothing, lose nothing, and gain nothing. However, you, Lord, will lose a generous spirit, someone who touched your very being, a loss etched into your memory for eternity.

11:14. Sitting among the heavenly saints and the Elders of the Universe, Arjuna struggles to understand the mystery of God's plan and his eternal journey through it, led by the divine spirit. He is amazed *(having been granted unique access to the inner mind of The Lord God)*. He bows before The Lord God and speaks these words.

Brahman is sitting on the throne, surrounded by the Elders of the Universe

11:15. **Arjuna:** O Lord, in this vision, I saw what your thoughts, plans, and desires were before anything came into existence. I saw Brahman sitting on the throne, surrounded by the Elders of the Universe and all the living entities.

I have gained some insight into your plan for creation, affirmed by signs from You. I saw the beginning, present, and future realms flash before me. I saw the Cosmos created by Brahman, atom by atom, each named and known by him. I saw the Universe come into being, piece by piece. The first subatomic particle was named 83.45. Each was lovingly created, entered into his inventory, and accounted for daily by Brahman. Each atom has a name and a place in your grand plan.

I saw the lives of ancient sages and the beginning and end of all things. All kinds of living things came to life. All were loved

and cherished, each according to its value.

11:16. Untold numbers of life forms on Earth and spiritual sanctuaries passed before me. I saw the beginning and end of all. You gave life and brought joy, pain and suffering into our lives, and in 'The Fullness of Time' (before The Day of The Lord), you made us whole (restored, made restitution) and wiped away all pain and suffering. You showed/proved that nothing thrives in the Universe at the expense of another. I comprehended your joy and sorrow from start to end.

In your first thought, I saw my name chosen with great care, written in your Eternal Books, sealed by your loving tears. I saw your excellent plan for me on Earth, in the spiritual sanctuary, and I beheld the very last thought of mine before the end of all creation.

All I saw had a beginning and an end. Yet, you have no beginning, middle, or end. You are The Lord of creation; the cosmos and my life rest in your hands.

Crowned with glory

11:17. Now I perceive you (not Brahman) surrounded by myriads of saints and Elders of the Universe offering prayers and hymns. You are seated in the centre of the Elders on your throne, crowned with the glory of your creation, spreading in all directions like a blazing sun. I comprehend all this, yet your true form is challenging to understand.

Arjuna's perception of God and humanity's purpose began to unveil

Gita 11:13-17 / Elaboration-Testimony F15-20.

F15. A considerate God created the Universe, in which all that has the breath of God goes through phases of joy, pain, and suffering. All are intentionally or not participants in contributing to God's kingdom on Earth and in Heaven. The Lord has designated this period on earth and heaven to train and perfect his chosen saints. Hence, a loving, benevolent God has the duty of care to compensate for the pain and suffering endured by all living entities (excluding the selfishness and evil brought by oneself), making fourfold restitution, sometimes on Earth, but mainly in the spiritual sanctuaries. That is a divine mystery unknown to most. Neither God nor His saints thrive at the expense of another. (Gita 3:31. 7:1-2. 11:1-4.)

F16. Fulfilling Brahman's laws, Gita 3:16: The Vedas (Scriptures) state that the Universe rotates on the axle of sacrifice. Brahman and I set this law in motion to train, discipline, and enlighten all in the principle of sacrifice. In heavenly realms, no adult living entity (exempting babies and young children), not even I, the Supreme Lord, thrive at the expense of another. Those who choose to live only for this world live in vain. Gita

---

3:16. 9:12.)

F17. Arjuna saw the law fulfilled in the end, just before the creation was dissolved. All were made whole, except the Evil ones. (Gita 3:10 15-17. 4:20 & 33. 6:3 & 47. 7:6. 9:22. 14:26.)

F18. Arjuna, resting on the divine palm, beholds his unique role in this excellent venture. Two beings, one a speck of dust, the other incomprehensible, building a place of love and acceptance—a home and a sanctuary of rest for all those worthy of The Lord's mercy and grace. (Gita 4:3. 11:47-48. 18:55.)

F19. Like most humans, Arjuna struggles to comprehend humanity's purpose in God's creative plan and God's expectations at the end of the creation, i.e. 'The Jewel,' the cleansed and purified spiritual people forged from the purifying fire of creation. (Gita 11:14. 2:50. 3:41. 7:2. 8:21. 11:7 & 45-48. 12:13-14. 13:1. 18:33 & 36. 18:50.)

F20. As a Father looks upon a son, he feels The Lord's thoughts, 'You matter more to Me than I matter to you. You are My joy, My delight. I did this so you (all devotees) and I could walk together as Father and (adopted) son/daughter one day.' (Gita 5:21. 7:17. 9:26. 6:20-23 & 47. 10:7. 18:55.)

11:18. Arjuna: You are the supreme reality, the refuge of all creation, the eternal, immortal spirit, and the guardian of all entities.

11:19. You have no beginning, middle, or end. Your glory fills the Universe. I see a blazing fire from your eyes and mouth and your radiance warming the Universe.

11:20. Your presence fills the Universe, and all are in awe of you.

11:21. All the hosts of Heaven and the cosmos tremble in fear and bow down before your throne. Saints with folded hands offer prayers and sing hymns, crying out peace to all.

11:22. All living entities from the cosmos are overwhelmed by you.

11:23. The entire Universe and I are terrorised at your sight.

11:24. O Lord, I perceive you surrounded by many radiant colours, with your open mouth and glowing eyes like fire. I tremble, and my courage and peace of mind flee from me.

11:25. With your wide-open mouth afire, I perceive your formidable nature swallowing the cosmos. O Lord, the refuge of the Universe, be gracious and have mercy upon me on that fearsome day (Day of The Lord).

On the Day of The Lord

11:26-29. On that fearsome day, I see Dhritarashtra's sons (all spiritually unsound and evil beings) and the allied kings with Bhisma, Drona, Karna, and all the warriors rushing towards their **deaths*** like moths into a flame.

> *Gita 11:26-29 / Elaboration-Testimony F21 deaths* *This is the second death (utter destruction). The first death was of the material body on Earth. On this fearsome day, it will be the death of the soul/spirit. Their Atman, however, will return to God, from whom it originally came. (Gita 2:18 & 20-25. 5:14.)*

The entire Universe bursts into fire

11:30. Filled with your terrible radiance on that fearsome day, the whole Universe bursts into fire, and you lap up all the ungodly into your mouth, devouring all.

11:31. I am bewildered as to who you are. I behold you as utterly fierce and destructive. I bow before you, all-pervading Lord.

Krishna, I am the destroyer

11:32. **Krishna:** I am time, and I am the destroyer. All the ungodly gathered on the Day of The Lord will perish. However, good, godly, honest, decent people will survive and continue to live.

> *Gita 11:11-32 / Elaboration-Testimony F22-31*

F22. Arjuna is given a unique privileged position sitting in the palm of The Lord. Like most mortals, he fails to grasp his influence with The Lord. He has the ear of the most powerful being in the Universe. So why does he not grasp the immense power and influence he commands? (Gita 11:9-30.)

F23. The answer is simple. At this early stage of his life, he has very little understanding of the workings of the mind of The Lord. For example, he prays but often does not see the prayer answered as requested. He fails to understand that God always responds to a prayer request, but not always as asked, since an answered prayer may have undesired repercussions that he is unaware of. (Gita 4:4. 7:2.))

F24. For example, a farmer prays for rain. Consider my ten-dimensional cube of the Universe (or Earth) No. 108 at the end of the book. Each sub-cube represents the atmospheric pressure or gravitational force over 27 Earth's or galaxy sectors. Changing the atmospheric pressure or the gravitational force in one sub-segment would require minimal changes in three other sub-cubes to restore the net outer balance of the cube, i.e., Earth or the Galaxy. Changing a single number in one sub-cube upsets the cube's total sum balance. (Gita 2:49. 4:20.)

F25. God always answers prayers, but not always in the way people want. If God answered the farmer's prayer for rain to fall over his land, the atmospheric pressure would change over his and three other sectors. Then, three other farmers will begin to pray because their environment has changed. It sets off a chain of undesirable reactions. (Gita 5:3.)

F26. Thus, waiting upon The Lord to see what He is about to do is far better. Find out the time, how and when He will answer the prayer and the reason for such action. This requires patience and good spiritual ears. Then, one can pray a specific prayer with a precise time, date, and outcome in line with God's will. One has established a sense of spiritual reality if it happens as prophesied. This is an excellent way to grow in faith and understand the workings of The Lord's mind. It also confirms that the walk with The Lord is genuine and not something brought about by good imagination. (Gita 6:13-14. 6:20-23 & 47. 7:1. 11:8. 10:7. 15:4.)

F27. When one connects with the most powerful being in the Universe, an electric current surges through, and the hair on the back of the neck rises with fear and joy. Spontaneously from the depth of one's being, a voice cries, 'Abba Father, Om-Tat-Sat. I am a speck of dirt, but I have the ear of the most *powerful being in the Universe.' (Gita 18:55 & 58 & 61 & 65 & 68-69.)*

F28. We are all spiritual orphans. *You may have heard or read accounts of adopted children and their intense need to find their biological parents. There is a deep need in us to find our sense of purpose, meaning, fulfilment, and a place of belonging. Some will suppress this need and get on with their worldly lives, while others will constantly pine to fill this void by seeking spiritual knowledge and experience. (Gita 2:41. 3:17 & 41. 4:33. 5:3. 11:7 & 45-46. 13:1. 16:23. 18:36.)*

F29. *Imagine standing in the presence of the Almighty, and you experience the warmth of a divine blanket that overshadows your whole being. All your worries, anxieties, and problems melt away under the power of that warmth. Your entire being crumbles down, soaked in love and acceptance. Tears of joy flow freely, and you cry with pleasure from your depths, 'Om-Tat-Sat.' Your spirit has finally found its true eternal home. (Gita 4:3. 6:20-23. 10:7. 15:4. 18:55.)*

F30. *You cry, 'I have found my spiritual home, parents, family. I am home, cherished, forgiven, wanted, loved.' (Gita 4:9. 8:28. 18:72.)*

F31. *From that moment, your whole being and life change. No amount of gold, silver, or adorations of others can supersede this experience, nor can all the gold on this Earth buy you this experience. (Gita 13:5. 15:4.)*

Fight the material and spiritual battle

11:33. **Krishna:** Arjuna, prepare to fight the material and spiritual struggle against darkness, ignorance, poverty, selfishness, and greed. Overcome them, and win glory on behalf of all people and your Lord.

Listen, Arjuna, conquer your greatest enemy: ignorance, selfishness, and fears. Build My kingdom of knowledge, truth, and justice in your heart and the hearts and minds of others, and bring light to the dark places in the Universe.

Dhritarashtra and his kind are mentally and spiritually unsound and doomed. These **ungodly**[1] children of darkness follow a path that leads to their doom. They are the living **dead**[2], though they appear alive.

Gita 11:33 / Elaboration-Testimony F32-33.

F32. The character of spiritually unsound (sightless) people and some of their destructive qualities: anger, hate, fear, shame, greed, self-pity, contempt, resentment, boredom, arrogance, jealousy, judgemental, uncontrolled desire, discomfort, lamentation, confusion.

Lacking: wisdom, universal love, kindness, holiness, purity of heart, and a sound mind subjugated to the Atman. (Gita 1:37-38 & 42. 16:9)

*F33. ² **dead** deemed spiritually dead. Temporarily kept alive as part of God's plan to expose the danger of ignorance, selfishness, and evil. Furthermore, to enlighten and perfect the godly-minded, until this fearsome day, many call 'The Day of The Lord - Judgement Day.' (Gita 2:42-43. 8:25-26. 14:17. 16:9. 2:50. 3:16. 4:15. 4:31-33. 15:20. 18:56)*

11:34. **Krishna:** All these people, Drona, Bhisma, Jayadratha, and Karna, have condemned themselves to their final (spiritual) death. Therefore, Arjuna, stand up, be courageous, and fight the adversary of ignorance, injustice, and darkness pervading Earth and the Cosmos. Do not hesitate to fight in this battle and conquer our enemies.

Saints bow down before The Lord while evil people flee

11:35. **Sanjaya**, the great sage, relays to King Dhritarashtra: Arjuna, feeling the weight of responsibility and trust placed on him, trembles in fear. He bows down before Lord God (Krishna) and speaks falteringly.

11:36. **Arjuna:** O Lord, it is fitting that the world delights and rejoices in your praise. Saints bow down before you while evil people flee from you.

You are the original Creator, Worthy of worship by all

11:37. O Lord, you are more significant than Brahman, the Creator. You are the original creator. How could they not worship you? You are limitless, the refuge of the Universe. You are The Lord of Lords. Only you are worthy of praise and worship.

11:38-39. You are the eternal, timeless Spirit, the resting place of all living entities. You pervade the entire Cosmos. You are the Father and

Grandfather of all creatures. You are inconceivable to the human mind (10:19). Yet, You reach out to the animals and us at a level all can comprehend. You are our Heavenly Father; none is turned away, and in 'The Fullness of Time', all will be reconciled, restored, and made whole— no one thrives in Your Kingdom at the expense of another. I bow before You. Only You are worthy of praise and worship. You are our final home.

11:40. You are everywhere I turn. You are all-knowing, and your power is immeasurable.

11:41-42. In our friendship, I was casual, disrespectful, and ignorant of your majesty in the past. Please forgive me, for I did not know of your greatness until now.

11:43. You are the Father of the Universe—the supreme teacher—and only you are worthy of worship by all. No one is greater than you are.

11:44. You are the Almighty God. I bow and prostrate myself before you. As a Father forgives his son, a friend forgives his friend, or a lover pardons a loved one, please forgive me for my past impudence. O, gracious, compassionate, and merciful Lord, I ask for mercy, forgiveness, and your blessing.

Simplicity

11:45-46. I rejoice in perceiving you and the purpose of creation as never seen before. The knowledge* you have entrusted me with is too much to comprehend. It overwhelms me. O Lord, I am trembling with excitement and fear at the amount of knowledge and trust placed upon me and at the sight of your awesome majesty. Please permit me to see you in a human form that I am comfortable with. (*Ref Gita 3:31. 7:1-2. 11:1-33.))

Gracious Lord

11:47-48. **Krishna:** Arjuna, by My grace, you have perceived My glorious, radiant, universal form and comprehended My cosmic eternal plans and your unique role in all this in a way no one has perceived or heard before. Unknown to you until now, you have featured from the beginning of my plans. Hence, I am placing all the resources you need to fulfil them at your disposal. All I need is your consent, willingness, and iron resolve to carry it out, not by your might, but by My might. Arjuna, such grace, and knowledge do not come from reading the Scriptures or performing sacrifices or rituals.

11:49. Do not be troubled by what you have seen or let your heart be bewildered. I shall continue to appear to you in the form that will make you feel comfortable until you are ready to see Me as I AM.

The familiar, friendly form of Krishna

11:50. Having spoken thus, The Lord assumed the human form Arjuna was familiar with.

11:51. **Arjuna:** Now that I see you in human form and as a friend, my mind is at rest.

One in purpose with The Lord

11:52-54. **Krishna:** Great saints and sages have desired to see your vision. Knowledge, austerity, and sacrifice cannot bring such a vision. To receive such visions, one needs to have a pure heart, a pure spirit, and a transformed mind in control of all the senses led by the inner Atman. Moreover, I can only be known or understood as I AM by My grace and through undivided devotional service to creation, humanity, and Me.

11:55. Moreover, those who act without selfish attachment, strive to fulfil My eternal plan, and are without malice towards all living things will abide by My side forever.

Chapter 12 – Charity, Faith, and Hope

This chapter begins with Arjuna asking Lord Krishna about the importance of devotion and faith in spiritual development.

Lord Krishna says that the love for God does not come naturally to struggling souls. It requires consistent effort to cultivate it. He understands that many find it challenging to meditate on His words or worship an invisible God. Therefore, if they find that difficult, they can serve Him by selflessly serving others on His behalf.

Lord Krishna further explains that the cultivation of knowledge is higher than mechanical ceremonial practice. Gaining the personal spiritual experience of Him is more elevating than academic knowledge. The rest of this chapter describes the characteristics of devotees who are very dear to Him.

---- ➤ ----

Perfect devotee

12:1. **Arjuna enquires:** Lord, who is considered more established in you? A devotee who worships and loves you or one who seeks the absolute truth?

Senses and mind under control

12:2. **Krishna:** Those engaged in My work with unfailing love and faith are established in Me. They will pass My test on the 'Day of The Lord.' Their actions will eventually produce good results, fulfilling My eternal plan on Earth and Heaven.

12:3-4. Those who seek the absolute truth, with their senses and minds under control, rendering service to Me and all creatures and humanity, will always find Me.

12:5. Those who cannot control their senses and minds will find serving Me and fulfilling My plans challenging.

The fear of death

12:6-7. As for the people who worship Me and carry out all their activities as an act of devotional love towards Me and humanity, I free them from the fear of death, for their consciousness has awakened their Atman. As a result, when they pass away on Earth, they leave behind a legacy of love, kindness, justice, and fairness, having enriched the lives of all around them.

To walk in the presence of The Lord

12:8. Arjuna, fix your mind and intellect on Me, and you will always abide beside Me.

12:9. If you cannot set your mind and intellect upon Me, learn to meditate on My words regularly.

12:10. If you lack the will for such discipline, engage in My work. Selfless service towards creation (welfare of society) on My behalf can still lead you to fulfilment.

12:11. However, if you cannot even do this, then engage in good works and take refuge in My presence.

Seek the good for others peacefully

12:12. Knowledge is better than the mere performance of rituals. Studying scriptures, understanding The Lord's will, and implementing it is better than knowledge. If one cannot do this, it is better to renounce personal ambitions and desires and peacefully promote the spiritual growth of others. By this, one attains peace.

The one I love

12:13-14. The ones I love are free from malice towards all living beings and are friendly, compassionate, kind, tolerant, and considerate. They gladly share their knowledge, wisdom, and all they have. They do not force or impose it on others. They do not think of themselves as proprietors but as stewards of mine. They are free of false egos and are equal in happiness and distress. They are always satisfied, content, self-controlled, at peace with others and themselves, engaged with all their heart and mind in My eternal purpose and plan*. Such persons are precious to Me.

[*My eternal purpose and plan.

Gita 12:13-14 / Elaboration-Testimony G1, The one I love understands' the cycle of the Cosmos, My plan, and goals from the beginning of time to the End. They comprehend their divine calling, Dharma (duty), and responsibilities in each realm. All this knowledge and wisdom are available to them. Furthermore, I release to them all the provisions necessary to accomplish My expectations. (Gita 4:3. 11:47-48. 18:55.)

12:15. They are not agitated by others and are steady in distress or happiness. They stay calm under fear or anxiety, unshakeable in their faith in Me. No one is put in a difficult situation by them.

12:16. The ones I love are not selfish; they are efficient, pure, and not anxious about the outcome. When the world around them seems to crumble, and events are beyond their capacity to change, they remain steady in faith, putting their trust in My divine provision. They constantly seek the best for others, friends and foes, acting selflessly and impartially.

12:17. They rise above pleasure and despair. They do not hanker obsessively after pleasant worldly situations nor run away from painful situations. Nor do they rejoice or grieve at the misfortune of others.

12:18-19. They regard friends and foes as equal, not elevated by praise, honour, or dishonour, and not buoyed by happiness or distress. They are not downtrodden by blame. They are free from selfish attachment to material objects or people. They live in harmony with everything. They remain firm in their faith.

12:20. Those who follow this path of devotional duty as their supreme goal and have faith in Me are My dedicated followers and dear to Me. ---- -ॐ------

Chapter 13 – The Field and Its Knower

This chapter presents us with two terms— *kshetra* (the field) and *kshetrajna* (spirit-knower of the field). To simplify, we may consider the 'field' as the body and mind, while the spirit* (soul and the Atman: I am, my consciousness) is the 'knower of the field.'

What a farmer sows in his field, he reaps. If he sows rice, he will harvest rice, not wheat. Similarly, we reap the results from the good or bad thoughts and actions we plant in our field (our body and mind). The Buddha taught, 'All that we are is the result of what we have thought; it is founded on our thoughts; it is made of our thoughts.' Thus, what we think, we become. Therefore, it is necessary to cultivate appropriate thoughts and actions in the field of the body.

Lord Krishna then describes the characteristics of a devotee as one who understands their true nature—a modest, wise person in control of their life.

Later, he describes the ultimate reality: Brahman, the all-pervading, omnipotent and aware of everything, existing outside and inside everything. He is beyond the power of the natural senses to see or know. Yet, to the knowledgeable (believer), He is very near.

He then discusses the duality of the mind and soul and who is responsible for suffering and enjoyment in the World and the Universe.

Furthermore, He says that when a person permits the Atman to guide the soul, it leads to enlightenment and spiritual growth.

Finally, those who see death as a transition from this life to the next and acknowledge the breath of God in all living entities see God's love everywhere. They do not harm themselves or others and advance in the spiritual world and understanding.

---- ➨ ----

Our material and spiritual nature

13:1. **Arjuna:** Lord, firstly, I wish to know about my material nature (prakrti-the field), and secondly, about my spiritual nature (purusa-my spirit, knower of my material nature). Also, the object of knowledge, life's purpose, and meaning.

Relationship between the field, spirit, and Divine Spirit

13:2. **Krishna,** The Lord God, replies: The brain, the material body, and all its senses, is called the field, and the one who knows this field is called the knower of the field, i.e., the person's spirit.

13:3. I am the supreme Divine Spirit. I am the knower of all living entities. For My devotees, the object of knowledge is to understand the relationship between these three:

a. Field (body, senses, and mind)

b. Knower (Atman and the soul, i.e., the spirit)

c. Divine Spirit (God)

13:4. Listen, Arjuna, and I will describe the nature of the field and the knower to you. How they are constituted, under whose control they function, and how changes occur in each.

13:5 The field (body and mind) is under the control of the body's five senses (seeing, hearing, smelling, tasting, and touching) and the three components of the mind:

a. Manas (rational faculty of mind)

b. Buddhi (intellectual faculty of mind)

c. Ahamkara (part of conscience, ego, attachment to the self)

Great sages and prophets from every race and tribe have sought this knowledge and tried to expound it in various ways. It has been stated in various Vedic hymns, especially in Vedānta-sūtra, with sound logic regarding its cause and effect.

The mind

13:6 Furthermore, the field comprises five significant elements: the ego, the intellect, the unmanifested primordial matter, the eleven senses (five knowledge senses, five working senses, and the mind), and the five objects of the senses.

13:7. In the mind arise desire, hatred, happiness, pleasure, pain, distress, aversion, false ego, intelligence, conviction, and the will.

Characteristics of devotees

13:8. Those close to the Supreme Lord (devotees) are above pride and deceit. They are gentle, forgiving, pure in thought, upright, and filled with inner strength and self-control. They are devoted to The Lord *(devotional service to The Lord God is to seek His happiness and that of His creation and all things contained in it and their happiness)*.

Devotees have the firm discipline to control their sensual gratification and self-will. They display humility, are not proud, adhere to non-violence, and do not cause distress to others.

Their tolerance, simplicity, cleanliness, and acts of devotion to God are part of their daily lives.

13:9 They comprehend The Lord's creative plan for the cosmos, their position in this plan, and the reason for joyful and painful lessons of life: the joy of family, friends, birth, suffering, disease, old age, and death. All these things are encountered in life and used for spiritual growth and advancement. Hence, they seek and are willing to learn from a spiritual master as they journey along this path.

13:10. Devotees are not compulsively entangled to possessions or family. They fulfil their responsibilities to all and are even-minded. They are unmoved by good and bad fortune.

13:11. They dedicate their lives to furthering God's and everyone's welfare, interests, and happiness. They enjoy solitude at times and refrain from following the crowd.

13:12. Devotees realise the importance of knowing themselves and the need to seek truth and justice.

Brahman and eternal life

13:13. They know what knowledge is needed to gain eternal life. Eternal life is to know the Supreme Lord and his subordinate, Brahman, who is without a beginning and is said to be neither being nor non-being.

13:14-15. Brahman lies beyond this material world and exists in all of His pervading forms in everyone and everything. He is all-pervading, omnipotent, and aware of everything, not motivated by senses nor attached to anything.

13:16. Brahman exists outside and inside everything. He is beyond the power of the natural senses to see or know. To the ignorant, He is incomprehensible and very near to the believer.

13:17. Various cultures perceive Brahman in different ways. However, He is the same Lord. He is indivisible yet appears as an individual breath of life in each creature. All life comes from Him and returns to Him and finally to God. *(In the Bible, he is 'The Word of God,' John 1:1).*

He is the light of the world

13:18-19. Brahman's breath of life, endowed to Him by the Supreme Lord, dwells in all. It is the source of knowledge, light, and life for all. Unity with Brahman and the Supreme Lord should be the object and goal of all.

The current goal of creation is the union of the person *(knower) and the body (field)]* with Brahman and the Supreme Lord. True devotees from all cultures and religions know these things, and all are worthy of being connected with the Divine. *(in the Bible, Book of John 14:6 & John 17:3).*

Pure consciousness

13:20. Arjuna, the breath of God, the Atman (Purusha, pure consciousness) is without beginning. The individual's transformation in this life is due to the interaction of their material nature (Prakriti), their spirit (duality of soul and Atman), and the divine influence on them or lack of it.

Different species, suffering, and enjoyment

13:21. The manifestations of different species of life are due to their diverse material natures. All material causes and effects are due to nature, while living entities cause all enjoyment and suffering in this world.

How a person thinks moulds the person

13:22. A person's spirit (duality of soul and Atman) identifies either with the material body (influenced by the **gunas***) or with the divine essence. And often both. How a person thinks moulds the person. For example, is his thinking led by his gunas or the indwelling spirit? Thus, according to their views, one comes across evil and good among all species.

[*Guna (Sanskrit: गुण) is a concept in Hinduism that translates as 'quality, peculiarity, attribute, properties. The three gunas are: Sattva (good, constructive, harmonious), Rajas (passionate, hasty, confused), and Tamas (darkness, destructive, chaotic).]

The Atman is the permitter

13:23. In the material body is the breath of God, the Atman. It is not the Atman that controls the body but the soul. The Atman is a guide, observer, permitter, and witness of individuals' actions.

13:24. When a person permits their Atman to counsel their soul, the liberated soul will lead them to the divine, here and hereafter.

13:25. Meditating on the Scriptures, gaining spiritual insight affirmed by signs and miracles from Me, and acting selflessly lead to enlightenment. By such means, a person grows in pure love for creation and Me.

13:26. Those who cannot grasp these paths can still develop closeness to God and creation by faithfully listening to their righteous spiritual teachers and following their instructions.

All life

13:27. Arjuna, wherever you see life, both moving and unmoving, it is born from the union of matter and the life-giving breath of God.

13:28. The spirit remains standing (alive) when the material body passes into death. When you grasp this, you will acknowledge the breath of God in all living entities.

13:29. People respecting the divinity in every being and creature see God's love everywhere. They do not harm themselves or others and advance in the spiritual world and understanding. How can one who sees the divine in all creatures injure another or walk away from an injured one? The one who does not perceive this separates himself from others, seeing some as friends and others as foes or creatures to exploit. *(Refer to 5:18)*

Some suppress divine guidance

13:30. Some want all the activities performed by the body under their control and choose to suppress divine guidance.

13:31. Though all creatures appear different, the same breath of God upholds them. The one who understands this identifies with Brahman and is on the path of purification.

Atman is eternal

13:32. Those with the vision of eternity can see that the Atman is imperishable and beyond the clutches of death. Despite contact with the material body, the Atman is not entangled by the body at death.

13:33. The sky does not mix with anything, although it is all-pervading. Similarly, the Atman, though situated in the body, does not mix with it.

Sharpening consciousness

13:34. As the Sun illuminates the whole world, the indwelling Atman illuminates the entire body by sharpening consciousness.

13:35. Those who understand the difference between the temporal body (field) and the indwelling spirit (knower) and the transition from the body to the spiritual world attain the supreme goal.

--------- ୨୨------

Chapter 14 – The Purpose of Life

In the previous chapter, Lord Krishna explained the differences between the material body, soul, and Atman. This chapter describes in more detail the nature of mind, matter, and human experience in terms of three qualities known as gunas (modes: the way a person behaves or acts)): Sattva (goodness), Rajas (passion), and Tamas (ignorance).

For the body, mind, and intellect to progress beyond the world of matter into the spiritual realms, they must deal with these three all-powerful forces. The combination of these gunas forms the basis of one's character.

Those in a mode of goodness display calmness, well-being, serenity, and knowledge and promote the welfare of society. Those in a mode of passion have endless desires and ambitions, and they strive to promote their happiness. Those in a mode of ignorance are driven by laziness, delusion, anger, hatred, and other vices.

For liberation from the clutches of these gunas, Lord Krishna reveals a simple solution to Arjuna: to affix his mind to God. He says that since the Supreme Lord is unaffected by these three modes, whoever connects their mind to God also rises from the material to the divine level.

Arjuna then asks Krishna to describe the qualities of those who have risen above these three gunas. Lord Krishna elaborates on the qualities of liberated souls as a person detached from the constant shifting and interaction of the gunas. They realise that the gunas and their play are external – even their emotions and thoughts are only the play of the material world.

In the end, Lord Krishna reminds him that the power of devotion and steadfast love can overcome the influence of the gunas.

---- ➤ ----

Knowledge of the world hereafter

14:1. **Krishna:** The Supreme Being said: Arjuna, I will explain how spiritual knowledge can take you into the next world and beyond at death. From this knowledge, the sages were able to reach perfection.

End of time: The Great Day of The Lord

14:2. This knowledge will open the passage to draw you closer to Me. On the *Day of The Lord*, before I annihilate the cosmos and create a new order, all shall stand before Me and be evaluated. You will stand by My side to see a new cosmos. There will be no more death for the sages who pass this testing point. (*Day of The Lord/some call it, The Judgement Day.)

Brahman and creation

14:3. Brahman existed before creation and (with My blessing) created the cosmic womb. I endowed the breath of life and the eternal spirit to Brahman, and He impregnated the cosmic womb with living entities. All life comes from the womb of creation.

14:4. All life forms came into being, from Me to Brahman and Him to all. I am the seed-giving Father. I am incomprehensible beyond the concept of the human mind *(Gita 10:19)*. Yet, I make myself known in a manner and at a level that humans and creatures can comprehend Me: as the Heavenly Father, since I sustain all.

The three gunas: Sattva (Goodness), Rajas (Passion), and Tamas (Inertia)

14:5. All living entities display the three gunas: goodness (Sattva), passion (Rajas), and ignorance (Tamas). These three modes govern their conduct according to their nature. Some living entities are calm; most are filled with restless energy, and others are lazy and unmotivated to act.

14:6. The mode of goodness is purer and more illuminating than the others, releasing one from selfish, sinful actions; thus, they display a sense of happiness and knowledge.

14:7. The mode of passion is fuelled by desire and longing for material possessions, fame, and self-gratification. This attachment binds a person to compulsive action.

14:8. The ignorance mode instils delusion, idleness, laziness, intolerance, overbearingness, and unreasonableness.

14:9. The mode of goodness conditions one to contentment, passion conditions one to constant activity, and ignorance clouds one's mind and judgement and leads to delusion.

All three modes are vying for supremacy

14:10. All three modes are continually vying for supremacy. The Sattva mode predominates when the Rajas and Tamas modes are subjugated. Rajas prevail when Sattva and Tamas are weak. Tamas prevails when Sattva and Rajas are weak.

14:11. When Sattva dominates, goodness, wisdom, and knowledge shine through.

14:12. When Rajas dominates, symptoms of selfishness, restlessness, and greed, driven by uncontrolled desire, manifest.

14:13. When ignorance dominates, darkness, confusion, frustration, and delusion manifest.

Heavenly places

14:14. Those who die in the mode of consistent goodness elevate to the purer, higher Holy sites in the sanctuaries where the sages live. All humans are tainted with flaws; none is entirely wholesome. Nonetheless, the Sattvic people leave behind a legacy of love, kindness, justice, and fairness, having enriched the lives of all around them.

14:15. Those who die in passion or ignorance are elevated to the heavenly places where others of similar nature dwell, leaving behind a mixed legacy of good and misery on Earth.

Fruit of the three Gunas

14:16. The fruit of righteousness (Sattva) is pure and said to be in the mode of goodness. The fruit in the manner of passion is misery. The fruit of Tamas is to sink into ignorance, confusion, darkness, and restlessness.

14:17. From the mode of goodness arises knowledge, understanding, and happiness. Passion creates greed and selfishness. Ignorance develops foolishness, delusion, anger, and pain.

14:18. Those in the mode of goodness gradually progress in this world and the next. Those stuck in passion are caught in earthly activities and remain in that worldly state in the hereafter. Those in ignorance sink even lower in this world and the afterlife.

14:19-20. All actions are permutations of the three modes (gunas). The struggle in life is to overcome the two inferior modes, reach goodness (Sattva), and ascend beyond. The person who climbs beyond all three modes is at the higher slopes of a spiritual mountain and remains free from material entanglement. He is finally free from the influence of birth, death, and old age distresses, and enters the mode of sturdy devotional service to others and Me.

Characteristics of spiritual masters who transcend the three gunas

14:21. **Arjuna** enquires: Lord, what are the hallmarks of those saints who have transcended the three gunas? How do they conduct themselves? How did they rise beyond these modes of nature?

14:22. **Krishna:** The Supreme Lord said: Those who overcome the natural modes (gunas) are, in essence, spiritual masters. They are aware of the power and influence of the gunas. They remain firm and sturdy in their spiritual knowledge, and the power that radiates from their spiritual strength overcomes the impact of the gunas.

14:23. Spiritual masters are unwavering and undisturbed by the gunas' actions. They are steady, strong, forceful, and unmoved. They have strong spiritual motivation and direction, which is more potent than the attraction to any gunas.

14:24. My devotees remain calm, steady, and confident in achieving their eternal goals. Therefore, they do not tie their moods to gunas-created circumstances and cease being uplifted or depressed by their likes or dislikes. They are alike in pleasure, pain, happiness, and distress, accepting blame and praise calmly. To them, a lump of clay, a stone, and a gold nugget are natural materials of short-term value, but the spiritual goal is eternal, of far greater value and worth. *(Gita 10:1)*

14:25. My devotees seek My assistance to overcome their selfish desires. They look upon a friend and foe, honour and dishonour alike, sailing above the power of gunas.

14:26. To transcend these modes of material nature is to serve humanity, creation, and Me and see the divinity in all others through total commitment to Me. Those who rise above their material nature are fit for union with Brahman and Me, and they will live to see a new order (Creation), a New Universe where the lion and lamb sit together and eat straw, and a child plays with them. *(Gita 10:6. 11:7-17 & 24-30. 14:2 & 26)*

I am the Light of the World

14:27. I am the foundation of the revealed and hidden Brahman, the immortal, imperishable, eternal, and unchanging. The source of truth and happiness. I am the light of the world.

---------- ᗴᎨ------

Chapter 15 – Self and Knowledge of God

This chapter is complex because it deals with theology and spiritual experience. In this chapter, Lord Krishna compares the material world to an upside-down mystical Ashvattha (sacred fig tree) tree, which sends its roots into the air and below into the Earth, like the banyan tree.

One cannot comprehend its origin, age, or how it continues to grow. God is the source of this tree; its roots face the sky, and its leaves reach downwards. The three *gunas* feed this tree, creating objects of the senses, like buds on the tree branches. These buds sprout aerial roots propagating this Ashvattha tree over a large area.

Lord Krishna declares that if we search for the Supreme Lord, we must first climb its branches and draw nourishment from the roots that reach upwards into Him. Once we surrender to Him, we gain God's abode, and we should prevent our return to this material world by cutting this tree at the earthly end with the axe of detachment.

He then describes the migration of the spirit from the material body at the time of death into the next world, carrying with it the mind and senses.

Lord Krishna reminds Arjuna that He has attributed his breath of life, Atman, to his inner self and each creature. At conception, the spirit (duality of Atman and soul) enters the body, which can grow and reflect all His characteristics. The spirit lodges in the body and then departs at death.

He often appears at a human level to reveal wisdom and knowledge *[i.e., as Krishna, or as the Word of God—Jesus Christ— in the Bible, the divine transformed into a being with whom we can relate]*.

On 'The Great Day of The Lord', *(also called 'Judgement Day' by Hindus, Christians, Muslims, Sikhs, and Jews)*, all beings will stand before Him and account for all their deeds. According to their deeds, they will be evaluated and awarded or denied their inheritance in God's Kingdom. The evil ones will perish.

Those who fail to measure up to his standards will lose their souls. He will separate their soul from the Atman, and without the Atman, they will perish. Life cannot exist without the breath of God. The Atman, once cleansed, will return to him without any memory. Those who pass the test will continue to live and grow.

The Atman is a gift of God for a limited period, and only those who cherish and nourish it will be allowed to retain it.

Avyayam Padam is the Hindu concept of our eternal home and our goal. Those who grasp Avyayam Padam will become enlightened; one day, they will fulfil their divine mission and the goal of creation/evolution.

Those unfamiliar with Hindu concepts, including many Hindus, may find this chapter challenging to comprehend.

---- ➤ ---

The mythical upside-down spiritual tree

15:1. **Krishna:** It is said that there is a mythical upside-down spiritual tree with its primary root reaching upwards towards Heaven and its branches, leaves, and secondary roots reaching down towards the Earth. The branches and leaves are made of Holy Scriptures. One who knows this tree understands the Vedas (Holy Scriptures).

15:2. The branches extend down towards Earth and upward towards God, nourished by the three gunas and the Atman. The twigs are compared to the human senses. Those branches and secondary roots going down correspond to attachments to worldly things that tie the individual to their earthly existence.

15:3. One cannot perceive the correct form of this tree in this world, neither its beginning nor its end. The tree symbolises spiritual and worldly life, and one must cut down this tree with the axe of detachment at the earthly end.

15:4 Free from attachment to the material world, one is ready to walk in the spiritual world with the Supreme Lord. With the eyes of spiritual vision opened, one's view of life changes.

Spiritual understanding of eternity

15:5. Those with the spiritual understanding of eternity find it easier to set themselves free from selfish desires, illusions, and bonds of attachment to the material world. Surrendering to the Supreme Being, the gate to God's kingdom is open, free from the dualities of happiness and distress.

Light from God

15:6. The Sun, Moon, and stars do not illuminate God's kingdom. The Sun illuminates the material world, while spiritual light from God permanently illuminates the inner spirit of a person and the heavenly realms.

Atman

15:7. A part of God's eternal spirit (Atman, the breath of God) enters the body at conception. It surrounds the developing senses, mind, and soul. Bound by material nature, the human spirit (duality of the soul and Atman) struggles with the senses and the mind for dominance until death.

Gita 15:7 / Elaboration-Testimony H1-2.

H1. [In most cases, the foetus emerges into the world surrounded by a shield of parental love. Sadly, this is not always the case. Regardless of the nature of their birth, floating in the air lurks a deadly foe that all breathe in: seeds of fear, self-doubt, denial, hypocrisy, dishonesty, resentment, anger, disrespect, contempt, frustration, cruelty, selfishness, greed, envy, hate, dissatisfaction, ignorance, darkness, disease, and more. Everyone inhales these seeds, where they lodge and take root. (Gita 2:31. 4:42. 5:16. 9:20. 10:9-10.)

H2. However, the seeds of kindness, gratitude, truthfulness, courage, sincerity, hope, love, generosity, humility, strength, and dedication do not float freely in the air. They have to be sought, cultivated, and constantly nourished. Gita is well-placed to do it. (Gita 2:52. 4:33. 7:3 & 16 & 18. 9:15 & 34. 11:7. 12:3-4. 13:12.)

Death and the Journey beyond

15:8-9. At the time of death, the human spirit (Atman and the soul) migrates from the material body to another body, as the wind carries a scent from place to place. The living entity, thus taking another body, obtains a different type of ear, eye, tongue, nose, and sense of touch.

Ungodly

15:10-11. The **ungodly**[1] people cannot understand that the soul resides in the body and enjoys sense objects, nor do they perceive it when it leaves the body and enters another body because their Atman has remained lifeless. They are unaware of the spirit that connects them to divine nature. As their souls migrate from one material body to another at the time of death, they become bewildered, frightened, and panicked as they enter another body. They enter a realm of their kind—not a pleasant thought. Those who strive resolutely to surrender to the Supreme Lord see all this.

Gita 15:10-11 Elaboration-Testimony H 3-4

H3. [**ungodly**[1]. *The character of the ungodly, spiritually blind people. Their destructive qualities are anger, hate, fear, shame, greed, self-pity, contempt, resentment, boredom, arrogance, jealousy, judgementalism, resentment, unkindness, uncontrolled desire, lamentation, and confusion. (Gita 2:31 & 62-63. 14:17. 16:4. 18:31.)*

H4. **Lacking:** *wisdom, universal love, kindness, holiness, purity of heart, and a sound mind subjugated to the Atman. (Gita 3:38. 8:25. 11:33. 17:10. 18:31.)*

I am the light of the world

15:12. **Krishna:** The light of the Sun, Moon, and fire that illuminates the world comes from Me. However, I am the true light that dispels all darkness.

15:13. My energy supports the Sun, moon, and the Universe, keeping the planets in their orbit. I supply light and warmth, the source of life, to all creatures and plants.

15:14. I am the energy source for all living entities, controlling all their outgoing and incoming breath.

All-pervading, omnipotent, omnipresent

15:15. My spirit resides in everyone and permeates every cosmic atom. All are accounted for, in My daily inventory. I am the source of proper knowledge and the understanding that dispels the darkness within all. I am impartial. All the Holy Scriptures in the world speak of Me. Indeed, I authorised them.

15:16. There are two types of beings in the world. In the material world, every living entity is Kshar (perishable); in the spiritual world, every living entity is Akshar (imperishable).

All Holy Scriptures declare Me as the Supreme Lord

15:17. But beyond these two is another, I, the Supreme Eternal Lord, who supports the entire cosmos and all living beings.

15:18. All Holy Scriptures from the Earth's four corners declare Me the Supreme Lord. I exist, the Eternal, unchanging, imperishable Lord, the source of all wisdom, worshipped by the inhabitants of the Universe.

15:19. Those who know Me as the Supreme Lord *(The same Supreme Lord called by different names: Jews/Christians call Me Jehovah/Yahweh, or LORD God Almighty. Sikhism: Akal Murati, the Eternal Being. In Islam Allah)* acknowledge the truth. Those who worship Me devote themselves to Me and My creation; they love Me and promote humanity and creation's welfare and happiness, including theirs.

The most intimate part of the Vedic Scriptures

15:20. This wisdom is the most secret part of the Vedic Scriptures I have shared with you and those willing to be in My kingdom. By obeying and participating in this wisdom, a person becomes enlightened and is on the path of union with Me. All who follow this Vedic teaching will become enlightened and fulfil their mission on Earth and Heaven.

> **Gita 15:20 / Elaboration-Testimony H5-8.**
>
> *H5. This is my understanding of the message of the Gita. The Supreme Lord: I*

am aware of the pain and suffering endured by all living entities, all contributing intentionally or unintentionally to My Kingdom for the perfection of My sages. Therefore, in the hereafter, I will reconcile, restore, and make restitution to all worthy living entities in the spiritual sanctuaries I have created with My saints and sages. *(Gita 3:31. 7:2. 8:16. 9:33. 11:7 & 16. 13:9. 14:2. 18:20.)*

H6. On 'The Day of The Lord', I will reveal why I allowed joy, pain, and suffering on Earth and how I, with My perfected saints, made appropriate restitution to all in the spiritual sanctuaries. *(Gita 2:11-12. 11:9. 14, 17 & 25. 11:21.)*

H7. On that day, all will render account to Me for their lives. I will evaluate all, rewarding the righteous and obliterating the evil. *(Gita 2:12 & 18. 10:38. 11:25 & 32. 12:2. 14:2.)*

H8. No one in the Cosmos can claim I perfected the saints at their expense and suffering. After 'The Great Day of The Lord', all enlightened beings will finally rest in peace in their new eternal home (Avyayam Padam). *(Gita 4:9. 4:38-39. 5:12 & 29. 6:3. 9:31. 11:16. 18:49-50 & 62 & 71.)*

It is a matter of Faith.

---------- ॐ-------

Chapter 16 – The Divine and Dark Nature of Humans.

And the struggle between good and evil in this world

This chapter describes the two kinds of human nature: the saintly that leads to spiritual growth, happiness and eventually liberation from worldliness, and the worldly nature, leading to suffering and enslavement of the spirit.

Lord Krishna explains that having a clear conscience, a sense of moral obligation towards society, and following the Scriptures' teachings purifies the mind and leads to the development of a holy character. A purified mind attracts divine qualities and cultivates modes of goodness in humans.

On the other hand, associating with modes of passion, ignorance, and materialistic lifestyles breeds a selfish nature. It generally gives rise to an unhealthy personality that can lead to a Hell-like existence. Such people often take a low view of human nature and cause suffering to themselves and others. They are arrogant, have insatiable selfish desires, and do not hesitate to get what they want, regardless of the impact on others.

Another unlikeable characteristic of 'selfish' personalities is their sense of self-importance. They like to be seen giving generous gifts, supporting charities, and offering ritual sacrifices, making them feel respectable, esteemed, and seen as good members of society. Lord Krishna allows them to enjoy their health, wealth, and power, but their destination is unhappiness and misery, as their karma bears fruit.

Towards the end, Lord Krishna reaffirms that knowledge of the Scriptures helps overcome ignorance, lust, anger, and passion, and elevates the person to a higher level. Therefore, we must understand the proper interpretation of Scripture teachings and injunctions and live according to their guidelines to make the right choices in life.

---- ➤ ----

Qualities one needs to nurture

Krishna

16:1. The Supreme Lord: Arjuna, you must nurture these qualities. Learn to overcome fear and walk in purity of heart and emotions. Study the Scriptures and grow in spiritual knowledge. Be compassionate and charitable, and have a clear conscience. Give freely and indulge in a duty of care and kindness towards all, especially the poor and vulnerable. Be self-controlled, sincere, and truthful. Nourish a spirit of giving and forgiveness.

16:2. Be compassionate and gentle. Control anger, avoid harming any living creature or being; bear no enmity, but show goodwill to all.

16:3. Cultivate patience, integrity, sincerity, and simplicity. Be truthful and loving. Turn away from worldly attachment or fault finding. Practise steady determination, vigour, fortitude, and cleanliness. Curtail envy, passion, and desire for honour. These qualities, Arjuna, belong to **godly people[1]**.

Gita 16:1-3 / Elaboration-Testimony J1-4. [1]Godly people; Characteristic.

J1. Their identity rests in knowing their unique position in God's kingdom, a sense of responsibility and duty (Dharma) in society and a good conscience. They are equal in happiness and distress, fortune, and misfortune. Self-contained, they remain unmoved, whether praised, blamed, honoured, or condemned. They do not distinguish between friends and enemies, but see all beings equally. (Gita 2:56. 6:9. 12:13-14 & 18-19. 13:9. 14:22 & 24-25.)

J2. Furthermore, their faith in The Lord reaffirms their belief that the Supreme Lord does not shield them from life's joys and miseries but helps overcome them, and He controls all the outcomes. Even our mistakes ultimately result in a good outcome. (Gita 2:49. 3:19. 4:20 & 22. 5:7. 13:22. 14:5 & 21. 18:17.)

J3. Their treasures are purity of heart, compassion, kindness, truthfulness, humility, tranquillity, non-attachment, discipline, non-violence, slowness to anger, patience, and more. Their hearts are filled with love, gratitude, and kindness, leaving no space for hatred, malice, or ill will towards anyone. (Gita

4:10. 6:41 & 46-47. 13:8. 16:1. 17:14-16.)

J4. They are honest, fair, and just in their conduct. These are some of the unseen but illuminated crowns they wear. Such beings are a joy to The Lord and illuminate His Kingdom. The nations of God's Kingdom are inspired and blessed by their light. (Gita 2:47. 3:19 & 25. 7:17. 10:9. 11:32. 17:14. 18:42 & 56.)

Qualities of ungodly people

16:4. Ungodly qualities are pride, arrogance, conceit, anger, quick, stern judgement, absence of moral character, inability to differentiate between right and wrong, truthfulness and falseness. These qualities belong to ungodly people.

16:5. Do not worry, Arjuna, for you have chosen to cultivate the divine qualities that lead to liberation. In contrast, degenerate people bring pain and suffering to themselves and others.

Two kinds of created beings

16:6. In this world, there are two kinds of people. One is called divine, and the other is called ungodly. I have described the godly, and now I will describe the ungodly.

Ungodly people

16:7. Ungodly people have no sense of uprightness or purity and have a degenerate moral conscience. They lack a sense of truth or correct conduct. There is little or no sacrificial goodness in them.

Ungodly people deny the existence of God

16:8. Ungodly people either have a perverted view of God or say there is no God, no spiritual law, and no moral order. To the unbelievers, the world is a random act of evolution, reproduction, sexual desire, and survival of the fittest.

Ungodly people are their own worst enemy

16:9. Adhering to this viewpoint, often the ungodly and people with a distorted view of God become their own worst enemy and the world's enemy. Without thinking of the consequences of their actions, they often cause destruction and suffering. If left to indulge in their selfishness, they will eventually destroy their communities, country, and themselves.

16:10. Many driven by false tenets or insatiable desires and delusions become arrogant, conceited, and proud. They live in an illusion—their actions sow seeds of pain and suffering on themselves, their families, and the world.

For the ungodly, to gratify the senses is the ultimate goal of life

16:11-12. Ungodly people, or people with perverted views of God, believe that indulging in their desires is the ultimate goal of life until death. They are often harsh and dominating and do not believe in life after death or have a perverted idea of the afterlife. Dominance, greed, anger, passion, and a desire to acquire material wealth govern their lives. Surrounded by their kind, they often live a fearful, meaningless life until death. Their every thought is to amass wealth or impose their tenets on others at any cost for self-gratification.

16:13. The ungodly person thinks: I want to be wealthy; hence, I will get what I desire regardless of the impact on others.

16:14. Often, the ungodly person says: If I have to, I will tread on and destroy my enemies, and all who oppose me will face my wrath. I will be successful, influential, and happy. I am The Lord of everything I own.

16:15. Some may say: I am rich and surrounded by wealthy family and friends. I can buy favours, prestige, and positions by making generous contributions to charity. I rejoice greatly in my generosity. This is how they delude themselves.

Meaningless life and self-promotion

16:16. Perplexed by meaningless life and greed, deluded, and attached to the gratification of senses, they spiral into a moral vacuum.

16:17. Deluded by self-importance, many ungodly people appear pious and participate in charitable acts or religious services, desiring to be seen as godly and righteous, but behind that façade lies self-promotion.

Ungodly people grieve The Lord's Spirit

16:18. Often unreasonable, arrogant, violent, and proud, driven by lust and anger, the ungodly grieve My indwelling spirit in their bodies. They deny My presence in themselves and others.

Ungodly people and the hereafter

16:19. These cruel, malicious, hateful, envious people, I cast them into the womb (spiritual sanctuaries) of their kind in the hereafter.

16:20. There, the ungodly will live in spiritual sanctuaries among their kind. Without My guidance, they will gradually sink to their worst possible depth.

16:21. They live in this self-destructive mode for three reasons: ignorance, worldly attitude, and spiritual blindness. A sane person should renounce these, for they lead to the degradation of the soul.

Those who seek Me will find Me

16:22. Those who turn away from these three gates of Hell and seek Me will find Me.

Ignoring the Scriptures

16:23. Those who ignore the Scriptures or My guidance and follow their impulses will not achieve perfection, happiness, purpose, or meaning in this life or the hereafter.

All Holy Scriptures came from Me

16:24. I am impartial. All Holy Scriptures came from Me to guide humanity. They show how to make the right choices. Therefore, one should understand the scriptural injunctions and teachings and act by them.   ---------- ᕙᕗ------

Chapter 17 – Those who ignore the Scriptures

Yet, have Faith and Worship God

In the previous chapter, Lord Krishna told Arjuna to follow the guidance given in the Scriptures. In this chapter, Arjuna wants to know about those who ignore the Scriptures yet have faith and worship God, and the relationship between faith and the three gunas – Sattva, Rajas, and Tamas.

Lord Krishna stresses the importance of faith. He says faith is part of human nature, and everyone holds a belief. Lord Krishna stresses that faith can have different qualities: *sāttvic, rājasic,* or *tamasic* (faith is used here to imply the sum total of values and what one considers crucial in one's life).

Sattvic faith comes from goodness, an unselfish desire to serve God and humanity through personal sacrifice, putting others' welfare and happiness ahead of personal comfort. Rajasic faith is dynamic but tainted with selfish motives, while Tamasic faith is self-centred and self-indulgent.

A person's faith generally determines their quality of life, character, behaviour, and food type.

Lord Krishna then applies the three gunas to worship and selfless service.

He then discusses the importance of tapas (austerity) and the discipline needed for spiritual growth. The Sattvic tapas are based on spiritual goals, and Rajasic tapas are performed to gain selfish ends. In contrast, in Tamas tapas, a person undergoes painful practices to gain power over others.

Toward the end of this chapter, Lord Krishna explains the relevance and importance of the ancient Hindu Mantra *'Om Tat Sat.'*

The syllable *'Om'* represents the Supreme Lord; *'tat'* is the supreme reality beyond language or thought uttered in ceremonies; the syllable *'sat'* signifies that which is eternal and good. Together, these words symbolise different aspects of the Absolute Truth.

Lord Krishna concludes this chapter by emphasising that all activities done without faith in the Supreme Lord are called 'Asat.' They are temporal and of little value in this life and the next.

---- ➤ ----

People of faith, who ignore the Scriptures

17:1. **Arjuna** enquires of Lord Krishna: What is the situation of those who disregard Scripture but still worship with faith? How does the nature of their faith lead them towards the mode of goodness (Sattvic), passion (Rajas), or ignorance (Tamas)?

Krishna

17:2-3. Lord God replies: Every person is born with a latent seed of faith, i.e., the sum total of their belief: what they value, hold important in life, and how they conduct their lives. All three modes of faith reside in a person – in goodness, passion, or ignorance – but there is always one dominant mode.

17:4. People in the mode of goodness worship Me. Those in the mode of passion worship power, wealth, or powerful men. Those in the mode of ignorance worship either a distorted version of Me, the spirits of the dead, or worldly goods and fame.

17:5-6. Some people inflict pain on themselves as part of their religious beliefs out of excessive pride, passion, hypocrisy, and egoism. This is foolishness, as it harms their bodies and grieves My indwelling Atman within them.

Nourishment of body and spirit

17:7. These three modes of faith generally express themselves in their eating and personal habits, work, and charitable acts. Now, hear of the distinctions between them.

17:8. The nutrients in food influence the body and mind and shape mental attitudes. Sattvic people generally eat food that promotes life's duration and provides strength, health, happiness, and satisfaction. Such foods are mild, fresh, juicy, tasty, wholesome, nourishing, and pleasing to the digestive system. Their habits, work, and actions bring peace, calmness, and joy.

17:9. Generally, but not in all cases, Rajasic people are fond of hot, bitter, salty, savoury, and spicy food. Such foods cause distress, misery, and disease. These people are often hot-tempered, rash, resentful, and envious, bringing grief, pain, and suffering to all.

17:10. Generally, but not in all cases, Tamasic people eat stale, old, tasteless food with little nutritional value. These people are often dull, aggressive, and violent, of unsound minds, bringing misery, pain, and suffering. They contribute little or nothing positive to society.

Sacrificial living

17:11. According to the Scriptures, the Sattvic people are respectful and perform good (sacrificial) acts as a duty to the Supreme Lord, humanity and all living entities. They desire no reward and have no expectations of reward.

17:12. The Rajasic people perform good (sacrificial) acts for show and material benefits.

17:13. Sacrificial acts, good or bad, performed without regard for the directions of Scripture, without solemnity, earnestness, prayers, or concern for the poor, come from the mode of ignorance (Tamasic) and improper faith.

Purification of thought and honouring parents

17:14. Service to the Supreme Lord consists of worshipping the Supreme Lord and respecting the spiritual master, parents, and Elders. All activities are conducted in purity, honesty, cleanliness, simplicity, and without violence.

Speak truthfully

17:15. Words that are truthful, kindly, pleasing, beneficial, and inoffensive while upholding the truth and regularly reading Scripture are the self-disciplines of speech and mind. Harsh and hurtful words inflict pain, damage confidence, and stunt spiritual growth in others. Therefore, shun words that incite negativity and always avoid flattery.

Purification of the mind

17:16. Lastly, consider the purification of the mind. Cultivate good thoughts, gentleness, self-restraint, purity of purpose, and noble sentiments: these are the self-discipline of the mind.

17:17. Practice this self-discipline with firm faith and without expectation of material benefit but as a way of life. Sages call this practice Sattvic.

17:18. Acts of purification performed to gain admiration, honour, or respect are said to be in the mode of passion (Rajasic). They have no merit.

17:19. Acts of purification performed without understanding, resorting to self-harm, or inflicting harm upon others are said to be in the mode of ignorance (Tamasic).

Charity and generosity

17:20. It is one's duty to give and cultivate inward compassion and care. Responsible, compassionate charity given with respect, without expectation of return, at the right time and place, and to a deserving person, is considered in the goodness mode (Sattvic).

17:21. Charity performed expecting favours or in a grudging mood is said to be in the mode of passion (Rajasic).

Giving disrespectfully

17:22. Giving at an inappropriate time and place to unworthy persons, or doing so disrespectfully or accompanied by an insult, is said to be in the mode of ignorance (Tamasic).

Devotion and the principle of sacrifice

17:23. At creation, Brahman chanted three words: Om (the Supreme Lord), Tat (one who is supreme reality), and Sat (eternal goodness) to represent the ultimate absolute truths. From Brahman came priests, Scriptures, and the principle of sacrifice.

Om, a tone of devotion

17:24. Om was the initial word spoken by the first-person Brahma and then used by his descendants while chanting the hymns and offering sacrifices to the Supreme Lord. Therefore, people utter 'Om' when offering prayers or singing mantras (hymns). This initiates a tone of devotion, love, and respect, purifying the mind.

Tat

17:25. Those seeking freedom from material entanglement without seeking any personal benefit add the word 'Tat' when performing various kinds of sacrifice, penance, and charity. The purpose is to become free from the sense of 'I' or 'mine' to reach out to 'The One who is Lord God.'

Sat

17:26-27. Worship in spirit and truth is the objective of devotional prayers and service. Uttering 'Sat' indicates that one is devoting one's life to good, worthy deeds in service of the Eternal Lord. Repeating Om, Tat, and Sat heightens spiritual awareness and pleases the Supreme Lord.

17:28. All activities of sacrifice, self-discipline, and giving without faith in the Supreme Lord are called 'Asat.' These activities are temporal and of little value in this life and the next.

Chapter 18 – Liberation and Perfection of Renunciation

This final chapter of the *Bhagavad Gita* is the longest, explicating many subjects. It starts with Arjuna requesting Lord Krishna to educate him on renunciation and explain the difference between Sanskrit words: Sannyasa *(rejection of action)* and Tyag *(renunciation of desires)*. Both come from the same root words that mean 'to abandon.'

A *sanyāsī* is a monk or a person who has renounced family and social life to practise *sādhanā;* giving up ordinary life to live an austere wandering life of a homeless person without any attachment to worldly goods. Lord Krishna says this kind of lifestyle should be renounced, and as long as we have a body, we have to maintain it with work and not burden others.

On the other hand, a *tyāgī* acts with selfish desires for the rewards of his actions. Lord Krishna again says that this kind of lifestyle should also be renounced and that devotional service, and nothing else, is the ultimate purpose of life.

Lord Krishna recommends that one should not drop out of life but engage in one's prescribed duty: works of sacrifice, charity, penance, spiritual discipline, etc. These duties aid in the purification and maturity of a person. Therefore, one should take control over their work and actions without attachment to their fruits since no one can command its result but should trust the Divine, who controls all the outcomes.

Lord Krishna describes five factors that contribute to a person's action, the three constituents of action, and the three factors that inspire action based on the three gunas (Sattvic, Rajasic, and Tamasic modes of nature) of that person. He gives a similar analysis of intellect, resolve, steadfast will, and happiness.

Further, in this chapter, Lord Krishna portrays the attributes of attaining perfection in spirituality and finding fulfilment and purpose in union with The Lord. He states the benefits of being surrounded by the divine presence and the freedom to stroll in the heavenly realms.

He concludes that one can unravel the secrets of the Supreme Divine Personality through loving devotion. Thus, one can overcome all difficulties and obstacles encountered in life through His strength and grace.

He warns Arjuna to share this knowledge selectively with deserving souls. Teaching others this truth while walking beside The Lord is the highest act of love cherished by the Supreme Lord.

Enlightened with divine knowledge, Arjuna tells Lord Krishna that all his doubts and illusions have been dispelled and that he is ready to act as instructed.

Later, Sanjay, who narrated this sacred dialogue to the blind King Dhritarashtra, states, 'Each time he recalls this conversation, he is amazed, his hair stands on end with ecstasy, and he experiences deep joy and bliss.'

He concludes the *Bhagavad Gita*—The Divine Song of God—by stating that wherever Krishna, The Lord of the Universe, and the likes of Arjuna (the devoted follower) are found, there will be goodness, honesty, peace, well-being, and wise conduct. ---- ➤ ----

Differences between Sannyasa and Tyaga

18:1. **Arjuna** asks: Lord Krishna, the illuminator of darkness, ignorance, and destroyer of evil, what is the difference between Sannyasa and Tyaga? Since both words mean renunciation, how does one differ from the other?

Giving up ordinary life is not recommended

Krishna

18:2. The Supreme Lord replied: For most people, I do not recommend giving up everyday life *(Sannyasa, renunciation)* to live an austere life as a monk and withdraw from family life. I also do not recommend selfish actions and desires for personal gain without concern for others (Tyaga). However, in some instances, renunciation can be positive, such as giving up part of one's wealth to those in need.

18:3. Some sages assert that all worldly activities should be given up, while other sages declare that one should never abandon acts of self-sacrifice, charity, and purification.

Three kinds of renunciation

18:4. Listen, Arjuna, renunciation is declared in the Scriptures as three types.

Sacrifice, charity, and self-discipline

18:5. Acts of sacrifice, charity, and self-discipline are desirable. These three are the highest deeds of human activity. They are essential for spiritual growth and the welfare of society, and should be the goal for all.

18:6. Perform these three activities without selfish desires or any expectation of rewards. Perform them as a matter of duty. The cosmos' primary law, providing sacrificial love, contributes to the world's purity by giving, not amassing. (Gita Chapter 3.14 & 3.16).

18:7. It is the sacred duty of all to carry out these three activities until death. Those who renounce these teachings are in a state of (tamasic) ignorance, neglecting their spiritual growth and the welfare of society.

Avoiding these three activities

18:8. To avoid these activities from fear of bodily discomfort or trouble comes from the mode of passion (Rajasic). There is nothing to be gained from it.

18:9. To perform these activities willingly as one's duty for others' good, with no desire for any reward, is in the mode of goodness (Sattvic).

Sattvic people

18:10. Sattvic people understand the purpose of renunciation. They regard pleasant or unpleasant work as part of their duties. They neither rejoice greatly nor mourn about their work. They do not hate anyone or anything.

To survive, it is essential to work

18:11. One should never give up work. It is crucial to support oneself in life and not burden others. True renunciation gives up personal reward in preference for promoting the well-being of all in equal proportion to the self.

Neglecting spiritual growth

18:12. Those attached to material things and ignoring their spiritual growth for selfish purposes will reap their rewards, here or hereafter. Their lives hereafter can be good, bad, or mixed, depending on their actions. Sattvic people have nothing to fear from death or the hereafter.

Five causes of all activities

18:13. According to the Vedanta, O mighty warrior Arjuna, five reasons affect one's lifestyle.

18:14. First, the body; second, the performer; third, the various senses; fourth, the will; and fifth, the spirit.

18:15. Whatever action, right or wrong, a person performs with their body, mind, or speech is caused by these five factors.

18:16. A person who does not understand that these five factors are involved in every action is not very thoughtful.

Brahman's long-term plans for the creation

18:17. A spiritual, mature person with the clarity of spirit understands Brahman's long-term plans for creation. They see all worldly activities, even life and death issues, as temporal and trust The Lord to turn them into a positive outcome in this life or the hereafter. Their and The Lord's actions have long-term objectives.

Factors that promote activity

18:18. Three factors promote activity: knowledge (information), the object of knowledge (reason), and the person involved. Also, these three—the means, the act itself, and the person—are the totality of action.

18:19. There are three kinds of people according to their modes.

A person in the mode of goodness, passion, or ignorance

18:20. A person in the goodness mode (Sattvic) acknowledges the divine spirit in him and all living things in the Universe. They see that each creature has the same divine breath, has a unique value to the Supreme Lord, and sees no separation between humans and other living entities. Pain, suffering, and the joys of life have cultivated and nourished the seeds of empathy in them. Thus, the enlightened sage experiences acute grief and despair for all creatures suffering. They will live to see a new order (New Creation): a New Universe where the lion and lamb sit together and eat straw, and a child plays with them. *(Gita 3:31. 7:2. 10:6. 11:7-17 &24-30. 14:2 & 26. īkṣate-one sees; tat – that; jñānam – knowledge; viddhi – know; sāttvikam – in the mode of goodness.)*

18:21. A person in the passion mode (Rajasic) sees all beings and creatures as separate and distinct.

18:22. In the mode of ignorance (Tamasic), a person has little or no spiritual knowledge and no sense of their value to society or the self. He sees a small part of the truth and mistakes it for the whole.

Work carried out in the different modes

18:23. All good work carried out for the good of society without the thought of personal reward, free from attachment and aversion, is in a goodness mode (Sattvic).

18:24. All work and obligations performed for the good of society for selfish desires and carried out with a false ego are done in the mode of passion (Rajasic).

18:25. All activities carried out without thinking or considering the distress they will cause others are said to be in the mode of ignorance (Tamasic).

Characteristics of people according to their modes

18:26. A Sattvic person is egoless, free of selfish desires and attachment, enthusiastic for society's good, and shows fortitude in success or failure.

18:27. A person in the mode of passion *(Rajasic, spiritual but materialistic)* has strong personal selfish desires and craves a reward for their action, with little consideration for others. They are liable to be greedy, envious, impure, and moved by joy and sorrow.

18:28. A desire for personal gain drives a person to the mode of ignorance *(Tamasic, worldly, materialistic disposition).* They are more inclined to be greedy, undisciplined, vulgar, stubborn, dishonest, destructive, and cruel. They are joyous or gloomy, depending on the success or failure of their acts.

Determination of mind

18:29. Listen, Arjuna. I will now tell you about intellect and determination of mind (will). Intellect refers to the faculty of understanding (buddhi), while the determination of mind (will) refers to the strength of convictions, resolve, and courage.

18:30. Sattvic intellect (buddhi) discerns between truth and falseness, right and wrong, when to act and refrain. What brings freedom or bondage? What is to be feared and not to be feared? What helps or hinders spiritual growth?

18:31. A Rajasic intellect has an unsound understanding of right and wrong. They twist the truth into falsehood and vice versa: greed, desire, anger, fear, and fanaticism cloud their judgement. For a Rajasic person, the end justifies the means, paying little or no attention to the harm they may cause to others or themselves.

18:32. A person in ignorance walks in spiritual darkness. They cannot distinguish good from evil or know when to act and refrain. Their life rotates solely around themselves.

Characteristics of Sattvic, Rajasic, and Tamasic minds

18:33. Sattvic determination *(free of selfish desires and attachment)* is unwavering in devotion to goodness. The activities of the mind, life, and senses are forced on the divine purpose to promote the welfare, interest, and happiness of The Lord, humanity, and creation above the self.

18:34. The Rajasic mind is governed by selfish desires for pomp, power, fame, and respectability, with some regard for society's welfare.

18:35. Tamasic determination shows itself in ignorance, fearfulness, lamentation, conceit, and illusion – such determination is in the mode of darkness.

Types of Happiness and Fulfilment

18:36. O, mighty warrior, there are three kinds of happiness. A materialistic person is engaged in the sense of gratification. Still, when they realise this is only repetitive, they may awaken to spiritual life and discover life's true purpose, meaning, fulfilment, and happiness.

18:37. Sattvic happiness permits the Atman to guide the spirit, mind, and senses. It takes practice, discipline, and hard work to bring the senses under the control of the Atman, rather than having the Atman suppressed by the senses. It is hard work initially and may feel like taking poison, but it tastes like nectar in the end.

18:38. Rajasic happiness based on the senses is just the opposite. It is a temporary pleasure derived from contact of the senses with their object, robbing one's spiritual growth and, at the same time, demeaning one's purpose and meaning in life. At first, it is bliss, but it eventually becomes poison.

18:39. Tamasic happiness comes from turning one's back on spiritual growth and deluding oneself. The only pleasure in this type of 'happiness' is acquiring possessions, sleep, laziness, intoxication, and sensual pleasure.

18:40. No one on Earth is free from these three modes of happiness born of their material nature.

Social responsibilities

18:41. Brāhmaṇas (priests), Kshatriyas (warriors), Vaiśyas (traders, farmers), and Sūdras (manual workers), distinguished by different responsibilities found in the social order, have their roots in accordance with their material modes and not by birth.

18:42. Brāhmaṇas (priests, educators, scientists, medics, counsellors, civil servants, people of learning, etc.). Their general characteristics are calmness, purity, patience, honesty, wisdom, tolerance, self-control, knowledge, and loving-kindness towards others. Their actions, generally but not always, are born from their nature.

18:43. Kshatriyas (warriors, police, firefighters, guardians of society). Their general qualities are cultivated and enhanced by their natural courage, heroism, determination, resourcefulness, generosity, and leadership.

18:44. Vaiśyas (merchants, skilled artisans, farmers). Trade, craft, and farming generally cultivate and enhance their natural characteristics. In contrast, service providers' natural inclination is usually enhanced by providing labour and vital services to others.

The Supreme Lord is impartial; to Him, all are essential equal members of society, contributing to society's welfare and His kingdom.

18:45. By following their natural abilities, people can become perfect and find fulfilment. Let Me show you how.

Achieving perfection

18:46. A person can achieve perfection by performing one's duties as devotional, sacrificial service for the welfare of all and as a devotee of the Supreme Lord.

Responding to the divine calling

18:47. It is better to engage in one's service for the welfare of all, even if one performs it imperfectly, than to engage in something one is good at for selfish enhancement.

18:48. Every endeavour is covered by some fault, just as fire is covered by smoke. Therefore, one should not give up one's endeavour (sacrificial service), even if such work is performed imperfectly.

Fulfilment and purpose

18:49. A self-controlled person free from selfish attachments who controls their body and passions will attain inner peace, fulfilment, and goal.

Fruit of being surrounded by the divine presence

18:50. Listen and learn from Me. Those who have achieved this state of inner peace, fulfilment, and purpose are on the path to perfection. They will gain a significantly higher level of knowledge of Brahman. They will cease to struggle in life and always feel the divine presence. (Gita 3:31. 11:7-17. 14:26).

18:51-53. Surrounded by My divine presence, they overcome the objects of self-gratification and passion. Freed from the clamour of likes and dislikes, they lead a simple life, eat moderately, and control their body, mind, and power of speech. Free from self-will, arrogance, aggressiveness, pride, anger, and the lust to possess people or things, they rest in the divine presence, in peace and contentment. They gladly share their wealth, knowledge and wisdom, but refrain from imposing it on others.

Gaining The Lord's favour and blessing.

18:54. United with Brahman, they are thus joyful, beyond the reach of desires and sorrows. They have high regard and respect for all living creatures, as I do, thus gaining My favour and blessing. (Gita 10:6. 11:17).

Gaining divine favour and Strolling in the heavenly realms

18:55. Thus, devotees gain My acceptance by aspiring to act as I do. I systematically reveal to them why I created all things, the purpose of creation, and their role in this life and the hereafter. I share plans for the future and their role in that domain, confirming My words with signs and miracles. Thus, such evidence establishes the reality of their spiritual path and inspires them to walk beside Me in My realms as I guide, correct, and prepare them for eternity. Although I am inconceivable *(Gita 10:19)* to the human mind, I reach out to humans and animals at a level where they can comprehend Me as their Heavenly Father. None is turned away, and in 'The Fullness of Time', all things will be reconciled, restored, and made whole—no one thrives in My Kingdom at the expense of another.

18:56. Therefore, My devotees look after My creation as stewards under My protection. As a sign of My approval and grace, I permit such enlightened beings to stroll in the Heavenly realms and spiritual sanctuaries (My abode). I am preparing and refining them so that in the hereafter, they will play a significant role in My Kingdom: reconciling, restoring, and making all creation whole—no one thrives in My realm at the expense of another. *(Gita 3:31. 7:2. 10:6. 11:7-17 &24-30. 14:2 & 26).*

18:57. Arjuna, dedicate every activity to Me, making Me your supreme goal. Depend upon Me, work under My protection, and you will feel My presence in all your activities.

The Lord's grace

18:58. If you learn to walk beside Me, you will pass by all life's obstacles by My grace. If you choose to follow your path, you will be lost and struggle alone.

Disengaging from the spiritual battle

18:59. If you do not engage in this spiritual and physical battle, your instinct to do your own things will take over, and you will struggle in life.

18:60. Guided by your understanding, you will hesitate to act according to My direction. Nonetheless, I know your nature; you will follow My advice.

Trusting The Lord and following the cosmic plan

18:61. Arjuna, I am The Lord of creation, situated in everyone's Atman. I seek to direct all creatures' wanderings by reasoning. All have free will.

Hence, I do not seek to persuade or impose anything on anyone except under exceptional circumstances. Therefore, trust Me and follow My great cosmic master plan. I will reason with you, gently guide, correct, counsel you, and affirm My teachings with signs and wonders. Follow My guidance, and you will always walk beside Me.

Surrender doubts and fears to The Lord

18:62. Surrender your doubts and fears unto Me. Abide in My grace, and you will attain that inner peace you seek. Follow Me and take your eternal place in My kingdom.

Precious wisdom

18:63. The wisdom I have passed on to you is very precious, and when you have thought on it thoroughly, you can use it to decide which path to follow.

18:64. Because I dearly love you, I have revealed knowledge hidden from others. I shared it with you and affirmed it with signs so that you and My devotees may benefit from it.

Walk in the ways of The Lord

18:65. Stay close to Me. Keep your mind and thoughts on the things I have taught. Walk in the ways I have instructed, and you will abide by Me and fulfil all our desires, My dear friend.

Trust The Lord

18:66. Abandon all varieties of religion and surrender unto Me. Put your trust in Me, and I shall deliver you from the snares of sinful actions. Do not worry. You will learn to walk away from wicked actions.

This wisdom is shared selectively

18:67. Devotees should not share this intimate knowledge with those who lack the desire to learn, whose interest lies in the material world, or those who sneer at Me.

Walking in this highest truth beside The Lord

18:68-69 Those who walk in this highest truth and teach others that hunger for this knowledge performs one of the highest acts of love. They will receive *(mam evaisyaty asamsayah)* an honoured place in My kingdom. There is no one more precious to Me than those who have sought Me and, through obedience, have earned the right to walk beside Me.

18:70. Whoever studies this sacred conversation and abides by it will worship Me with devotion and understanding.

Eternal home

18:71. Anyone who listens, exercises faith, and places their trust in Me will become free from sinful actions. Hereafter, they shall gain an eternal home in the spiritual sanctuaries where the pious dwell.

18:72. O mighty warrior, conqueror of evil, darkness, and selfishness, have you listened with an attentive mind? Are the doubts and confusion in your mind now dispelled?

Acting according to The Lord's instructions

18:73. Arjuna said: My dear Lord Krishna, my illusions are gone. By your mercy, I have regained my composure. I stand firm, with my doubts gone. I am now prepared to act according to your instructions.

Wonderful message

18:74. Sanjaya, the great mystic seer, has finished his narration. Later, he comments to the king: Whenever I recite this wonderful conversation between the Supreme Lord Krishna and Arjuna, the noble son of Pritha, my hair stands on end.

18:75. My spiritual Master, Vyāsa, taught me the Kly-son ability, a unique spiritual ability to hear and see events happening in a distant place. Hence, I gained insight into the most confidential talks between the Master of all mysticism, Krishna, and Arjuna.

18:76. O King, I am thrilled and pleased whenever I recall this wonderful and holy dialogue between Krishna and Arjuna.

Love, grace, and mercy of the Supreme Lord

18:77. Each time I remember the Supreme Lord Krishna's extraordinary form, love, grace, and mercy, I am struck with wonder and great rejoicing.

18:78. Whenever Krishna, The Lord of the Universe, and devotees like Arjuna are found, there will be goodness, honesty, peace, well-being, and wise conduct.

END

Bless you. May your journey on this Earth be fruitful and pleasing in the eyes of The Lord and His creation. One day, the true devotees of the Heavenly Father with good hearts and clear consciences, untainted by blood or violence, from all faiths, shall meet in this life and supper together or in the hereafter. That is The Lord God's supreme desire.

Part 2
Hereafter and Scriptures

Chapter 1 The Hereafter and Scriptures

Death comes to all

It was early evening. Martin parked the car and walked into the house. "Hi, Kathy, I'm home," he shouted.

His wife put her arms around him, tears on her face. "Andy came home from school, Martin," she sobbed. "His best friend's mother died in a car crash yesterday." T

"That is awful," he said as he held her tight.

"Andy wanted to know if she has gone to **Heaven[1].**"

"And you said?"

"I told him there is no Heaven or Hell. People die, and that is part of life."

He stepped away from her. "Kathy, he is only five."

"I thought you would support me," she said. "You always go on about being honest."

"I will go and see how he is," he said. He turned and climbed the stairs, and entered the boy's room. The young child ran up and flung his arms around his father.

He sobbed, "Dad, Tim says his mum has gone to Heaven, but Mum says there is no such place."

He kissed the young boy's forehead and tucked him into the bed. "Tim's mum was a wonderful woman. Nice people go to **Heaven[2].**"

The young boy closed his eyes. In a few minutes, he was fast asleep. Martin closed the door, entered the kitchen, and poured a drink.

He sat down on the settee. His mind drifted back to when he was eleven and had a near-death **experience.**[3] He remembered floating in the air, drifting towards a **bright light**[4] and catching a brief glimpse of a beautiful garden.

He had been confused by what he had witnessed, so he had shared this experience with his grandmother. She had given him a book called *The Spiritual Sanctuary* to read.

His grandmother had said, "Martin, there are more than two billion Christians and Muslims who believe in the hereafter. Another two billion people in the Far East believe that their souls travel on to join their ancestors."

He had asked her many questions regarding the hereafter, but she answered, "Martin, read this book."

His mind drifted back to the vision of the garden. After a brief glimpse of it, just as he was getting comfortable in his new surroundings, the noble **person**[5]**,** surrounded by white light, said he had to return to Earth.

His thoughts drifted to the book his grandmother had given him. He opened it and started to read.

---- ➤ ----

Bible (NKJV)	Bhagavad Gita (translated by Hari Patel Amazon.com)
[1] 1 Corinthians 15:12, If Christ is proclaimed raised from the dead, how can some of you say there is no resurrection of the dead?	[1] Chapter 8:20, Beyond this material world lays the invisible spiritual reality that cannot be destroyed. Spiritual reality will remain when this world is gone.
[2] John 14:2, Many dwelling places exist in my father's house. If it were not so, would I have told you that I was going to prepare a place for you?	[2] 2:13, The Atman dwells in a body for a while in each being. It experiences the body through childhood, youth, and old age. Just as a caterpillar casts off its cocoon and attains another
[3] Isaiah. 26:19, Your dead shall	

live; Together with my dead body, they shall arise.

4-5 Exodus 23:20, I will send an angel in front of you to guard you on the way and bring you to the place that I have prepared.

--x--

Koran

2 6:36, As for the dead, God will bring them back to life. Then to Him, they shall return.

1, 3, 5 6: 61-62, When death overtakes one of you, Our envoys take him away, and they never fail. Then, they are brought back to God, their True Master.

--x--

2, 3 (Buddhism) *Wheel of Life and Death.* When one dies, one's consciousness leaves and enters one of the six paths of rebirth.

--------- ᛜ------

body, the spirit reaches another body at death. These changes do not delude the wise

3, 4, 5 8:23-25, There are two paths at the point of death. Those who know Me pass through the northern tunnel that leads towards light, brightness, goodness, and Me. V25 The selfish and evil follow the southern tunnel that leads towards the path of smoke and night towards a darker, unpleasant place, leaving behind a legacy of greed, selfishness, and misery.

---x---

(Sikhism) Shri Guru Granth Sahib

1 Section 25 - Part 022, I do not know what will happen in the world hereafter; I am so confused – please teach me, Lord!

2 Section 05 - Siree Raag - Part 036 For the soul's journey, gather those supplies that will go with you here and hereafter.

3 Section 05–Pt 008. In this world, people are engrossed in false pursuits, but in the world hereafter, only the account of your true actions is accepted.

--------- ᛜ------

Chapter 2

Near-death experience

It was a warm spring day. The young schoolchildren were in high spirits, glad to be out of the stuffy, humid classroom. They were on a field trip with their adored young blonde teacher.

The teacher said, "Today, we are going to study metamorphosis. Does anyone know what metamorphosis is?"

The children looked at each other. No one answered. She turned around, walked towards a tree, and then reached out and pulled a branch down so the children could look at the leaves. On the underside of the leaves were caterpillars.

"Does anyone know what will happen to these caterpillars in a few days?"

"I know, Miss," one bright boy called out. "In a few days, they will weave cocoons and sleep. When they come out of their cocoons, a miracle will happen. They will have **changed**[1] into beautiful butterflies."

"Thank you, Jeff." She turned to face the class. "It is amazing what (God via) evolution has come up with. Evolution is just amazing. It has created many diverse ways for species to survive."

"Miss, do humans undergo **metamorphosis**[1]**?**" the boy asked.

"What do you think?" asked the teacher.

He paused to consider and replied, "Many people believe that **life goes on**[2] in some other form after **death**[3]. Perhaps that is why we have churches and other places of worship. Maybe when we die, we change into something else."

She nodded. "You have a point." It was getting warm, and the children were getting bored. The teacher said, "Children, you have twenty minutes to play."

A couple of girls ran to a nearby playground. They were playing on the swings when they heard a cat mewing.

A young woman called Sam was passing by. One of the girls ran up to her and said, "Miss, there is a cat in the tree. Can you help the cat? It looks like she's stuck."

The young woman looked towards the tree and saw the cat was in distress. Without hesitation, she started to climb the tree. She got close to the cat and grabbed hold of it. But just then, Sam's foot slipped, and as she panicked, she clutched the nearest branch.

The rotting branch broke, and Sam fell heavily onto the hard ground. The back of her head struck a rock, and she passed out. A small pool of blood formed around her head.

Sam seemed to leave her body and started to float **upwards**[4]**.** She looked down and saw her body on the ground, surrounded by the children. As she watched, she was drawn towards the mouth of a tunnel.

Slowly, she drifted into the tunnel. For a while, she was in darkness. Then, a bright light appeared at the other end of the **tunnel.**[5] She walked towards the light and **emerged**[6] from the tunnel.

---- ➤ ----

Bible (NKJV)	Bhagavad Gita (translated by Hari Patel Amazon.com)
[1] 1 Corinthians 15:51, Listen, I will tell you a mystery! We will not all die, but we will all be changed (transformed).	[1] 14:1, Krishna: The Supreme Being said: Arjuna, I will explain how spiritual knowledge can take you into the next world and beyond at death.
[2] Luke 9:30, Suddenly, they saw two men, Moses and Elijah, talking to him. (*Moses and Elias, who had died years earlier, appear to Jesus.*)	[2] 6:41-44, When people who have accepted Me die, they go to a spiritual realm where the
[3, 4] 1 Corinthians 15:44, It is sown a	

natural body; it is raised a spiritual body. There is a natural body, and there is a spiritual body.

[5] 1 Corinthians 15:54. So when this corruptible has put on incorruption, and this mortal has put on immortality, then shall be brought to pass the saying that is written: "Death is swallowed up in victory."

[6] Luke 16:22-23, The poor man died and was carried away by the angels to be with Abraham. The rich man also died and was buried. In Hades, where he was being tormented, he saw Abraham far away with Lazarus by his side. "

--x--

Koran

[1] 6:36, As for the dead, God will bring them back to life. Then to Him, they shall return.

[5,6] 13:23, Everlasting gardens, which they will enter, along with the righteous among their parents, spouses, and descendants. And the angels will enter upon them from every gate

righteous live.

[3, 4] 7:29, Many take refuge in Me, seeking liberation from old age and death. Having acquired a spiritual life, they begin comprehending Brahman in their inner self. They will be united with Me at death.

[5, 6] Ch 8:24. Those who know Me pass through the northern tunnel that leads towards light, brightness, goodness, and Me, whether the time of death is auspicious or not, leaving behind a legacy of love, kindness, justice, and fairness, having enriched the lives of all around them.

---- ----

Shri Guru Granth Sahib

[1, 2] Section 05 – Siree Raag – Part 030. Those who serve the True Guru receive a place in the world hereafter. O my mind, praise the Creator.

[2, 6] Section 05 – Siree Raag – Part 032. In His Sanctuary, there is eternal peace. He is the Supreme Lord God, the Creator.

[3] Section 05 Siree Raag-Part 008 To reach your True Home after you die, you must conquer death while still alive   -------- ᕯ-------

Chapter 3

Garden

Sam saw a beautiful place with lush green **meadows[1]**, clear lakes, and beautiful forests. The grass was green and velvety. Clean air and a fresh fragrance filled the atmosphere, and no signs of decay existed. It was the most **beautiful place[2]** she had ever seen, making her feel **safe and secure[3]**.

A noble-looking man approached her. "Welcome to my garden. My name is **Tenzin[4]**."

She stood dumbfounded and then said, "I am Sam. Tenzin, what is this place?"

Tenzin replied, "It's a sanctuary for people to come to terms with death and the afterlife. I am here to help and guide you. I must leave now, as I am needed somewhere else, but I will see you soon. Meanwhile, make yourself at home. This is a safe place. No harm will come to you here."

A heavy load of fear and anxiety was lifted from her shoulders. A tremendous sense of love, acceptance, and **peace[5]** surrounded her. The whole place had a pleasant atmosphere of peace and harmony, something she had never experienced before.

She walked around this delightful garden and noticed that her physical body's basic faculties were still intact. She could see, smell, taste, and feel heat and cold. But she realised there were also differences in her new body. It was different from the **physical body[6]** she had on Earth. It was much lighter. ---- ➤ ----

Bible (NKJV)	Bhagavad Gita
[1] 1 Corinthians 2:9, But, as it is written, "What no eye has seen, nor ear heard, nor the human	[1] 8:5-6, Devotees who remember Me at the time of death will come to Me. This is certain. At the point of death, one's spirit travels

heart conceived, what God has prepared for those who love him."

[2] Isaiah 55:12, For you, shall go out in joy, and be led back in peace; the mountains and the hills before you shall burst into song, and all the trees of the field shall clap their hands.

[3, 6] Isaiah 65:22-25, They shall not build, and another inhabit; they shall not plant and another eat; for like the days of a tree shall the days of my people be, and my chosen shall long enjoy the work of their hands.

[4] Exodus 32:34, "Now, go, lead the people to the place of which I have spoken to you. Behold, My angel shall go before you.

[5] Micah 4:4, But they shall all sit under their vines and fig-trees, and no one shall make them afraid.

[6] 1 Corinthians 15:54, When this perishable body puts on imperishability, and this mortal body puts on immortality, then the saying that is written will be fulfilled: "Death has been swallowed up in victory

wherever one's true self belongs.

[6] 15:8-9, At the time of death, the human spirit (Atman and the soul) migrates from the material body to another body as the wind carries a scent from place to place. The living entity, thus taking another body, obtains a different type of ear, eye, tongue, nose, and sense of touch.

--------- ❡ -------

Chapter 4

Other people and animals

The garden was filled with various fruit trees, and a lovely, clear stream ran through the middle. There were plenty of **animals and birds[1]** living in harmony. She spent many delightful days playing with them, and they seemed to enjoy her company.

To her amazement, the whole place was teeming with life. Not just animals, either; she found some of her previous neighbours who had passed away before her, alive again, living peaceful, happy existences in this garden.

She was delighted to meet her elderly **grandmother[2]** and her respected elderly schoolteacher and her husband, both still deeply in love. Then there was her kind great-aunt, who had always been good to her on Earth, not to mention all the strangers. There was an overwhelming sense of the communal spirit of oneness.

Along the banks of the **stream[3]** grew fruit trees suitable for food; their leaves did not wither, nor did their fruit fail. They came to fruition every month, and the fruit was delicious and nourishing.

---- ➤+ ----

Bible (NKJV)	Bhagavad Gita
[1,] Ecclesiastes 3:19, For the fate of humans and animals is the same; as one dies, so dies the other. They all have the same breath, and humans have no advantage over animals, for all is vanity. **Isaiah 65:25,** The wolf and the lamb shall feed together, and the lion shall eat straw like the ox. **Isaiah 34:16-17,** Search the book	[1] 9:29, I look upon all creatures equally. Nevertheless, whoever renders caring service to My Creation and Me is My friend. **13:29.** People respecting the divinity in every being and creature see God's love everywhere. They do not harm themselves or others and advance in the spiritual world

of the LORD and see what he will do. None of these birds and animals will be missing, and none will lack a mate. He surveyed and divided the land and deeded it to those creatures. They will possess it forever, from generation to generation.

[2] Romans 8:38-39, For I am convinced that neither death, nor life, nor anything else in all creation, will be able to separate us *(one another)* from the love of God in Christ Jesus our Lord.

[3] Ezekiel 47:12, On the banks, all kinds of trees will grow for food on both sides of the river. Their leaves will not wither, nor will their fruit fail, but they will bear fresh fruit every month because the water flows from the **sanctuary**. Their fruit will be for food, and their leaves for healing.

and understanding. 9:6. All creatures and created beings rest in Me, just as the mighty wind moves everywhere and comes to rest in the sky.

[2] 2:12, Your Atman and that of these kings and soldiers have always existed and will continue to live hereafter. Their physical bodies may cease to live, but their spirits (Atman and soul) will continue to live.

---x--

--------- ॐ ------

Chapter 5

The caterpillar

Sitting on the bank of a clear stream in deep thought, Sam looked up and saw a magnificent **lion**[1] on the other side. He waded across the water and sat beside her. Neither said a word.

A beautiful butterfly flew across the meadow and landed on her shoulder. Sam stretched out her right arm and opened her hand, and the butterfly flew onto her palm. She and the butterfly looked into each other's eyes.

Sam was the first to speak, asking, "How did you get here?"

"In the same way you did," the butterfly replied. "I was what you call a happy **caterpillar**[2] on Earth, full of praise for the Lord, minding my own business, and then I noticed some changes in my body. I seemed to age, and one day, I began to weave a cocoon and went to sleep.

"The next thing I remember is emerging into a brilliant light. My whole body had changed entirely. Previously, I had many legs and a big, fat, round body, but now I have a small body with beautiful wings. My wings were weak, but in a few minutes, they strengthened, and I could fly. I flapped them and found myself floating in the air.

"I looked down and could see the shell of my old **body**[3]. Everything looked different from the air, and I was happily hovering over the trees. It was a nice, warm day, and everything looked beautiful. I flew upwards to look at the ground, when suddenly I felt a sharp blow on my neck and passed out. When I woke up, I found myself in this wonderful garden."

---- ➤ ----

Bible (NKJV)	Bhagavad Gita
[1] Isaiah 65:25 The wolf and the lamb shall feed together, and the <u>lion shall</u>	[1] 9:6. All <u>creatures</u> and created beings rest in Me, just as the mighty

eat straw like the ox; **Isaiah 34:16-17,** Search the book of the LORD and see what he will do. None of these birds and animals will be missing.

[2] Colossians 1:23, The gospel you heard has been proclaimed to every creature under heaven.

[2,3] Romans 8:19-23, 19 For the earnest expectation of the creation eagerly waits for the revealing of the sons of God. For the creation was subjected to futility, not willingly, but because of Him who subjected it in hope; because the creation will also be delivered from the bondage of corruption into the glorious liberty of the children of God. We know the whole creation groans and labours together with birth pangs.

---X--

wind moves everywhere and comes to rest in the sky.

[2] 4:14. No work affects Me. I am involved in every activity of creation but am not attached to any material activities of the world nor seek any reward. All creatures reap what they sow.

[3] 13:35. Those who understand the difference between the temporal body (field) and the indwelling spirit (knower) and the transition from the body to the spiritual world attain the supreme goal.

---X--

--------- ⇜------

Chapter 6

New skills

Sam learnt from her neighbours that the garden was linked to their minds and **thoughts.**[1]

The garden's continued existence, its trees, lakes, and meadows, depended on their mental effort. They learnt to **work**[2] as a team, controlling and creatively directing their thoughts. They did not seem to have any **tools**[3] beyond this.

The senior neighbours encouraged her to participate, joining them in **reshaping**[4] the garden with their thoughts. Seeds were planted and nourished daily. Over time, these turned into plants, trees, and shrubs.

The garden began to grow bigger and more **beautiful**[5]. More of Sam's time and energy were devoted to its maintenance. She enjoyed this work, and she acquired new skills. The art of co-coordinating the body and mind strengthened her **bonds**[6] with the people. She made friends and became a valuable member of this vital community.   ---- ➤ ----

Bible (NKJV)	Bhagavad Gita
[1] 2 Corinthians 10:5, we take every thought captive to obey Christ.	[1] Ch 2:61. Healthy and wise is the person who subdues his senses and keeps his mind ever-absorbed in me. **Ch 6:5,** Those who aspire to grow should transform themselves by renewing their minds and not allowing their minds to degrade them. The mind can be a friend or an enemy.
[2] Genesis 2:15. The LORD God took the man and put him in the Garden of Eden to till it and keep it.	
[3] Exodus 20:25, But if you make an altar of stone for me, do not build it of hewn stones; for if you use a chisel upon it, you profane it. **Hebrews 9:11,** But Christ came as High Priest of the good things to come, with the greater	[2] Ch 7:28, I forgive the mistakes and sinful actions of pious people

and more perfect tabernacle not made with hands, that is, not of this creation.

[4] **Genesis 1:1,1**. Then God said, "Let the earth put forth vegetation: plants yielding seed, and fruit trees of every kind on earth that bear fruit with the seed in it." And it was so.

[5] Romans, 8:17-26, and if children, then heirs, heirs of God and joint-heirs with Christ—if we suffer with him, we may also be glorified with him. V19, For the creation, waits with eager longing for the revealing of the children of God; for the creation was subjected to futility, not of its own will but by the will of the one who subjected it, in the hope that the creation itself will be set free from its bondage to decay and will obtain the freedom of the glory of the children of God. We know that the whole creation has been groaning in labour pains until now, and not only the creation but we, who have the first fruits of the spirit, groan inwardly while we wait for adoption, the redemption of our bodies.

[6] Philippians 2:2 fulfil my joy by being like-minded, having the same love, and *being* of one accord and mind.

who give up their evil and selfish ways and engage in service for the good of all.

[4, 6] Ch 5:7. A mature, enlightened person provides selfless services, learns to control his senses and mind, and sees the divine in all creatures. Though engaged in work, he is never entangled in worldly actions and is not disappointed or happy due to the outcome, but leaves the result in My care.

–x–

[1, 2, 3] **Buddism.**

The Noble eightfold path. Right:- view, Thought, Speech, Conduct, Livelihood, Effort, Mindfulness, Concentration.

--------- ᛅ-------

--------- ᛅ-------

Chapter 7

Mobility and travel

Each day seemed to bring new delights and **experiences[1]**. Sam discovered a new, exciting freedom: travel was instantaneous.

Whenever she focused her thoughts on a place outside the sanctuary, she travelled there. She just had to think of a **place[2]**, and she would be there.

Initially, she made several mistakes and travelled all over the place. After much practice, she mastered the art of focusing her thoughts on a specific location.

In pursuit of meaning

As time passed, an inner longing began to surface among the inhabitants, thoughts regarding the meaning of life, purpose, and fulfilment.

Some began to wander away from the garden to pursue adventure, hungering for new realms and challenges in life. To them, the garden was just a transitional place, somewhere to rest, to gather strength before moving on.

---- ➤ ----

Bible (NKJV)	Bhagavad Gita
[1] Numbers 14:8 "If the LORD delights in us, then He will <u>bring us into this land </u>and give it to us, a land which <u>flows with milk</u> and honey." [2] Ephesians 2:6 and <u>raised us with him and sat</u> us with him in the heavenly places in Christ Jesus,	[1,] 6:42-43. Or they may move (metamorphose) into the realm of a great spiritual master. Such a move is rare. Their divine consciousness is <u>reinvigorated </u>by the great spiritual masters, and with their help, they are encouraged to make further progress. [2] 6:45. These <u>disciplined people</u> in

--x--	their <u>new realms</u> progress further as their selfish desires are purified. Moving upwards towards <u>higher realms,</u> they eventually attain the seventh Heaven, the supreme goal of all. --x--

---------- ᐊᐅ-------

Chapter 8

Kingdoms

Sam often sat down with her remaining friends and shared their experiences of travelling to different realms. Some of these realms were incredibly beautiful **places[1]**, well-governed and joyous.

There were differences between them: some were places of art and pageantry, others of quiet reflection, bright and exuberant, each a perfect home for its inhabitants. Others were simple, straightforward gardens, like in Sam's realm.

Despite these differences, in each **realm[2]**, their leaders were modest and compassionate and manifested marvellous abilities. The inhabitants were kind and generous.

However, most of Sam's friends only got a few glimpses of these realms, and they were not always welcomed. ---- ➤ ----

Bible (NKJV)	Bhagavad Gita
[1] 1st Corinthians 2:9 But, as it is written, "What no eye has seen, nor ear heard, nor the human heart conceived, what God has prepared for those who love him." [2] 2 Corinthians 12:2 I know a man in Christ who fourteen years ago — whether in the body I do not know, or out of the body I do not know, God knows — such a one was caught up to the third heaven ----x---	[1,2] 6:45. These disciplined people in their new realms progress further as their selfish desires are purified. Moving upwards towards higher realms, they eventually attain the seventh Heaven, the supreme goal of all. --------- ↬------

Chapter 9

Steward of the garden

Many people have mentioned that they have found themselves in such gardens at the point of death. They often describe meeting a close relative, a friend, or a noble **person.**[1] Some said the noble person was an angel or an enlightened being (Christ or Lord Krishna).

Sam soon came to know such a person, and as time passed, their friendship grew. He was called Tenzin. There was nothing distinct about him. He was of average height and slim build, with a pleasant, round face and a carefree way of smiling that made her feel at ease.

However, his eyes seemed to penetrate her soul when he looked at her. It was as if he could **read**[2] all her thoughts. In the beginning, she would avoid meeting his gaze. Then, as she got to know him better, she began to feel less threatened.

Her early impression was that he was an angel, but she later decided she had been wrong. He was a human, albeit unique, with some extraordinary spiritual **abilities.**[3]

---- ➤ ----

Bible (NKJV)	Bhagavad Gita
[1] Exodus 23:20. I will send an angel in front of you to guard you on the way and bring you to the place that I have prepared.	[1] Ch 4:34. Follow the guidance of a spiritual master and render service unto him. The spiritual master can instruct you in this wisdom.
[2] 1 Corinthians 2:16 But we have the mind of Christ. Matthew 9:4 But Jesus, knowing their thoughts, said, "Why do you think evil in your hearts?	[3] Ch 2: 54. My Lord, tell me about the enlightened people. How do they talk, sit, move, and conduct themselves? ---x--

[3] Matthew 25:15 And to one he gave five talents, to another two, and to another one, to each according to his <u>ability</u>; and immediately he went on a journey. ---x--

---------- ৭৴------

Chapter 10

Communication

On her very first encounter with Tenzin, she was amazed. She found that he would often communicate by telepathy, revealing more of his thoughts to her as she got to know him better. Stage by stage, he opened up her **understanding**[1] of her surroundings.

One of the things she learnt from him was, *"It is never wise to reveal all at once, nor is it to the person's benefit to know all **mysteries**[2] before their time. Knowledge brings responsibility, and a person needs appropriate maturity to deal with this knowledge. With maturity, one learns to acquire wisdom, empathy, and ability. A confident, mature person is happy to be **accountable**[3], has a sharp awareness and a clear **conscience**[4] that leads them on the right and just path."* ---- ➤ ----

Bible (NKJV)	Bhagavad Gita
[1] Jeremiah 3:15. I will give <u>you shepherds</u> after my own heart, who will feed <u>you with knowledge and understanding.</u>	[1] Ch 4:34. Follow the guidance of a spiritual master and render service unto him. The spiritual master can instruct you in this wisdom.
[2] 1st Corinthians 4:1. Think <u>of us</u> in this way, as servants of Christ and stewards of <u>God's mysteries.</u>	[2] 11:1. My Lord, you have kindly given me insight into the mystery of the spiritual realms, confirming Your words with signs and miracles.
[3] Romans 14:12, each of us shall give an <u>account</u> of himself to God.	[4] 2:6. If I let my evil cousin win this battle, then evil will prevail, and I will have failed to do my duty to protect society and our kingdom. How could I live with a <u>clear conscience</u> if I engaged in this battle and killed family members? ---x--
[4] 1 Timothy 3:9 holding the mystery of the faith with a pure <u>conscience.</u>	
---x--	

Chapter 11

Tenzin's mind

He had a marvellous **mind**[1], very quick and logical. He could analyze a situation, work out a solution, think through its implications, and quickly modify it to achieve the desired result.

Through the sheer strength of his mind, the garden and everything in it was adequately supervised and maintained by him. He could accurately account for every tree, shrub, and animal at any moment. If a single leaf fell to the ground, he knew about it.

Visitors to the garden were under his authority and supervision. He was the **caretaker**[2] of the garden, and his role was to prepare the new **arrivals**[3] for their future roles in their new realms.

(Kly-son);

He also had a unique ability (Kly-son); he could focus his mind on any new arrival and, in a flash, access complete knowledge of their **past life**[4]. He could evaluate it and form a correct and precise understanding of the person.   ---- ➤ ----

Bible (NKJV)	Bhagavad Gita
[1] 1st Corinthians 2:16. Who knows the mind of the Lord, that he may instruct him? But we have the mind of Christ.	[1] 2:40. This path is called Karma Yoga: the oneness of mind with Me through Action. Even a little spiritual advancement on this path will protect you from your greatest fear.
[2] Titus 3:7, so that, having been justified by his grace, we might become heirs according to the hope of eternal life.	[2] 3:42. Senses are superior to the body, and the mind can rise above the senses. Intelligence can rise above the mind, and the spirit can rise above intelligence.
[3] 1st Peter 4: 6. This is why the gospel was proclaimed even to the	

dead, so that, though they had been judged in the flesh as everyone is judged, they might live in the spirit as God does.

[4] 1st Corinthians 6:3. Do you not know that we are to judge angels—to say nothing of ordinary matters? 2 Timothy 3:17. so that everyone who belongs to God may be proficient, equipped for every good work. ---x--

[3] 4:33. The primary purpose of creation is the spiritual advancement of all, and the secondary purpose is sharing My eternal plan with those who seek it with all their hearts, minds, and strengths. Signs and wonders accompany sacred knowledge and are not revealed to those who place little value on it

---x--

---------- ᐦ-------

Chapter 12

Kly-son

Tenzin could also telepathically project memories of people's lives into their minds—a phenomenon often described as "seeing your life flash before your eyes." He called this ability **Kly-son.** [1]

As Sam got to know him better, their companionship grew, and she learnt many things from him, including how he was able to **evaluate**[2] a person's life.

For him, it was simple. He would use his **wonderful gift**[3] to see whether the person had lived a self-centred, selfish life or had lived to promote others' interests and happiness. In short, had they loved their neighbours as themselves?

In the tunnel of life and death, selfish, **self-centred people**[4] received no sympathy or help from him. On the other hand, he warmly welcomed those who had devoted their lives to the good of others. He gladly supported them in their transition from death to the Garden of Peace.

She could understand and appreciate his reasoning. The garden's welfare depended on the **people**[5] working together with a communal spirit, shared for the benefit of all, not for the individual alone.

---- ➤ ----

Bible (NKJV)	Bhagavad Gita
[1] 2 Timothy 3:17. So everyone who belongs to God may be proficient, equipped for every good work.	[1] 11:15. Arjuna: O Lord, in this vision, I saw what your thoughts, plans, and desires were before anything came into existence.
[2] 1 Corinthians 2:16 For "who has known the mind of the LORD that he may instruct Him?" But we have	[3,] 2:69. Material things take precedence over everything to the worldly-minded person, obscuring

the <u>mind</u> of <u>Christ</u>.

[3] Ephesians 1:3 Blessed be the God and Father of our Lord Jesus Christ, who has <u>blessed</u> us with <u>every spiritual blessing</u> in the heavenly places in Christ,

[4] Hebrews 4:2. For this good news — God has prepared this rest — has been announced to us just as it was to them. But it did them <u>no good</u> because they didn't share the faith of those who listened to God.

[5] Acts 4:3.2 Now, the <u>whole group</u> of those who believed were <u>of one heart and soul</u>, and no one claimed private ownership of any possessions, but everything they owned was held in common.

---x--

their spiritual existence. To the spiritually minded, worldly things are temporary; spiritual things are tangible, visible, and clear as day.

[4] 3:13. Those who carry out all life tasks for <u>selfish enjoyment</u> abide in My displeasure.

[5] 3:14 The whole of creation depends on <u>selfless service and sacrifice</u>. All living things are nourished and sustained by food provided by the gifts of others. Plants and trees sacrificially give their fruit, flowers, and shade without complaining, and if someone cuts them down, they remain free from malice and the desire for revenge. Sun, clouds, and rain <u>work together selflessly</u> to offer warmth and water freely to benefit all. They all provide service without expecting a return. The performance of prescribed sacrificial duties sustains all life. One who takes more often than gives is selfish and not sacrificial. ---x--

---------- ᎒-------

Chapter 13

Make whole

It was a warm day with a gentle breeze, and the buffaloes and antelopes[1] were grazing peacefully near the riverbank.

Sam turned and looked at Tenzin. She said, 'Tenzin, you and Brother Stefan are very dedicated to us, the people here, and this garden. You could have chosen to be anywhere in the Universe. Why did you choose this garden?'

Tenzin replied, 'The Master chose[2] every person in this garden and desires that everyone here be given a chance to be made whole.'

'I don't understand.'

'He wants to undo the harm that each person suffered on Earth: to reconcile[3] them, where possible, with their families, loved ones, and neighbours, and to compensate[4] them and make restitution for their suffering and loss. We volunteered to work under his supervision, but we are limited in what we can do by some parameters.'

Sam said, 'Like consent?'

'Yes. We cannot use the power of force[5] or persuade or coerce anyone. We can only reason or plead. We believe our duty as warrior priests is to make everybody here whole. Our salvation and inheritance in God[6] lie in the healing and restoration programme. We find it **joyful**[7] to be here.'

'Are you going to make all the people here whole?'

'With the Lord's help, we will endeavour to fulfil our mission. We will reconcile your family and loved ones if we get their consent and willingness and make more than adequate restitution for your and their pain, suffering, and loss on Earth. We do this because we love the Master and because it is a programme to perfect[8], purify and make us wholesome and fit to receive our inheritance.'   ---- ➤ ----

Bible	Bhagavad Gita
[1] Isa 65:25 The wolf and the lamb shall feed together, The lion shall eat straw like the ox, And dust *shall be* the serpent's food. They shall not hurt nor destroy in all My holy mountain," Says the LORD.	[1] 5:18. My devotees have equal regard for all. They see the same self (the breath of God) in a learned scholar, an outcast, a cow, an elephant, and a dog. ~Hence, as they progress in their spiritual growth, they regard all life forms as part of their and God's extended family.
[2] Eph 1:4 He chose us in Him before the foundation of the world, that we should be holy and without blame before Him in love,	[2,3,4,5] 3:31. Duties performed as a selfless way of life with the interests of others in mind without complaining and established in faith are pleasing to Me. Such people do not have to worry about offending Me. I guide, correct, and refine their activities. I take responsibility for their work. I brought joy, pain and suffering into the world. In 'The Fullness of Time'(*a period between now and 'The Day of the Lord'*), I will make restitution to all affected and make them whole again, wiping away all tears. There will be no more tears. Therefore, no one in the Universe can say we thrived at their expanse. [*Gita 14:2, 14:26. 3:16.*]
[3] Col 1:20 and by Him to reconcile all things to Himself, by Him, whether things on earth or things in heaven, having made peace through the blood of His cross.	
[4] Luke 19:8 And Zacchaeus stood, and said unto the Lord; Behold, Lord, the half of my goods I give to the poor; and if I have taken anything from any man by false accusation, I restore *him* fourfold.	
[5] Philemon 1:14 But without your consent, I wanted to do nothing, that your good deed might not be by compulsion, as it were, but voluntary.	
[6] 1 Peter 1:4 To an inheritance incorruptible, undefiled, and that fadeth not away, reserved in heaven for you.	[2] 11:16 ~In your first thought, I saw my name chosen with great care, written in your Eternal Books, sealed by your loving tears.
[7] Philippians 2:2 fulfil my joy by being like-minded, having the same love, *being* of one accord and mind.	
[8] 2 Timothy 3:17 That the man of God may be perfect, thoroughly furnished	[3-8] 4:3. To a select few, I revealed My existence and plans for

unto all good works.

---------- ᛮ------

eternity (past, present, and future worlds to come). You are My friend and devotee, and in due time, as you gain My favour, I will **reveal*** these mysteries and explain your role here on Earth, in the spiritual world, and in the far distant future. You and other trusted devotees will build My material and spiritual kingdoms in this world and hereafter and walk beside Me in all My realms. I will guide and teach you all as a Father.

[5] 10:7. People who understand My mystic power are engaged in devotional service to My creation and walk beside Me.

[7] 6:20-23. In union with the Me (Samadhi), the sensory and emotional feelings are subjugated to contemplate the spiritual. They begin to fill up with inner joy and fulfilment. They now walk in truth and are free from all miseries from material contact.

[8] 2:16 A spiritual.....~ Thus, such evidence establishes reality in their spiritual walk and inspires them to walk beside Him as He guides, corrects, and prepares them for eternity. -------- ᛮ------

Chapter 14

Thirst for knowledge

Sam had a keen mind and a thirst for knowledge. She questioned Tenzin at every opportunity. She still struggled to comprehend the new environment and had much to learn.

Slowly, step by step, Tenzin taught her how his great **mental powers[1],** refined and purified by the Holy Spirit, controlled the **whole garden[2]**. Each new leaf or blade of grass and each interaction with a person in the garden were meticulously analysed and considered for a specific outcome.

He would organise his plans or events so the outcome would fulfil a more excellent long-term goal, written in the **Eternal Scroll**.[3]

Aunt Millie

One day, while they were playing in the garden, Tenzin came to see them. He had a visitor with him.

As they approached, Sam burst into a big smile. She rushed up to the middle-aged woman with distinguished white hair and hugged her.

"Hello, Aunty Millie!" she said. "I am so pleased to see you." They hugged as Tenzin watched.

Tenzin smiled and said, "I will leave you with your aunt."

"Wait," Sam cried out. She turned to Tenzin. "This is my favourite aunt." Then, turning to her aunt, she said, "This is my friend, Tenzin."

They exchanged polite greetings, and then Tenzin left them.

Hours went by. There was much to catch up on. Sam had many questions, but some of these, her aunt refused to answer. She explained that revealing everything before its time was **not wise***.

They hugged each other as Tenzin approached. It was time for her aunt to leave. Sam said, "Goodbye, Aunt Millie; I hope to see you again."

Her aunt smiled and replied, "I'll be back soon." Then Tenzin and Aunt Millie left.

A few hours later, Tenzin turned up. There was confusion on Sam's face. She said, "Aunt Millie was a very old lady, but now she seemed so young. There were no signs of old age! How old does my Aunt Millie look to you?"

He paused and said, "Well, that depends on who is looking; she may appear thirty or ninety years old."

He saw the confusion on her face.

He explained that age is irrelevant here. The actual appearance of a person depends on their character and personality. Your aunt chose to appear in a form you were used to and displayed glimpses of what she is now. It was the appearance you would feel most **comfortable**[4] with."

Wise*. *[Liz's Tenet 1];- It is not wise to reveal all before its time.*

---- ➤ ----

Bible (NKJV)	Bhagavad Gita
[1] Isaiah 51:16. And I have <u>put My words in your mouth</u>; I have covered you with the shadow of My hand. That I may plant the heavens, Lay the earth's foundations, And say to Zion, 'You are My people.'	[1] 6:5-7. Those who aspire to grow should transform themselves by <u>renewing their minds</u> and not allowing their minds to degrade them. The mind can be a friend or an enemy. People <u>who renew their minds</u> by the scriptures' teaching rather than yielding to sense objects discover that their minds are their best friends. For those who yield to sense objects, the sense objects will remain their worst enemy. One whose mind is
[2] Isaiah 55:11, so shall my word go out from my mouth; it shall not return to me empty, but <u>it shall accomplish </u>that which I purpose,	

and succeed in it.

[3] Ephesians 3:11. This was in accordance with the eternal purpose he carried out in Christ Jesus our Lord. Ephesians 1:11. In Christ we have also obtained an inheritance, having been destined according to the purpose of him who accomplishes all things according to his counsel and will,

---X--

renewed by the divine scriptures lives in peace. In servitude to Me, a person's resolve is unmoved by happiness, distress, cold, heat, pain, or pleasure.

[3] Further light on Gita 1:26-46 /Elaboration A9. *Arjuna's mind wandered to the beginning of time when he was just a thought in the Lord's mind before anything came into being.~ A11, In a different time and place, when Arjuna was just an essence in the Lord's mind, he had perceived creation as a beautiful plan. The Universe teeming with all sorts of plants, happy people, and animals. His essence had rejoiced at the very idea of God's creation.*

[4] 11:49. Do not be troubled by what you have seen or let your heart be bewildered. I shall continue to appear to you in the form that will make you feel comfortable until you are ready to see Me as I AM

---X--

---------- ᕐᕈ------

Chapter 15

Eternal plan

As her knowledge and understanding grew, she asked more complex questions such as, "What is the rest of the Universe like? What is the Great **Eternal Plan**[1] you mentioned? When will you show me the other realms?

"What is the great **mystery**[2] hidden since the **beginning**[3] of time, revealed now to a **select few**[4]? What is the great Day of Judgement, and what will happen afterwards?" ---- ➤ ----

Bible (NKJV)	Bhagavad Gita
[1] Acts 15:18. "Known to God from eternity are all His works.	[1,2] 11:14. Sitting among the heavenly saints and the elders of the Universe, Arjuna struggles to understand the mystery of God's plan and his long eternal journey through it, led by the divine spirit. He is amazed (having been granted unique access to the inner mind of the Lord God). He bowed before the Lord God and spoke these words.
[2] 2nd Timothy 1:9, who saved us and called us with a holy calling, not according to our works but according to his purpose and grace. This grace was given to us in Christ Jesus before the ages began,	
[3] Ephesians 2:10. For we are what he has made us, created in Christ Jesus for good works, which God prepared beforehand to be our way of life.	[2,3,4] 11:1-2. Arjuna: My Lord, you have kindly given me an insight into the mystery of the spiritual realms. My delusions are diminished. You have shown me your limitless power and eternal existence in visions and revealed the secret of the beginning and end of all creatures and creation. ---x--
[4] Psalms 139:16, You saw me before I was born. Every day of my life was recorded in your book. Every moment was laid out before a single day had passed.	

Chapter 16

Outside the garden

One day, he took her to a place that looked like a massive stadium. She was surprised to see people from almost every **race**[1], nationality, and tribe. It was like attending a carnival, with people enjoying different forms of entertainment. It was full of life and diverse activities, and she found the whole atmosphere most enjoyable.

A few days later, while she was sitting near the lake, Tenzin approached her. There was excitement in his voice.

"Come, hurry, Sam. We need to go to the mouth of the tunnel." On the way, he explained, "We are going to collect a female called Kwan-yin. She is about to pass away on Earth."

They met Kwan-yin in the tunnel, looking very frightened and lost. She was a dignified young woman, aged before her time, with a sad face. Sam noticed that behind that pleasant face was a woman with a broken **heart**[2] and emotional wounds that needed healing.

They escorted her through the tunnel and brought her safely to the garden. Tenzin gave her a small section of **land**[3] as her property in the northern part of the garden. He then left her with Sam and departed.

Kwan-yin was immediately engrossed in her new environment. She had had a difficult life on Earth, as reflected in her approach to others. It was as if a high wall guarded her inner self. Her confidence and self-esteem were low, and she had difficulty trusting people, though she seemed to trust Tenzin. She was a wonderful person, a loner who liked her privacy.

Tenzin understood her and decided it would be better for Sam to **help her**[4]. The interaction between the two women would help them both. It would induce friendship, maturity, and understanding and give them insight into each other's lives.

Sam understood what Tenzin had in mind. He needed people like her, who could win Kwan-yin's respect, trust, and confidence so that together they could heal Kwan-yin's wounded soul.

Over the next few days, Sam stayed with Kwan-yin and got to know her better. She began to express her thoughts, saying, "I am interested in you. You have a lovely soul, but it is hidden. I want to be your friend and work **with you**[5] to help each other heal our wounds."

Tenzin was hoping that, with Sam's help, he could make Kwan-yin relax, be more comfortable, and help her blossom. He wanted to reassure her that they would not judge or try to undermine her. She was now in a secure place where she could feel safe and grow.

---- ➤ ----

Bible (NKJV)	Bhagavad Gita
[1] Revelation 5:9. They sing a new song: "You are worthy to take the scroll and to open its seals, for you were slaughtered and by your blood, you ransomed for God saints from every tribe and language and people and nation;	[1] 11:14. Sitting among the heavenly saints and the elders of the Universe, Arjuna struggles to understand the mystery of God's plan and his long eternal journey through it, led by the divine spirit. He is amazed *(having been granted unique access to the inner mind of the Lord God).* He bowed before the Lord God and spoke these words.
[2] Matthew 12:20. He will not break a bruised reed or quench a smouldering wick until he brings justice to victory.	[2] 8:16. Every person and creature on earth is subject to pleasure, pain, and suffering. However, those attaining My Abode acquire the strength to overcome their pain and suffering.
[3] Micah 4:4, but they shall all sit under their vines and fig-trees, and no one shall make them afraid; for the mouth of the LORD of hosts has spoken.	[3] 18:57. Arjuna, dedicate every activity to Me, making Me your supreme goal. Depend upon Me,
[4] Deuteronomy 4:14. And the LORD charged me to teach you	

statutes and ordinances to observe in the land you are about to cross into and occupy.

[5] Zak's Tenet – Consent. "Guide you with my eye. I respect your privacy. I can only reason with you; I will not press or persuade you without your consent."

work under My protection, and you will feel My presence in all life activities.

[4] 13:11. Devotees dedicate their lives to furthering God's and everyone's welfare, interests, and happiness. They enjoy solitude at times and refrain from following the crowd.

[5] 12:16. The ones I love are not selfish; they are efficient, pure, and not anxious about the outcome. When the world around them seems to crumble and events are beyond their capacity to change, they remain steady in faith, putting their trust in My divine provision. They constantly seek the best for others, friends and foes, acting selflessly and impartially.

---x--

---------- ᛘ------

Chapter 17

World of imprisoned souls

One day, Tenzin called out for Sam. "Come, let me show you something. You may see some unpleasant things, but do not be afraid. Watch and learn from what you see. Hold my hand and close your eyes."

They drifted through space and ended up in a cold place.

"You can open your eyes now," Tenzin whispered.

She tightened her grip on his hand. A shiver went through her.

"What do you see?" he asked.

"This is a terrible, foul-smelling place – like burnt hair and flesh. The air is cold, stale, suffocating, and damp. It is dark, but I see dungeons with low ceilings and rough-hewn walls. Tenzin, can we please leave?"

"Not yet. Look inside the **dungeons.**[1] What do you see?"

"I **see bodies**[2] made of some grey-white substance. Some are chained to the walls, while others are on the floor."

"Have a closer look."

"I think... they're dead."

"Take a closer look."

She bent over a body and sprang back in terror. "They're alive!" She paused and said, "They seem to have **lost the will to live**[3]**.** Who are these people? Why are they here?"

---- ➤ ----

Bible (NKJV)	Bhagavad Gita
[1] 1 Peter 3:19, in which also he went and made a proclamation to the spirits in prison,	[1] 8:25. The selfish and evil follow the southern tunnel that leads toward the path of smoke, of night, towards a darker, unpleasant place, leaving behind a legacy of greed, selfishness and misery.
[2] 1st Peter 4:5-6. But they will have to give an accounting to him who stands ready to judge the living and the dead. For this reason, the gospel was proclaimed even to the dead so that, though they had been judged in the flesh as everyone is judged, they might live in the spirit as God does.	[2] 9:20. Those who study the Holy books and worship Me free themselves from ignorance, darkness, fear and evil. They attain a spiritual place in the heavenly realms and enjoy My divine blessing.
[3] Job 38:15. Light is withheld from the wicked, and their uplifted arm is broken.	[3] 18:32. A person in ignorance walks in spiritual darkness. They cannot distinguish good from evil nor know when to act and refrain. Their life rotates solely around themselves.

---------- ᴕ-------

Chapter 18

Selfishness and evil

Tenzin said, "If you look closely, you will notice that their life force, creative will, and determination to get up has gone, or has been taken away. Some people have been here for a long time, while others have just arrived. We should go."

"Why?" Sam asked.

"If we stay, what you see and hear will be unpleasant. I don't want you to see any more."

"I am not afraid. I want to know why **these people are here[1].**"

She watched and saw that now and then, guards, almost human but too tall, too strong to be ordinary people, would bring in more bodies.

She tried to talk to and revive some of these prisoners, but her efforts were fruitless. With tears in her eyes, she looked at Tenzin to find the meaning of this unpleasant prison.

"I wanted you to know that some awful places exist in the Cosmos. One day, you will understand. Selfishness, self-centredness, pride, and **greed[2]** can have unpleasant consequences."

"Who are these people? What is this place?" she asked nervously.

After an awkward pause, he said, "These people had brought great pain and suffering to others. Many were individual petty criminals, but others were leading members of their country who committed crimes against humanity and intelligent animals or incited others to carry them out. Sadly, these people are still honoured and admired as great leaders among their fellow citizens.

"They await the Great Day. People call it by various names: **Judgement Day[3],** The Day of the Supreme Being, and The Final Judgement.

"There are **places**[4] like this in the Cosmos that are very dangerous. You should never come here on your own."

---- ➤ ----

Bible (NKJV)	Bhagavad Gita
[1] Daniel 12:2. Many of those who sleep in the dust of the earth shall awake, Some to everlasting life, Some to shame and everlasting contempt.	[1-3] 11:25-32. With your wide-open mouth afire, I perceive your fearful nature, swallowing the whole cosmos. O Lord, the refuge of the Universe, be gracious to me and have mercy upon me on that fearsome day (Judgment Day). On that fearsome day, I see Dhritarashtra's sons (all spiritually blind and evil beings) and the allied kings with Bhisma, Drona, Karna, and all the warriors rushing towards their deaths* like moths into a flame. Filled with your terrible radiance on that fearsome day, the whole Universe bursts into fire, and you lap up all the ungodly into your mouth, devouring all.
[2] James 1:21. So get rid of all the filth and evil in your lives, and humbly accept the word God has planted in your hearts, for it has the power to save your souls.	
[3] Romans 14:12. So then, each of us will be accountable to God.	
[4] Jude 1:6. And the angels who did not keep their position, but left their proper dwelling, he has kept in eternal chains in deepest darkness for the judgment of the great Day.	[4] 11:31-32. I am bewildered as to who you are. I behold you as utterly fierce and destructive. I bow before you, all-pervading Lord. **Krishna:** I am time, and I am the destroyer. All the ungodly gathered on Judgment Day will perish. However, good, godly, honest, decent people will survive and continue to live.
---x--	---------- ↬------

Chapter 19

My paternal father

One day, Sam was pleading with Tenzin, tears in her eyes. "My father passed away years ago. I assume he is in one of these sanctuaries. I would like to see my father. I have missed him. Where can I find **him?**[1] Please, can you take me to him?"

Tenzin replied, "All I can tell you for the present is that your father is a great and virtuous man who has moved on to a different realm. He knows you are here.

"He has asked me to look after you. When the time is right, I will take you to meet him. Unfortunately, you can't meet him yet.

"I cannot explain because you will not understand. I want you to **trust me**[2]. Come with me, and I will show you something that will prepare you to meet your father someday."

She followed him. They came to a new part of the garden, where she had never been before, and sat by the side of the lake.

Tenzin said, "Close your eyes and listen to the music."

At first, there was complete silence, and then, slowly, music started to come from all directions. It began very slowly, sad and gloomy, and engulfed her whole being. The music awakened all her fears and anxieties while on Earth. It was as though all the past pain was running through her again.

She recalled how evil men, disease, and ill health had ruined her parents' lives. Her kind, gentle, and considerate parents had died in poverty, driven to an early grave by the acts of selfish people who only cared for themselves. They had trodden on others to get what they wanted, irrespective of other people's needs.

The cries of all the innocent victims of violence and abuse, including animals eaten while still alive by predators, seemed to flow through her, crying out for justice.

They were followed by a menacing, haunting quietness, conveying that life is **without purpose[3]**, meaning or hope. There was nowhere in this bottomless pit to hide.

The sad music had sucked all the strength, will, and life from her. It gave way to complete stillness, like being in a vacuum, awaiting a merciful end to all feelings, thoughts, and energy. How could a divine being create or allow such evil to flourish?

"If there is a God," she cried aloud, "I will make Him/It answer for all the crimes against my parents, kin and Creation."

A profound pessimism set over her. She cried out, "Please, someone, **help me[4]**."

A bright light and a great sense of energy and power surrounded her. Slowly, the despair and loneliness began to fade. The utter loneliness and misery that had filled the air began to be replaced by **hope[5]**.

A new form of positive energy flowed through the song. It became more assertive and more powerful.

---- ➤ ----

Bible (NKJV)	Bhagavad Gita
[1] Romans 8:35. Who will separate us from the love of Christ? (Or those in Christ) Will hardship, distress, persecution, famine, nakedness, peril, or sword? [2] Ecclesiastes 3:1-2. For everything under heaven, there is a season and a time for every	[2] 12:16. The ones I love are not selfish; they are efficient, pure, detached, and not anxious about the outcome, but put their trust and faith in My divine provision. ~ They constantly seek the best for others, friends, and foes, <u>acting selflessly</u> and impartially.

matter: a time to be born, to die, to plant, and to pluck up what is planted;

[Liz's Tenet 1 – It is not wise to reveal all before its time.]

[3] Matthew 4:4. But he answered, "It is written, 'One does not live by bread alone, but by every word that comes from the mouth of God.'"

[4] Job 10:1 My soul loathes my life; I will give free course to my complaint and speak in the bitterness of my soul.

[5] Psalms 78:7 That they may set their hope in God, And not forget the works of God, But keep His commandments;

---X--

[3] 18:36. O, mighty warrior, there are three kinds of happiness. A materialistic person is engaged in the sense of gratification. Still, when he realizes this is only repetitive, he may awaken to spiritual life and discover life's true purpose, meaning, fulfilment, and happiness.

[3, 4] 3:32. However, those who complain and ignore the Scriptures lack knowledge. They are deluded, spiritually lost, and devoid of hope of enlightenment in life.

[5] 4:38. Nothing in this world purifies like spiritual knowledge. Living in conjunction with it is the pinnacle of perfection hoped for by all the saints. One who practices this wisdom comes to enjoy inner peace.

---X--

--------- ꝗ→------

Chapter 20

Earth will pass away

The song filled her with power, strength, and joy; she felt hopeful, radiant, and confident. Everything—every experience, good or bad, in her life— seemed to float past her. Every thought, every moment, was bathed in a brilliant white light. It seemed to say, "I **will convert**[1] all these feelings into a positive experience, which will mould your character and personality into a thoughtful, compassionate person."

This brilliant white light left a deep impression on her that what it had **begun**[2] had the ability and power to bring to fullness in time.

A strong voice seemed to come from within her. [Kate Adin's Tenet 1] "All you have seen and felt will be taken care of, accounted for, justified, and all your losses compensated, and restitution made **fourfold**.[3]

"Know this: every grain of sand you have come across, every atom, every quark (a subatomic particle) is known, accounted for, and has a purpose.

"One day, you will understand that all the suffering in the cosmos has a **purpose**[4] and will be accounted for. Compensation and restitution will be made for those who suffer pain, anguish, and loss.

"Those who have inflicted pain on others and have not changed their ways will be **separated**[5]. Darkness is more significant than evil, and light is more excellent than night. The night will give way to light.

"When that is achieved, the **New Children**[6] of the Cosmos will be free of pain and suffering, and the Cosmos will finally be at peace.

"Earth will eventually pass away (die, burn up) filled with joy after seeing her newborn cosmic children reach adulthood."

It was too much for Sam to comprehend. She was exhausted and fell into a deep sleep. Tenzin found her asleep under the fig tree. He covered her with a blanket. She slept for a long time, and when she woke up, she found Tenzin beside her.

She shared her experience with him and asked, "What does it mean?"

He was in deep thought. "That song was written honouring your father and you," Tenzin explained. "It should have given you a glimpse into how your **father felt**[7] and overcame the struggles of his life on Earth. He has now moved on to a higher level. One day, when the time is right, and you have reached a certain level of growth, you will be able to meet your father."

"I still don't understand," Sam said.

[Kate Adin's Tenet 2]. Tenzin replied, "Trust me. You are unique. There is a greater power that guides your path. Everything that has been made and created is made for you (those like you). Some things and mysteries are hidden until the fullness of time—called Awara-nar."

Sam replied, "You say I am unique, but I don't feel it."

---- ➤ ----

Bible (NKJV)	Bhagavad Gita
[1] Romans 12:2. Do not be conformed to this world, but be transformed by renewing your minds to discern God's will—what is right, acceptable, and perfect.	[1] 3:30. Arjuna, fix your mind on Me and surrender all your works unto Me. Fulfil My divine plan to improve all creatures' welfare, interest, and happiness. Do it without any desire for personal gain.
[2] Philippians 1:6. I am confident that the one who began a good work among you will complete it by the day of Jesus Christ.	[2] 1:2. The Supreme Lord has granted Sanjaya incredible spiritual power (Kly-Son ability) to see and hear what was happening on the battlefield.
[3] Luke 19:8. Zacchaeus stood there and said to the Lord, "Look, half of my possessions, Lord, I will give to	[4] 2:50. Devotional service aims to

the poor; and if I have defrauded anyone of anything, I will pay back four times as much."

[4] 1st Peter 1:11, searching what, or what manner of time, the Spirit of Christ who was in them was indicating when He testified beforehand the sufferings of Christ and the glories that would follow.

[5] Matthew 25:32. All the nations will be gathered before him, and he will separate people one from another as a shepherd separates the sheep from the goats,

[6] "[Janet Warrington's Tenet 1]. We will use everything that happened to you as a positive force for good. Every experience, good and bad, every thought, feeling, and tear you have shed, and all laughter and joy, we will turn into a positive force for good. It will be used for your spiritual growth and maturity to fulfil your place among us. You are not alone. We are with you and will be with you until the end of time."

[7] [King David's Tenet – A Father's love for his child]. "I understand the pain and sorrow in your heart. When a loving, devoted father leads his child through the valley of death, he has a good reason and purpose. He will shed more tears than you because he will

free you from self and attachment to the material world. Secondly, it lifts you into My presence and enlightens you with My purpose for creation. Thirdly, to instil in you a sense of oneness with all life.

[4] 11:7. In My body, you will perceive the whole cosmos cycle passing before your eyes. Whatever you want to see, the past, present, future, Creation, earth, and Spiritual sanctuaries will flash before you. You will find answers to questions regarding the terms 'in the fullness of time' and 'the end of all material and spiritual worlds' and your purpose on earth and in the heavenly realms. The mysteries of the universe are available to all brave enough to seek them.

[5] 16:19-20. These cruel, malicious, hateful, envious people, I cast them into the womb (spiritual sanctuaries) of their kind in the hereafter. There, the ungodly will live in spiritual sanctuaries among their kind. Without my guidance, they will gradually sink to their worst possible depth.

[6] 11:14. Sitting among the heavenly saints and the elders of the Universe, Arjuna struggles to understand the mystery of God's plan and his long eternal journey through it, led by the divine spirit. He is amazed *(having been granted unique access to the inner mind of*

allow your pain to continue. His motives, his intentions, are for your betterment and growth. Your tears will inflict deep wounds on him, yet he has chosen this path for both of you. Love comes at a high cost. Moral character and compassion are refined in the fires of grief, suffering and joy, just as gold is refined in the fire."

---X--

the Lord God). He bowed before the Lord God and spoke these words.

---X--

---------- ⤴------

Chapter 21

The aborted babies

[Rev Jim Hammond's Tenet]. [All he could say was, 'We came across a field covered with white, blue, and red earthen pots that held the testimonies of miscarried and aborted embryos and foetuses.']

Sam was walking in the orchard when she saw Tenzin near a mature fruit tree. She greeted him.

Tenzin smiled at her. "I have something to show you. Come with me."

He led her past the orchard to a field that was new to her. The area was divided into square sections. Each ten-furlong square had **stone pots/jars¹** laid out in neat, straight rows. The colours of the earthen pots in each division were different.

They came to a section that had white pots.

Tenzin told Sam, "Pick up a pot, and tell me what happens."

Sam picked up a white stone pot the size of a small pebble. She held it in her palm, closed her eyes, and sensed that it contained the testimony of an embryo. When she held the jar in her palm, it started to speak to her.

"You have come to the resting place where each **pot holds²** the spirit and testimony of an embryo or a foetus that lived for a few days or months. Unfortunately, each of our mothers had a natural miscarriage. In most cases, our parents were unaware they had conceived or lost us."

---- ➤ ----

Bible (NKJV)	Bhagavad Gita
¹ Joshua 4:21. Then he spoke to the children of Israel, saying: "When your children ask their	¹ 1:40-41. When families break up, the widows and orphans are left desolate and vulnerable to

parents in time to come, saying, 'What are these <u>stones</u>?'

[2] Matthew 3:9. I say that God can raise children to Abraham from these stones. 2 Exodus 28:12, "And you shall put the two stones on the shoulders of the ephod as memorial stones for the sons of Israel. So Aaron shall bear their names before the LORD on his two shoulders as a memorial.

corruption. The unity of the family declines, and the country is plunged into chaos.

---- ➤ ----

---------- ⤳------

Chapter 22

Nothing in the Cosmos is irrelevant

"Each pot contains a detailed history and background of an embryo or a **foetus,**[1] including information such as the parents' ancestry and country of origin, location, the time and circumstances of conception, and the events that led to the miscarriage.

"It contains details of its parents' thoughts, emotions, desires, perceptions, and reactions before, during, and after the miscarriage.

"It contains the details of the parents' circumstances, their positions in society, their financial means, and their ability to look after the embryo/foetus or not. It records whether they were loving or unconcerned parents. Every thought of the parents is recorded in detail, and could fill a couple of books. They rest here, waiting for their parents or foster parents to claim them."

She turned to Tenzin and asked, "Why so detailed?"

He replied, [Liz's Tenet 2] *"It is recorded so that it can be used in the future for forgiveness and reconciliation. Nothing in the Cosmos is irrelevant. The Cosmos has invested a vast amount of energy because it has an eternal plan, a desire for life to flourish, and where possible, reconcile, restore, and make all things whole."*

Sam stated, "Whosoever has compiled these testimonies has done so with care, tenderness, and dedication." Solemnly, she returned the pot to its place.

Tenzin replied, "When life is viewed in terms of a lifespan of seventy years, there is not **enough time**[2] for minute details. When time becomes part of eternity, details matter, and each event has long-term repercussions **for the future**[3]. The universe was born in a day (short time), but its repercussions are forever."

He paused, then continued, "One day, when you have a deeper understanding of the laws of the Cosmos, we believe you will take part in compiling and logging some of these details."

"For what purpose?" she inquired.

"If there is to be eternal peace in the Cosmos, then everything has to work in harmony. When that harmony is disturbed, it has unpleasant **repercussions**[4], where darkness, ignorance, and evil thrive. Hence, we must work hard to reconcile, restore, and make all things **whole**[5] so that peace, order, and harmony prevail."

She replied, "I don't understand. Such analytical work requires **special talents (Kly-son)**[6]. You have this ability, but I do not."

"These are early days. With our guidance, you will acquire this skill." (Refer to Chapter 45 – Elders.)

[6] *Kly-son. A unique blessing from God/Cosmos that gives a person instant insight into a person's life with a single glance. They can assess every thought, motive, and detail of that person's history, ancestry, and effect on others. They can weigh up all the good and bad that person has done, their character, personality, past or future intentions, and the implications for others. If they conclude that the person will greatly add to the suffering of others, they will intervene to stop them."* ---- ➤ ----

Bible (NKJV)	Bhagavad Gita
[1] Job 5:23. For you shall have a covenant with the stones of the field, And the beasts of the field shall be at peace with you.	[2] 8:17. A thousand years are like a day and a night to Brahman.
[2] Psalms 90:4. A <u>thousand</u> years in Your sight Are like yesterday.	[3] - [6] 2:11-12. Lord Krishna says: My friend, your words may feel wise, but those spiritually in tune with Me can <u>see the whole picture</u> through the windows of past, present, future, and eternity. Grieve neither for the living nor for the dead. Your Atman and that of these kings and soldiers
[3] Luke 8:17. <u>Nothing is hidden</u> that will not be disclosed, nor is anything secret that will not	

become known and come to light.

[4] Revelation 12:7-8 And war broke out in heaven: <u>Michael</u> and his angels fought with the dragon, and the dragon and his angels fought, but they did not prevail, nor was a place found for them in heaven any longer.

[5] Colossians 1:20. By Him to reconcile all things to Himself, by Him, whether things on earth or <u>things in heaven</u>, having made peace through the blood of His cross.

[6] 1st Chronicles 22:12. Only the LORD <u>grant you insight</u> and understanding so that when <u>He gives you charge</u> over Israel, you may keep the Law of the LORD your God. ---x--

have always existed and will continue to live hereafter. Their physical bodies may cease to live, but their spirit will continue to live.

[4] 3:23-24. If I cease to work, all creation will follow My example, and there will be <u>cosmic chaos</u> and the destruction of humanity.

[5] 4:7-8. Whenever there is a decline in Dharma (devotional duty) and humanity's goal is lost, I (or My Apostles, prophets or Gurus) appear in every age <u>to restore Dharma</u>, re-establish religion, protect civilisation, and destroy evil.

[5] *Gita 1:26-46/Elaboration A6 The spirit of the Lord in Arjuna reveals that even in Heaven, the work of counselling, reconciliation, restoration, restitution, and making each whole has to continue if there is going to be eternal peace. That would require the special abilities, time, and effort of Godly eternal warrior-priests like him to restore and heal until all are made whole. The daunting task ahead and hereafter demoralises him and subdues his spirit. (Gita 11:1-31).*

[6] 1:2. The Supreme Lord has granted Sanjaya incredible spiritual power to see and hear what was happening on the battlefield. 3:11. Participate in this <u>sacrificial service</u> to My creation, and you will receive. ---x--

Chapter 23

Spiritual parents

Tenzin led her to the next section. In this part of the field, all the pots were purple. She picked one up.

It told her, "You have come to the resting place where each pot holds the spirit and testimonies of much-**wanted pregnancies**[1] that didn't come to term. Our parents cried and grieved when they miscarried."

She could feel the pain of the foetuses and their parents. These were loved and wanted babies who never made it to birth through no one's fault. She returned the pot to its place.

The following field had red pots. She picked up a small pot, and a sad, haunting feeling went through her body.

"We are foetuses **deliberately aborted**[2]. We were unwanted, unloved babies. We were a problem—an inconvenience to our parents. We are orphans in the cosmos."

Her body shook as blood trickled out of the pots, changing the earthen pots' colour to red. She bent down, stroked her stomach, and started to cry. Tenzin placed his hand on her shoulder. Gently, she returned the pot to its place. He led her away from the field and back to her garden.

---- ➤ ----

Bible (NKJV)	Bhagavad Gita
[1] 2nd Samuel 12:22-23. And he (King Davis) said, While the child was yet alive, I fasted and wept: for I said, Who can tell whether GOD will be gracious to me, that the child may live? But now he is dead, wherefore should I fast? can	[2] **Further light on Gita 1:26-46. Arjuna at the battlefield elaboration.** [2] A2 *He regarded himself as more than a prince. This role was temporary. His eternal role was as a*

I bring him back again? I shall go to him, but he shall not return to me.

² Genesis 4:10. And He said, "What have you done? The voice of your brother's blood cries out to Me from the ground.

---X--

warrior priest of the Supreme Lord of the Universe set apart to serve Him and others for eternity[1], to seek and promote their eternal welfare[2]. He looks at all those gathered on the battlefield, good, decent people on both sides mingled among the evil, amoral leaders[3]. How could he, with good conscience, engage in this destruction? (Gita [1]2:3. [2]3:1-2. [3]16:9)

A:3 If he survived the carnage of war (or Abortion, etc.), he would need to devote his life to reconstructing both sides. The role of cementing, reconciling, restoring, and making restitution for all the victims of war (Abortion), friends and foes, would fall on his kind. (Gita 4:33. 10:11-18)

---X--

---------- ᎧᎧ------

Chapter 24

All this suddenly means very little

They sat on the banks of the lake. It was a warm day. For a long time, neither of them said anything. He sat beside her, his presence a source of comfort, as she pondered what she had seen. The encounter with the pots had deeply moved her. She rested against the tree trunk and fell into a restless sleep.

He placed a blanket on her and left. Even in this beautiful and peaceful sanctuary, he understood that this encounter had stirred up an intense sense of pain and helplessness in her.

He felt the sadness that was in her. She was beginning to understand the message he was trying to get across. There were some unpleasant truths in the Cosmos.

She was coming to terms with some defining moments in her past that had carved out her future forever, often in an undesired direction.

The delicious fruit and lovely music, the companionship of pleasant neighbours, now added to her grief. All the garden's beauty and peace suddenly became meaningless when strong emotions swept through her. She **cried**[31] in her sleep until she was exhausted and fell into an even deeper, dreamless place. When she woke up, Tenzin was sitting near her.

"Why are you so sad?" he asked.

She stood up, pointed at the garden, and said, "All this suddenly means very little. It has lost its charm."

"Why this sudden change?" he asked.

She thought for a while and replied, "I am unsure how to answer. I feel, but I cannot rationalise it or put it in words. It has made me question what kind of person I am and what type of person I would like to be.

"To have the privilege to live here and do nothing for those babies makes me feel selfish, self-centred and mean. On the other hand, I have no means of helping them. I feel so frustrated, so angry, and utterly helpless."

He looked into her sad eyes and said, "What you feel is benevolent and compassionate love. Sadly, it is a quality that is lacking in some parts of the Cosmos."

She looked at him and said, "My feelings are not enough. I need to channel them in **practical ways,**[2] to take those feelings and put them to some use, like helping those babies." ---- ➤ ----

Bible (NKJV)	Bhagavad Gita (Hindu Scripture) by Hari Patel Amazon.com
[1] 2nd Corinthians 1:7. Our hope for you is steadfast because we know that as you are <u>partakers of the sufferings</u>, you will also partake of the consolation.	[2] 3:11. Participate in this sacrificial service to My creation, and you will receive My blessing. Collaboration between humankind and creation brings prosperity to all.
[2] Ezekiel 36:26. A new heart will also give you, and a new spirit will I put within you: I will take away the stony heart out of your flesh, and I will give you a heart of flesh.	[2] 8:28. Study the scripture, give selfless service to others, live modestly, and give to the poor. This selfless duty to others and devotion to My teachings will guide you to your spiritual home, My abode.

---------- ᕃ------

Chapter 25

A spiritual mother

Tenzin smiled. "Now you are speaking like a mother, a spiritual mother. There are **many teachers**[1] in the Cosmos, but not many spiritual <u>fathers and mothers</u>."

She looked at him with pleading eyes. "I want to be a spiritual mother to the orphans."

"If you want to be a spiritual parent, you will need to learn all about the duties and responsibilities of a spiritual parent. It is not like on Earth, where anyone can be a parent. Here, anyone desiring to be a <u>spiritual parent</u>[2] undergoes a vigorous training programme and must pass it."

"I understand. I have a question, something that is of interest to me. What happens when these fostered foetuses grow and ask about their **biological parents**[3]? What will happen when they come face-to-face with their Earthly parents?"

He did not reply. He thought for a while.

Sam said, "Could you come with me to the field of truth and reconciliation?"

They walked up to the field of coloured pots.

Tenzin asked, "Why have we come here?"

She looked at Tenzin, sadly saying, "I can feel part of me was here. My aborted baby's spirit was in the red pots. It isn't here now. Why not?"

He replied, carefully choosing each word, "We moved it to another place, where it is looked after and cared for."

"Why?"

"It hurts me to remind you that yours was an unplanned pregnancy, the product of rape. You could not look after that child on Earth, and are still not emotionally able to look after that child.

"You have many issues, like anger and hatred for the child's father and others who mistreated you. You must deal with these issues. You harbour anger towards the parents you love. You blame them for your misfortune in life. A burning fire inside you is slowly draining your life force. You have to be free of it."

"How can I be free of it?"

"It starts with understanding your past feelings and their damage to you."

Sam admitted, "I know I have mixed feelings. I have unresolved issues to deal with about the multiple times I was raped. My child's father was my abuser and rapist, and I don't know how to deal with it."

"We understand how you feel, and we sympathise with you. We have undertaken to help you deal with your issues. We will arrange for you to receive therapy, counselling, and guidance.

"When the time is right, we will take **each event**[4] and teach you to learn from it and show you how to overcome it and grow. I do not expect you to understand; just trust me. Please follow me."

He led her to another part of the field—a small, well-tended section bordered with scented shrubs. In the middle stood a fountain that watered this section. At the base of the fountain lay a neat row of pots.

Sam ran towards the fountain and picked up a small, bright red pot. "This holds my child's spirit." ---- ➹ ----

Bible (NKJV)	**Bhagavad Gita**
[1 - 2] 1st Corinthians 4:15. Though you might have ten thousand instructors in Christ, you do not	[1] 4:34. Follow the guidance of a spiritual master and render service unto him. The spiritual master can

have many fathers; for, in Christ Jesus, I have begotten you through the gospel.

³ Numbers 27:11. And if his father has no brethren, then you shall give his inheritance unto his relative that is next to him of his family, and he shall possess it:

⁴ Ro 12:2. Do not be conformed to this world, but be transformed by renewing your mind so that you may prove God's good, acceptable, and perfect will. Philippians 3:21, who will transform our lowly body that it may be conformed to His glorious body, according to the working by which He can even subdue all things to Himself.

---x--

instruct you in this wisdom.

² 6:10. People who aspire to grow spiritually should always have their bodies, minds, and self in servitude to My creation and Me. 10:9. My devotees' thoughts and lives centre on Me. They derive tremendous satisfaction and happiness from their service to society and Me. Teaching one another and conversing about Me, they enlighten one another.

³ 18:68-69 Those who walk in this highest truth and teach others that hunger for this knowledge performs one of the highest acts of love. They will receive *(mam evaisyaty asamsayah)* an honoured place in My kingdom. There is no one more precious to Me than those who have sought Me and, through obedience, have earned the right to walk beside Me. ---x--

Chapter 26

Reconciliation

Tears started to run down Sam's cheeks until her hands and the jar were soaked. "Please help me, Tenzin," she pleaded. She began to sob over the pot with the foetus and cried, "I am so sorry I had to take your life away. Please forgive me."

The pot began to change colour and turned from red to white. It was as if the spirit in the pot could understand her grief and remorse. She replaced the jar under the fountain once more.

Tenzin said softly, "We will help you to meet him one day. We will see to it that you have a second chance.

"When you meet, you will have grown into a more mature adult, the flaws in your character smoothed out. In time, you will have proved you have become a loving, caring foster mother to other children. It will be a happy day when we will unite you with your child. **Reconciliation**[1] will be easier when you have earned your child's respect and your child is proud of you."

"What is happening to my child?"

"Some of his father's family members have tried to claim him. We must find a way to **link him**[2] with his relatives and past grandparents from both sides of the family. It is a complicated affair."

"His father was a killer."

"Yes, but his ancestors on his father's side do not share his father's crime. They have a claim over him."

"He is my child. I am his guardian. Why should his ancestors have a claim? Why should they care for a product of rape, shame, and dishonour?"

---- ➔ ----

Bible (NKJV)	Bhagavad Gita
[1] Ephesians 2:16, He might reconcile them to God in one body through the cross, thereby putting hostility toward each other to death.	[1] 4:35. Having gained spiritual wisdom, you will not be deluded again. You will see that all living entities are part of the divine plan, part of one family, and have the same breath of life from the divine.
[2] Exodus 6:14. These are the heads of their fathers' houses: The sons of Reuben, the firstborn of Israel, were Hanoch, Pallu, Hezron, and Carmi. These are the families of Reuben. **Numbers 4:29.** "As for the sons of Merari, you shall number them by their families and by their father's house. ---x--	[2] 1:40-43. When families break up, the widows and orphans are left desolate and vulnerable to corruption. The unity of the family declines, and the country is plunged into chaos. Social upheaval is hell for the family, society, and those who destroy families. It eliminates the spiritual foundation laid down by our ancestors. Thus, the unity and the spiritual foundation for families and the morals of society are degraded. ---x--

---------- ॐ-------

Chapter 27

Spiritual parents

Tenzin replied, "Families matter. Family history reconnects a person to their routes and their identity. People without a family history are like boats drifting without a rudder in a sea. Therefore, in the child's interest, we try to link them to their family from both their parents' sides. People with no ties to the past have difficulty facing the future. The sanctuaries are full of troubled children with no past or future unless someone tries to intervene and change their paths. The Cosmos is very short of **spiritual parents.**[1]"

"You mean there is a shortage of beings like you," Sam said.

He laughed. "What do you think?"

She replied, "I don't know."

He led her back to her garden. Her friend, Kwan-yin, was waiting for her. He left the two women and went away.

Sam shared her experiences with her friend.

After an awkward pause, Kwan-yin said, "I was fourteen when I became pregnant. The baby's father forced me to sell my body for money, and I was beaten if I did not obey him. A few months later, I became pregnant. I was desperate to have the child, the only thing I could call mine, but my pimp had my pregnancy terminated." She started to cry. "I hated him. I would have killed him if I'd had the strength and the opportunity."

Sam suggested, "Next time Tenzin is here, you can ask him about your baby. I am sure he will be able to help you."

They were walking through the garden when, in the distance, they saw Tenzin talking to someone they had not seen before. They ran up to the men. Tenzin turned around and faced them.

He smiled and said, "Let me introduce you to Brother Stefan."

A small, well-built man stepped forward and shook their hands. He had a friendly face and easy manners that instantly made him approachable.

Sam asked, "Have you just joined us?"

Stefan laughed, and Tenzin joined in.

Tenzin said, "Brother Stefan has decided to rejoin us."

Stefan added, "I used to live here. I left to visit some family members, probably before you two came here." He paused and then said, "You have to excuse me. I need to go and see some friends. I will join you later on."

Once he had gone, Tenzin asked, "How can I help you both?"

Kwan-yin replied, "I need your help. I want to know about my child. Can you help?"

He paused and said with a gentle, sympathetic tone, "Your child's pot was in the red field. When you came to this sanctuary, we moved it and placed it next to the fountain. You were in a difficult situation at the time of its conception. The biological father controlled every aspect of your life and terminated the child. You were vulnerable and defenceless, and there was nothing you could do.

"One day, your child will know that his father subjected you to extreme pain and suffering. This knowledge will be a heavy burden for him. You both have issues and will need our help to deal with them before you can be reconciled."

Kwan-yin pleaded, "I want to prove that I can change given a second chance. I want to learn to be a good spiritual foster mother. I want to earn the respect of my child so that we can be reconciled and be together forever."

He looked at the two women and said, "What you desire will happen in time. You two need to learn a lot and grow stronger here. You had very little love in your past lives. We want you to experience love, peace, tenderness, and things you had previously missed. There are many good things you need to experience and feel. We want you to learn to trust again, to enjoy life and companionship."

They nodded in agreement.

---- ➤ ----

Bible (NKJV)	Bhagavad Gita
[1] 1st Corinthians 4:15. Though you might have ten thousand instructors in Christ, you do not have many fathers; for, in Christ Jesus, I have begotten you through the gospel. ---x--	[1] 4:34. Follow the guidance of a spiritual master and render service unto him. The spiritual master can instruct you in this wisdom. ---x--

---------- ᕀᛏ------

Chapter 28

Frontiers of the spiritual realms

[1] *[Kate Adin's 3rd Tenet.]* *She saw red, blue, and yellow flowers: simple words used here to convey a complex spiritual experience with no equivalent expression in earthly human life. It is a spiritual experience in a different dimension, not constrained by the material world's laws, including time. The colours we see reflect light from an object, whereas, in the spiritual realm, it is the inner beauty of an item or a being's virtue. These experiences are given to people during difficult periods to strengthen them.*

Words cannot convey things beyond the limits of our language. There are no words to describe things about another dimension the human eye has not seen, nor has the human ear **heard**[1]. How shall one describe such things?

2 Corinthians 4:18: We do not concentrate on the things that are seen, but on the things that are not seen: for the things that are seen are temporal; but the things that are not seen are eternal.

One day, Tenzin took Sam to visit one of their neighbours, Kenneth.

"Let me show you around my **vineyard**[2]," Kenneth told them.

It was a **beautiful**[3] garden. On the garden's northern side were shrubs with hundreds of red flowers, and on the eastern side were flowers of various shades of blue. In the south were shrubs with many shades of yellow flowers. It was the most beautiful, colourful garden Sam had ever seen. ---- ➤ ----

Bible (NKJV)	Bhagavad Gita
[1] John 3:12, "If I have told you earthly things and you do not <u>believe</u>, how will you <u>believe</u> if I	[1] 13:9. They comprehend the Lord's creative plan for the cosmos, their position in this plan, and the reason for joyful and painful lessons of life:

tell you heavenly things?

2 Isaiah 5:1, Now let me sing to my Well-beloved A song of my Beloved regarding His vineyard: My Well-beloved has a vineyard On a fruitful hill.

3 Isaiah 61:3, To appoint unto them that mourn in Zion, to give unto them beauty for ashes, the oil of joy for mourning, the garment of praise for the spirit of heaviness; that they might be called trees of righteousness, the planting of the LORD, that he might be glorified.

3 Isaiah 35:10, And the ransomed of the LORD shall return, And come to Zion with singing, With everlasting joy on their heads. They shall obtain joy and gladness, And sorrow and sighing shall flee away. ---x--

the joy of family, friends, birth, suffering, disease, old age, and death. All these things are encountered in life and used for spiritual growth and advancement. Hence, they seek and are willing to learn from a spiritual master as they journey along this path.

2 2:69. Material things take precedence over everything to the worldly-minded person, obscuring their spiritual existence. To the spiritually minded, worldly things are temporary; spiritual things are tangible, visible, and clear as day.

---x--

---------- ᎒᎒------

Chapter 29

The eternal song

As they walked through it, a symphony of **delightful song**[1] and music started to accompany them. The flowers, plants, and trees seemed caught in the symphony and released a powerful fragrance.

Bright light and pleasant air surrounded them as if someone had placed a warm, compassionate blanket over them, overwhelming them with intense love and joy.

She was caught in an atmosphere where everything in her life seemed to have a **purpose,**[2] a plan, a destiny. She wanted to be part of this grand plan—a sea of **possibility**[3] in which her doubts and fears had disappeared. She felt a surge of new energy, optimism, and hope, as though she could live forever.

She was overwhelmed; her mind seemed to overflow with joy and emotions beyond her understanding. She sat down to rest, her legs weak and fell into a deep sleep.

When she awoke, she found herself back in her garden. Most of what she had seen, heard, or felt in the symphony had left only a vague memory. Hard as she tried to recollect it, most had vanished.

Kwan-yin came over and asked her what the neighbour's garden looked like. She thought for a minute but could not find adequate words to express the vast range of colours or the music's beauty and meaning.

"Kwan-yin, it's difficult to describe. You have to see it to appreciate it. I can only describe it as a beautiful garden with red, blue, and yellow flowers." That was all she could say.

---- ➤ ----

Bible (NKJV)	Bhagavad Gita
[1] Isaiah 55:12, "For you shall go out with joy, And be led out with peace; The mountains and the hills Shall sing before you, And all the trees of the field shall clap their hands.	[2] 5:24. The wise find joy, happiness, purpose, and fulfilment within their inner-self and attain freedom in Me.
[2] Romans 8:28, And we know that all things work together for good to those who love God, to those called according to His purpose.	[3] 9:20. Those who study the Holy books and worship Me free themselves from ignorance, darkness, fear and evil. They gain a spiritual place in the heavenly realms and have access to My wisdom and blessings.
[3] 2 Corinthians 5:17, Therefore, if anyone is in Christ, he is a new creation; old things have passed away; behold, all things have become new.	---x--
---x--	

---------- ஒ-------

Chapter 30

Go out with joy

Sam was sitting on a rock in the garden when she noticed Tenzin walking towards her. Everything changed. The atmosphere started to come alive, **joyous**[1] and full of life. Everything began to radiate energy and acknowledge **his authority**[2].

She was pleased to see him looking so tall and majestic. His demeanour, how he walked and held his head, spoke of nobility, maturity, humbleness, and humanity. He wore no crown or sumptuous garments, only a simple tunic.

His presence inspired **confidence**[3] and brought out the good in others. She was overwhelmed by his virtues. He had been kind, gentle, and patient with her and had never rebuked her.

He was confident his love and care would eventually inspire trust, confidence, and **respect.**[4] In time, she would grow in wisdom and maturity and aspire to be like him and follow his example.

He was deep in thought as she walked beside him. They did not speak. He was contemplating while she was enjoying his company.

A small sparrow flew towards him and sat on his shoulders. In her beak, the sparrow held a small olive branch. Her eyes showed admiration.

He gently laid his finger on her. Immediately, the little bird was transformed, filled with great joy. She lost her balance, fell off his shoulder, and landed on the ground, unhurt and seemed drunk with pleasure.

A few moments later, she flew away, full of happiness.

---- ✈ ----

Bible (NKJV)	Bhagavad Gita
[1] Isaiah 55:12. For you shall go out in joy, and be led back in peace; the mountains and the hills before you shall burst into song, and all the trees of the field shall clap their hands.	[1] 18:17. A spiritual, mature person with the clarity of spirit understands Brahman's long-term plans for creation. They see all worldly activities, even life and death issues, as temporal and trust the Lord to turn them into a positive outcome in this life or the hereafter. Their and the Lord's actions have long-term objectives.
[2] 2nd Corinthians 13:10. Therefore, I write these things being absent, lest being present I should use sharpness, according to the authority the Lord has given me for edification and not destruction.	[2] 6:30. I am ever-present to those who have realised Me in every creature. Seeing all life as My manifestation, they are never separated from Me.
[3] 2nd Corinthians 2:3. And I wrote this very thing to you, lest, when I came, I should have sorrow over those from whom I ought to have joy, having confidence in you all that my joy is the joy of you all.	[3] 4:38. Nothing in this world purifies like spiritual knowledge. Living in conjunction with it is the pinnacle of perfection hoped for by all the saints. One who practices this wisdom comes to enjoy inner peace.
[4] 1st Thessalonians 5:15 See that no one renders evil for evil to anyone, but continuously pursue what is good both for yourself and all.	---X--
---X--	

---------- ᴓ------

Chapter 31

Forbidden frontiers of a spiritual world

The sanctuary that Tenzin controlled was one of many. There were **other**[1], similar places controlled by different **beings**[2]. Travelling from one garden to another required **permission**[3] from the owners, which was not always granted.

One day, Sam decided to travel to Kenneth's sanctuary without seeking his permission. She was confident she knew the way and assumed that Kenneth would be pleased to see her. She focused on him, thinking she would be transported to his rainbow garden.

Instead, she found herself in a vast, dark space and began to panic. She could not make her way back home or to Kenneth's garden. She was lost in the vast expanse of the universe. Distressed and panicked, she called out to Tenzin, but oddly, she could not contact him telepathically. Perhaps she had travelled beyond the range of telepathy.

She had not realised that wandering in the vast space outside her garden was dangerous. The more she panicked, the darker the surroundings seemed to get. She tried to relax and concentrate her thoughts on Tenzin.

Time passed, and she became weaker. She was losing hope of ever being reunited with Tenzin and her friends. She began to cry in despair and frustration. Then she saw a ray of light coming towards her. It got brighter and brighter until she looked up and saw Tenzin standing beside her. She hugged him with delight and relief.

"I am sorry; I shouldn't have left the garden without your permission. Please forgive me."

He looked into her eyes and said, "You matter more to me than I do to you." *[Kathy Cochrane's Tenet 1 – A person, or a relationship, is of greater eternal value than what we participate in.]* He gently escorted her back to the safety of her garden. ---- ➤ ----

Bible (NKJV)	Bhagavad Gita
[1] Colossians 2:15. Having disarmed principalities and powers, He made a public spectacle of them, triumphing over them. [2] Ephesians 3:10. So that God's wisdom in its rich variety might now be made known to the rulers and authorities in the heavenly places through the church. [3] Romans 13:1. Let every person be subject to the governing authorities; for there is no authority except from God, and God has instituted those authorities that exist. ---X--	[1-3] 4:3. To a select few, I revealed My existence and plans for eternity (past, present, and future worlds to come). You are My friend and devotee, and in due time, as you gain My favour, I will reveal these mysteries and explain your role here on Earth, in the spiritual world, and in the far distant future. You and other trusted devotees will build My material and spiritual kingdoms in this world and hereafter and walk beside Me in all My realms. I will guide and teach you all as a Father. ---X--

---------- ५५------

Chapter 32

Meeting her Father

Sam had been with Tenzin for a while now. She had learnt a lot and was adapting to her new environment. Tenzin decided that it was time for her to meet her father.

Together, they set off on the journey to the City of Light. As they travelled, he pointed out, on the far horizon, what looked like a rising sun. That, he explained, was the place where her father lived. As they made their journey, they came across several people. They were **gentle**[1] and hospitable, in harmony with one another and their surroundings. They were imperfect but radiated inner peace and contentment and could read each other's **thoughts.**[2]

Her thoughts were all **over the place**.[3] She had anger and discontent to deal with, which made her feel uncomfortable because all her inner conflicts were **exposed**[4] to these enlightened people.

He sought to reassure her. "No one **condemns you**[5] but you." He held her hand, and the warmth reassured and comforted her. She had much to learn. With his guidance, she would grow to be like the people here.

As they progressed, the character of the people they encountered seemed to change. The closer they got to the city, the brighter their **garments**[6] appeared to be, and they seemed more knowledgeable and mature.

She also noticed she appeared to be more like a child, younger, immature, ignorant, and naive. Her knowledge, ability, and powers seemed limited, and she felt out of place. However, Tenzin's presence was of great comfort.

People displayed more remarkable abilities as they approached the City of Light. Her life—every action, every thought, good or evil—was exposed and transparent to them. She started to feel uncomfortable. She would have returned home if it were not for Tenzin's reassuring presence.

They came to the city gates and entered.

---- ➤➤ ----

Bible (NKJV)	Bhagavad Gita
[1] 1st Peter 3:4 Let it be the hidden person of the heart, with the incorruptible beauty of a gentle and quiet spirit, which is very precious in the sight of God. [2] 1st Timothy 5:25, Likewise, the good works of some are evident, and those that are otherwise cannot be hidden. [3] Matthew, 10:26-27. "Therefore, do not fear them, for nothing is covered that will not be revealed and hidden that will not be known. "Whatever I tell you in the dark, speak in the light, and what you hear in the ear, preach on the housetops. [4] 2nd Corinthians, 4:2. We have renounced the shameful things one hides. We refuse to practice cunning or falsify God's word. We tell the truth before God, and all who are honest know this. [5] Romans 8:1, There is no condemnation to those in Christ Jesus, who do not walk according to the flesh, but according to the	[1] 5:7. A mature, enlightened person provides selfless services, learns to control his senses and mind, and sees the divine in all creatures. 3:7. Conversely, the better option is for the mind to learn to control one's senses for selfless service for the higher good of all. 5:10. Those walking in the divine presence and learning to surrender all selfish attachments to the Supreme Lord are like the leaf of a lotus plant floating clean and dry in muddy water. Similarly, those who submit all selfish attachments to the Supreme Lord no longer have the desire to sin. [2] 3:33. Even men of knowledge act according to their mode of nature. All creatures follow their heart. It is rooted in their thoughts and their tendencies. ~What is the use of repressing one's material nature? [3] 6:33-34. **Arjuna** responds: My Lord, my mind is restless and unsteady. How can one control one's thoughts? The mind is powerful, turbulent, and wild; trying to control it is like restraining the wind.

Spirit.

[6] Job 29:14, I put on righteousness, which clothed me; My justice was like a robe and a turban.

---x--

[4] 4:22-23. The wise person is steady in success and failure and does not compete or compare with others. He is free of envy, content with whatever the outcome, and safe in knowing that all results are under My divine control. The wise person, purified in the knowledge of My divine nature and freed from selfish desires, performs his duties in the spirit of sacrifice as an act of devotion and offering.

[5] 4:36. Spiritual knowledge is liberating. Even if you were once the most sinful of all sinners, once you board the boat of spiritual experience, you could sail beyond the ocean of your sins.

[6] 6:32. People who see equality in all beings and creatures have profound empathy for all and respond to their joy and sorrow as their own. They have attained one of the higher states of spiritual union with Me and My creation. (Refer to 5:18)

---- ➤ ----

---------- ୨୨-------

Chapter 33

Journey back to the garden

Her father was waiting in the courtyard, and she looked at him in amazement. Her emotions were mixed—ecstatic yet confused. Her father seemed so noble, so capable, and yet so humble. He had grown in stature and **authority**[1], and her life was transparent to him. There was not a single thought she could hide from him.

She ran to him and threw her arms about his neck.

"Hello, Sam," he murmured.

Their time spent together was happy and joyous, though fleeting. It passed almost as a blur. Her father told her of things he had been doing, watching over her, weeping at her suffering, and rejoicing when he found out he would finally see her again.

"Father, will you come back with me to the sanctuary?" Sam asked.

Her father's eyes filled with tears, and he held her close. "Sam," he said, "it has been so good to see you, and I wish we had more time. Nevertheless, you have much to learn before we can live together. I promise we will see each other again when the time is right."

Too soon, the time came for them to part.

"I have one request to make," her father said. "Trust Tenzin. Do what he asks you, obey him, and follow his **instructions**[2]. I have complete confidence in him." He turned to face Tenzin and said, "Please, **look after her**[3]."

"I will," Tenzin answered. "I won't let either of you down."

They set off, and soon, once more, her father was out of sight. Sam made her journey back to the garden in silence with a heavy heart, Tenzin at her side, each preoccupied with their thoughts. ---- ➤ ----

Bible (NKJV)		**Bhagavad Gita**
[1] Psalm 132:9, Let your priest be clothed with righteousness, and your saints shout for joy. [2]1st Corinthians, 12:28. God has appointed these in the church: first apostles, second prophets, third teachers, after that miracle, gifts of healings, helps, administrations, varieties of tongues. [3] Colossians, 1:28 We preach Christ, warning every man and teaching every man in all wisdom, that we may present every man perfect in Christ Jesus. ---x--		[1] **6**:45. These disciplined people in their new realms progress further as their selfish desires are purified. Moving upwards towards higher realms, they eventually attain the seventh Heaven, the supreme goal of all. [2 & 3] 14:23. Spiritual masters are unwavering and undisturbed by the gunas' actions. They are steady, strong, forceful, and unmoved. They have strong spiritual motivation and direction, which is more potent than the attraction to any gunas. ---x--

Chapter 34

Laws regarding the sanctuary

[Personal spiritual experiences are individual to each person and are difficult for others to comprehend unless they have had the same experience.]

All those who were fortunate enough to enter the garden came under the authority and supervision of Tenzin. His task was to help them learn **new skills**[1] and acquire new abilities to settle into this new community.

The garden was composed of a substance Tenzin called "Kari-so-Masma" or "K-Mass." Part of it existed in the universe before the material universe was formed. It was, and is, a form of energy. It combines with some sub-atomic particles (quarks, leptons, bosons, hadrons, and trions) to produce high-energy, subatomic substances. Like matter, this energy could be focused into any **shape**[2] and held together by powerful, gifted spiritual beings.

The talent to shape K-Mass was a learned one. Just as human hands can shape the earth, dig the ground, and plant seeds, a spiritual being could shape K-Mass. People's capacity to shape K-Mass grew at different **levels**[3] and rates. It took hard work and dedication for the spirit to learn to shape K-Mass and transform it into beautiful objects.

Shaping and nourishing the K-Mass exercised the spiritual beings' **minds**[4]. Yet not all minds were creative; many spiritual beings were happy to work in the garden under an elder's supervision.

---- ➤ ----

Bible (NKJV)	Bhagavad Gita
[1] Ephesians 4:7, To each of us, grace was given according to the measure of Christ's <u>gift</u>. 2 Timothy	[1] - [4] 6:42-45. Or they may move (metamorphose) into the realm of a great spiritual master. Such a move is rare. Their divine consciousness is

1:6, Therefore, I remind you to stir up the gift of God in you by laying on my hands.

[2] Genesis 1:3. Then God said, "Let there be light," and there was light.

[3] Ephesians 3:7, I became a minister according to the gift of the grace of God given to me by the effectual working of His power.

[4] Ephesians 1:3. Blessed be the God and Father of our Lord Jesus Christ, who has blessed us with every spiritual blessing in the heavenly places in Christ, 2 Corinthians 9:15. Thanks be to God for His indescribable gift!

---X--

reinvigorated by the great spiritual masters, and with their help, they are encouraged to make further progress. Due to their disciplined lives, they will become attracted to the new realm. Inquisitive disciples who contemplate Me rise above those who perform rituals. These disciplined people in their new realms progress further as their selfish desires are purified. Moving upwards towards higher realms, they eventually attain the seventh Heaven, the supreme goal of all.

---- ➤ ----

---------- ↬ ------

Chapter 35

Judgement Day

Sam was sitting on a large, flat rock on the bank of the lake. By her side stood Tenzin. They were both in deep thought. She was the first to speak.

"Tenzin, tell me about **Judgement Day.**[1]"

He glanced over the waters and took a deep breath. "Some people believe in Judgement Day; others do not."

"What do you believe, Tenzin?" she asked.

He thought for a while. "I believe we shall all stand before the **Judgement Seat of God**[2]."

"Why?"

"**To account**[3] for every thought, every deed in our lives. But not everyone believes it. I believe its purpose is not to condemn us but to evaluate us and show our true character and the potential we have to improve—to smooth out the flaws in our character and be greater than we are."

She inhaled deeply and asked, "Who will be the judge?"

"Some say, God, others say that a panel of good, enlightened beings like the **Elders and the Master**[4] will be the ones to judge. Some beings have a unique ability (Kly-son) to see through a person and to review other people's lives. Many Christians believe Jesus Christ will judge all."

Sam: "You have a special gift. Will you be part of this judgement?"

Tenzin: "No. I have a role to play in this sanctuary. Some of us have a unique skill called Kly-son, which we use to allow people to see their past errors and effects on others. We help them to learn and amend their ways and to reconcile, restore, and make them whole.

"All over the Cosmos, people are given a chance to make restitution for their misdeeds. Those who refuse to **make restitution**[5] will lose their inheritance in God's Kingdom.

"Brother Stefan and I are here to learn and to help you and others to progress in your spiritual journey. The Master has appointed me as a **steward**[6] for this garden."

She thought about it for a while. "What will happen to me on Judgement Day? I have wronged my family, neighbours, and Mother Earth, for which I am truly sorry."

He placed his right hand under her chin and lifted it tenderly. she looked into his eyes. He said softly, "Rest assured, everyone in this place will pass Judgement Day. The Master would not have brought you here otherwise. By that day, you would have amended all the wrongs you did with our help, and you would have made restitution to all. No one will say you thrived at their expense.

"For you and all present here, that 'Day of the Lord' will be a day of rejoicing and celebration. A day when all your hard work and worth will be recognised, and you all will receive your crowns."

---- ➤ ----

Bible (NKJV)	Bhagavad Gita
[1] Revelation 20:12, I saw the dead, small and great, stand before God. The books were opened, and another was opened—the Book of Life. According to their works, the dead were judged on things written in the books. Daniel 7:10, A stream of fire issued and flowed out from his presence. A thousand served him, and ten thousand stood attending him. The court sat	[1 & 3] Ch 12:2. Krishna: Those engaged in My work with unfailing love and faith are established in Me. They will pass My test on the 'Day of The Lord.' Their actions will eventually produce good results, fulfilling My eternal plan on Earth and Heaven.

[2] 11- 26- 29. On that fearsome day, I see Dhritarashtra's sons (all spiritually unsound and evil beings) and the allied kings with Bhisma, |

in judgement, and the books were opened.

[2] 2 Corinthians 5:10, For we must all appear before the judgement seat of Christ, that each one may receive the things done in the body, according to what he has done, whether good or bad. **Romans 14:10**, But why do you judge your brother? Or why do you show contempt for your brother? For we shall all stand before the judgement seat of Christ.

[3] Romans 14:12, So, each of us shall give an account of himself to God.

[4] 1st Corinthians 6:2. Do you not know that the saints will judge the world?

[5] Luke 19:8. Then Zacchaeus stood and said to the Lord, "Look, Lord, I give half of my goods to the poor; and if I have taken anything from anyone by false accusation, I restore fourfold." **2 Samuel 12:6**. He shall restore the lamb fourfold because he did this and had no pity.

[6] Luke 12:42. The Lord said, "Who then is that faithful and wise steward, whom his master will make ruler over his household, to give them their portion of food in due season?

Drona, Karna, and all the warriors rushing towards their deaths like moths into a flame.

[4] 10:6. The mighty seven sages (archangels, guardians of the Universe), the four great ancestors (elders), and the fourteen Manus (ancestors of all humanity) came from Me—born from My mind. All beings populating the various continents, planets, and universes descend from them. I, the Supreme Lord, passed unto Brahman the breath of life. From Brahman came the *seven great sages, four great thinkers, Sanka, Sananda, Santana, Sanat-kumara, and fourteen Manus. Together, they form the twenty-five Elders of the Universe.

[6] 2:71. My devotees are free when they give up selfish material desires and false egos. They hold all proprietorship as My stewards rather than as owners, taking what they need to sustain them. Such devotees attain inner peace and remain calm at the prospect of death.

---- ➤ ----

Sikhism. Scripture, Shri Granth Sahib. Section 22 – Pt 075

[1] Hereafter, they are called to account in the Court of the Lord; the false ones are struck down and humiliated.

Koran. [1] Ch 37: 20-21. They will say, "Woe to us. This is the <u>Day of Judgment,</u> which you used to deny." ---X--	[2] Section 13 - Part 026. <u>God has saved me, both here and hereafter</u>. He has not taken my merits and demerits into account. [2] Section 19-Pt 003 Do not think you will automatically find a place of rest hereafter. According to the actions one has committed, so does the mortal become. ---X--

---------- 9)------

Chapter 36

Second chance

"On the other hand, Sam, on Judgement Day, many will discover that their sorrow and grief will be no atonement for the harm they have done to others. The blood of the innocent cries out for justice. We all have to learn from our errors. Here, we have a second chance to mend our ways and make restitution for our misdeeds to others."

"I'm still worried. The great day frightens me."

He laid his hand on her shoulder. "All of us have done wrong to others and Mother Earth. The Eternal Spirit of the LORD (*to some: Holy Spirit, Atman*) is with us, and **it will help us**[1] to make restitution for each wrong we have done to all living things. Look around you at all these people and animals. That work has just started. I feel its power within my spirit. Some call it faith."

"I have done much wrong; it will take a long time to put right."

He nodded. "Sam, the great day is a very long time away. Meanwhile, we have a lot to do. To **live in eternity**[2], we need to have a **clear conscience,**[3] free of all wrongdoings. The Eternal Spirit will help us."

Sam: "What happens after I have made restitution to all?"

Tenzin: "Your conscience will be clear, but it will never be clean."

She inhaled deeply and then muttered, "Why?"

Tenzin explained, "'Sam, you acknowledge that you have done wrong to others and want to make restitution. We will teach you to examine your actions one at a time. Our Kly-son ability will show you the harm inflicted on others and its ongoing repercussions. Then, you can discover the reason why you acted in that form. Was it self-preservation, selfishness, greed, or something else? Next, we will teach you to make appropriate restitutions and make them whole. This process will help to reconcile you with your victims. Hence, your conscience will begin to clear.

He continued, "In the past, you acted selfishly, but now you have taken responsibility and want to make an informed decision from the knowledge you have acquired. Your spirit was once illuminated by fear, selfishness, and ignorance, but now it is inspired by light. God is pure light, and your spirit is headed towards that light.

"In time, wounds will heal, but the **scars*** will remain. You will carry the knowledge of their pain, grief, and scars for eternity. Those scars can never be washed away. They are there to remind you, through eternity, of the great cost that was paid by Mother Earth and all her children (all living things) for your spiritual growth."

She started to cry. "I can feel the pain."

His gaze darted over her anxious face. "The pain will worsen. We and all in the Cosmos will help you amend your ways and make restitutions to others for the hurt you brought them so that, by Judgement Day, no one, nothing will cry out for vengeance against you. Your hands **will be clean**[4], though your conscience will bear the scars forever."

* [_Su Anne's_ Tenet 1 —Wounds heal, but scars are for eternity]

Evil will live with evil

Selfishness will live with selfishness

Goodwill with goodwill

And the Cosmos will exert its final say.

A caterpillar goes to sleep,

And is transformed into a butterfly with wings,

Humankind into spiritual beings.   ---- ➤ ----

Bible (NKJV)	Bhagavad Gita
[1] John 6:63. "The Spirit gives life; the flesh profits nothing. The words that I speak to you are spirit, and they are life. John 6:27. "Do not labour for the food which perishes, but for the food which endures to everlasting life, which the Son of Man will give you because God the Father has set His seal on Him." [2] John 17:3. "This is eternal life, that they may know You, the only true God, and Jesus Christ whom You have sent. [3] Hebrews 13:18. Pray for us: we are persuaded that we have a good conscience, desiring to live honourably in all things. [4] Jude 1:24. Now to Him who can keep you from stumbling, And present you faultless Before the presence of His glory with exceeding joy, [4] 2nd Corinthians 11:2. For I am jealous for you with godly jealousy. For I have betrothed you to one husband, that I may present you as a chaste virgin to Christ. ---X--	[1] 7:26. I am the Eternal One. The past, present and future are known to me and every living entity by their names and deeds. I regularly take an inventory of their thoughts, motives and actions. Hence, I know all there is to know about them; however, no one knows Me thoroughly. [2] 8:11. I am impartial. All Holy Scriptures reveal that those who worship Me are sacrificial, relinquishing selfishness and materialism. They seek to promote the welfare, interest, and happiness of others and Mine. Such people find salvation and eternal life in Me. [3-4] 16:1. The Supreme Lord: Arjuna, you must nurture these qualities. Learn to overcome fear and walk in purity of heart and emotions. Study the Scriptures and grow in spiritual knowledge. Be compassionate and charitable, and have a clear conscience. Give freely and indulge in a duty of care and kindness towards all, especially the poor and vulnerable. Be self-controlled, sincere, and truthful. Nourish a spirit of giving and forgiveness. ---X--

---------- ૧૩------

Chapter 37

Truth and Reconciliation (Part 1)

Sam and Kwan-yin played together happily for quite a while. Then Kwan-yin said, "Come, Sam, let's go for a walk."

They walked across the **beautiful meadow**[1], covered in soft green grass scattered with small plants and lovely flowers. They had become used to the scenery and paid scant attention to it.

Soon, the meadow gave way to an orchard with hundreds of fruit trees, which would bloom at different times to ensure an adequate supply of **tasty fruit.**[2] The soil and the trees were in tune with the **inhabitants' needs**[3] and were happy to produce fruits for their enjoyment and nourishment.

They came to a corner of the orchard and beheld a vast field covered with smooth round stones arranged in straight rows, placed a foot apart. Sam and Kwan-yin came close to the stones and could see that **each stone had a name.**[4]

They carefully avoided stepping on the stones as they walked into the field. It was a vast field stretching away to the horizon. There must have been millions of these stones. They stood there for a long time, speculating on what this could mean.

Kwan-yin said, "I think it's some kind of memorial place." They looked at each other, confused.

Sam replied, "You could be right. It looks like a **memorial.**[5] However, the names are strange. They don't sound like people's names."

Kwan-yin glanced nervously at the names. "Come, let's go back to our garden. Maybe we shouldn't be here. This place looks like a consecrated ground, and we may be intruding."

"We will ask Tenzin. He will know about this place. He knows about everything that exists here."

---- ➤+ ----

Bible (NKJV)	Bhagavad Gita
[1] Exodus 15:17. You will bring them in and plant them In the mountain of Your inheritance, In the place, O LORD, which You have made For Your dwelling, The sanctuary, O Lord, which Your hands have established. [2] Genesis 1:12. And the earth brought forth grass, the herb that yields seed according to its kind, and the tree that produces fruit, whose seed is in itself according to its kind. And God saw that it was good. [3] Ezekiel 34:27. "Then the trees of the field shall yield their fruit, and the earth shall yield her increase. They shall be safe in their land and know that I am the LORD when I have broken the bands of their yoke and delivered them from the hand of those who enslaved them. [3] Genesis 9:15-16. "I will remember My covenant between Me and you and every living creature of all flesh; the waters shall never again become a flood to destroy all flesh. The rainbow shall be in the cloud, and I will look on it to remember the everlasting covenant between	[1-2] 4:35. Having gained spiritual wisdom, you will not be deluded again. You will see that all living entities are part of the divine plan, part of one family, and have the same breath of life from the divine. [3] 6:30–31. I am ever-present to those who have realised Me in every creature. Seeing all life as My manifestation, they are never separated from Me. Enlightened people worship Me by showing kindness to all living things. Wherever they may live, they abide in Me. Hence, all their actions proceed from Me. ---X--

God and every living creature of all flesh on earth."

[4] Exodus 28:9. "Then you shall take two onyx stones and engrave the names of the sons of Israel on them.

[5] Exodus 28:12. "And you shall put the two stones on the shoulders of the ephod as memorial stones for the sons of Israel.

---X--

---------- 𝕎------

Chapter 38

The place of truth and reconciliation

They made their way back to their garden.

Sometime later, Tenzin came to see them. They greeted him, and Kwan-yin said, "Tenzin, can you tell us about the field next to the orchard? The one with rows of neatly marked stones."

He replied, "It is time you knew about the stones. Come, let us go there."

They walked through the meadow and came to the field. They stood looking at the area and the endless rows of stones. There was an atmosphere of sorrow and sadness.

Sam asked, "What is this place?"

He replied, "It's a sacred place of truth and reconciliation. See that stone? Can you read what's written on it?"

Sam read the name on the stone aloud. "Misti."

Tenzin picked up the stone. There was a slight noise behind them. They turned around and saw a young puppy running towards them. He came bouncing up to them and licked their hands. It was apparent he was delighted to see them, particularly Tenzin.

He calmed the puppy and led them to a corner of the field. They sat down in a circle. Tenzin passed the stone to Sam and said,

"Close your eyes and feel the stone, then pass it to Kwan-yin."

After a while, Sam passed the stone to her friend. Kwan-yin rolled it in her palm, felt its smoothness, and then passed the stone on to Tenzin.

Tenzin said softly, gently, "Close your eyes and let the **stone speak to you[1].**"

Soon, tears ran down the faces of the women. They closed their eyes. As soon as they did that, a voice came out of the stone and recited that it contained the testimony of a little dog called Misti.

A few words escaped between their sobbing, phrases like, "I'm so sorry, it's so sad; I feel for you. They were awful to you. I am ashamed of what my fellow humans did to you."

They looked at Tenzin and then at the puppy.

Kwan-yin said to the puppy, "You are Misti. The voice we heard was you."

He nodded.

Tenzin explained, "What you heard was the testimony of his life on Earth written on the stone. You have only heard a small part of his testimony. This area is called the Zone of **Truth and Reconciliation[2].**"

Tenzin continued, "Now you know something about Misti's past life, his parents, his home, his master, the village he grew up in and much more.

"You know intimately how cruelly his master and other animals treated him and how disease and malnutrition weakened him.

"All his life, he was bullied, attacked, and mauled by bigger dogs and humankind. He had a tough, painful, short life. You now know about him.

"This knowledge will take some time to sink in. It is a lot to take in during a single sitting."

Sam faced the dog. "I am so sorry." She leaned down and patted the dog. "Does he know anything about us?" she asked.

Tenzin nodded. "He knows a lot about you two. He knows and understands much about your past, parents, village, childhood, and miscarriages. He knows and understands how you felt then and how you feel now. He knows you almost as well as you know yourselves."

Kwan-yin asked, "How does he know?"

"This is a unique, sacred place to reconcile people and creatures. Here, the past is shared, mistakes, wrongs and righteousness acknowledged, and a plan for restitution and making each whole is formulated and implemented. One day, all creatures will be at peace and reconciled **with one another[3].** All will be made whole. There will be no more tears. This second chance in life is offered to all good, honest people and creatures."

Tenzin whistled, and a lion and a cow came running to meet him. He introduced them to Sam and Kwan-yin. They sat down in a circle.

Tenzin asked the lion, "Leo, could you tell them your story. Your life in Masai Mara National Reserve."

Leo took a deep breath and said, "I grew up on the reservation. In the beginning, life was good. Then, when I was an adult, my brother and I took over a neighbouring pride from an old male. Each day was filled with anxiety and fear. We set out on petrol daily, trying to hold onto over territory and drive away groups of wondering single males or hyenas. There were regular fights and ambushes, and our bodies were covered with battle scars. The tension and stress prematurely weakened and aged us. One evening, we were isolated by three young males in their prime. My brother was the first to die. The next day, they came for me. I fought and managed to kill one of them but was gravely wounded and ran for my life. The next day, I struggled to walk. I was unable to hunt and slowly starved to death. I woke up, and I was here. I am eternally grateful to Tenzin for helping me to resettle **here[4].** Life is good, and I am at peace with everyone. That is my **story[5]."**

Zebu the cow began to recount her story, "I, too, was born in the same reservation. Well, on the fringe of the reservation among the tribal people. My childhood was happy following my mother as we were led to graze. Then, I saw the cruelty of the tribal people. Regularly, they would tie my mother, cut her vein, collect her blood and milk, mix it and drink it. When a human came near my mother, she would be petrified. She would break into a sweat, her heart beat faster, and a low moan escaped her lips. I would feel her anxiety and her stress. There was nothing I could do. I hated our life. My soul would cry out to God. It was useless. No deliverance came.

"In her old age, after years of loyally providing them with her blood, milk and faithful service as their slave, they rewarded her by slitting her throat in front of us all. They cooked her in our sight and used her skin to make shoes, belts and jackets. From that day, we knew that would be our reward for years of slavish service to humans. We feared and hated humans.

"One sweltering hot day, the guard fell asleep while we were grazing in the wilderness. I took the opportunity to run away. I successfully escaped. I joined a herd of Zebras and wildebeest. For three wonderful days, I enjoyed my freedom. Then Leo's pride of lions caught me. My demise was painfully quick. I, too, am eternally grateful to Tenzin for helping me to resettle here. I can sleep peacefully for the first time without fearing Leo or any previous predators. It is paradise here. And I am grateful to the Master and our God. He has finally redeemed us, and now, with the help of people like Tenzin, Brother Stefan and all the other animals here, he is restoring, **reconciling**[6] and making us whole."

"Look around. All around us, you find Beasts of burden and other animals: Cows, horses, sheep, goats, pigs, ducks, chickens, guinea pigs, minks and others. Many of us, cows, goats, buffaloes, and camels, acted as surrogate mothers to their infants, providing vital milk for their children who would otherwise have suffered poor health, and some may even have died. Other animals provided transport, companionship, meat, skins etc. Yet, after all that service we provided to humans, most of them never acknowledged or appreciated our contributions to their welfare."

She looked at Tenzin with tears rolling down her cheek. "Thank you."

Tenzin said, "Actually, I am grateful to you all and the Master for entrusting me with this wonderful task of restoring all. It brings great joy to me. I feel so full of life, so honoured and privileged. You are now my **eternal family**[7]. We all have felt the joy and dread of life on earth, and this place helps us to learn so much about ourselves, our desires, dreams, aspirations and our sense of value, appreciation, and gratefulness. We are very blessed. We are a family and children of God."

---- ➤ ----

Bible (NKJV)	Bhagavad Gita
[1] Luke 19:40. But He answered and said to them, "I tell you that if these should keep silent, the stones would immediately cry out."	[1] 7:2. As you grow spiritually, I will declare unto you, Jnana: the highest kind of spiritual **knowledge,** direct revelation from Me. Furthermore, I will declare *Vijnan*: the intimate understanding of **Creation,** how every subatomic particle was created and is accounted for daily, how the Universe is balanced, and the mindset behind this design, affirmed with signs and miracles.
[2] Colossians 1:20, by Him, to reconcile all things to Himself, whether things on earth or things in heaven, having made peace through the blood of His cross.	
[3 - 6] Ephesians 1:10, in the fullness of the times He might gather together in one all things in Christ, both in heaven and on earth — in Him. Ephesians 1:17-23 that the God of our Lord Jesus Christ, the Father of glory, may give you the spirit of wisdom and revelation in His knowledge. The eyes of your understanding being enlightened; that you may know what the hope of His calling is, what are the riches of the glory of His inheritance in the saints, and what is the exceeding greatness of His power toward us who believe, according to the working of His mighty power which He worked in Christ when He raised Him from the dead and seated Him at His right hand in	[2] 6:20-23. In union with Me (Samadhi), the sensory and emotional feelings are subjugated to contemplate the spiritual. They begin to fill up with inner joy and fulfilment. They now walk in truth and are free from all miseries from material contact. Here, they desire only to please Me. The joys or sorrows of life do not govern their life, but My divine influence.

[3] 16:2. Be compassionate and gentle. Control anger, avoid harming any living creature or being, bearing no enmity but showing goodwill to all.

[3 - 6] 18:20. A person in the goodness mode (Sattvic) acknowledges the divine spirit in him and all living |

the heavenly places. Far above all principality, power, might, dominion, and every name that is named, not only in this age but also in what is to come. And He put all things under His feet and gave Him to be head over all things to the church, His body, the fullness of Him who fills all in all.

4, 5 Isaiah 11:7 The cow and the bear shall graze; Their young ones shall lie down together; And the lion shall eat straw like the ox.

---X--

things in the Universe. They see that each creature has the same divine breath, has a unique value to the Supreme Lord, and sees no separation between humans and other living entities.

3 - 7 5:18. My devotees have equal regard for all. They see (vidya-vinaya-sampanne) the same self (the breath of God) in a learned scholar, an outcast, a cow, an elephant, and a dog. All are contributing directly or indirectly towards God's kingdom and our salvation. Therefore, they (panditah) have a heightened appreciation and a duty to care for and promote everyone's welfare. Hence, as they progress in their spiritual growth, they regard all life forms as part of their and God's extended family.

---X--

---------- ৭১-------

Chapter 39

Scars remain forever

Sam said with tears in her eyes, "Misti's master was cruel to him. It is easy to look at others and point out their acts of cruelty and unkindness.

"I, too, have done bad things to others and mistreated many animals. Maybe not as evil as others, but they were still thoughtless, selfish, self-centred, cruel acts.

"I am truly sorry for that and, if possible, I would like to make restitution for my acts, my cruel behaviour. I deeply regret it now."

Kwan-yin sobbed and cried out, "Me too. I am **truly sorry for the selfish**[1] cruelty I displayed in the past."

Tenzin said, in a gentle voice, devoid of any accusation, "I know both of you are sorry and full of remorse for those acts, but that is not enough.

"You will have to learn from your mistakes, and you will have to make restitution to those you have hurt.

"We, with the help of the **Holy Spirit**[2], will help you and show you the way. We will take every good and negative act, analyse it, and see its impact on you and others. We will help you to **learn from it**[3]. Turn the whole experience into motivation for the future good and make that your new way of life. You will gain knowledge and wisdom from everything that has happened to you."

Kwan-yin asked, "What happens after that?"

"You will find that the saddest aspects of life are wounds, physical or emotional. The wounds you inflicted on others will heal, but their scars will remain forever, and you will bear that on your conscience. Their scars are the cost they paid for your edification."

Sam asked, "Does that mean we will be in debt to them forever?"

"Yes. The scars on your conscience will remind you to be **humble**[4], act humbly, and inspire you to think, restrain, and be cautious. Your training will teach you to consider the consequences before you act and to count the cost of your actions. Every emotion of life—every tear, joy, and sadness—is logged. Take heart; nothing in the universe is without purpose.

"God has given you a second life here. All your past pain and suffering going to waste would be a terrible loss to God and us. We will help you put your past life to **good use.**[5] Nothing in the universe is ever wasted."

The girls listened patiently to Tenzin, but his words made little sense. Still, they trusted him and knew that many things he said were words of wisdom, carried life, and someday would make sense. There was a time and place for everything.

---- ➤ ----

Bible (NKJV)	Bhagavad Gita
[1] Isaiah 66:2. For all those things My hand has made, And all those things exist," Says the LORD. "But on this one will I look: On him who is poor and of a contrite spirit and trembles at My word.	[1] 4:36. Spiritual knowledge is liberating. Even if you were once the most sinful sinners, once you board the boat of spiritual experience, you could sail beyond the ocean of your sins.
[2] *(Christians, Jews, and Hindus should read as the Holy Spirit/Divine Spirit, the Supreme Being).* Daniel 4:18. "This dream I, King Nebuchadnezzar, have seen. Now you, Belteshazzar, declare its interpretation since all the wise men of my kingdom cannot tell me the interpretation, but you can, for the Spirit of the Holy God is in you." Mark 1:8. "I indeed baptized you with water, but He will baptize	[3] 7:19. Overcoming many trials and errors, the wise continue to persist and freely follow My ways based on informed choice, realising I encompass everything. Such souls are rare, leaving a legacy of love, care, and goodness wherever they go. ---X--

you with the <u>Holy Spirit</u>."

[3] Ezekiel 18:31. "<u>Cast away from you all the transgressions</u> you have committed, and get yourself a new heart and spirit. For why should you die, O house of Israel?

[4] Psalms 10:17. LORD, You have heard the <u>desire of the humble</u>; You will prepare their heart; You will cause Your ear to hear,

[5] 2nd Timothy 2:21. Therefore, if anyone cleanses himself from the latter, he will be a <u>vessel for honour,</u> sanctified and <u>useful for the Master,</u> prepared for every good work.

---X--

---------- ᐱᐱ------

Chapter 40

Spiritual home

They were sitting, enjoying each other's company in the garden. Sam turned to Tenzin.

"Tenzin, can I ask you about something that's haunted me for a long time?"

He replied, "It is about your parents. You want to know about them."

Sam nodded. "It happened when I was about eight years old. My father was a schoolteacher. One day, rebel soldiers came to our village. There was a lot of shooting. People were running about in panic. Some of the houses were burning. Then, the shooting stopped.

"Some soldiers came to our house. They dragged my father out of the house. My mother ran after the soldiers, pleading with them to let my father go. We were petrified.

"The soldier dragged my father and mother into the street and shot them. There were many dead people in our village. When the rebels left, our neighbour came and helped us."

"I remember. They took you to an orphanage."

"Yes, I was separated from my brothers and sisters and taken to an orphanage."

"I know you had a hard life there. You were always hungry and cold and **often beaten.[1]**"

"Did you know I was raped in the orphanage when I was fourteen? We were made to **beg[2]** and then beaten if we didn't bring back enough money. I had my first miscarriage when I was fifteen years of age." Tears rolled down her cheeks. Her voice was low. ---- ➤ ----

Bible (NKJV)	Bhagavad Gita
[1] Philippians 4:12. I know how to live on almost nothing or with everything. I have learned the secret of living in every situation, whether with a full stomach or empty, with plenty or little. [2] 1st Corinthians 1:28-29. God chose what is low and despised in the world, things that are not, to reduce to nothing things that are so that no one might boast in the presence of God. ---x--	[1 & 2] 1:40-41. When families break up, the widows and orphans are left desolate and vulnerable to corruption. The unity of the family declines, and the country is plunged into chaos. ---- ➤ ----

---------- ᎒------

Chapter 41

Anybody who has shed human blood cannot enter this sanctuary

Kwan-yin was also crying. She sobbed, "I had a similar experience. We lived in Bangkok, and when I was eleven, my parents died in a bus accident. I was alone in a big city, with no family to look after me.

"I joined a street gang for protection. Our gang leader sent us out to beg for money. He would beat us if we came back with little money. He was ruthless. He would shout and swear at us. We had to sleep in the gutters or derelict buildings."

She paused and then continued, "When I turned fourteen, he started to rape me and sell me to other men. I was fifteen when I became pregnant. He forced me to take some drugs to induce an abortion. After that, he had a birth control device fitted inside me."

Tenzin spoke slowly. "You both had hardship in your lives—so much suffering for young people. Sometimes, I wanted to intervene, but the Lord would not allow it.

"He didn't abandon you. He ensured that some kind families were around to give you food and clothes. When you were sick, he ensured you went to the temple and received care from the monks."

Both girls were sobbing now. He gave them each a hug and wiped their tears away.

"You are safe here. This is your home now and your **sanctuary.** [1] Those kinds of things will not happen to you again. Those evil people will not be allowed to come into this sanctuary."

Sam said nervously, "I am afraid. I saw my parents murdered. The memory still haunts me. Sometimes, I dream the killers are after me."

Tenzin said, "This is a sacred place", in a gentle, reassuring voice. Anybody who has shed **human blood**[2] cannot enter. This applies to all humankind.

"Unfortunately, some of your relatives, including Kwan-yin's father, are barred because they have shed blood. It does not matter if it was to protect others or in self-defence. You will meet kind priests and other selected people who will never harm or mistreat you. Come with me, and I will show you something."

Kwan-yin asked, "Does that mean I will never see my father?"

"Not in this sanctuary, but you will meet him in another realm after he has been cleansed and purified. He will need to make restitution.

"He will have to undergo many things before he is **purified**[3], but his past deeds and shame will stay with him forever. This is stamped on his forehead; others will see it and know he has shed blood."

---- ➤ ----

Bible (NKJV)	Bhagavad Gita
[1] Exodus 15:17. You will bring them in and plant them In the mountain of Your inheritance, In the place, O LORD, which You have made For Your dwelling, The sanctuary, O Lord, which Your hands have established. Exodus 36:1, and every gifted artisan (Tenzin and Stefan) whom the LORD has given skill and understanding to know how to do any work in the construction of the sanctuary shall work in accordance with all that the LORD has commanded.	[1, 3] 4:10. My followers taking refuge in My abode are set free from the slavery of fear and selfish attachment. Their greed, anger, and love are slowly refined, cleansed, purified, and sanctified in My presence
	[2] 1:31. I see no good in killing my kin in this battle. Causing death and destruction is not how I want to be victorious and win back my kingdom.
	---X--
[2] 1st Chronicles 28:3, "But God said to me, 'You shall not build a house for My name because you have	

been a man of <u>war and have shed blood</u>.' Hebrews 12:14. <u>Follow peace</u> with all men, and holiness, without which no man shall see the Lord:

[3] Daniel 12:10. "Many shall be <u>purified, made white,</u> and refined, but the wicked shall do wickedly; none of the wicked shall understand, but the wise shall understand.

---X--

---------- ⁊⁊------

Chapter 42

The mind, a human library

One day, Sam was sitting near the shores of the lake, deep in thought. Her mind was troubled.

Tenzin approached and put his hand on her shoulder. "Come, let's go for a walk."

They walked towards the orchard and came across Kwan-yin.

"Kwan-yin," Tenzin called out. "Come join us."

She ran up to them, a broad smile on her face.

Sam glanced at her friend. "You look cheerful."

Kwan-yin replied, "I am. And I'm always glad to see you, Sam." She looked at Tenzin, then reached out and hugged him on an impulse.

He smiled. "It brings me great pleasure to see you."

She smiled back at him. "Do you have a lesson for us?"

He nodded. "Yes. But first, let's find a nice, comfortable place to sit." They walked up to a huge tree and sat in its shade. He inhaled deeply and said, "There are some things I need to teach you. It is time to broaden your knowledge about the garden's workings. To do that, you need to understand how your thoughts must change."

He paused to give them time to focus on what he was about to say. He continued, *[Janet Warrington's Tenet 2]* "Your **brain is like a library**[1] *holding many books. In each book, each chapter is about an experience in your life—some good and pleasant, some sad, while others are horrible and painful.*

"When you have settled here, we will take each experience in your past life, good or bad, and turn them into positive experiences, and the lessons you learn from them will turn into books of wisdom and knowledge.

We will **examine**[2] one book at a time, analyse it, and observe its impact on you and others. We will turn all you learn from the books into seeds, then take one seed at a time and cultivate them to grow into plants and trees of knowledge and wisdom.

"An orchard of knowledge and wisdom will reside in your mind and spirit, benefiting many people.

---- ➤ ----

Bible (NKJV)	Bhagavad Gita
[1] Romans 12:2. Do not be conformed to this world, but be transformed by renewing your minds to discern God's will—what is right and acceptable and perfect.	[1] 2:40. This path is called Karma Yoga: the oneness of mind with Me through Action. Even a little spiritual advancement on this path will protect you from your greatest fear.
[2] Hebrews 4:12, God's word is quick, powerful, and sharper than any two-edged sword, piercing even to the dividing asunder of soul, spirit, joints, and marrow, and is a discerner of the thoughts and intents of the heart.	[2] 2:53. When you have clarity of mind, apprehending your closeness with Me, your consciousness will begin to merge with My Will. Then, you will start to comprehend your goal in life.
---x--	[2] 2:55. Lord Krishna replied: An enlightened person learns to subjugate his selfish desires and all types of sensual gratification. Having his mind purified of selfish desires, he is satisfied with his true self. He is said to have risen above his natural state.
	[2] 2:64-65. However, a person who

has his senses under control is free from attachment and aversion. His mind is at peace. The power of material existence has no decisive influence. Instead, intelligence and spiritual wisdom guide him.

[2] 2:66. A mind not in tune with Me is far from wise; how can it maintain stability? How can it be at peace? Without inner peace, how can one know real joy or happiness?

[2] 3:41-43. Therefore, Arjuna, learn to bring your senses, mind, and intellect under My supervision with all your strength. Conquer your worst enemy, selfishness, destroyer of My divine purpose that abides in you. The senses are superior to the body, and the mind can rise above the senses. Intelligence can rise above the mind, and the spirit can rise above intelligence. Thus, your true self, the indwelling spirit, imparting My divine spiritual strength, can guide your intellect, mind, senses, and desires. Therefore, your true self gives you the power you need to overcome this insatiable enemy known as selfishness.

---------- ၅၅------

Chapter 43

Pain and sorrow

"You will realise that all the **pain, sorrow**[1], and goodness in your former life have played a valuable and essential part in your growth.

"On Earth, it was a terrible burden, a drain on your life and happiness. Here, it will become a tremendous blessing; by the Day of Judgement, it will have become fruit. Nothing in the cosmos is wasted."

The two girls remained quiet, not sure what to say.

He smiled. "We will do one thing **at a time.**[2] Here, time is on our side."

Kwan-yin said, "Thank you. When do we start?"

He smiled again. "Not today. I want you to think it over for a few days."

While the girls were considering his words, Stefan walked up to them. They greeted him, and the monk left them again after some polite conversation.

Tenzin asked, "Tell me what you make of Brother Stefan."

Sam answered, "He is like an older brother to us. He looks after us like a guardian. He is very kind, gentle, and very wise. We have a lot of respect and admiration for him. He is good to us."

Kwan-yin nodded in agreement.

Tenzin remarked, "He was not always like that. He was once a soldier and did many bad things, although he had never killed. Yet what he saw and was forced to do by his superiors—stealing from the weak, taking from those who already had so little—appalled him, so he could not continue that way.

"So, one stormy night, risking death, he sneaked out of the camp and began the perilous journey through the forests and mountains. Finally, he crossed the border and sought refuge in another country.

"There, he found a monastery. He **renounced his past,**[3] took a vow never again to do the things he had done before, and joined the monks' ranks. He devoted the rest of his life to helping others."

Sam said, "That was in the past. What he is now matters, not the past."

Tenzin replied, "Are you sure?" Something in the way he said it made her pause and think.

Sam glanced at him, puzzled. "Whatever he was in the past is gone. He has changed, having given up those things. I know Brother Stefan deeply regrets what he did then."

"Come with me."

He led the girls back to the field, covered in stones. He pointed at a stone with Sam's father's name on it, and next to it was a stone with her mother's name.

Sam asked, "Why did you bring us here?"

"Among the group of soldiers who came to your village and killed your parents," Tenzin said, "was Brother Stefan."

---- ➤ ----

Bible (NKJV)	Bhagavad Gita
[1] Isaiah 35:10. And the ransomed of the LORD shall return, And come to Zion with singing, With everlasting joy on their heads. They shall obtain joy and gladness, And <u>sorrow</u> and sighing shall flee	[1] 6:20-23. In union with Me (Samadhi), the sensory and emotional feelings are subjugated to contemplate the spiritual. They begin to fill up with inner joy and fulfilment. <u>They now walk in truth and are free from all miseries from</u>

away

2 Colossians 1:25-27, of which I became a minister according to the stewardship from God which was given to me for you, to fulfil the word of God, the mystery which has been hidden from ages and from generations, but now has been revealed to His saints. To them, God willed to make known the riches of this mystery's glory among the Gentiles: Christ in you, the hope of glory.

3 2nd Corinthians 4:2. But we have renounced the hidden things of shame, not walking in craftiness nor handling the word of God deceitfully, but by manifestation of the truth commending ourselves to every man's conscience in the sight of God.

---x--

material contact. Here, they desire only to please Me. The joys or sorrows of life do not govern their life, but My divine influence.

1 6:32. People who see equality in all beings and creatures have profound empathy for all and respond to their joy and sorrow as their own. They have attained one of the higher states of spiritual union with Me and My creation.

2 3:7. Conversely, the better option is for the mind to learn to control one's senses for selfless service for the higher good of all

3 4:41. Those people established in devotional service, having renounced selfishness and overcoming their doubts through spiritual wisdom, live in freedom.

---- ➤ ----

---------- ᠹ-------

Chapter 44

The Eternal Court and the Elders

Sam and Kwan-yin wandered around the orchard, looking for ripe fruit. The trees produced fruit, just as a mother has milk for her baby. A mother feels the pleasure of feeding her baby and strengthening their bond. Similarly, the trees gave their fruit to the inhabitants and strengthened the bond between the people and the sanctuary.

It was a warm, pleasant day. They were happy and relaxed, enjoying each other's company and laughing at Sam's jokes. From the corner of her eye, she noticed Tenzin and Stefan walking towards them.

"Tenzin and Stefan are here," Sam said as her face lit up in joy.

Kwan-yin whispered to Sam, "I wonder what brings them here? Whatever it is, it must be important."

They all exchanged greetings. Tenzin turned to face the women and, in a melancholy voice, said, "We want you to come with us. It would be best if you remained quiet at all times. Do not speak or ask any questions. We want you to observe everything that you see and hear. Sam, you take hold of my hand, and Kwan-yin, you hold Brother Stefan's hand. Close your eyes and come with us."

They seemed to drift through space and then land on soft ground.

Tenzin said, "You can open your eyes now." Before them stood a massive, magnificent structure that looked like a **grand courthouse.**[1] Its appearance radiated immense power and authority.

They walked into the building. The inner hall radiated power; it was enormous and majestic. In the hallway was a large round table, and at its far end stood a very **distinguished person**[2]**.** His garment was white as snow, and the hair of His head was like pure wool. He was addressing the Council.

On either side of Him sat **twelve beings³**. Some Elders had human features, and some had strange-looking, non-human features. The table and chairs were of plain wood, with no carving, inlay, or embossing. They exuded simplicity, modesty, and humility.

There was some kind of session going on. One of the Elders stood up and addressed the Council. When he stopped talking, there was silence for a while. Then, all the Elders started to raise their hands.

The speaker looked around. The Elders' decision was unanimous. The speaker wrote something on parchment and, with his fist, thumped down twice on the table.

---- ➤ ----

Bible (NKJV)	Bhagavad Gita
¹ Ezekiel 10:4. Then the glory of the LORD went up from the cherub and paused over the temple threshold; the house was filled with the cloud, and the **court** was full of the brightness of the LORD'S glory. ² Daniel 7:9. "I watched till thrones were put in place, and the Ancient of Days was seated; His garment was white as snow, And the hair of His head was like pure wool. ³ Daniel 7:27. Then the kingdom and dominion, And the greatness of the kingdoms under the whole heaven, Shall be given to the people, the saints of the Most High. His kingdom is everlasting, And all dominions shall serve and	²⁻³ 10:6. The mighty seven sages (archangels, guardians of the Universe), the four great ancestors (elders), and the fourteen Manus (ancestors of all humanity) came from Me—born from My mind. All beings populating the various continents, planets, and universes descend from them. I, the Supreme Lord, passed unto Brahman the breath of life. From Brahman came the *seven great sages, four great thinkers, Sanka, Sananda, Santana, Sanat-kumara, and fourteen Manus. Together, they form the **twenty-five Elders** of the Universe. ²⁻³ 11:9-12. Having spoken these words to Arjuna, the Lord God reveals his exalted form and unveils his divine plan for creation. Sitting on the palm of the Lord, he sees a

obey Him.' ---x--	multitude of Saints singing hymns and praising the Lord. He hears their intercession to relieve humanity's and the Earth's creatures' suffering. (Continue to read the whole 11:9-33)~. **11:14.** Sitting among the heavenly saints and the elders of the universe, Arjuna struggles to understand the mystery of God's plan and his long eternal journey through it, led by the divine spirit. He is amazed *(having been granted unique access to the inner mind of the Lord God).* ---- ➤+ ----

---------- ꝗ-------

Chapter 45

The site of imprisoned spirits

Immediately, two guards came out of a side door and approached him. They were strong and well-built, like those guards Sam had seen in prison. The speaker gave the parchment to the guards, who read it, nodded, and walked towards the main entrance.

Tenzin gave Sam a gentle tug, and they followed the guards. Stefan and Kwan-yin followed them out of the building. Tenzin ordered the two women to close their eyes. They began to drift into space; soon, it felt cold and uncomfortable.

Tenzin whispered, "You can open your eyes, but do not let go of our hands."

They were in a place that was cold, **grey, and misty.**[1] Tenzin had brought Sam here before; she recognised this place, the site of imprisoned spirits.

One of the guards was unfastening chains from the wall while the other stood on guard. All the prisoners had chains around their arms and legs. They looked miserable. The guards freed one of the prisoners from the wall and led him away.

Tenzin commanded, "Close your eyes."

They drifted through space once more. The atmosphere started to feel warmer and more welcoming.

Stefan said, "You can open your eyes now and let go of our hands."

---- ✈ ----

Bible (NKJV)	Bhagavad Gita
[4] Ezekiel 26:20. I will <u>send you to the pit</u> to join those who	[1] 11:16. Untold numbers of life forms on Earth and spiritual sanctuaries

descended there long ago. Your city will lie in ruins, buried beneath the earth, like those in the pit who have entered the world of the dead. You will have no place of respect here in the land of the living.

---x--

passed before me. I saw the beginning and end of all. You gave life and brought joy, pain and suffering into our lives, and in 'The Fullness of Time' (before The Day of The Lord), you made us whole (restored, made restitution) and wiped away all pain and suffering. You showed/proved that nothing thrives in the Universe at the expense of another. I comprehended your joy and sorrow from start to end.

---- ➤ ----

---------- ⇥------

Chapter 46

They found themselves back in the sanctuary.

Tenzin said, "Excuse me now; I have to go. I will leave you in Stefan's care; he will happily answer your questions."

The two women were intrigued. Kwan-yin was the first to speak. "What was that great building? It looked like a courthouse."

Stefan replied, "That was part of the Great Hall of Justice. It is called the Eternal Court, the highest courthouse in the cosmos. The twenty-four Elders and the Leader are **appointed to implement justice.**[1] They are the final authority among all beings, apart from God."

Sam asked, "What's so special about them?"

"These Elders are very gifted. They have **unique special abilities**[2] that make them the masters of the cosmos. They can weigh all the good and bad that a person has done and their character, personality, future intentions, and implications for others. A glance can give them instant insight (Kly-son) into a person's life. If they conclude that the person will greatly add to the suffering of others, they will intervene to stop them."

"How?"

Stefan replied, "What you saw was decreed by the Elders to take the prisoner from this location to a far more secure site. **Dangerous prisoners,**[3] the worst ones in the Cosmos, are taken to **'the Bottomless Pit'**[4], where there is no escape. There, they are held for an indefinite time."

Kwan-yin asked, "Does Tenzin have a similar skill?"

Stefan replied, "Yes. I believe it is still in the early stages of growth."

Sam asked, "Does that mean he could make mistakes?"

"Yes. And, like most beings, he is learning from his mistakes. The Elders monitor his performance and teach him to spot and correct his mistakes." He continued, "The Elders have placed you under Tenzin's supervision, and they have made available all the resources of the **Universe**[5] at his disposal to be used for your growth. Everything that **happens in your life**[6], good and evil, is used for your good. You may find this hard to understand, but seeing it from the viewpoint of eternity, it makes perfect sense to me."

They reflected on his words. Kwan-yin asked, "If we are away from the safety of the sanctuary, will we be safe from those who raped us or murdered Sam's parents?"

---- ➤ ----

Bible (NKJV)	Bhagavad Gita
[1] Daniel 7:27. Then the kingdom and dominion, And the greatness of the kingdoms under the whole heaven, <u>Shall be given to the people, the saints of the Most High.</u> His kingdom is everlasting, And all dominions shall serve and obey Him.'	[1-2] 10:6. The mighty seven sages (archangels, guardians of the Universe), the four great ancestors (elders), and the fourteen Manus (ancestors of all humanity) came from Me - born from My mind. All beings populating the various continents, planets and universes descend from them.
[2] 1st Chronicles 22:12. Only the LORD <u>grant you insight</u> and understanding so that when <u>He gives you charge</u> over Israel, you may keep the Law of the LORD your God.	The Supreme Lord passed unto Brahman the breath of life. From Brahman came the *<u>seven great sages</u>, <u>four</u> other great thinkers, Sanka, Sananda, Santana and Sanat-kumara, and **fourteen Manus** were manifested. Together, they form **twenty-five Elders** of the Universe.
[3] 1st Peter 4:5-6. They will give an account to Him, who is ready to judge the living and the dead. For this reason, the gospel was <u>also preached to those dead,</u> that they might be judged according to men	[2] 3:12. I will meet all your basic needs during your selfless service to humanity, creation and Me. One

in the flesh but live according to God in the spirit.

[3] 1 Peter 3:19 By which also he went and preached to the spirits in prison; who in former times did not obey, when God waited patiently in the days of Noah, during the building of the ark, in which a few, that is, eight persons, were saved through water.

[4] Revelation 9:2 He opened the bottomless pit, and smoke arose out of the hole like the smoke of a great furnace.

[5] Ephesians 1:3-23 Blessed be the God and Father of our Lord Jesus Christ, who has blessed us with every spiritual blessing in the heavenly places in Christ,

[6] Romans 8:28 And we know that all things work together for good to those who love God, to those who are the called according to His purpose.

---x---

who takes from the world without selfless service is a thief.

[3-4] 15:10-11. The ungodly people... >> They enter a realm of their kind—not a pleasant thought. Those who strive resolutely to surrender to the Supreme Lord see all this.

[4] 3:11. Participate in this sacrificial service to My creation, and you will receive My blessing. Collaboration between humankind and creation brings prosperity to all.

[6] 5:3. A person in devotional service to Me can overcome his material nature, whereby he neither hates nor desires personal sense gratification beyond everyday needs. Such a person is singular in purpose, liberated, and free from all paths, so whatever he does, he does for Me. I ensure that all his actions, intentional or not, including his mistakes, will eventually bear good results.

---x---

---------- ᚱ------

Chapter 47

Making the cosmos a safer place

Stefan gave Sam an embarrassed look. He had been sickened by the rebels' attack on her village and their disregard for the suffering of others. He had not taken part in her family's death, but his presence amongst the rebel soldiers had, in a small way, empowered them to commit crimes against innocent villagers.

She looked back at him; there were tears in her eyes. "You were forced to join the rebel group. That's in the past. We are a family now. But are we safe from others?"

There were tears in Stefan's eyes, too. He did not want to alarm the women, nor did he want to hide the truth.

"You are safe here," he replied.

Kwan-yin remarked, "You don't sound very convincing."

Stefan nodded. "Nothing in the cosmos is ever truly safe. Not until the end times. That is why we must work and help each other to make the cosmos a **safer place**[1].

"There are some very evil beings in the universe. They have their sanctuaries and their own rules and governments. They want to rule over the cosmos to enslave others. Tenzin says we will have to go to war with **them**[2] one day."

He could sense the fear and anxiety building up in the women. They had suffered enough on Earth, and now those fears were resurfacing. He had undermined their newfound security; perhaps he had said too much. He looked at the two women, who were both in distress.

Stefan: "I am sorry. I should have explained better. Tenzin wanted you to see the Eternal Court and the prisoners to show you the consequences for those seeking to harm you. If anyone attempts to harm you here, our Master will intervene to protect you."

"Why are the Elders and the Lord interested in us?" Sam asked.

"You have suffered enough. This place is a sanctuary under the protection of our Lord and the Eternal Council. They have a plan for **our future**[3]. A good plan and hard work await us, supervised by virtuous people like Tenzin."

"I still do not understand why the Elders are interested in us."

"We are part of the Lord's family. I believe they love and care for us. They have ambitious goals for our spiritual maturity. They chose us very carefully because they saw our potential in us. They have confidence that we will not let them down. In return, they will not let us down.

"I do not have answers to everything. I know we are loved and wanted here, unlike on Earth, where we felt unloved. We are now part of a **loving, caring family.**"[4]

Sam asked, "Will everyone from Earth come here someday?"

Stefan replied, "Not everyone, only those our Lord has **chosen**[5] for this place. There are other sanctuaries, and he may send other people there. He would choose the best place for them."

Kwan-yin asked, "How does he choose?"

"That is a hard question, difficult to answer. Tenzin looks at **people's hearts**[6]. In its simplest form, people who promote the interests and well-being of others and are **not selfish**[7] find their way here. These people are willing to confront their true natures and desire to change, forgive, and seek forgiveness. They have an openness to be reconciled, learn from the past, and forge a better future. You two are a good example of that."

The women were full of questions, and Stefan took the time to answer them.

Sam started to tremble. "After what we saw earlier, I don't feel secure. I'm worried."

Stefan replied, "I can understand how you feel. All your past difficulties, pain, rejection, and suffering have moulded your spirit. Those wounds will heal, but the scars and some memories will always stay with you. Those scars will help you grow into a better person."

They were in deep conversation, totally engrossed, when Tenzin approached them. He sat down quietly and listened.

---- ➤ ----

Bible (NKJV)	Bhagavad Gita
[1] Ezekiel 34:27. "Then the trees of the field shall yield their fruit, and the earth shall yield her increase. They shall be <u>safe in their land</u> and know that I *am* the LORD when I have broken the bands of their yoke and delivered them from the hand of those who enslaved them.	[3] 3:30. Arjuna, fix your mind on Me and surrender all your works unto Me. <u>Fulfil My divine plan</u> to improve all creatures' welfare, interest, and happiness. Do it without any desire for personal gain.
[2] Revelation 12:7 <u>And war broke out in heaven</u>: Michael and his angels fought with the dragon, and the dragon and his angels fought.	[3] 4:3. To a selected few, I revealed My existence and plans for eternity (past, present, and <u>future worlds</u> to come). You are My friend and devotee, and in due time, as you gain My favour, I will <u>reveal these mysteries</u> and explain your role here on Earth, in the spiritual world, and in the far distant future.
[2] Ephesians 6:12. For we do not wrestle against flesh and blood, but against principalities, against powers, <u>against the rulers of the darkness of this age</u>, against spiritual hosts of wickedness in the heavenly places.	[4] 13:29. People respecting the divinity in every being and creature <u>see God's love everywhere</u>. They do not harm themselves or others and advance in the spiritual world and understanding. How can one who sees the divine in all creatures injure
[3] Ephesians 1:11. In Him also we have obtained an inheritance,	

being predestined according to the purpose of Him who works all things according to the counsel of His will,

[4] Hebrews 12:1. Therefore we also, since so great a cloud of witnesses surrounds us, let us lay aside every weight and the sin which so easily ensnares *us*, and let us run with endurance the race that is set before us,

[5] Ephesians 1:4-5, just as he chose us in Christ before the foundation of the world to be holy and blameless before him in love. He destined us for adoption as his children through Jesus Christ, according to the good pleasure of his will.

[6] Matthew 5:8. Blessed are the pure in heart, For they shall see God

---x--

another or walk away from an injured one?

[5] 11:16. Untold numbers of life forms on Earth and spiritual sanctuaries passed before me. I saw the beginning and end of all. You gave life and brought joy, pain and suffering into our lives, and in 'The Fullness of Time' (before The Day of The Lord), you made us whole (restored, made restitution) and wiped away all pain and suffering. You showed/proved that nothing thrives in the Universe at the expense of another. I comprehended your joy and sorrow from start to end.

[6] 9:26. I accept with joy any devotional service offered with a pure heart, a leaf, a flower, a fruit, or water.

[7] 6:45. These disciplined people in their new realms progress further as their selfish desires are purified. Moving upwards towards higher realms, they eventually attain the seventh Heaven, the supreme goal of all.

Chapter 48

Supreme Leader of the cosmos

The four of them were sitting on the bank of the lake. Ducks and other birds were swimming on its surface. It was a lovely, warm day; some **animals**[1] had come to the lake to wash or drink. It was quiet and peaceful.

Lions, antelopes, buffaloes, and other animals grazed together. They fed on what Mother Nature willingly gave them, like a mother breastfeeding her child, because there was a **covenant**[2] between the Lord, the land, and all who lived on it.

They ate the same food together; no one was afraid or lived in fear of the others.

Amos and Niza, two lions, came and sat with them. The male laid his head on Tenzin's lap and went to sleep. The lioness sat next to Sam, who reached out and massaged her.

Suddenly, everything went quiet. They looked at each other in alarm. Then, a slight sound came from the orchard and the woods. All the creatures stopped whatever they were doing and stood still, heads bowed. The trees and plants seemed **to twist and clap**[3] their hands.

Walking towards them from the orchard was the **Leader**[4] of the twenty-four Elders, still dressed in a simple tunic. Tenzin and Stefan knelt respectfully and kept their gazes firmly on the ground.

---- ➤ ----

Bible (NKJV)	Bhagavad Gita
[1] Isaiah 11:6. "The wolf also shall <u>dwell with the lamb</u>, The leopard shall lie down with the young goat, The calf and the young lion and the fatling together; And a little child	[1] 5:7. A mature, enlightened person provides selfless services, learns to control his senses and mind, and sees the <u>divine in all creatures</u>. Though engaged in work, he is never

shall lead them.

² Hosea 2:18. On that day, I will make a covenant for them with the beasts of the field, With the birds of the air and the creeping things of the ground. I will shatter the bow and sword of battle from the earth, To make them lie down safely.

³ Ezekiel 34:27. "Then the **trees** of the field shall yield their fruit, and the earth shall yield her increase. They (animals) shall be safe in their land; they shall know that I am the LORD when I have broken the bands of their yoke and delivered them from the hand of those who enslaved them. ³ᵇIsaiah 55:12. "For you shall go out with joy, And be led out with peace; The mountains and the hills Shall break forth into singing before you, And all the trees of the field shall clap their hands.

⁴ Psalms 106:4. Remember me, O LORD, with the favour You have toward Your people; Oh, visit me with Your salvation,

---X--

entangled in worldly actions and is not disappointed or happy due to the outcome but leaves the result in My care. ¹ᵇ**6:28-29**. Those collaborating with My divine spirit are happy and free from material worldly ties. They see My divine nature within and in all creatures and creation.

² 13:29. People respecting the divinity in every being and creature see God's love everywhere. They do not harm themselves or others and advance in the spiritual world and understanding. How can one who sees the divine in all creatures injure another or walk away from an injured one? The one who does not perceive this separates himself from others, seeing some as friends and others as foes or creatures to exploit.

⁴ 6:42-43. Or they may move (metamorphose) into the realm of a great spiritual master. Such a move is rare. Their divine consciousness is reinvigorated by the great spiritual masters, and with their help, they are encouraged to make further progress.

---- ➤ ----

---------- ᠙----

Chapter 49

Brilliant light

The two women kept their gaze on the **Leader**[1]. They were surprised to see him and didn't know how to react or what was expected of them.

He approached them and said, "**Come, follow me**[2]." His voice was gentle but **authoritative.**[3]

The **two women**[4] walked with him in silence around the lake. The two lions followed while all the animals watched them. Everything else in the sanctuary stood still.

Tenzin[5] and Stefan knelt at the sight of the Lord, with seven mighty, angelic beings accompanying him. One of the angels approached them and placed a shield around them. Immediately, a brilliant light surrounded them. They stayed in that position for a long time. Then, the light faded, and the angel removed the shield.

Tenzin and Stefan became aware that the **Lord**[6] and the women were standing near them.

---- ➤ ----

Bible (NKJV)	Bhagavad Gita
[1] Hebrews 5:5. So also Christ did not glorify himself in becoming a high priest, but was appointed by the one who said to him, "You are my Son, today I have begotten you";	[1] 9:20. Those who study the Holy books and worship Me free themselves from ignorance, darkness, fear and evil. They attain a place in the heavenly realms and have access to My wisdom and blessings.
[2] John 10:27-28. My sheep hear my voice; I know them, and they follow me, and I give them eternal life. They shall never perish;	[2] 10:37. The name Lord Krishna represents My divine nature and opulence among many cultures.

neither shall any man pluck them out of my hand.

³ Hebrews 10:19-24. My friends, we have the confidence to enter the sanctuary by the blood of Jesus and by the living way he opened for us through the curtain (that is, through his flesh).

⁴ Ephesians 3:11-19. This was in accordance with the eternal purpose that he has carried out in Christ Jesus our Lord, in whom we have access to God in boldness and confidence through faith in him. I pray that, according to the riches of his glory, he may grant that you may be strengthened in your inner being with power through his Spirit and that Christ may dwell in your hearts through faith, as you are being rooted and grounded in love. I pray that you may have the power to comprehend, with all the saints, what is the breadth and length and height and depth, and to know the love of Christ that surpasses knowledge so that you may be filled with all the fullness of God.

⁴ Hebrews 9:11. Christ came as High Priest of the good things to come, with the greater and more perfect tabernacle not made with hands, not of this creation.

⁵2nd Corinthians 6:16. For we are the temple of the living God; as

³ 13:24. When a person permits his Atman to consul his soul, the liberated soul will lead the person to the divine, both here and hereafter.

⁴ 13:20. Arjuna, the breath of God, the Atman (Purusha, pure consciousness) is without beginning. The individual's transformation in this life is due to the interaction of their material nature (Prakriti), their spirit (duality of soul and Atman), and the divine influence on them or lack thereof.

⁵ 6:20-23. In union with Me (Samadhi), the sensory and emotional feelings are subjugated to contemplate the spiritual. They begin to fill up with inner joy and fulfilment. They now walk in truth and are free from all miseries from material contact. Here, they desire only to please Me. The joys or sorrows of life do not govern their life, but My divine influence.

⁸ 6:19. As a lamp is steady in a windless place, so is a calm mind able to be steadfast in My divine presence.

---- ➤ ----

God said, "I will live in them and walk among them, and I will be their God, and they shall be my people.

[6] Ephesians 1:11. In whom also we have obtained an inheritance, being predestinated according to the purpose of him who worketh all things after the counsel of his own will:

---X--

---------- ⌇⌇------

Chapter 50

War on horizon

He looked at the two men and said, "Look after them. **Teach[1] them my ways.[2]**" Then the **Master[3]** and the angels walked towards the forest and vanished.

As Tenzin and Stefan stood up, they noticed that one of the angels had stayed behind.

"Come," he said to Tenzin. "We need to talk." The two of them walked away from the others. When they were far away, the angel Nan-ya said, "We have a problem."

Tenzin replied, "Yes, a big one."

Nan-ya stared at the sky for a minute. "The Archangel **Michael[4]** and the others are concerned and say it will not be easy."

Tenzin glanced at the sky, too. "What about our foes?"

Nan-ya replied, "They have found a strong leader and are gathering under his banner, preparing for **war[5].**"

"We cannot be complacent; we must be prepared."

---- ➤ ----

Bible (NKJV)	Bhagavad Gita
[1] Hebrews 3:1. This is why I, Paul, am a prisoner for Christ Jesus for the sake of you Gentiles—; [2A] Hebrews 4:15. But speaking the truth in love, we must grow up in every way into him who is the head, into Christ. [2B] Ephesians 1:5. Having predestinated us to the	[1] 10:9. My devotees' thoughts and lives centre on Me. They derive tremendous satisfaction and happiness from their service to society and Me. Teaching one another and conversing about Me, they enlighten one another.

adoption of children by Jesus Christ to himself, according to the good pleasure of his will. **2C** Ephesians 2:10. For we are his workmanship, created in Christ Jesus to good works, which God ordained that we should walk in them.

3 Hebrews 2:17. Wherefore in all things it behoved him to be made like to his brethren, that he might be a merciful and faithful high priest in things pertaining to God, to make reconciliation for the people's sins. **3B** Romans 8:29-30. For whom he did foreknow, he also did predestinate to be conformed to the image of his Son, that he might be the firstborn among many brethren. Moreover, whom he did predestinate, them he also called: and whom he called, them he also justified: and whom he justified, them he also glorified.

4, 5 Revelation 12:7. And war broke out in heaven: Michael and his angels fought with the dragon, and the dragon and his angels fought,
---X--

2 8:28. Study the scripture, give selfless service to others, live modestly, and give to the poor. This selfless duty to others and devotion to My teachings will guide you to your real spiritual home, My abode.

3 9:3. Those who reject the teachings of My holy scriptures (*sacred teachings given to various nations, races, and tribes*) are walking away from their place in My eternal spiritual home.

---- ➤ ----

---------- ꙩ------

Chapter 51

Humanity cannot live by bread alone

Matthew 19:29, And everyone who has left houses, brothers, sisters, father, mother, wife, children, or lands for My name's sake shall receive a hundredfold and inherit eternal life.

The two women, Sam and Kwan-yin, were getting familiar with the **garden.**[1] It was set in a secluded part of a large valley bordered by mountains. The melting snowcaps formed a clear stream that **watered**[2] the valley.

They had begun to relax and enjoy the pleasures of the **peaceful**[3] garden. However, it seemed too quiet, and the daily routine became dull. Other people were in the valley, but those people preferred spending time with their families.

The two women missed having families and friends with whom they could spend time. An inner longing burned in their hearts as if their lives had no meaning, no purpose. They had easy access to tasty food and everything to sustain their bodily needs. They had Stefan and Tenzin's companionship, not to mention all the others, but something was still **missing.**[4]

Stefan told Tenzin, "They were happy to have escaped their earthly lives when they came here. They started to relax, enjoy this life, and interact with others. Despite their agitation, they have integrated into the community well. The wounds of their previous suffering and grief are healing. Nonetheless, they are getting restless."

Tenzin replied, "They have settled well and are making good progress, though their emotional wounds are still far from healing. But you are right. They have become restless. They see others have close-knit families—a shared identity they don't have."

"Perhaps the time has come. What does the Lord think?"

Tenzin replied, "He is aware."

"Perhaps you should remind Him."

Tenzin nodded. "I will go and see Him. I think He will agree with our plan."

He got up and left. He was gone for a short time and returned with a broad smile.

"He has agreed. Now it is up to us."

Stefan asked, "What did the Lord agree to?"

---- ➤ ----

Bible (NKJV)	Bhagavad Gita
[1] Micah 4:4. But everyone shall <u>sit under his vine,</u> and his fig tree and no one shall make them afraid; For the mouth of the LORD of hosts has spoken. [2] Jeremiah 31:12. They shall come and sing aloud on the height of Zion, and they shall be radiant over the goodness of the LORD, over the grain, the wine, the oil, and the young of the flock and the herd. Their life will be like a <u>watered garden,</u> and all their sorrows will disappear. [3] Proverbs 3:24. When you lie down, you will not be <u>afraid</u>; Yes, you will lie down, and your <u>sleep will be sweet.</u> [4] Luke 4:4. But Jesus answered him, saying, "It is written, 'Man	[1-2] 13:29. People respecting the divinity in <u>every being and creature see God's love everywhere.</u> They do not harm themselves or others and advance in the spiritual world and understanding. **4:35.** Having gained spiritual wisdom, you will not be deluded again. You will see that all living entities are part of the divine plan, part of one family, and have the same breath of life from <u>the divine.</u> Hence, as you progress in your spiritual growth, you will regard all life forms as an extension of The Lord and your family. **6:28-29.** Those in collaboration with My divine spirit <u>are happy and free</u> from material worldly ties. They see My divine nature within and in <u>all creatures and creation.</u> [3] 2:64-65. However, a person who

shall not live by <u>bread alone</u>, but by every word of God.' "

---X--

has his senses under control is free from attachment and aversion. His mind is <u>at peace</u>. The power of material existence has no decisive influence. Instead, intelligence and spiritual wisdom guide him.

[3-4] 4:33. The primary purpose of creation is the spiritual advancement of all, and secondary sharing My eternal plan with those who seek it with all their heart, mind, and strength. Signs and wonders accompany sacred knowledge and are not revealed to those who place little value on it.

[3, 4] 2:70. Many rivers flow into the ocean, but the sea never fills up. Similarly, selfish desires and attachments continuously flow into a person's mind, which remains unsatisfied. However, wise person asserts control over their mind, never yielding to them. Such a man dwells in peace, which is not so with the person who strives to satisfy his unrestrained desires.---x--

---------- ૭૭------

Chapter 52

Tsunami

"He gave me **three names[1]** and said we should go to Sector Five."

"Why Sector Five?"

Tenzin. "That is where we will find the three."

"Do we take the women with us?"

"Yes."

They went in search of Sam and Kwan-yin. When they found them, Tenzin called them over.

Tenzin said, "You need to come with us. Hold our hands, and close your eyes." They drifted through space, entered the Tunnel of Death, and came out at the other end. They were on Earth.

They were on the shore of the mainland where a tsunami had hit. There was utter destruction everywhere. Fields and houses were submerged in muddy water. The air felt heavy and smelt terrible, and it was very humid. Pieces of wood, trees, and homes were floating in the water, with dead bodies of people and animals everywhere.

They reached higher ground and came across distressed people, many crying over the bodies of dead friends, neighbours, and family members.

Besides the ruin of a mud hut, a young mother was crying over the bodies of her two young children and husband. Nearby, a father and mother were grieving over their dead baby and elderly parents. People were suffering everywhere. They had lost everything: homes, crops, animals, and, worse still, their families.

The two women were shocked, but Stefan held their hands firmly.

"Do not let go of my hands," he said to them. "Tenzin has work to do here."

They watched as Tenzin walked among the destruction and searched for the three souls he had come to collect. He soon found them scattered among the debris.

Stefan recognised the body of a man taking his last few breaths, lying among the dying and the dead. "Wait," he said. "I knew this man. He did a lot for his people. He was a pillar of his society, loved and respected by everyone. We must take him with us."

Tenzin replied, "I am sorry, Brother Stefan. He was a good man, but he **killed**[2] a person. The rules are clear. No one who has shed human blood, regardless of the reason, can enter our sanctuary."

Sam asked, "What will happen to him?"

"That is for the Master to decide. There are **other sanctuaries**[3] where he could go. There, he will have to undergo a cleansing and purification process."

Stefan said anxiously, "He won't be able to go through the cleansing alone."

"It will take someone a lot of time and effort to help him," Tenzin replied. "Perhaps one of his relatives may take an interest in him. This one is not our concern. I have to go and pick up the ones the Master has chosen. Go back to the sanctuary, and wait for me there."

"Close your eyes," Stefan ordered the women, and they all drifted back to their garden through the tunnel.

"It is good to be back home," Sam murmured.

A little while later, they saw Tenzin walking up to them.

He told the two women, "Go to the orchard with Brother Stefan. There, you will meet three very distressed children. You are to help Stefan to settle the children here. You will look after the children and help them mix into this community. Stefan will look after their spiritual needs. He will teach them about their faith and their religion."

Sam said, "We will look after them, but I have a question. What if all three of them are of **different faiths?**"[4]

Tenzin replied, "In our sanctuary, people of all faiths, and some atheists, are welcomed. Our Lord chooses them. We do not judge them but guide them according to their beliefs until they are ready to join their families, or someone from their faith is willing to take over the responsibility. I have to go now and report to the guardian of the realm. Stefan will guide and help you both."

---- ➤ ----

Bible (NKJV)	Bhagavad Gita
[1] Ephesians 1:4. just as He chose us in Him before the foundation of the world, that we should be holy and without blame before Him in love,	[1] 7:26. I am the Eternal One. The past, present, and future are known to me. I know every living entity by its names and deeds and regularly take an inventory of its thoughts, motives, and doings. Hence, I know all there is to know about them; however, no one knows Me thoroughly.
[2A] Genesis 9:6. "Whoever sheds man's blood, by man his blood shall be shed; For in the image of God, He made man.	
[2B] Lamentations 17:4. "He has shed blood, and that man shall be cut off from among his people,	[2] 1:31 I see no good in killing my kin in this battle. Causing death and destruction is not how I want to be victorious and win back my kingdom.
[3] De 4:41-42. Then Moses set apart three cities of refuge east of the Jordan River. Anyone who killed another person unintentionally,	[3A] 15:1. **Krishna:** It is said that there is a mythical upside-down spiritual tree with its primary root reaching upwards towards Heaven and its

without previous hostility, could flee there to live in safety.

[4] Revelation 5:9 And they sang a new song, saying: "You are worthy to take the scroll, And to open its seals; For You were slain, And have redeemed us to God by Your blood Out of every tribe and tongue and people and nation,

---X--

branches, leaves and secondary roots reaching down towards the Earth. The branches and leaves are made of Holy Scriptures. One who knows this tree understands the Vedas (Holy Scriptures).

[3B] 8:11. I am impartial. All Holy Scriptures (All Faiths) point to the eternal truth that those who worship Me are sacrificial, relinquishing selfishness and materialism. They seek to promote the welfare, interest, and happiness of others and Mine. Such people find salvation and eternal life in Me.

[4A] 15:15. My spirit resides in everyone and permeates every cosmic atom. All are accounted for in My daily inventory. I am the source of proper knowledge and the understanding that dispels the darkness within all. I am impartial. All the Holy Scriptures in the world speak of Me. Indeed, I authorised them.

[4B] 15:18. All Holy Scriptures from the Earth's four corners declare Me the Supreme Lord. I exist, the Eternal, unchanging, imperishable Lord, the source of all wisdom, worshipped by the inhabitants of the Universe. ---X--

---------- ॐ------

Chapter 53

The three children

Sam and Kwan-yin went to meet the children. Two boys and a girl were playing on the stream's banks, and one of the boys was very excited. He was dancing. Ahmet ran to the girls, shouting, "Look, I can run. I was a cripple all my life, yet I am finally like the other people in this place. I have arms and **legs[1].**" He grabbed Sam's hands. "Look, I have arms and legs. Now, I can play with the others."

His face was radiant, full of happiness. He turned to Kwan-yin. "Look, I am normal. How did this happen?"

"Ahmet, this is my friend Sam, and my name is Kwan-yin. My friend will explain." Kwan-yin said. "Let us find a nice place to sit, and Sam will explain."

They sat down on the velvety green lawn. Couples of birds were noisily feeding, and a few yards away, the deer were grazing.

Sam began. "The man that brought you here, his name is Tenzin. He told us all about your past. You were born with a disability and spent most of your life in a wheelchair. When you were seven years old, you watched some children playing in the sea. They were happy, but there were tears in your eyes because you wanted to be like them, to play with them. You sat in the wheelchair and cried. You cried out to God (Supreme Lord, Jehovah, Allah). You pleaded with God to make you the same as the other children.

"He heard your prayer and saw your **tears[2]**. We don't know why he did nothing then. However, he never forgot you." She wiped away the tears of joy from his face. "It was the Lord who sent Tenzin to bring you here. Perhaps it is here that God has chosen to answer your prayer, to make you **whole[3],** to restore the years the locusts have devoured." There were tears of joy in their eyes.

The second child, a small, shy Indian girl called Dipa, was watching them. She grabbed Sam's hand to draw attention to her. "Look," she said, her voice full of passion and excitement. "My face is normal. I saw my reflection in the water; no scars on my face, shoulder, or arms. I am, finally, like other children. My mother used to read the Gita and pray to the **Supreme Lord**[4,] and now he has answered her prayers."

Joseph was tugging at Kwan-yin's arm. "Look, I can see and hear. I was born with poor eyesight and was deaf, but now I am normal. I am like Ahmet and Dipa, normal. My mother used to pray to lord Jesus to make me better, and now I am complete." He hugged her. After a while, he released her. "Please," he pleaded. "Can you tell us where our parents are?"

There was silence. Suddenly, there was a chill in the air. The two women looked at each other.

Finally, Sam looked at the children and answered, "We don't know. We were asked to look after you to make you feel at home here. When Master Tenzin comes, he may be able to answer your questions."

Some distance away, Sam saw Tenzin. She ran up to him, her face covered in tears of joy. "Tenzin," she cried, "Come see the children. They are whole, normal!"

"I know."

"But you don't sound joyful."

He hesitated and replied, "They were healed because Master took an interest in them. We saw othere people and we could not help them. Master asked us to bring only these three here."

"Why were you not allowed to help others?"

"I cannot answer **that**[5.]*"

* [Liz's Tenet 1:-] It is not wise to reveal all before its time.

---- ➤ ----

Bible (NKJV)	Bhagavad Gita
[1] Leviticus 21:21 No descendant of Aaron with a defect may approach the altar (Sanctuary) to present special gifts to the LORD. Since he	[1] **Gita 1:26-46 elaboration** *A:6 The spirit of the Lord in Arjuna reveals that even in Heaven, the*

has a defect, he may not approach the altar to offer food to his God (enter into his presence). Leviticus 21:23, 'Only he shall not go near the veil or approach the altar, because he has a <u>defect</u>, lest he profane My sanctuaries; for I the LORD sanctify them.'

[2] Psalms 31:22 For I said in my haste, "I am cut off from before <u>Your</u> eyes"; Nevertheless You <u>heard</u> the voice of my supplications when I cried out to You.

[3] Job 5:18 For He bruises, but He binds up; He wounds, but His <u>hands make whole.</u>

[1-5] Heb 11:13 All of these died in faith without receiving the promises, but they saw and greeted them from a distance. They confessed that they were strangers and foreigners on Earth.

---X--

work of counselling, reconciliation, restoration, restitution, and making each whole has to continue if there is going to be eternal peace. That would require the special abilities, time, and effort of Godly eternal warrior-priests like him to restore and heal until all are made whole. The daunting task ahead and hereafter demoralises him and subdues his spirit. (Gita 11:1-31)

[2] *A:15 "Your enemies are not flesh and blood but darkness, ignorance, selfishness, greed, apathy, injustice, and spiritual darkness that pervades the universe and within you. So, fight the good fight. Follow My guidance, and I (the Supreme Lord) will wipe away all tears. I will make all things whole." (Gita 14:5-10)*

[3] *A:20 With My assistance, make all who cross your path, friend and foe, whole, and claim your inheritance as my joint heir and my (adopted) son.'(Gita 18:55-58).*

---X--

Chapter 54

<u>Truth and reconciliation¹ (Part 2)</u>

The two women were sitting under the shade of a tree on the shores of the lake. The two lions, Amos and Niza, were **<u>asleep near them</u>²**. About a dozen antelopes, deer, and zebras grazed nearby. The two women were deep in conversation and did not notice Stefan approaching them. Amos was the first to see him, raising his big head in greeting.

Stefan came and sat down next to Amos. His presence seemed to have stifled the conversation between the two women. There was an awkward silence. Sam looked embarrassed while Kwan-yin toyed with a piece of straw.

"I apologise," said Stefan. "I didn't mean to intrude."

He got up and was about to leave when Kwan-yin called out. "It's okay. You don't have to leave. Please join us."

He sat down again, but a cold silence filled the air.

"No, I should go," said Stefan.

The lioness Niza got up, strode over to Stefan, and put her head in his lap, almost as if to say, "You should stay."

Kwan-yin looked pleadingly at Sam. "I think you should tell Brother Stefan how you feel."

"I cannot," replied Sam. "I don't know how to say it. I am confused; my emotions and feelings are irrational. There's no logic to them. Yet, I can't suppress my feelings, no matter how hard I try." There were tears in her eyes.

Amos got up and went over to Sam. He put his right paw on her shoulder and gently licked her face.

Niza, the lioness, looked at Kwan-yin with gentle pleading; she seemed to say, "Perhaps you should tell Brother Stefan."

The monk looked at Sam, encouraging her to speak.

Kwan-yin avoided eye contact with Stefan and muttered, "It has to do with her parents." She paused, still toying with the piece of straw.

Stefan took a deep breath and leaned backwards; he raised his right hand and brought it across his mouth, subconsciously trying to stop himself from speaking. Yet, a tiny gasp escaped him. It was almost as if someone had stabbed him.

He and Tenzin had talked about this moment a few times. They had rehearsed what to say, but all that seemed to evaporate in an instant of emotional upheaval. It was his turn to avoid eye contact, and he looked at the ground and shook his head.

"I am sorry," he said and started to cry. He could not look Sam in the eyes; no one spoke for a long time. Their **thoughts engulfed them[3].**

---- ➤ ----

Bible (NKJV)	Bhagavad Gita
[1] Colossians 1:20, and through him to <u>reconcile all things unto himself</u>, having made peace through the blood of his cross; through him, I say, whether things upon the earth or things in the heavens.	[1, 2, 3] 6:20-23. In union with Me (Samadhi), the sensory and emotional feelings are subjugated to contemplate the spiritual. They begin to fill up with <u>inner joy and fulfilment</u>. They now walk in truth and are free from all <u>miseries</u> from material contact. Here, they desire only to please Me. The joys or sorrows of life do not govern their life, but My divine influence.58fd69+
[2] Ezekiel 34:25, "I will make a covenant of peace with them, and cause wild beasts to cease from the land, and they will <u>dwell safely</u> in the wilderness and <u>sleep in the woods.</u>	[1, 2] 18:30. Sattvic intellect (Buddhi) discerns between <u>truth and falseness,</u>

[3] 1st Corinthians 12:26, And if one member suffers, all the members suffer with it; or if one member is honoured, all the members rejoice.

---x--

right and wrong, and when to act and refrain. What brings freedom or bondage? What is to be feared and not to be feared? What helps or hinders spiritual growth?

[3] 8:16. Every person and creature on Earth is subject to pleasure, pain, and suffering. However, those attaining My Abode acquire the strength to overcome their pain and suffering.

[3] 13:9 They comprehend the Lord's creative plan for the cosmos, their position in this plan, and the reason for joyful and painful lessons of life: the joy of family, friends, birth, suffering, disease, old age, and death. All these things are encountered in life and used for spiritual growth and advancement. Hence, they seek and are willing to learn from a spiritual master as they journey along this path.

---- ➤ ----

---------- ↬ ------

Chapter 55

Field of stones

Kwan-yin was the first to break the silence. She wanted to act as the peacemaker, but could not find the appropriate words.

She stammered. "You were with the soldiers." She could not bring herself to finish the sentence.

He nodded and then looked at Sam. Amos was consoling her. He brought his big paw up underneath her jaw and gently lifted her head so that she was now facing Stefan.

Amos pleaded. "You should tell Stefan how you feel."

She stammered. "Part of me struggles to let go of the past. I remember you and the soldiers coming to our house. I can still see the hate-filled faces of those who killed my parents while the other soldiers stood by and tried not to watch. I couldn't understand why they wouldn't stop it or why they didn't help us if they knew it was wrong."

"**I'm so sorry**[1]; I stood by and did nothing. I was forced to join the rebels. Please **forgive**[2] me." Stefan whispered.

Sam, "I try to tell myself you were a victim too, that you couldn't have turned on the others, but…." She trailed off. Suddenly, she got up and hugged him fiercely.

He gently pushed her away so that he could look into her eyes. Then he said softly, "Come with me."

She took hold of his hand. As he led her away, he glanced back at Kwan-yin and said, "You too."

She followed them with the lions on either side of her, followed by the herd of herbivorous animals.

He led them through the orchard to the field of **stones³** that held all the creatures' **testimonies⁴.** They stepped through the area, avoiding stepping on the stones. They walked for a very long time. No one spoke.

---- ➤ ----

Bible (NKJV)	Bhagavad Gita
¹ Colossians 3:25, But he who does wrong will be repaid for what he has done, and there is no partiality. ² Mark 11:25. "And whenever you stand praying, if you have anything against anyone, forgive him, that your Father in heaven may also forgive you your trespasses. ³ Joshua 4:6. "This may be a sign among you when your children ask in time to come, saying, 'What do these stones mean to you?' ⁴ Ecclesiastes 3:19. For what happens to the sons of men also happens to animals; one thing befalls them: as one dies, so dies the other. Indeed, they all have one breath; man has no advantage over animals, for all is vanity.---**X**--	² 16:1. The Supreme Lord: Arjuna, you must nurture these qualities. Learn to overcome fear and walk in purity of heart and emotions. Study the Scriptures and grow in spiritual knowledge. Be compassionate and charitable, and have a clear conscience. Give freely and indulge in a duty of care and kindness towards all, especially the poor and vulnerable. Be self-controlled, sincere, and truthful. Nourish a spirit of giving and forgiveness ---**X**--

---------- ↬------

Chapter 56

Monument of truth and reconciliation.

They came to a vast, four-sided stone monument. On each side was a pot from which a flame glowed. Underneath each pot flowed a spring of clear water.

The memorial held the **records**[1] of every living thing on "Tenzin's Patch", his land. He was responsible for every seed, plant, tree, insect, or person, down to the smallest living organism.

Stefan let go of Sam's hand, knelt next to one of the pots, put his hands over the flame, and then scooped up some water and washed his face. He got up and asked the women to do the same. He stood next to the lions as the women knelt and did as he had asked. He asked them to form a small circle, and they all knelt.

Stefan spoke. "We have come to the monument of **truth and reconciliation.**[2] The fire represents burning and purifying the past; the water represents cleansing and washing away." He paused as the two lions and the herd of herbivores walked up to the monument, raised their legs over the fire, and then washed their faces in the water. They then came and joined them in the circle.

Stefan continued. "I am a simple monk. My understanding is, likewise, simple. One day, we shall see the **whole picture**[3]. You may find my belief challenging to understand, and you have the right to have a different viewpoint. But this is what I believe.

"We all came from a world where all living things lived off each other. We have all participated in the killing, be it of our kind or other living creatures. Sometimes, we did so knowingly; other times, we were unaware of our actions, such as stepping on ants or small insects."

He paused for his words to sink in and said, "On Earth, whatever we did, we did to survive. We lived off each other, the prey and the predators—even herbivorous creatures preyed on living things, like plants and grass.

"It does not justify what we did to survive; I merely state how it was. This is a place of truth and reconciliation **for prey and predators**[4] coming together to tell their story."

---- ➤ ----

Bible (NKJV)	Bhagavad Gita
[1] Matthew 10:26. "Therefore, do not fear them. Nothing is covered that will not be revealed and hidden that will not be known.	[2] 16:1. The Supreme Lord: Arjuna, you must nurture these qualities. Learn to overcome fear and walk in purity of heart and emotions. Study the Scriptures and grow in spiritual knowledge. Be compassionate and charitable, and have a clear conscience. Give freely and indulge in a duty of care and kindness towards all, especially the poor and vulnerable. Be self-controlled, sincere, and truthful. Nourish a spirit of giving and forgiveness
[2] 2nd Corinthians 5:18. Now all things are of God, who has reconciled us to Himself through Jesus Christ and has given us the ministry of reconciliation,v19 that is, that God was in Christ reconciling the world to Himself, not imputing their trespasses to them, and has committed to us the word of reconciliation.	[2] 13:12. Devotees realize the importance of knowing themselves and the need to seek truth and justice.
[3] 1st Corinthians 13:12, For now, we see in a mirror, dimly, but then face to face. I know partly, but then I shall know just as I am known.	[2, 14] 14:27. I am the foundation of the revealed and hidden Brahman, the immortal, imperishable, eternal, and unchanging. The source of truth and happiness. I am the light of the world.
[4] Ezekiel 34:28, "And they shall no longer be a prey for the nations, nor shall beasts of the land devour them, but they shall dwell safely, and no one shall make them afraid.	[3, 11] 11:7. In My body, you will perceive the entire cosmos cycle passing

---X--

before your eyes. Whatever you want to see, the past, present, future, **creation** (*refer to the end of the book),* Earth, and spiritual sanctuaries will flash before you. You will find answers to questions regarding the terms 'in the fullness of time' and 'the end of all material and spiritual worlds' and your purpose on Earth and in the heavenly realms. The mysteries of the Universe are available to all brave enough to seek them.

---X--

---------- ᐊᐅ------

Chapter 57

Accountability

He paused again as he gazed over them and continued, "We came from a world where survival is a **cycle of life and death**[1].

"God is our father, mother, guardian and the creator of all things, including the universe's pain, **suffering**[2] and joy. He takes all responsibility and acknowledges that He is accountable for all his actions. No one is higher than him, so He has decreed that anyone can challenge Him to justify His actions and has **set a day for it**." [3]

There was a long, awkward silence. Stefan tried to see if they had understood him, but their faces were blank.

His gaze darted between their faces. He inhaled deeply and said, "We, all living things, have appointed the Lord and the Elders to judge Him and all the beings in the universe, including us. Everything in the universe must be held accountable, including God.

"To be seen as just, the cosmos (God) has bestowed **special powers**[4] on the Elders so they can fulfil their tasks. Our Lord, the Elders, and the LORD God Almighty have appointed a 'Day of the Lord.' On that day, all the universe will account for their lives, **including God**."[5]

He paused. He looked at each of them once more. Only the lions and the herbivores seemed to comprehend him. Humans are arrogant, proud species who wrongly consider themselves above every other species because of their higher intelligence. They are more intelligent, but although a lion is more intelligent than a sheep, the Elders of the universe do not place the lion above the sheep. In the sanctuary, all animals are equal.

He reflected on what he was saying. He did not have Tenzin's gift of timing or the wisdom to know if it was the right time to speak.

He continued, "I do not understand this very well. You will have to ask Tenzin to clarify it. My limited understanding is that God gave us all a **second chance**[6] in the sanctuaries spread across the universe to make restitution for the past. He has created shelters that give us all, whether people, lions, herbivores, or insects, a new home and life.

---- ➤ ----

Bible (NKJV)	Bhagavad Gita
[1] Genesis 3:21, Also, for Adam and his wife, the LORD God made tunics of skin (he killed animals) and clothed them.	[2] 8:16. Every person and creature on Earth is subject to pleasure, pain, and suffering. However, those attaining My Abode acquire the strength to overcome their pain and suffering.
[2] Isaiah 45:7. I form the light and create darkness, make peace and create calamity; I, the LORD, do all these things.'	[2, 3, 4, 5] 7:2 **Vijnan** (Wisdom of Divinity): According to our good pleasure, Brahman and I made atoms and many universes (the visible and the invisible). We gave life to all and brought joy, pain and suffering into the world, and in 'The Fullness of Time,' We shall make all whole: restore, reconcile and make restitution and wipe away all pain and suffering (Gita 14:26). The cost of purification of Saints borne by Creation will be redeemed and restitution made. We will purge all the unclear/defiled consciousness that pervades the Universe. All will be accounted for. We shall demonstrate to the Universe that nothing thrives in the Universe at the expense of another.
[3] Daniel 1:17. 'You shall not show partiality in judgment; you shall hear the small as well as the great; [3b] Ecclesiastes 8:6. Because for every matter there is a time and judgment,	
[4] Exodus 9:16. "But for this purpose, I have raised you, that I may show My power in you, and that My name may be declared in all the earth.	
[5] Matthew 7:2. "For with what judgment you judge (O lord), you will be judged; and with the measure you use, it will be measured back to you (O Lord).	
[6] 1st Corinthians 15:22, For as in	

Adam all die, so also in Christ shall all be made alive. [7b] 1st Corinthians 15:45, So also it is written, The first man Adam became a living soul. The last Adam became a life-giving spirit. [7c] 1st Peter 2:24, Who bare our sins in His own body on the tree, that we, being dead to sins, should live to righteousness: by whose stripes ye were healed.

---x--

---x--

---------- ᕦ------

Chapter 58

A second chance in the sanctuaries

"The sanctuary provides us with food and shelter, as a mother produces milk for her child, so no one has to prey on another. Here, we can learn to, value and respect all life, grow in wisdom, and understand the consequences of our past behaviour and the joy and pain it brought to others and us. We have another chance to learn to choose a **better way.**[1]

"We learn to love instead of hate, to let go of our **selfishness**[2], and grow into saints. No one can escape their past life, but they can work to undo the wrong done to others by facing up to their past and acknowledging that they preyed on others to survive. They hurt others and are willing to make and receive restitution, forgive, be forgiven, and be reconciled."

He looked at them; the animals nodded in agreement, but the women looked blank and puzzled.

Tenzin had told Stefan, "You humans consider yourselves the most intelligent species, but sometimes you are the stupidest, most conceited, and vain creatures in the universe."

Kwan-yin asked, "What if someone doesn't want to change or is not willing to admit to the wrong they have done? What if they don't want to be saints?"

He replied, "The Sovereign God gives everyone, good or bad, man or creature, a second chance in the sanctuaries. I do not know how it works, but those unwilling to change end up in shelters with their kind.

"Evil or selfish, materialistic people will share with others like **themselves**[3]. Unfortunately, their experience will lack love, respect, understanding, and compassion. I cannot see how their sanctuary can be a happy place.

"I believe we will all stand before the Lord's judgement seat one day. It is not a day of punishment. It will be a day when good and evil are **separated forever.** [4]

---- ➤ ----

Bible (NKJV)	Bhagavad Gita
[1] Colossians 1:20, And, having made peace through the blood of his cross, by him to reconcile all things to himself; I say, whether they be things on earth or in heaven. Romans 5:10, For if, when we were enemies, we were reconciled to God by the death of his Son, much more, being reconciled, his life shall save us. [2] Romans 6:13 And do not present your members *as* instruments of unrighteousness to sin but present yourselves to God as being alive from the dead, and your members *as* instruments of righteousness to God. [3] Luke 16:22-26. (*Parable of Lazarus and Abraham*).*v26,* 'And besides all this, between you and us, there is a great gulf fixed so that those who want to pass from here to you cannot, nor can those from there pass to us.' [4] Matthew 25:32. And before him, shall be gathered all nations: and he shall separate them one from another, as a shepherd divides his	[1] 3:41. Therefore, Arjuna, learn to bring your senses, mind, and intellect under My supervision with all your strength. Conquer your worst enemy, selfishness, destroyer of My divine purpose that abides in you. [1] 5:10. Those walking in the divine presence and learning to surrender all selfish attachments to the Supreme Lord are like the leaf of a lotus plant floating clean and dry in muddy water. Similarly, those who surrender all selfish attachments to the Supreme Lord no longer have the desire to sin [2] 3:26. Do not neglect the ignorant attached to selfish work, but show them by example that works done with the right spirit can be made sacred to improve the welfare of others. [3] 16:11-12. Ungodly people, or people with perverted views of God, believe that indulging their desires is the ultimate goal of life until death. They are often harsh and dominating and do not believe in life after death or have a perverted idea of the afterlife. Dominance, greed, anger,

sheep from the goats:

---X--

passion, and a desire to acquire material wealth govern their lives. Surrounded by their kind, they often live a fearful, meaningless life until death. Their every thought is to amass wealth or impose their tenets on others at any cost for self-gratification.

[3, 4] 9:3. Those who reject My holy scriptures' teachings (*sacred teachings given to various nations, races, and tribes*) are walking away from their place in My eternal spiritual home. They will pass from physical death to the spiritual realm appropriate to their nature and then pass away into their final demise.

---- ➤ ----

---------- ↳-------

Chapter 59

Spiritual adults

"When that time comes, hopefully, we will have changed, made restitution for our destructive ways and, more importantly, have grown spiritually. The suffering, the pain, and the goodwill have made us better creatures, compassionate, thoughtful, **caring, and kind.**[1]

"I may be wrong. I believe God's only way to perfect and metamorphose us from physical to **spiritual adults**[2] is to use the universe's pain, suffering, and joy to refine and purify us. All creatures, after death, desire to be reunited and reconciled with their families and friends will, where possible, be reunited. For every tear we shed on Earth, restitution will be made to us here, so in the end times, no one could say they lost out.

"As I have said, those unwilling to change will live in sanctuaries with their kind. Some would call this Heaven; others would **call it Hell.**[3]

"The worst among them are held in the grey, misty world, or the Bottomless Pit. Cosmos gave the caterpillar an evolutionary path to metamorphose into a butterfly, tadpoles into frogs, and humanity into spiritual beings.

"Suffering is part of all living things on Earth. It should remind us of the high cost to others and ourselves for our spiritual growth. We owe it to God and all living things to take this second chance and become **worthy,**[4] so that all our past sacrifices were not in vain.

"Humans think love and loss are unique to them. This is not true. All living things feel love, pain, grief, **loss**[5], and joy. It is part of our awareness."

They sat in silence, each lost in their thoughts.

---- ➤ ----

Bible (NKJV)	Bhagavad Gita
[1] Hebrews 13:21. Make you perfect in every good work to do his will, working in you that which is well-pleasing in his sight, through Jesus Christ; to whom be glory forever and ever. Amen.	[1] 12:13-14. The ones I love are free from malice towards all living beings and are friendly, compassionate, kind, tolerant, and considerate.
[2] 1st Corinthians 15:47 The first man was from the earth, a man of dust; the second man is from heaven.	[2] 4:33. The primary purpose of creation is the spiritual advancement of all, and the secondary purpose is sharing My eternal plan with those who seek it with all their hearts, minds, and strengths.
[3] Hebrews 10:29. How much worse punishment do you think will be deserved by those who have spurned the Son of God, profaned the blood of the covenant by which they were sanctified, and outraged the Spirit of grace?	[3] 16:19-20. These cruel, malicious, hateful, envious people, I cast them into the womb (spiritual sanctuaries) of their kind in the hereafter. There, the ungodly will live in spiritual sanctuaries among their kind. Without My guidance, they will gradually sink to their worst possible depth.
[4] Acts 3:19 Repent therefore and be converted, that your sins may be blotted out, so that times of refreshing may come from the presence of the Lord,	[4] 4:36. Spiritual knowledge is liberating. Even if you were once the most sinful of all sinners, once you board the boat of spiritual experience, you could sail beyond the ocean of your sins.
[5] Romans 8:22. For we know that all creation has been groaning as in the pains of childbirth right up to the present time. ---X--	[5] 8:16. Every person and creature on Earth is subject to pleasure, pain, and suffering. However, those attaining My abode acquire the strength to overcome their pain and suffering. ---X--

---------- ॐ ------

Chapter 60

Future aspiration

On one of his visits to the sanctuary, Sam asked Tenzin:

"What kind of people will eventually inhabit the cosmos?"

"Come, let us sit down under the shade of the big tree," he suggested.

When they had made themselves comfortable under the shade of the tree, he asked:

"In what kind of world would you like to live? What kind of person would you like to be in this future world?"

She thought about it for a while. Something Tenzin had once said sprang to her mind: that to live in the future; one must have "clean hands."

She considered the words. She knew she lacked the intelligence and maturity to comprehend their meaning. Her simple understanding was that her spiritual growth had been at a cost to others.

Those who had suffered due to her actions would receive more than adequate restitution for their **loss.**[1] She acknowledged that her spiritual growth would not have been possible without their involvement in her life, often resulting in their joy, pain, and suffering.

The Cosmos had been like a mother, father, brother, sister, family, and teacher to all. She appreciated her love. The combination of the world's good, bad, and evil and God's love allowed her to grow spiritually and enter the realms of enlightenment.

"And what are your aspirations today?" he inquired.

"I am beginning to understand that every living thing, every atom, or subatomic particle has contributed to my spiritual growth.

"I am beginning to comprehend that all living things have an equal right to live. Everything in the universe is valuable. A bacterium has as much right to live in the cosmos as I do.

"Yet I have a different value from a bacterium or an animal because I have a more remarkable ability, and because of that gift, I have greater responsibility and accountability.

"All my life, I have received from the cosmos and often taken, stolen, from other living entities without their consent to survive. Therefore, to convey my debt, gratitude, and remorse, I want to **make restitution**[2] to all.

"I hope, one day, to have a **clear conscience**[3]. I want to be free of all obligations so I can hold my head high, not with pride, but in the most profound humility, not as a lord but as a servant.

"I want to **serve,**[4] not to lord it over others, but I cannot achieve it alone."

"That is a noble aspiration you have," he said. "You are right; you cannot do it on your own. But you are not alone. You have the **family of the Elders**[5] and the Lord, and with their help, you can achieve your goal.

"Trust me. The Elders have the ability and means to make it happen. All they need is your **commitment.**[6] They will guide and lead you, though it will take a long time and hard work."

"I am willing to try."

---- ➤ ----

Bible (NKJV)	Bhagavad Gita
[1, 2,] Luke 19:8. Then Zacchaeus stood and said to the Lord, "Look, Lord, I give half of my goods to the poor; and if I have taken anything from anyone by false accusation, I	[1, 2, 3] 16:1. The Supreme Lord: Arjuna, you must nurture these qualities. Learn to overcome fear and walk in purity of heart and emotions. Study the Scriptures[2] and grow in spiritual knowledge. Be compassionate and

restore fourfold."

[3] Hebrews 10:22. Let us draw near with a true heart in full assurance of faith, having our hearts sprinkled from an evil conscience, and our bodies washed with pure water

[4] Matthew 20:28. "the Son of Man did not come to be served, but to serve and give His life a ransom for many."

[5] Hebrews 12:22. But you have come to Mount Zion and to the city of the living God, the heavenly Jerusalem, to an innumerable company of angels,

[6] Romans 12:1. I appeal to you, therefore, brothers and sisters, by the mercies of God, to present your bodies as a living sacrifice, holy and acceptable to God, which is your spiritual worship

---x---

charitable, and have a clear conscience[3]. Give freely and indulge in a duty of care[1] and kindness towards all, especially the poor and vulnerable. Be self-controlled, sincere, and truthful. Nourish a spirit of giving[2] and forgiveness.

[4] 2:41. Those who desire to serve Me and creation (all life forms and humanity) will attain a singular purpose with great resolve. For those who lack resolution, life's decisions will divert them from Me to material things.

[4] 3:17. People who have found their true self and purpose for life in Me are content and happy. Serving humanity, My creation, and Me is a privilege and a pleasure for them.

[4] 14:26. To transcend these modes of material nature is to serve humanity, creation, and Me and see the divinity in all others through total commitment to Me. Those who rise above their material nature are fit for union with Brahman and Me, and they will live to see a new order (Creation), a New Universe where the lion and lamb sit together and eat straw, and a child plays with them.

[5] 4:35. Having gained spiritual wisdom, you will not be deluded again. You will see that all living entities are part of the divine plan, part of one family, and have the same breath of life from the divine.

[6] 3:10. The Supreme Lord of creation continued: At the beginning of creation, I blessed creation and set in motion the principle of selfless, sacrificial service to promote the welfare, interest, and happiness of all creation. Thus, through this selfless service, all creation would be prosperous and fruitful and fulfil its desires.

[6] 2:2. The Supreme Lord turns to Arjuna and says: My dear friend, where does all this despair and confusion come from? You are an honourable man called to live a life of Dharma (duty), sacrifice, and righteousness. This lack of weakness and clarity in a crisis is not worthy of you.

[6] 3:9. Selfish action imprisons a person in the material world. Therefore, always act selflessly, performing your duties as a service to humanity and Me without thinking of personal benefit.

---- ➤➤ ----

---------- ৭৮-------

Chapter 61

I am not ashamed to call you brother/sister.

It was mid-morning. Underneath the shade of the tall papaya tree lay Tenzin, fast asleep. The whole area changed when **the Master descended with two of his angels.** [1]

Everyone and everything in the garden **bowed down**[2] as the Lord and his angels strolled through the garden. They walked past the sleeping Tenzin and sat on the stream's banks.

The two angels, Benin and Abinar, sat around the Lord. He looked at Benin and said, "Well?"

"Master, the **sanctuary**[3] I visited was amazing. The steward had turned it into a beautiful garden full of life, ten times bigger and better than the last time we visited."

He turned to the second angel, Abinar, who gave a similar report. "Master, the sanctuary was five times bigger and better than on our previous visit."

He asked them, "Are they according to **the pattern**[4] shown in the scriptures?"

Again, they reported glowingly, but they both added that there were minor deviations. Each steward had followed the scriptures' pattern but added their personal touch to the sanctuary.

He glanced around the garden and at the steward of this garden, Tenzin, fast asleep under the papaya tree. The garden looked neglected. The trees looked unkempt; the green grass was tall and, in places, trampled down.

---- ➤ ----

Bible (NKJV)	Bhagavad Gita
1 Genesis 18:1-2. Then the LORD appeared to him by the terebinth trees of Mamre as he was sitting in the tent door in the heat of the day. So he lifted his eyes and looked; behold, three men were standing by him, and when he saw them, he ran from the tent door to meet them and bowed to the ground.	**1** 8:20. Beyond this material world lays the invisible spiritual reality that cannot be destroyed. Spiritual reality will remain when this world is gone.

1 Genesis 18:1-2. Then the LORD appeared to him by the terebinth trees of Mamre as he was sitting in the tent door in the heat of the day. So he lifted his eyes and looked; behold, three men were standing by him, and when he saw them, he ran from the tent door to meet them and bowed to the ground.

2 Isaiah 55:12. "For you shall go out with joy, And be led out with peace; The mountains and the hills Shall break forth into singing before you, And all the trees of the field shall clap their hands.

3 Exodus 15:17. You will bring them in and plant them In the mountain of Your inheritance, In the place, O LORD, which You have made For Your dwelling, The sanctuary, O Lord, which Your hands have established.

3 Ezekiel 37:26-28. And I will make a covenant of peace with them, an everlasting covenant. I will give them their land, increase their numbers, and put my Temple among them forever. I will make my home among them. I will be their God, and they will be my people. And when my Temple is among them forever, the nations will know that I am the LORD, who

1 8:20. Beyond this material world lays the invisible spiritual reality that cannot be destroyed. Spiritual reality will remain when this world is gone.

2 11:21. All the hosts of Heaven and the cosmos tremble in fear and bow down before your throne. Saints with folded hands offer prayers and sing hymns, crying out peace to all.

3 18:56. Therefore, My devotees look after My creation as stewards under My protection. As a sign of My approval and grace, I permit such enlightened beings to stroll in the Heavenly realms and spiritual sanctuaries (My abode). I am preparing and refining them so that in the hereafter, they will play a significant role in My Kingdom: reconciling, restoring, and making all creation whole—no one thrives in My realm at the expense of another.

---X--

makes Israel holy."

[4] Exodus 25:9. "According to all that I show you, the pattern of the tabernacle and all its furnishings so that you can make it. [4b] Acts 7:44. "Our fathers had the tabernacle of witness in the wilderness, as He appointed, instructing Moses to make it according to the pattern that he had seen,

---X--

---------- ᙁ------

Chapter 62

Heir

In places, the stream was muddy. Overall, the site was neglected, but according to the pattern. There was no personal image of Tenzin. Following the scriptures, he **created the garden**[1] with the help of the people.

The Lord said, "Not perfect, but perfect where it matters. I see the work of a contrite and **humble**[2] spirit."

"Master," said the angel Benin, "shall we wake him up?"

The Lord shook his head. "On your next visit, tell the other stewards I am pleased."

They looked at Tenzin, slumped under the tree, and laughed.

The second angel said, "Lord, you gave him a special gift **(the mind of Christ)**,[3] to create, from a thought, energy, spiritual energy, atoms, and life forms. No previous prophet was called to learn to be a creator, a judge, a consoler, etc. or to be your joint **heir**[4]. You appointed him to be a steward over your sanctuary. A great privilege, and he sleeps in the middle of the day!"

The angel Benin woke Tenzin up. "Come, hurry. The Master requires you."

He got up, ran up to the Master, and bowed. "Sire, I apologise."

The Lord waved towards the garden. "**Report.**[5]"

"My Lord, I have looked after the garden. I apologise for its condition. I have tried to look after it according to your vision. I realise it is full of errors, and things are not as they should be. I have tried to stay true to the vision."

His lordship nodded. "It is one thing to have a gift and another to know how to harness its power. Call all the people. I want to hear from them.

---- ➤ ----

Bible (NKJV)	Bhagavad Gita
[1] John 14:12. "Most assuredly, I say to you, he who believes in Me, the works that I do he will also do; and more wondrous works than these he will do, because I go to My Father. [2] Isaiah 57:15. For thus says the High and Lofty One Who inhabits eternity, whose name is Holy: "I dwell in the high and holy place, With him who has a contrite and humble spirit, To revive the spirit of the humble, And to revive the heart of the contrite ones. [3] 1st Corinthians 2:16. But we have the mind of Christ. [4] Galatians 4:7. Therefore, you are no longer a slave but a son; if a son, then an heir of God through Christ. [5] Matthew 25:15. "And to one he gave five talents, to another two, and another one, to each according to his ability; and immediately he went on a journey. V 19 After a long time, the lord of those servants came and settled accounts with them. ---	[2] 2:40. This path is called Karma Yoga: the oneness of mind with Me through Action. Even a little spiritual advancement on this path will protect you from your greatest fear. ---------- ↬-------

Chapter 63

Leah

Tenzin blew the trumpet, and the entire congregation gathered. Benin questioned their leaders while Master listened, but no one found fault with Tenzin.

Then, the angel asked all the **animals**[1] to assemble before the Lord.

Leah, the rabbit, and her three siblings were there. They stood next to Tenzin. Their happy faces radiated their joy and gratitude to Tenzin for making them whole, compensating for their pain and suffering on Earth (Haringey).

Behind Leah stood the fox and his family, beaming with pleasure. The fox was reconciled with Leah, the rabbit he had killed in Haringey. Now, they were the best of friends. Again, no one found fault with Tenzin.

Next, the angel questioned the chief rock, which overlooked all the other **stones**[2]. Not a single stone found fault with Tenzin.

Looking at the Lord, the first angel said, "Master, his workmanship is shoddy, but no one finds fault with him, and he has been true to the pattern shown."

The Lord asked Tenzin, "What do you say?"

"Lord, their struggle with life and death on Earth allowed me to grow spiritually. I appreciate their trust and owe them gratitude for entrusting me to be their steward. I won't let them down."

The Master said, "I gave you a gift of salvation that kings and **prophets**[3] have sought and not been granted. I asked you to build me a spiritual **sanctuary**[4], the likes of which have never been made, one on Earth and one in a spiritual realm (Heaven)—a task no one on Earth has ever been called to do. ---- ➤ ----

Bible (NKJV)	Bhagavad Gita
[1] Genesis 2:19. Out of the ground, the LORD God formed every beast of the field and every bird of the air and brought them to Adam to see what he would call them. And whatever Adam called each living creature, that was its name.	[1] 11:16. Untold numbers of life forms on Earth and spiritual sanctuaries passed before me. I saw the beginning and end of all. You gave life and brought joy, pain and suffering into our lives, and in 'The Fullness of Time' (before The Day of The Lord), you made us whole (restored, made restitution) and wiped away all pain and suffering. You showed/proved that nothing thrives in the Universe at the expense of another. I comprehended your joy and sorrow from start to end.
[2] Luke 19:40. But He answered and said to them, "I tell you that if these should keep silent, the stones would immediately cry out.	
[3] Luke 10:24, "for I tell you that many prophets and kings have desired to see what you see, have not seen it, hear what you hear, and have not heard it."	[3] 9:33. Even kings and those of noble birth seek My attention. All are born in this transient world of sacrificial love, pain, suffering and joy. Therefore, engage in loving service to My creation and Me.
[4] Hebrews 8:5, who serve the copy and shadow of the heavenly things, as Moses was divinely instructed when he was about to make the tabernacle. For He said, "See that you make all things according to the pattern shown you on the mountain." [4b] 1st Peter 1:10 -16. This salvation was something even the prophets wanted to know more about when they prophesied about this gracious salvation prepared for you. They wondered what time or situation the Spirit of Christ within them was talking about when he told them in advance about Christ's suffering and his great	[4] 18:71. Anyone who listens, exercises faith and places his trust in Me will become free from sinful actions. Hereafter, he shall gain an eternal home in the spiritual sanctuaries where the pious dwell.

---- ➤ ---- |

glory afterwards. They were told that their messages were not for themselves <u>but for you.</u> ---x--	

---------- ֎------

Chapter 64

Eternal City

The Master said, "Soon, we will ask you to join us, Tenzin. We are building the walls of the coming Kingdom, atom by atom. We have long waited for a man worthy of laying the walls of the **eternal city**[1] with us. You shall walk among us in the city of your Lord God, you and your children's children."

"Lord, I am honoured," replied Tenzin.

"You, Tenzin, will continue to look after my interests in the **New Heaven**[2] and Earth for me. For the present, this is your Kingdom. You are undoing the pain and suffering we brought upon them on Earth. I leave it to you to make a **hundredfold restitution**[3] for their pain. The Holy Spirit will guide you and empower you."

He let the words sink in. The Lord turned to face him and smiled. "Don't call me Lord. Call me **Mōtā bhai**[4-M1]. Come, we can live in each other's visions as a family. Bapuji (Father) calls; we have work to do."

"Yes, Master."

The angels smiled and burst out into laughter. They all laughed together.

---- ➤ ----

Bible (NKJV)	Bhagavad Gita
[1] Revelation 21:1-2. Now I saw a New Heaven and Earth, for the first heaven and the first earth had passed away. Also, there was no more sea. Then I, John, saw the holy city, New Jerusalem, coming down out of heaven from God, prepared as a bride adorned for	[1,2] 4:9. Those who know My true nature and follow My teachings will take their rightful place in My eternal home upon leaving this material world. Where I am, they will be. [4-M1] Mota Bhai. (Elder/big brother – a term used in my mother tongue,

her husband.

[2] Matthew 19:29. And everyone who has left houses, brothers, sisters, father, mother, wife, children, or lands for My name's sake shall <u>receive a hundredfold</u> and inherit eternal life.

[3] Hebrews 2:11. The one who sanctifies and those who are sanctified have <u>one Father</u>. For this reason, Jesus is not ashamed to call them brothers and sisters.

---X-----

Gujarati, with respect for an elder brother, who is the head of the family in the father's absence). I am not ashamed to call you Nano Bhai (little brother)."

---- ➤ ----

---------- ᚸ------

Chapter 65

Tenzin, standing before the Council of Elders.

Daniel 11:35 Some wise shall fall, so that they may **be refined, purified[1]**, and cleansed, until the end, for there is still an interval until the time appointed.

The senior **Elder[2]** asked, "Tenzin, tell us, what is your vision? What are your aspirations?"

"A Universe where **Nothing gains[3]** at the expense of another." Replied Tenzin.

"How do you **refine silver[4]?**" asked the Elder.

"I was taught we use fire to refine silver and gold, but we make **good the earth[5], restore it**, make **restitution[6]**, and our Lord has **set a day[7]** when Earth (and its people), and the Lord can ask us to **account[8]** for our actions."

A second elder asked, "Gold and silver have one standard: purity. Is there a single **standard[9]** for all on Judgment Day?"

---- ➤ ----

Bible (NKJV)	Bhagavad Gita
[1] Daniel 11:35. Some of the wise shall fall, so that they may **be refined, purified[1]**, and cleansed, until the end, for there is still an interval until the time appointed.	[1,] 4:10. My followers taking refuge in My abode are set free from the slavery of fear and selfish attachment. Their greed, anger, and love are slowly refined, cleansed, purified, and sanctified in My presence.
[2] Revelation 4:4. Around the throne were twenty-four thrones, and on the thrones, I saw twenty-four elders sitting, clothed in white	[2] 10:6. The mighty seven sages (archangels, guardians of the Universe), the four great ancestors

robes; they had crowns of gold on their heads.

³ Exodus 20:15. "You shall <u>not steal</u>.

⁴ Zechariah 13:9. I will bring the one-third through the fire, <u>refine them</u> as <u>silver is refined</u>, And test them as gold is tested. They will call on My name, And I will answer them. I will say, 'These are My people; 'each one will say, 'The LORD is my God.' "

⁵ Isaiah 49:8. Thus says the LORD: "In an acceptable time I have heard You, And in the <u>day of salvation</u> I have helped You; I will preserve You and give You <u>As a covenant</u> to the people, To **restore the earth,** To cause them to inherit the desolate heritages;

⁶ Exodus 22:5. When someone causes a field or vineyard to be grazed over or lets livestock loose to feed in someone else's field, restitution shall be made from the best in the owner's field or vineyard.

⁷ Daniel 11:35. Some of the wise shall fall so that they may be <u>refined, purified, and cleansed, until the end</u>, for there is still an interval until the time appointed.

⁸ Romans 14:12. So, each of us shall give an <u>account</u> of himself to

(elders), and the fourteen Manus (ancestors of all humanity) came from Me - born from My mind. All beings populating the various continents, planets and universes descend from them.~~ Together, they form <u>twenty-five Elders</u> of the Universe.

⁴ 6:45. These disciplined people in their new realms progress further as their selfish desires <u>are purified</u>. Moving upwards towards higher realms, they eventually attain the seventh Heaven, the supreme goal of all.

⁵ 18:56. My devotees look <u>after My creation</u> as stewards under my protection. As a sign of my approval and grace, I permit such enlightened beings <u>to stroll in the heavenly realms</u> and spiritual sanctuaries (My abode). I am preparing and refining them so that in the hereafter, they will play a significant role in My Kingdom.

⁷ 2:18. Your body is temporary and may perish in this conflict. Your Spirit (soul and Atman) will continue its journey until the 'Day of The Lord' (Judgement, Evaluation Day) and perhaps beyond. Therefore, I call upon you to fight.

⁸ 11:32. Krishna: I am time, and I am the destroyer. All the ungodly gathered on Judgment Day <u>will perish</u>. However, good, godly,

God. [9] 1st Peter 4:5. They will give an <u>account</u> to Him who is ready to judge the living and the dead.--**x**-- ---**x**--	honest, decent people will survive and continue to live. ---**x**--

---------- 9)------

Chapter 66

A greater hand guides your destiny

Tenzin thought for a while. In spiritual terms, he was just a child, and this knowledge was beyond him.

The second Elder said, "To refine gold, we need fire. To refine life, we need competition, in other words, evolution, unfairness, and inequalities. A dog-eat-dog world."

Tenzin replied, "Competition is not perfect. It is a process where one often thrives at the expense of another by stealing and killing, contrary to moral law. (You shall not steal from man, animals, or anything in the universe.)"

"Do you know of any other way?"

"No."

The Holy Spirit lifted him into the **past**[10], and he stood with the Elders. A long time ago, the Elders and the Lord had met to discuss the pain of the universe. They had **formulated a plan**[11] to deal with it and free the universe from its stranglehold. He had the gist of their plan. But Tenzin's mind was clouded with worries about his current 'patch'. Things were not going his way. He was troubled. One of the Elders turned to him.

"We will take care of it. Rest in peace. A greater hand **guides**[12] your destiny."

The Lord added, "We want you to grasp what we are about to share with you. You must have a firm understanding of the matter we will reveal to you." ---- ➤ ----

Bible (NKJV)	Bhagavad Gita
[10] 1st Corinthians 2:7. But we speak the wisdom of God in a mystery,	[10, 11] Chapter 11:7. In My body, you will perceive the entire cosmic cycle

the <u>hidden</u> wisdom which God ordained <u>before the ages</u> for our glory,

[11] Revelation 13:8, the <u>Lamb slain</u> from the foundation of the world.

[12] [Kate Adin's Tenet-2]. "You are unique. There is a greater power that guides your path. Everything made and created is set up for you (for those like you). Some things, some mysteries, are hidden until the fullness of time called 'Awaranar'.

---X--

passing before your eyes. Whatever you want to see, the past, present, future, **creation** (*refer to the end of the book*), Earth, and spiritual sanctuaries will flash before you. You will find answers to questions regarding the terms 'In the Fullness of Time' and 'The end of all material and spiritual realms' and your purpose on Earth and in the heavenly realms. The mysteries of the Universe are available to all brave enough to seek them.

[12] 4:3. To a selected few, I revealed My existence and plans for eternity (past, present, and future worlds to come). You are My friend and devotee, and in due time, as you gain My favour, I will **reveal*** these mysteries and explain your role here on Earth, in the spiritual world, and in the far distant future. You and other trusted devotees will build My material and spiritual kingdoms in this world and hereafter and walk beside Me in all My realms. I will guide and teach you all as a Father.

---X--

---------- ૧૧------

Chapter 67

Divine gift

The second Elder said, "We are aware of the pain of all **living things in the universe.**[1] We need beings who understand, have experienced pain and suffering, and are willing to work with us to bring healing to all who need it. We want them to be filled (**baptised**[2]) with the Holy Spirit with their informed consent.

"The ability to **empathise**[3] with someone suffering is one of life's greatest gifts. The ability to reach out and help someone overcome their problem is an even more excellent gift.

"The strength and ability to carry weak, frail, venerable, and frightened people across the troubled bridge; this is a **divine gift**[4]."

"Lord, is this a good time? I am weak and vulnerable. It would be better to ask when I am well and of sound mind." (**Zak's Tenet**[5])

"Yes, we will wait."

The senior Elder said, "Our core value is to try to undo the **pain**[6] of the universe and bring all to maturity and **perfection**[7]. Think about it. We want you to be part of it (undo, reconcile, restore, heal, make whole)."

---- ➤ ----

Bible (NKJV)	Bhagavad Gita
[1] Romans 8:22, For we know that the whole creation groans and labours with birth pangs together until now.	[1] 8:16. Every person and creature on Earth is subject to pleasure, pain, and suffering. However, those attaining My Abode acquire the strength to overcome their pain and suffering.
[2] Mr 1:8 He will baptize you with the Holy Spirit."	[3] 6:32. People who see equality in all beings and creatures have profound empathy for all and respond to their
[3] Hebrews 4:15. This High Priest of	

ours understands <u>our weaknesses</u>, for he faced the same testings we do, yet he did not sin.

[46] 1st Peter 4:11. Whoever speaks must do so as one speaking the very words of God; whoever serves must do so with the strength that God supplies, so that God may be glorified in all things through Jesus Christ. To him belong the glory and the power forever and ever. Amen.

[5] [Zak's Tenet; - Consent. *"Guide you with my eye. I respect your privacy. I will reason with you and not press or persuade you without your consent."*

[6] Colossians 1:20, and by Him to <u>reconcile</u> all things to Himself, whether on earth or in heaven, having made peace through the blood of His cross.

[7] Hebrews 6:1 Therefore, leaving the discussion of the elementary principles of Christ, let us go on to <u>perfection</u>, not laying the foundation of repentance from dead works again and of faith toward God, ---X--

joy and sorrow as their own. They have attained one of the higher states of spiritual union with Me and My creation.

[4] 8:11. I am impartial. All Holy Scriptures reveal that those who worship Me are sacrificial, relinquishing selfishness and materialism. They seek to <u>promote the welfare</u>, interest, and happiness of others and Mine. Such people find salvation and eternal life in Me.

[6] 13:9 They comprehend the Lord's creative plan for the cosmos, their position in this plan, and the reason for joyful and <u>painful lessons of life:</u> the joy of family, friends, birth, suffering, disease, old age, and death. All these things are encountered in life and <u>used for spiritual growth</u> and advancement. Hence, they seek and are willing to learn from a spiritual master as they journey along this path.

---X--

-

--------- 9?------

Chapter 68

Clear conscience

The Lord, two angels, and Tenzin were standing on the shores of the lake. It was a warm day, and the animals were resting in the background, chewing the cud.

The Lord asked Tenzin, "Why did you choose to follow me?"

"I am not clear about my reasons."

Lord, "Others chose the simple path, but you chose the harder path. Here, in the sanctuary, you insisted on learning to **form/create**[1] every atom, grain of sand, leaf, and tree. With the help of the Holy Spirit, you studied and brought back to life every living thing that was once on your patch on Earth. You sat with them, **shared their pain**[2], consoled and **healed**[3] them and made restitution for their pain and suffering on Earth. Why?"

"Lord, if I may speak freely, it was the right thing to do. I am grateful for your help **(salvation**[4]**)** and the resources you provided. I couldn't have done it without your help."

"But why?" asked the angel.

"To have a clear **conscience**[5]. I believe nothing in the universe has a right to thrive at the expense of another. On Earth, I had little choice. In the sanctuary, I chose to make amends to all. I chose a different path from the others."

The angel asked, "How do you feel now?" ---- ➤ ----

Bible (NKJV)	Bhagavad Gita
[1] John 14:12, "Most assuredly, I say to you, he who believes in Me, the works that I do he will also do; and	[1] 4:33. The primary purpose of creation is the spiritual advancement of all, and the secondary purpose is

more wondrous works than these he will do, because I go to My Father.

[2] Romans 8:17, and if children, then heirs of God and joint heirs with Christ, if indeed we suffer with Him, that we may also be glorified together.

[3] Luke 4:18, "The Spirit of the LORD is upon Me Because He has anointed Me To preach the gospel to the poor; He has sent Me to heal the brokenhearted, To proclaim liberty to the captives And recovery of sight to the blind, To set at liberty those who are oppressed;

[4] Psalms 40:10, I have not hidden Your righteousness within my heart; I have declared Your faithfulness and Your salvation; I have not concealed Your lovingkindness and Your truth From the great assembly.

[5] Acts 24:16. "This being so, I always strive to have a conscience without offence toward God and men. 1Ti 3:9, holding the mystery of the faith with a pure conscience

---x--

sharing My Eternal plan with those who seek it with all their hearts, minds, and strengths. Signs and wonders accompany sacred knowledge and are not revealed to those who place little value on it. Sacrifices made to promote spiritual understanding are better than material offerings. The fruit of spreading spiritual knowledge in the community is love, joy, peace, longsuffering, gentleness, goodness, righteousness, and truth. The fruit of righteousness is sown in peace by those who make peace.

[2] 9:27-28. Whatever you do, the food you eat, the help you offer others and the suffering you endure, do it as an offering to Me. In this way, you will be free from the bondage to duty and, from its result, both pleasant and painful. With your mind fixed on Me, you liberate yourselves from material existence to serve My creation (all life forms and humanity) and Me.

[3] 3:10. The Supreme Lord of creation continued: At the beginning of creation, I blessed creation and set in motion the principle of selfless, sacrificial service to promote the welfare, interest, and happiness of all creation. Thus, through this selfless service, all creation would be prosperous and fruitful and fulfil its desires.

[4] 8:11. I am impartial. All Holy

Scriptures reveal that those who worship Me are sacrificial, relinquishing selfishness and materialism. They seek to promote the welfare, interest, and happiness of others and Mine. Such people find salvation and eternal life in Me.

[5] 16:1. The Supreme Lord: Arjuna, you must nurture these qualities. Learn to overcome fear and walk in purity of heart and emotions. Study the Scriptures and grow in spiritual knowledge. Be compassionate and charitable, and have a clear conscience.

---X--

--------- ५१------

Chapter 69

What inspires me to live?

Tenzin replied, "I feel good now. I do what I believe to be the right thing. Many times, I have thought about the question of life. What is the point? I still struggle with it. Our Lord exists; He has no choice but to live and create. We can choose to live or die. We have something he does not have: this choice. When I first came here, I just wanted to lie down and **sleep for good[1]**, but with your help, I dealt with many issues. I am sorry if I was a disappointment to you." There were tears in his eyes.

Lord said, "Come. I will show you things that make me want **to live and create[2]**. Walk with us."

Tenzin replied, "Lord, my spirit is tired. I saw the terrible price all the creatures of **Earth paid[3]** for your creation. I sat in the sanctuary, listened to their tales, and shared their pain and anguish. Your spirit helped me understand them better—all the **pain and suffering they endured.[4]** My spirit is leaden with all that pain, and I bear a heavy burden. This knowledge brought me joy, as well as a lot of grief. I ask myself, "What was it all for?"

---- ➤ ----

Bible (NKJV)	Bhagavad Gita
[1] Psalms 90:10. The length of our lives is seventy years, and if by reason of strength, it is eighty years, yet the best of them brings toil and sorrow; for they pass quickly, and we fly away.	[3, 4] 8:16. Every person and creature on Earth is subject to pleasure, pain, and suffering. However, those attaining My Abode acquire the strength to overcome their pain and suffering.
[2] John 6:27. "Do not labour for the food which perishes, but for the food which endures to everlasting life, which the Son of Man will give	---X--

you because God the Father has set His seal on Him."

[3, 4] Romans 8:221-22, the creation will also be delivered from the bondage of corruption into the glorious liberty of the children of God, for we know that the whole creation groans and labours with birth pangs together until now.

---X--

Chapter 70

Suffering is part of all living things

The Lord replied, "God needed you and bought your redemption with a heavy price so that you could understand the longing in His heart for a family, a place to **dwell**[1] and make a home."

Tenzin replied, "Lord, I mean no disrespect or ingratitude. You have done a lot for me, but if I may speak freely. My redemption is valuable to you, but I place no value on it. I am nothing; it is how I feel."

The Lord said, "Walk with us. It is not a command but a request. Join us."

"Lord, I need to rest. My spirit is exhausted. I have seen and felt too much pain and suffering of others and my own."

The angel Benin said, "Brother Tenzin, the Lord wanted you and us to learn the importance of sacrificial **love**[2]. He tried to confer this to us so that we could deliver care and healing. Not just empathy but also the ability to meet the needs of all living things. To talk to them, reassure, inspire, and make them whole, so they are in a better and stronger position to cope with their problems in life."

The second angel, Abinar, said, "You learnt that **suffering**[3] is part of all living things. It is a reminder of the cost to others for your spiritual growth. Their suffering paid for it. You owe more than gratitude to the universe and those who have suffered. You should take this second chance to make restitution to them."

Benin added, "The **first-born**[4] in Christ always owes gratitude for the **perfection of their salvation**[13] to those who were victims of their perfection.

"There is an eternal obligation by the firstborn in Christ to all living things. The Lord God goes to great lengths in the sanctuaries to make restitution, through the firstborn, to all living things.

"The firstborn can then have a clear conscience that the Lord paid for their perfection. The firstborn will be allowed to enter and exit the city gates. The second-born, the latecomers, will live outside the **city gates[5]**."

The second angel, Abinar, said, "Humans think love and loss are unique to them. This is not the case. All living things feel love, loss, pain, and grief in distinct ways.

"The human brain has the potential to uncover the universe with the help of the indwelling Holy Spirit. Your spirit can be bigger than everything contained in the universe. The cosmos is a mathematically **balanced entity.[6]**"

The Master stretched forth his arm before Tenzin, and the powers of the cosmos passed by: incredible energy, resources, and the will to undo the pain and suffering of all.

Master said, "It is nothing. It came from a thought, a tear, and a singularity into the cosmos. Creating a universe is simple, but bringing a free moral life form to perfection (to God's standard) is **incredibly difficult[7]**."

---- ➤ ----

Bible (NKJV)	Bhagavad Gita
[1] Revelation 21:3. I heard a loud voice from heaven saying, "Behold, the tabernacle of God is with men, and He will dwell with them, and they shall be His people. God Himself will be with them and be their God.	[2] 3:9. Selfish action imprisons a person in the material world. Therefore, always act selflessly, performing your duties as a service to humanity and Me without thinking of personal benefit.
[2] 1st John 4:12. No one has seen God at any time. God abides in us if we love one another, and His love is perfected in us.	[3] 8:16. Every person and creature on Earth is subject to pleasure, pain, and suffering. However, those attaining My Abode acquire the strength to overcome their pain and suffering.

[3] Hebrews 5:8, though He was a Son, He learned obedience from the things He suffered.

[12] Romans 8:29. For whom He foreknew, He also predestined to be conformed to the image of His son, that He might be the firstborn among many brethren.

[4] Hebrews 6:9. Even though we speak in this way, beloved, we are confident of better things, such as things that belong to salvation.

[5] Revelation 11:2. "But leave out the court which is outside the temple, and do not measure it, for it has been given to the Gentiles. And they will tread the holy city underfoot for forty-two months.

[6] Hari's cube is a ten-dimensional cube (a Universe model) that equals 777 or 108 at every corner.

[7] *Author: - I understood what he meant, though I have no idea how to convey this. It is a form of understanding, an appreciation of a priceless object's value and cost. One perfect life form is worth more than the universe to the Lord God. Many more life forms are a bonus to him.*

To some, it may not make sense. A lonely being with all the universe's resources at his disposal and no one to share it with lives in a self-

[5] 8:11. I am impartial. All Holy Scriptures reveal that those who worship Me are sacrificial, relinquishing selfishness and materialism. They seek to promote the welfare, interest, and happiness of others and Mine. Such people find salvation and eternal life in Me.

[7] Hari's cube is a ten-dimensional cube (a Universe model) that sums up 777 or 108 at every corner

---x--

created Hell (not a place but a condition of the mind and spirit). God knows what it feels like; he has lived there for billions of years before creation.

For billions of years, God lived in isolation and loneliness and was deprived of conversation. Creation, before he created humans and animals, gave him joy. He wanted to share this joy, so he made life to share all he had with living entities, giving him greater pleasure.

A spiritual baby smiling back at him brings Him a lot of pleasure. The spiritual sanctuaries are the second phase of creation.

Heaven is a place, a state of mind, and the joy of sharing life with all as equals.

---X--

--------- ϟ------

Chapter 71

Free will has a cost

The Master said, "We have invested so much in you, yet you do not choose to cross the bridge with us?"

Tenzin just sat there, gazing into the distance. He had no long-term purpose, no meaning to his life, except to see those under his care live their lives until the **fullness of their time**[1].

A cloud of sadness hung over the sanctuary. They felt his sadness.

As the Master and the angels **ascended to heaven**[2], tears were in their eyes.

The angel Abinar said, "Master, we have to find a way. We invested so much in this man, who scaled the heights of the heavens and beyond, and now he slides out of our hand."

Lord replied, "We can only try to reason; we **cannot persuade**[3]. (Zak's Tenet.) So near and yet so far."

"Master, he is one of those rare people who dared to question the Heavenly Father about the wisdom of **creation**[4]. He has perceived to a high level the Father's mind and comprehended the cost of pain and suffering to the Father, us, and all creatures.

"Moreover, in His mercy, the Heavenly Father has responded to the **tears**[5] of that 10-year-old child, now an adult. It would tear apart our Father's heart to lose one who has wrestled fearlessly with him. We have to reconcile them." ---- ➤ ----

Bible (NKJV)	Bhagavad Gita
[1] Ephesians 1:10. That in the dispensation of the <u>fullness of the</u>	[1] 2:18. Your body is temporary and may perish in this conflict. Your Spirit (soul and Atman) will continue its

times He might gather together in all things in Christ, both in heaven and which are on earth — in Him.

[2] Genesis 28:12. Then he dreamed, and behold, a ladder was set up on the earth, and its top reached heaven; the angels of God were ascending and descending on it.

[3] Psalms 32:8. I will instruct and teach you how you should go and guide you with My eye.

[4] Romans 8:20. For the creation was subjected to futility, not willingly, but because of Him who subjected it in hope;

[5] Isaiah 25:8. He will swallow up death forever, And the Lord GOD will wipe away tears from all faces; The rebuke of His people He will take away from all the earth; For the LORD has spoken

---X--

journey until the 'Day of The Lord' (Judgement, Evaluation Day) and perhaps beyond. [3] 12:13-14. The ones I love are free from malice towards all living beings and are friendly, compassionate, kind, tolerant, and considerate. They gladly share their knowledge, wisdom, and all they have. They do not force or impose it on others. They do not think of themselves as proprietors but as stewards of mine. They are free of false egos and are equal in happiness and distress. They are always satisfied, content, self-controlled, at peace with others and themselves, engaged with all their heart and mind in My eternal purpose and plan*. Such persons are precious to Me.

[4] 2:50. Devotional service aims to free you from self and attachment to the material world. Secondly, it lifts you into My presence and enlightens you with My purpose for creation. Thirdly, to instil in you a sense of oneness with all life.

[4] 3:10. The Supreme Lord of Creation continued: At the beginning of creation, I blessed creation and set in motion the principle of selfless, sacrificial service to promote the welfare, interest, and happiness of all creation. Thus, through this selfless service, all creation would be prosperous and fruitful, fulfilling its desires. --------- ᷍------

Chapter 72

To account

The Master said, "Yes. He has an incredible grasp of the value of life and the length and **breadth**[1] the Heavenly Father is willing to go to achieve his ultimate goal for a family. He also understood the moral duty to make creation whole for its pain and **suffering**[2]."

The angel Benin said, "He is the first one who undertook to **account**[3] for every thought, string of energy, atom, leaf, tree, and living thing in his patch and make **restitution**[4] to all. He felt their pain and suffering. It spurred him to **remind**[5] you and the father to make all things whole again (to restore, reconcile make whole). No one has done that before."

The Lord said, "He is fragile. The weight on his shoulders could destroy him."

Benin, "Surely our father knows the future. He has willed that Tenzin comes out well."

Lord: "I don't think our father wants to know the future. It is something he chose to leave open. He respects free will. He is willing to invest and let Tenzin slip out of his hand. Perfect **love**[6] allows a person to walk away. It comes with no strings attached. Our Father has chosen to honour free will; hence, no outcome is predestined."

(King David's Tenet:

[< Father's love for his child>]. "I understand the pain and sorrow in your heart. When a father leads his child through the valley of death, he has a reason and a good purpose. He has shed more tears than you because his loving hand has allowed your pain to continue. His motives, his intentions, are for your betterment and growth. Your tears inflict deep wounds on him, yet he has chosen this path for both of you. Love comes at a high cost. Moral character and compassion are refined in the fires of grief, suffering, and joy, just as gold is refined in the fire."

Benin said, "He loves us; he loves our Heavenly Father. So, what can

separate[7] him from us?"

The Lord replied, "**The desire to live[8]**. He may choose to pass away. He is a broken man."

"Why doesn't the father intervene?"

"Father cannot force someone to live."

"Why?"

"Maybe to make us appreciate the value of each life. We have gone to all lengths and breadths to bring Tenzin to this high spiritual growth level, with no certainty, while he exercises his free will. Nothing can separate us from him, but he can walk away, and there is nothing we can do."

The angel Abinar added, "We could try to persuade him, twist his arm a bit." He smiled.

The Lord said, "We can reason with him with his consent. Nothing more. (Zak's Tenet.) Losing him would be an immense loss to us. It is like selling everything we have to buy the **field[9]** with the biggest diamond in the world. We work for months and years and finally extract the diamond. Our joy is great for a season."

The second angel, Benin, said, "Only to discover the diamond chose to disintegrate when we extracted it. The price of free will."

Abinar added, "Wounds heal; spiritual scars remain. This maketh a saint."

"Or destroys a saint," added the Master.

"Such is life," added Abinar   ---- ➤ ----

Bible (NKJV)	Bhagavad Gita
[1] Ephesians 3:18-19. May be able to comprehend with all the saints the <u>width, length, depth,</u> and	[1-9,] 11:16. Untold numbers of life forms on Earth and spiritual sanctuaries passed before me. I saw

height to know the <u>love of Christ</u> which passes knowledge; that you may be filled with all the fullness of God.

2 Romans 8:22, For we know that the whole <u>creation groans and labours</u> with birth pangs together until now.

3 1st Corinthians 4:1. Let a man <u>consider us</u> servants of Christ and <u>stewards of the mysteries</u> of God.

4 Colossians 1:20, And, having made peace through the blood of his cross, by him to <u>reconcile</u> all things unto himself; I say, whether they be things on earth or in heaven.

5 Habakkuk 1:2, O LORD, <u>how long shall I cry</u>, And You will not hear. Even cry out to You, "Violence!" And You will not save.

6 1st John 4:18. There is no fear in <u>love</u>, but <u>perfect love</u> casts out fear; fear has to do with punishment, and whoever fears has not reached perfection in <u>love</u>.

7 Romans 8:35, who will <u>separate us</u> from the love of Christ? Will hardship, distress, persecution, famine, nakedness, peril, or sword?

8 Luke 4:4, But Jesus answered him, saying, "It is written, 'Man

the beginning and end of all. You gave life and brought joy, pain and <u>suffering</u> into our lives, and in 'The Fullness of Time' (before The Day of The Lord), you <u>made us whole</u> (restored, made restitution) and <u>wiped away</u> all pain and <u>suffering</u>. You showed/proved that nothing thrives in the Universe at the expense of another. I comprehended your joy and sorrow from start to end.

In your first thought, I saw my name chosen with great care, written in your Eternal Books, sealed by <u>your loving tears</u>. I saw your excellent plan for me on Earth, in the spiritual sanctuary, and I beheld the very last thought of mine before the end of all creation.

All I saw had a beginning and an end. Yet, you have no beginning, middle, or end. You are The Lord of creation; the cosmos and my life rest in your hands.

---X--

shall not live by <u>bread alone,</u> but by every word of God.' "

[9] Matthew 13:44, "Again, the kingdom of heaven is <u>like treasure hidden in a field,</u> which a man found and hid; and for joy, he sells all that he has and buys that field.

"I will gladly sacrifice my life to have lived for a year, a month, like Sam or Tenzin. I would honour their memory by making the most of my remaining life worthwhile in doing well towards others and serving my Lord.

"A month, a day, a moment's intensity of love could be far more sustaining than a long, mundane, loveless life." H p

---X--

--------- ᕱᕱ-------

Chapter 73

Festival of celebration

Stefan came up to the girls. They greeted him.

"Come," he said, "we have to go to the orchard and collect fruit, berries, and Mocca (a range of vegetables, some sweet and others spicy)."

"Why?" asked Kwan-yin. "We have enough here for our needs."

Stefan replied, "It's not for us. All of us have to bring enough food to last a week. Soon, it will be time for the Festival of **Remembrance**[1].

Kwan-yin, "We will collect the fruit first and then look for Mocca."

Sam said, "Collecting fruit will be easy, but finding Mocca will be difficult. It only grows in certain places in thick woodlands."

Stefan: "I agree, it is going to be difficult. We must collect enough to last a week, and there will be many people to feed."

Kwan-yin asked, "Why do we have the Festival of **Remembrance**[2]?"

"It is a festival where we meet other members of our sanctuary. Besides food, we share stories about our lives on **Earth**[3]. And it is a time to **thank**[4] the Lord for bringing us to this safe, secure, **peaceful land**[5].

"We learn from each other, and it helps us bond with one another and our Lord. This is our **home**[6]. We are protected here, looked after, and loved. We care for and delight in our neighbours, animals, and surroundings. We have chosen to live in **peace**[7] and harmony with all in our sanctuary.

"We chose Brother Tenzin to guide us to be our spiritual parent. We can leave anytime, but we have decided to remain here.

---- ➤ ----

Bible (NKJV)	Bhagavad Gita
1 Daniels 8:18, "And you shall remember the LORD your God, for it is He who gives you the power to get wealth, that He may establish His covenant which He swore to your fathers, as it is this day.	**1** 8:28. Study the scripture, give selfless service to others, live modestly, and give to the poor. This selfless duty to others and devotion to My teachings will guide you to your real spiritual home, My abode.
2 1st Chronicles 16:15. Remember His covenant forever, The word which He commanded, for a thousand generations. Isaiah 46:9 Remember the former things of old, For I am God, and there is no other; I am God, and there is none like Me,	**2** 14:14. Those who die in the mode of consistent goodness elevate to the purer, higher, holy places in the sanctuaries where the sages live.
3 Ezekiel 36:24. "For I will take you from among the nations (Earth), gather you out of all countries and bring you into your own land.	**3, 4, 5** 18:56. My devotees look after My creation as stewards under my protection. As a sign of my approval and grace, I permit such enlightened beings to stroll in the heavenly realms and spiritual sanctuaries. I am preparing and refining them so that in the hereafter, they will play a significant role in My Kingdom.
4 1st Chronicles 29:13. "Our God, We thank You And praise Your glorious name.	**5** 6:41. When people who have accepted Me die, they go to a spiritual realm where the righteous live (reborn, metamorphosed in sanctuaries). Whenever My devotees pass away into the hereafter, they leave behind a legacy of love, kindness, justice, and fairness, having enriched the lives of others.
5 Joshua 1:13. "Remember the word which Moses the servant of the LORD commanded you, saying, 'The LORD your God is giving you rest and is giving you this land.'	
6 Deuteronomy 30:4. "If any of you are driven out to the farthest parts under heaven, from there the LORD your God will gather you, and from there He will bring you.	**6** 11:16. Untold numbers of life forms on Earth and spiritual sanctuaries passed before me. I saw the beginning and end of all. You gave life and brought joy, pain and suffering into our lives, and in 'The Fullness of
7 Deuteronomy 27:7. "You shall	

offer <u>peace</u> offerings, and shall eat there, and rejoice before the LORD your God.

---X--

Time' (before The Day of The Lord), you made us whole (restored, made restitution) and wiped away all pain and suffering. You showed/proved that nothing thrives in the Universe at the expense of another. I comprehended your joy and sorrow from start to end.

In your first thought, I saw my name chosen with great care, written in your Eternal Books, sealed by your loving tears. I saw your excellent plan for me on Earth, in the spiritual sanctuary, and I beheld the very last thought of mine before the end of all creation.

---X--

--------- ५५------

Chapter 74

Remembrance of grief

"Look around the sanctuary. **All the things[1]** in it wish us well. This sanctuary has put extra effort into producing the best fruit and Mocca to help us celebrate the festival.

"All things here work together for **the good[2]** of us all. It is time to be happy and to rejoice with one another. It is time to thank one another for our contributions to the sanctuary—a time to **thank our Heavenly Father[3]** for his blessings."

Kwan-yin said, "I am so excited to meet others and share their experiences."

"Me too," added Sam. "I want to hear their stories. I want this to be the best festival I've ever attended."

They collected **plenty of fruit[4]** from the **orchard[5]** and brought it to a big barn they had built, making many more trips until it was almost full.

Stefan said, "Now comes the hard part: the search for Mocca. I hope the animals have left some for us. I bet they're out in the woods searching for it. They look fat."

On the way to the woodland, Sam asked Stefan, "What happens after the festival?"

"We have another festival for a week."

"What kind? I hope it's another nice one."

"It is a week of **remembrance of grief [6].**"

"That is an odd festival to have."

Stefan nodded. "It will be a period of sadness. During the Grief Festival, the sanctuary is transformed. The sky will lose its brightness; the trees will shed their leaves, the fruit will drop off the trees, and the Mocca will grow dull. There will be no music in the air.

"The sanctuary will begin to look like Earth. All the fruit, vegetables, and Mocca will lose their **sweetness**[7] and flavour. The water will lose its clarity and sparkle. Everything will feel and look like life on Earth, albeit without illness.

"We live as if we were on Earth for a week. It's a reminder of our past and heightens our appreciation of the good things in this sanctuary. It teaches us to appreciate and thank the Lord and the Elders for their kindness to us."

The two women nodded in agreement.

Sam smiled. "Yes, taking things for granted is easy until we face hardship."

Kwan-yin murmured, "We all do it all the time."

---- ➤ ----

Bible (NKJV)	Bhagavad Gita
[1-2] Romans 8:28, We know that all things work together for good to those who love God and are called according to his purpose. [3] Jeremiah 30:19. Then out of them shall proceed thanksgiving And the voice of those who make merry; I will multiply them, and they shall not diminish; I will also glorify them, and they shall not be small. [4] Ezekiel 36:30, And I will multiply	[1, 2, 3] 3:10. **The Supreme Lord** of creation continued: At the beginning of creation, I blessed creation and set in motion the principle of selfless, sacrificial service to promote the welfare, interest, and happiness of all creation. Thus, through this selfless service, all creation would be prosperous and fruitful, fulfilling its desires. [6] 9:3. Those who reject My holy scriptures' teachings (sacred

the fruit of your trees and the increase of your fields so that you never need again bear the reproach of famine among the nations.

⁵ Deuteronomy 11:12, "a land for which the LORD your God cares; the eyes of the LORD your God are always on it, from the beginning to the end of the year.

⁶ Psalms 143:5, I remember the days of old, I think about all your deeds, I meditate on the works of your hands.

⁷ Jeremiah 4:27, For thus says the LORD: "The whole land shall be desolate, Yet I will not make a complete end.

---X--

teachings given to various nations, races, and tribes) are walking away from their place in My eternal spiritual home. They will pass from physical death to the spiritual realm appropriate to their nature and then pass away into their final demise.

---X--

--------- ᛩᛮ------

Chapter 75

Tanza, Ka-ark

The four of them sat in a circle a few paces away from the others. Sam asked Tenzin, "You once said there would be a New Jerusalem and Heaven after **Judgement Day.**[1]"

Tenzin replied, "You mean the **Holy City**[2]?"

"Yes, what will lie beyond New Jerusalem?" Sam asked.

Kwan-yin remarked, "I, too, would be interested in knowing. I thought the Eternal City was the final destination of the saints?"

Tenzin thought for a minute. "Well," he said, "enlightened spirits have their own beliefs, which vary from person to person. No one I know claims to have the **absolute truth.**[3]"

"What about the Elders and our Lord?" Sam asked.

"Let's just say they have their **aspirations for the future**[4]."

Stefan said, "I would like to know what you believe."

"I can only tell you of my experience. I am unsure if it was a real experience or a vision." Tenzin paused. "I will be back in a little while."

He returned with one of his **diaries**[5] and glanced at his writing.

"Beyond the Eternal City, I travelled into the future, when life in a sanctuary, the Judgement Day, and our life in the Sacred City (Zion, the Golden City) will have passed.

"I was thinking beyond even that. This is towards the **end of time**[6], beyond the limits of our knowledge. As I said, my beliefs formed after I had a vision. I think some beings will continue beyond the Golden City."

Stefan asked, "Why some and not all?"

"In due time, I will explain, but not now. Let me tell you what lies beyond the city. It is a very different place. No words can describe this region, so I will only use the language and terms you can comprehend.

"Beyond the City lies a steep valley, and on the other side lies an area I call Tanza. To get to Tanza, one has to cross the valley.

"Few are those brave enough to venture beyond the city gates and enter the valley. Very few cross the valley, climb the cliff at the other end, and reach Tanza."

"What makes the journey so difficult?" asked Sam.

"It is a lonely journey. It is also a test of the person's determination and will. The Master says, [**Sue Anne's Tenet 2**], "Only those who have the will to empty the ocean with the palm of their hand manage to get across."

Sam said, "Tell us what happened to you when you reached Tanza in your vision. Everything there must have been different, scary, and lonely."

"Tanza was a bleak, isolated, barren area where nothing seemed to survive for long unless it had some unknown ability or energy. It is outside time and space. In Tanza, God or the cosmos only exists in people's minds and imaginations."

"Is that true?" Sam asked.

"For some, it may be."

"Go on. Tell us about Tanza." ---- ➤ ----

Bible (NKJV)	Bhagavad Gita
[1] Revelation 21:1, I saw a <u>new heaven and a new earth</u>: for the	*Cosmic Cycle: Mysteries of the universe*

first heaven and the first earth were passed away; there was no more sea.

² Revelation 21:2, Then I, John, saw the holy city, New Jerusalem, coming down out of heaven from God, prepared as a bride adorned for her husband.

³ 1st Corinthians 13:12, For now, we see in a mirror, dimly, but then face to face. Now I know in part, but I shall know just as I am known.

⁴ Revelation 21:5. Then He who sat on the throne said, "Behold, I make all things new."

⁵ Proverbs 7:3. Bind them on your fingers; Write them on the tablet of your heart.

⁶ Daniel 8:17. So he came near where I stood, and when he came I was afraid and fell on my face; but he said to me, "Understand, son of man, that the vision refers to the time of the end." Da 12:4 But thou, O Daniel, shut up the words, and seal the book, even to the time of the end: many shall run to and fro, and knowledge shall be increased. Da 12:9 And he said, Go thy way, Daniel: for the words are closed up and sealed till the end. --
-X--

[1-6] 11:7-8. In My body, you will perceive the whole cycle of the cosmos pass before your eyes. Whatever you want to see, the past, present, future, Creation, earth, and Spiritual sanctuaries will flash before you. You will find answers to questions regarding the terms 'in the fullness of time' and 'the end of all material and spiritual worlds' and your purpose on earth and in the heavenly realms. The mysteries of the universe are available to all brave enough to seek them.

[1-6] 11:8. Humans cannot see spiritual things with physical eyes. However, they can receive spiritual insight and vision from Me. I grant such knowledge *(Gita 7:2)* and wisdom to spiritually hungry people with the courage and tenacity to wait upon Me and claim them.

---X--

Chapter 76

Part II, Tanza

Tenzin replied, "It is challenging to convey a spiritual experience. Sometimes, there are no words to describe it. Perhaps the best way to tell you about my experience is to say it in story form.

"This is my story. Soon after I reached Tanza, I discarded my crowns. I wandered in Tanza for a long time. Then, I came across a warrior priest who was from another faith. He had seen me discard the crowns. He was lost, so he followed me from afar. After a while, I stopped and waited. He came up to me."

"Sir," he asked, "why have you discarded your **crowns?**[1] These are much sought after. They are symbols of your talent and virtue. They display your glory and authority. You are a prince among your people."

"They mean nothing. They have value only to those who want to give them value," I told him.

"Sir," he called out again, "you cannot go beyond here."

"Why not?" I asked him.

"There is nothing out there but a chasm." He paused. "Out there, sir, is darkness, the unknown. They that go beyond this zone never come back. It is not permitted to go beyond Tanza."

"Who has laid down this law?" I asked.

"The LORD God Almighty, He whom no one has seen. The Lord God, who is **merciful and gracious**[2]."

He bowed and prostrated himself upon the ground in reverence to his God as he cried out, "He who is most holy, the noblest, and king of all kings."

Slowly, he got up and came to me. "Who are you, sir?"

"I am nobody," I said to him.

"But, my lord," he said, glancing at my discarded medals, "you are a prince, the **anointed**[3] one of the highest."

Before he could continue, I stopped him. "I am nothing; I am no one. I am not worthy of any crowns, medals, praise, or honour. Those crowns have value only to those who gave them to me, Ka-ark."

"You know my name?" he asked in amazement.

"Yes," I replied, looking him in the eyes.

"Have you heard of me?" Ka-ark asked.

"No."

He looked puzzled.

"I **perceived**[4] you. In a split moment, your whole existence passed before me. We call it Kly-son," I explained to him.

"You saw through me. You read me." He looked bewildered.

"I read what I require for the moment, for what is relevant to us. You are Ka-ark, a prophet of the Supreme Lord. You are greatly respected and revered by your people," I said to him.

It was a shock to him that I could know him, as his spirit knew him just by looking at him.

He began to murmur, "I remember now. I saw you a long time ago. You were a young man, then. You were anointed by the Holy One, Prince from the **Golden City**[5] (Holy City) of the house of Benjamin. A man who has the key to our Sacred City. You have sat in the Council of our Elders." A deep sense of reverence seemed to sweep over him.

"I am nobody. I am no one," I repeated. "What you say has value only to you. But it has no value to me, for I am nothing."

My grief and loneliness had begun to creep over me. I began to walk away from him. I left the area and wandered into the outer emptiness to be alone in space. "I am nothing. I cannot create anything," I reminded myself.

A deep sense of loneliness and despair began to engulf me. All the works of my being, the achievements and the glory that preceded them, meant nothing.

I fell asleep. Like my blood, the memory of my past began circulating through my being. Every minute detail of my life stood crystal clear before me.

Tenzin paused.

---- ➤ ----

Bible (NKJV)	Bhagavad Gita
[1] 1 Peter 5:4, and when the Chief Shepherd appears, you will receive the crown of glory that does not fade away. Revelation 3:11 Behold, I am coming quickly! Hold fast what you have, that no one may take your crown.	[2] 10:11. I am warm, generous, forgiving, compassionate, and merciful.
[2] Nehemiah 9:31, For You are God, gracious and merciful.	[4] 10:40. There is no limit to My divine power. I have shown you a fraction of My infinite energy in a manner you can comprehend.
[3] Psalms 45:7. You love righteousness and hate wickedness; Therefore, God, Your God, has anointed You With the oil of gladness more than Your companions.	---X--

[4] John 1:48. Nathanael said to Him, "How do You know me?" Jesus answered and said to him, "Before Philip called you when you were under the fig tree, I saw you." Ps 139:16. You saw me before I was born. Every day of my life was recorded in your book. Every moment was laid out before a single day had passed.

[5] Revelation 21:2, Then I, John, saw the holy city, New Jerusalem, coming down out of heaven from God, prepared as a bride adorned for her husband.

---X--

--------- ᛃᛃ------

Chapter 77

Part III, Tanza

In a quiet voice, Sam said, "Please, Tenzin, go on."

Stefan muttered, "Sounds to me like you were depressed. Why so?"

"Give me a moment to think," he replied. "You have to remember; I'm speaking from the future when all the things we see today will have passed away."

Kwan-yin walked up to him and put her hand on his shoulder. "Please go on."

After an awkward pause, Tenzin continued to tell his story in his own words. "I remember now," he said, as if in a trance or hallucinating.

"It was not my life in the sanctuary that concerned me, but my previous life on Earth, in a world of astonishing beauty and suffering. A world of immense **sorrow and grief**[1], its rivers and oceans filled with tears and blood of humankind and creatures of the Earth.

That sorrow, grief, and sadness were engulfing me. I was unable to move. It began to rise from my feet, then through my legs and then my arms. It began to cover my face, and slowly, I began to cease to think.

Gradually, the feeling passed. I was left devoid of emotion, without any sense of life, pain, or sorrow. I was aware of only myself.

"Why, Lord God, did you **create me**[2]? Why did you give me life?" I cried out. It was a cry of a being devoid of pride or worth—a simple cry born out of despair.

There was no answer. My helplessness began to overwhelm me again.

"Why did you create me, Lord? You owe me an answer." It was a simple plea. I sat in silence for a long time. Then I heard a gentle voice from far away say, "I made you."

"Why?"

"I made you **for myself [3]**," a clear voice rang out.

"Lord," I said. "You gave me no choice. You made me without my consultation. That is not fair; it is not morally right! It was an act of selfishness on your part. You taught me that selfishness has no place in the cosmos."

His presence drew closer. "I had no choice."

It took me a while to understand. God had always existed. By creating us, He had made us in His image.

He explained, "I have no choice whether to live or die. **I exist[4].** True to my nature, I have brought others into existence after my **image[5]**. I have not been untrue to myself."

I understood Him much better than I could ever express to anyone. *(I do not have words to describe this side of my spiritual nature.)*

There was a long silence, and then He remarked.

---- ➤+ ----

Bible (NKJV)	Bhagavad Gita
[1] Romans 8:21-22, the creation will also be delivered from the bondage of corruption into the glorious liberty of the children of God. We know the whole creation groans and labours with birth pangs together until now.	[2] 10:11. I am warm, generous, forgiving, compassionate, and merciful. I dwell in My devotee's hearts and minds, dispelling the darkness born from ignorance with the shining touch of knowledge, affirmed with signs and miracles. Hence, my devotees follow my

[2] Job 14:1. "Man born of woman Is of few days and full of trouble. Jeremiah 1:5, "Before I formed you in the womb I knew you; Before you were born, I sanctified you; I ordained you a prophet to the nations."

[3] Ephesians 1:4, even as he chose us in him before the foundation of the world, that we should be holy and without blemish before him in love:

[4] Revelation 22:13, "I am the Alpha and the Omega, the Beginning and the End, the First and the Last."

[5] Genesis 1:26. Then God said, "Let Us make man in Our image, according to Our likeness;

---X--

example.

[3] 11:15. Arjuna: O Lord, in this vision, I saw what your thoughts, plans, and desires were before anything came into existence.

[4] 11:2. You have shown me your limitless power and eternal existence in visions and revealed the secret of the beginning and end of all creatures and creation.

---X--

--------- ᛤ------

Chapter 78

Craving for a family

"The Lord God said, "We **created you,**[1] to teach you everything you need to know about our work, motives, and us. Son of man, you have something we do not have. You have something we can never have."

"What, Lord? How can I have something that you do not have?"

"You have a unique quality, free will. You can choose to live or die. We cannot die. We exist forever. You have true choice and true freedom."

He let me ponder this. How can the created have more choice and freedom than the creator?

"Son of man, what do you see?"

"Lord," I said, "Before time, before Bi-kly-son, it was just you and your loneliness and pain. That bitter, sad existence, which was neither life nor death. A place of despair, and your longing for something better, perhaps a **craving for a family**[2]? A period you call Kly-so-ak.

"It was an empty world, like where we now stand. Your first tears, the first tears of joy, turned into pure energy. From all that pain and suffering came the writing of the Holy **Eternal Scrolls**[3]. It was followed by what we humans understand as the **beginning**[4].

"From the tears came the creation of the angelic and spiritual world, then the universe, creation, Earth, life forms, humankind, sanctuaries, epochs and millenniums, Judgement Day, a new Eternal City, Tanza, Divana, Nazar, Awara-nar. A place where past, present, and future co-exist as one." I stopped.

The Lord replied, "You have seen all you **need to see**[5]. All that is sufficient for you to make an informed choice."

---- ➤ ----

Bible (NKJV)	Bhagavad Gita
[1] Psalms 104:30, You send forth Your Spirit, they are <u>created</u>, And You renew the face of the earth.	[2] 15:18. All Holy Scriptures from the four corners of earth declare Me, the Supreme Lord. <u>I exist,</u> the Supreme Lord, the eternal, unchanging, imperishable Lord.
[2] Romans 8:15, For you, have not received the spirit of bondage again to fear; but you have received the <u>Spirit of adoption</u>, whereby we cry, Abba, Father. 2 Corinthians 6:18 And will be a Father unto you, and <u>ye shall be my sons and daughters</u>, saith the Lord Almighty.	[1, 4, 5] 18:55. Thus, devotees gain My acceptance by aspiring to act as I do. To them, I systematically reveal who I am (the supreme Personality of Godhead and Father of all creation), why <u>I created all things</u>, the purpose of creation, and their <u>role</u> in this life and the hereafter. Furthermore, I share My <u>future plans</u> and their role in that domain with them. Such knowledge motivates and inspires them to walk beside Me in My realms (kingdoms) as I guide, correct, and <u>prepare them</u> for eternity.
[3] Revelation 5:9, And they sang a new song, saying: "You are worthy to take <u>the scroll,</u> And to open its seals; For You were slain, And have redeemed us to God by Your blood Out of every tribe and tongue and people and nation,	---------- ॥-----
[4] John 1:1, In the <u>beginning,</u> was the Word, and the Word was with God, and the Word was God.	
[5] 1st John 1:1. That which was <u>from the beginning,</u> which we have heard, which <u>we have seen with our eyes,</u> which we have <u>looked upon,</u> and our hands have handled, of the Word of life; ---x--	

Chapter 79

Two doors

He brought me before two doors. They looked alike to me.

The Lord God said, "Son of man, you must experience everything and gather sufficient knowledge and wisdom to make an informed choice. After that, you will be well placed to exercise your free will.

"You needed the life you lived to exercise that freedom. Now, you are in a position to make an **informed choice[1]**.

"There are two doors before you. Beyond the right door, marked Nazar (Nirhodha), lies emptiness and freedom from life's pain, suffering, and joy. It's a path most people choose because they have no desire or inclination to be accountable or take responsibility for their actions. They have no desire to amend their way and make appropriate compensation and restitution. These people desire a simple life, to survive and **pass away[2]** in the fullness of time. Hence, they give up their **inheritance[3,]** as adopted children of God, and if they are God's children, then they are **heirs of God[4]**. Their inheritance will be given to others.

"Beyond the left door, marked Divana, **lies spiritual life[5]** with us and everything that goes with it. It is a long, rugged, and difficult path that eventually leads to a meaningful, creative life.

"I know you. You will choose this more challenging path. There will be times when you wish you were never born. Sometimes, you will want to crawl into a hole and die.

"Because you have seen all, felt all, you can now choose what you desire. Once you go through one of these doors, you may not be able to come back."

---- ➤ ----

Bible (NKJV)	Bhagavad Gita
[1] 1 Corinthians 13:12, For now, we see in a mirror, dimly, but then face to face. <u>I know partly, but then I shall know just as I</u> am known.	[1] 7:19. Overcoming many trials and errors, the wise continue to persist and freely follow My ways based on <u>informed choice</u>, realizing I encompass everything. Such souls are rare, leaving a legacy of love, care, and goodness wherever they go.
[2] Revelation 2:11. "Anyone with ears to hear must listen to the Spirit and understand what he says to the churches. Whoever is victorious will not be harmed <u>by the second death.</u>	[2, 5] 11:13-14 Arjuna: Lord, you have revealed all this to me, but this plan is vast and beyond my comprehension. You have invited me to share your goals and be part of them. If I choose to <u>go my own way,</u> as some have done, and <u>die in the natural order,</u> I will remember nothing, lose nothing, and gain nothing. However, you, Lord, will lose a generous spirit, someone who touched your very being, a loss etched into your memory for eternity.
[3] Hebrews 9:15 And for this reason, He is the Mediator of the new covenant, by means of death, for the redemption of the transgressions under the first covenant, that those who are called may receive the promise of the eternal <u>inheritance</u>. 1 Peter 1:4, to an <u>inheritance</u> incorruptible and undefiled and that does not fade away, reserved in heaven for you,	---------- ↭------
[4] Galatians 4:7, Therefore you are no longer a slave but a son, and if a son, then an <u>heir</u> of God through Christ.	
[5] Titus 1:2, in the hope of <u>eternal life,</u> which God, that cannot lie, promised before the world began. ---**X**--	

Chapter 80

In the fullness of time

A warm mist of love surrounded me.

"In the fullness of time, I have given you two choices. You can choose to be free from existence or join us and live."

While the door on the right, Nazar, had no lock, the door on the left, Divana, did.

"Lord, why does the door on the left have a lock?"

"You cannot go through it **without my permission.**[1] Those who go beyond it are true to my nature. They have chosen to walk with Me. They made an **informed choice,**[2] free from all interferences, pressure, and fear."

"What if I choose to walk through this door of Divana and join the overcomers?"

"That will be your informed choice. Before I unlock it, you must return to the beginning. Open the **Holy Eternal Scrolls**[3] and the **Lamb's Book of life**[4] and **write your name**[5] in them. It's your choice."

"And if I do that?"

"Then you have given Us and the universe **your informed consent**[6]**.**"

"What happens after that?"   ---- ➤ ----

Bible (NKJV)	Bhagavad Gita
[1] Luke 18:18, A certain ruler <u>asked</u>, " Good Teacher, what shall I do to <u>inherit eternal life</u>? [2] Acts 13:48 And as the Gentiles	[1, 2] 7:19. Overcoming many trials and errors, the wise continue to persist and freely follow My ways based on <u>informed choice</u>, realizing I encompass everything. Such souls are

heard this, they were glad, and glorified the word of God: and as many as were <u>ordained to eternal life believed.</u>

[3] Revelation 5:9, And they sang a new song, saying: "You are worthy <u>to take the scroll</u>, And to <u>open its seals</u>;

[4] Revelation 13:8. All who dwell on the earth will worship him, whose names have not been written in the <u>Book of Life of the Lamb</u> slain from the foundation of the world.

[5] Revelation 21:27. But there shall by no means enter anything that defiles or causes an abomination or a lie, only those written in the <u>Lamb's Book of Life.</u>

[6] 1st Corinthians 13:12, For <u>now, we see</u> in a mirror, dimly, but then face to face. <u>I know partly, but then I shall know just as I</u> am known.

---X--

rare, leaving a legacy of love, care, and goodness wherever they go.

[1, 5-6] 11:13-14 **Arjuna**: Lord, you have revealed all this to me, but this plan is vast and beyond my comprehension. You have invited me to share your goals and be part of them. If I choose to <u>go my own way</u>, as some have done, and <u>die in the natural order</u>, I will remember nothing, lose nothing, and gain nothing. However, you, Lord, will lose a generous spirit, someone who touched your very being, a loss etched into your memory for eternity. Sitting among the heavenly saints and the Elders of the Universe, Arjuna struggles to understand the mystery of God's plan and his eternal journey through it, led by the divine spirit. He is amazed *(having been granted unique access to the inner mind of The Lord God)*. He bows .

[3-6] 13:9 They comprehend the <u>Lord's creative plan</u> for the cosmos, <u>their position</u> in this plan, and the reason for joyful and painful <u>lessons of life</u>: the joy of family, friends, birth, suffering, disease, old age, and death. All these things are <u>encountered in life</u> and <u>used for spiritual growth</u> and advancement. Hence, they <u>seek and are willing to learn from a spiritual master</u> as they journey along this path. --------- ᴖ-----

Chapter 81

The Lord's creative plan

The Lord God, our Heavenly Father, said, "Then, the full power of this universe will be unleashed to help you reach Awara-nar. You can choose your time and place of birth, your parents, your life choices on Earth, and the number of days there. You can write in the **Eternal Book**[1] all things you will need for your **journey**[2].

"You can choose the sanctuary, your spiritual fathers, your role in the Sacred City. The whole universe will work with you and empower you to **accomplish**[3] what you have chosen.

"All that you write in the **Eternal Books**[4] will come to pass because you made an informed choice. Consider before you write your name and give your consent. If you exercise your informed free will, you become jointly responsible and accountable for your part in the **suffering and pain**[5] the universe is undergoing. Think before you decide on your journey."

---- ➤ ----

Bible (NKJV)	Bhagavad Gita
[1] Hebrews 10:7, Then I said, 'Behold, I have come — In the volume of the book it is written of Me — To do Your will, O God.' Revelation 20:12, And I saw the dead, small and great, standing before God, and books were opened. And another book was opened, which is *the Book* of Life. And the dead were judged according to their works, by the things written in the books.	[1-5] 13:9 They comprehend the Lord's creative plan for the cosmos, their position in this plan, and the reason for joyful and painful lessons of life: the joy of family, friends, birth, suffering, disease, old age, and death. All these things are encountered in life and used for spiritual growth and advancement. Hence, they seek and are willing to learn from a spiritual master as they journey along this path
[2] Ephesians 1:3, Blessed *be* the	[2-5] 2:53. When you have clarity of

God and Father of our Lord Jesus Christ, who has <u>blessed</u> us with <u>every spiritual blessing</u> in the heavenly *places* in Christ,

[3] 2nd Peter 1:3, as His divine <u>power</u> has given to us all things <u>that pertain to life</u> and godliness, through the knowledge of Him who called us by glory and virtue,

[4] 2 Corinthians 3:18, But we all, with unveiled face, beholding as in a mirror the glory of the Lord, are being <u>transformed into the same image</u> from glory to glory, just as by the Spirit of the Lord.

[5] Romans 8:17-19, And since we are his children, we are his heirs— heirs of God and joint-heirs with Christ, if indeed we <u>suffer</u> with Him, that we <u>may also be glorified together.</u>

---X--

<u>mind</u>, apprehending your closeness with Me, your consciousness will <u>merge with My Will</u>. Then, you will start <u>to comprehend your goal</u> in life.

---X--

--------- ૐ-------

Chapter 82

Freedom from the cycle of life and suffering

I looked at the <u>door marked Nazar</u>*. Part of me wanted to choose the other door and continue my life. And yet, as I considered it now, I realised I had exhausted my sense of purpose and meaning. I was tired of **living[1]** in his vision.

All I wanted was an end, and for me, this door could lead to that end, to freedom from the cycle of life and suffering. It gave me the option to cease to exist.

I walked up to the door marked Nazar and gave it a final glance. I felt his sadness. Then, I walked through. The spirit of all creation surrounded me. Creation (Ma-Mother) could not bear seeing me pass away. She desired **me to live[2].** I was her child, a product of her love and compassion. A blanket of life and warmth surrounded me.

Mother Earth, Sanctuary, and God took on a new meaning and understanding for me. The Holy Spirit cried out, "Your journey through Earth, the sanctuary, the Sacred City, Tanza, has a meaning, a purpose. Walk with Us, and live for the greater **good of all[3]** and for the people who will go through the door of Divana and beyond to Awara-nar.

"Their names were written in the **sacred book[4]** from the beginning. Your **life's work[5]** will help them fulfil their destiny. They will continue to grow. We will grant you Our peace if you desire to leave Us. We are grateful for your life. You will rest in Our peace **forever[6].**"

To walk through the door of Nazar, one reaches the final resting place; some would call it nirvana, to be one with the universe. It is an informed choice to enter a place of peace and oneness. It will be as if one never existed, but Cosmos will retain their emotions and experience and use these to build Awara-nar, adding to its formation's building blocks.

----➤----

Bible (NKJV)	Bhagavad Gita
1 Luke 4:4, But Jesus answered him, saying, "It is written, 'Man shall not live by bread alone, but by every word of God.' "	**2** 2:52. When your intelligence has overcome the dense forest of delusion, you will become indifferent to worldly things. You will seek eternal values over material values.
2 Ezekiel 18:32, "For I have no pleasure in the death of one who dies," says the Lord GOD. "Therefore, turn and live!" **3** Titus 2:14, He gave Himself for us, that He might redeem us from every lawless deed and purify His special people, zealous for good works.	**3** 3:17. 3:17. People who have found their true self and purpose in life in Me are content and happy. Serving My creation and Me is a privilege and a pleasure for them.
4 Philippians 4:3, I urge you, faithful companion, to help these women who laboured with me in the gospel, with Clement, and the rest of my fellow workers, whose names *are* in the Book of Life.	**5** 3:20. The great King Janaka found solace and favour in My presence by performing his duty sacrificially and selflessly with others' welfare always in mind. Similarly, do your work with the interest of others in mind.
5 Ephesians, 2:10. We are His workmanship, created in Christ Jesus for good works, which God prepared beforehand that we should walk in them.	**6** 4:39. Those who take spiritual knowledge as their highest goal and have it validated by the Supreme Lord, remaining steadfast in the faith, with senses controlled, attain wisdom and peace.
6 Hebrews 4:10, For he who has entered His rest has also ceased from his works as God did from His. --------- ꝗ------	**6** Samadhi: a state where all the senses and emotions are under control and the spirit is free (Mukta). ---X--

Chapter 83

Alone in the Universe

I walked a few more paces. As time passed, I realised I was alone for the first time. There was no one. That atmosphere—that sixth sense of His presence, which had always existed even in my darkest hour—was gone.

Slowly, the sense of utter aloneness overcame me. There was no one to hold my hand, no light or fear of darkness to govern or influence my thoughts. I came face-to-face with my being. I saw myself as I **was.**[1]

My mind was crystal clear. Three things stood out.

1: The lack of any outside (His) presence/influence.

2: The faculties of my reasoning were clear. They were sharper than ever before, untainted by anyone or anything.

3: There was a final door in front of me.

I sat and reflected while time stood still. The door behind me led back to Tanza.

The one in front led to **oblivion**[2]; some would call it the door to nirvana.

I pondered. So far, I have lived in the vision of the creator. It was his vision: the beginning, creation, the Golden City. I was part of his vision and his creation.

He had once said, "Man cannot live without vision." I had lived in his vision, starting as an essence in the beginning, later as a lifeform on Earth, in my 'patch'. The presence of people and all living and non-living things (atoms, Earth) gave me an excellent opportunity to grow spiritually. I was grateful to all from Earth, but a small, significant part of me was missing from my life. I had no vision of my own and no desire to exist.

I had felt the pain and sorrows of all in my '**Patch³**'—their daily struggle to put food on the table. I grew spiritually by living among them; therefore, I felt obligated to share my spiritual blessing and its glory.

They (humanity and creatures) had undergone pain and suffering on Earth. I had a sense of debt owed to them. I wanted to **repay that debt⁴** by ensuring that all were given a second chance in the hereafter. Moreover, the Lord had **empowered⁵** me with his Holy Spirit to make it happen.

I wanted to give meaning and purpose to my existence—something to love, cherish, and delight by overseeing the broken-hearted, distressed, downtrodden beings and creatures returned to life. To restore them to good health, the joy of life, family, friends, and loved ones, and to restore my faith in God and myself.

However, to truly live, I needed to be free, to be me—aspiring to be creative, with a will to grow and live. I looked at myself. I was too young. In spiritual terms, I was a five or six-year-old child, too young to decide. I was here before my time.

Slowly, I got up and walked back through the door I had entered towards Tanza. As I travelled through Tanza, certain things became clear. I began to understand all the mysteries of the cosmos, creation, judgement, and the Sacred City. The knowledge and the **secrets of the universe⁶** started to make sense. I could now comprehend the bigger picture.

I had walked into this place (Tan-kly-son: the cycle of Cosmos) of my free will. I was completely free and independent—a free, independent person with no more obligations to his past master.

I was aware of my pain and despair. I could finally make sense of the world of saints, sinners, joy, pain, and the struggle for survival in a dog-eat-dog universe. However, knowledge did not relieve the pain. Even in this place, I felt my struggle and pain surface and my inability to bear it. I crouched and began to cry in sheer frustration. Overcome with tears of pain, sorrow, and grief. A product of the world of prophets and liars and my anguish.

From a distance, from another time, came a voice. "A broken and **contrite heart[7]**," said the Lord God, "is more precious than all knowledge, wisdom, or power."

---- ➤ ----

Bible (NKJV)	Bhagavad Gita
[1] 1 Corinthians 2:11, For what <u>man knows</u> the things of a man except for the spirit in him? Even so, no one knows the things of God except the Spirit of God. [2] Daniel 9:14. 'Let Me alone, that I may destroy them and <u>blot out their name</u> from under heaven, Ex 32:32 "Yet now, if You will forgive their sin — but if not, I pray, <u>blot me</u> out of Your book which You have written." [3] Romans 8:19, For the earnest expectation of the **creation** eagerly waits for the revealing of the sons of God. [4] 1st Samuel 12:3 Behold, here I am: witness against me before the LORD, and before his anointed: <u>whose ox have I taken?</u> or whose ass have I taken? or who have I defrauded? Who have I oppressed? Or of whose hand have I received any bribe to blind my eyes in addition to that? And I will	[1] 4:19. A wise person is said to be <u>fully knowledgeable</u> when all his undertakings are free from anxiety about the result and devoid of the selfish sense of gratification. The fire of My divine wisdom has consumed all his selfish desires. [3-4] 4:21. The wise person acts with his mind and intelligence perfectly controlled, regarding all his possessions as Mine, and uses only the necessities of life. He serves <u>humanity's interests and Me</u>. Hence, he incurs no sin (displeasure from Me) in his activities. [4] 6:32. People who see equality in all beings and creatures have profound empathy for all and <u>respond to their joy</u> and sorrow as their own. They have <u>attained one of the higher states</u> of spiritual union with Me and My creation. 7:17. One in search of life's meaning and purpose, unwavering in devotional service to humanity, creation, and Me, surpasses all the others. <u>They are My</u>

restore it to you.

5 Psalms 45:7. Thou lovest righteousness, and hatest wickedness: therefore God, thy God, hath anointed thee with the oil of gladness above thy fellows.

6 Matthew 13:11. He answered, "Because it has been given to you to know the mysteries of the kingdom of heaven, but to them, it has not been given.

7 Isaiah 57:15. For thus says the High and Lofty One Who inhabits eternity, whose name is Holy: "I dwell in the high and holy place, With him who has a contrite and humble spirit, To revive the spirit of the humble, And to revive the heart of the contrite ones.

--------- ᕯ-------

joy, and I am their joy.

5 9:22. But I uphold and provide for all the needs of those fully committed to serving My creation and Me.

6 4:3. To a selected few, I revealed My existence and plans for eternity (past, present, and future worlds to come). You are My friend and devotee, and in due time, as you gain My favour, I will reveal these mysteries and explain your role here on Earth, in the spiritual world, and in the far distant future. You are one of My most trusted architects. You and other trusted devotees will build My material and spiritual kingdoms in this world and hereafter and walk beside Me in all My realms. I will guide and teach you all as a Father.

7 11:52-54. **Krishna:** Great saints and sages have desired to see your vision. Knowledge, austerity, and sacrifice cannot bring such a vision. To receive such visions, one needs to have a pure heart, a pure spirit, and a transformed mind in control of all the senses led by the inner Atman. Moreover, I can only be known or understood as I AM by My grace and through undivided devotional service to creation, humanity, and Me.---**x**--

---------- ᕯ-------

Chapter 84

Why, O God? Why?

I felt His warmth, affection, and care towards me. It lasted a few moments and disappeared, but it did nothing to relieve my inner struggle.

I was independent of Him now, free. I had to overcome my fears. I had to come to terms with my inner self. Inside me was a struggle for life over death. Moreover, death seemed sure to prevail.

There was no angel of death, no rebellion towards God, no ingratitude, just pain and anguish.

Slowly, I slid into sleep. So little happiness, a life that had seen so much suffering and so little joy. The **cries of creatures[1]** that lived on my 'patch' came to haunt me as predators tore into their bodies.

Their cries of pain and tears haunted my spirit as they were eaten alive. They cried out to me as predators tore into their limbs. "Why has God of love created me to die in such an awful way? My little ones will starve to a slow, lingering, painful death. We did not seek to be born for such a life."

"Why, O God? Why?" A deep sense of anger and hopelessness flooded me. I grew to hate the hands that had **created life[2]**, pain and suffering for their **good pleasure[3]**. The creatures' despair ran like hot iron through my soul.

I cried out, "I hate this creation, this life. I did not like to think that innocent creatures' blood was shed for my, for our, **redemption[4]**. My conscience was defiled: I participated in their daily destruction and suffering to survive, to grow—all at their expense. A broken, bruised, and contrite heart may be precious to God. Nevertheless, a broken heart full of anguish and sorrow cannot live without a clear conscience. Eventually, a broken, grieving heart gives in.

I was a corrupt, defiled, parasitic child of the Cosmos, feeling alone, lost in time and space, and badly in need of a vision to live a good, clean life without thriving at the expense of another. I looked at my feet. There were three **drops of water**[5] (three strings of energy)—the first water I had seen in Tanza.

---- ➤ ----

Bible (NKJV)	Bhagavad Gita
[1] Romans 8:21-22, because the **creation** will also be delivered from the bondage of corruption into the glorious liberty of the children of God. We know the whole **creation** groans and labours together with birth pangs.	[1-4] 3:10. **The Supreme Lord** of creation continued: At the beginning of creation, I blessed creation and set in motion the principle of selfless, sacrificial service to promote the welfare, interest, and happiness of all creation. Thus, through this selfless service, all creation would be prosperous and fruitful and fulfil its desires.
[2] Genesis 1:1. In the beginning, God created the heavens and the earth.	[5] 5:19. Such people have conquered the fear of life and death. They rest in the perfect Brahman and Me as they are gradually refined and made flawless
[3] Philippians 2:13, God works in you to will and do for His good pleasure.	---X--
[4] Exodus 29:36. "And you shall offer a bull every day as a sin offering for atonement. You shall cleanse the altar when you make atonement for it and anoint it to sanctify it.	
[5] 1st Corinthians 13:13. And now abide faith, hope, love, these three; the greatest of these is love. --------- ↬-------	

Chapter 85

A place where the wolf and the lamb would feed together

My tears changed to ones of joy and excitement. Yes, I wanted to live, to create a world of **beauty and order.**[1] A place where the **wolf** [2] and the lamb would feed together. The lion would eat straw like the ox; rivers would flow with love and kindness, mountains full of compassion, and trees would wave their branches with music and harmony.

My joy died upon realising I had no power to create or bring it about by myself.

I called out, "Heavenly Father, help me." I picked up the teardrops (faith, hope, love), the first water I had seen in Tanza.

To my surprise, The Master appeared before me.

"Sire, you are here!" I called.

He said calmly, "Father **sent me.**[3]"

I nodded. "Thank you, Master, for coming."

He smiled. "You have found a vision—a purpose and meaning for your life—but lack the power to bring it about. Come follow me, and we will fulfil your vision."

"Thank you, Lord."

He smiled. "Nothing is impossible with our Father. We will show you things **hidden**[4] from eternity, the mystery that will make you joyous." He paused, letting his words take root in me.

He continued, "Do not call me Master. In the past, I chose you. Now, you have called me and chosen me. So, I am here."

"What do I call you?"

He replied, "**Mota Bhai[5]**" (a term used in my mother tongue, Gujarati, for 'elder brother', regarded as the head of the family in the father's absence). "I am not ashamed to call you Nano Bhai ('little brother'). Come, we can live in each other's visions as a family. Bapuji (Father) calls; we have work to do."

Tenzin said, looking at the small group of people before him, "That was my experience. I do not wish to impose it on anyone. It's my calling, which helps me with my spiritual journey. You have to find your **calling,[6]** your path, your Tallack."

They sat silently for a long while; each lost in their thoughts.

Stefan was the first to break the silence. "Tenzin, with all respect to you, I do not believe in a creator or God. We are all Masters and the Elders, a product of evolution and metamorphosis."

Tenzin put his arm around Stefan's shoulders and said, "Brother Stefan, you may be right. Many in our sanctuary share your beliefs. We each have our own Tallack to follow. Come, it's time we had something to eat."

---- ➤ ----

Bible (NKJV)

[1] Isaiah 34:16-17. Search the book of the LORD and see what he will do. None of these birds and animals will be missing, and none will lack a mate, for the LORD has promised this. His Spirit will make it all come true. He surveyed and divided the land and deeded it to those creatures. They will possess it forever, from generation to generation. Re 7:17. "for the Lamb amid the throne will shepherd them and lead them to living fountains of waters. And God will

Bhagavad Gita

[1 - 2] 5:18. My devotees have equal regard for all. They see the same self (the breath of God) in a learned scholar, an outcast, a cow, an elephant, and a dog.

[2] 5:19. Such people have conquered the fear of life and death. They rest in the perfect Brahman and Me as they are gradually refined and made flawless.

[3] 11:38-39. You are the eternal, timeless spirit, the resting place of all

wipe away every tear from their eyes."

2 Isaiah 65:25. The wolf and the lamb shall feed together, The lion shall eat straw like the ox, And dust shall be the serpent's food. They shall not hurt nor destroy in all My holy mountain," Says the LORD.

3 John 14:20. "At that day, you will know I am in My Father, and you in Me, and I in you. Revelation 22:3-4. And there shall be no more curse: but the throne of God and the Lamb shall be in it; his servants shall serve him: And they shall see his face;

4 1 Corinthians 2:9, But as it is written: "Eye has not seen, nor ear heard, Nor have entered into the heart of man The things which God has prepared for those who love Him."

5 Hebrews 2:11. For both He who sanctifies and those who are being sanctified are all of one, for which reason He is not ashamed to call them brethren,

6 Hebrews 4:1-16. Therefore, since a promise remains of entering His rest, let us fear lest any of you seem to have come short of it. Indeed, the gospel was preached to them and us, but the word they heard did not profit them, not

living entities. You pervade the whole cosmos. You are the father and grandfather of all creatures. You are inconceivable to the human mind (10:19). Yet, You reach out to the animals and us at a level all can comprehend. You are our Heavenly Father; none is turned away, and in 'The Fullness of Time', all will be reconciled, restored, and made whole—no one thrives in Your Kingdom at the expense of another. I bow before You. Only You are worthy of praise and worship. You are our final home

5-6 2:53. When you have clarity of mind, apprehending your closeness with Me, your consciousness will merge with My Will. Then, you will start to comprehend your goal in life.

---x--

being mixed with faith in those who heard in time of need. ---x--	

---------- ٩٩------

Chapter 86

Second visit: the leader

The two girls and Stefan sat on the stream's edge, happily singing a new song they had learnt during the festival while Amos and Niza, the lion and lioness, played in the water. A small group of deer grazed around them.

Tenzin walked up to them, joining in the **singing**[1] as he sat near them.

They greeted him cheerily.

Tenzin told them, "I have some good news. Our Lord will visit us and be here soon, so I need your attention."

Stefan looked at Tenzin. He got up and said to the girls, "Excuse me. I think Tenzin has an important message for you. I will leave you in his care."

He departed, and the lions followed him.

"Listen carefully," said Tenzin. "When our Lord comes to the sanctuary, do not bow, but look him in the **eyes**[2]. Do not speak until he addresses you. If you have any questions, wait until he asks you. When he departs, do not bow. Stand still. Do not move until he has gone."

"Why?" [3] asked Sam. Both girls looked confused.

"In this garden, all things rotate on the axle of **love**[4], not fear. When you get to know the Master better, you will kneel of your **accord**[5], motivated by love and reverence. He requires no pretence, no fear, and no **falseness**[6]. Even though he is the Master, he likes to earn his subjects' trust, respect, and honour. He wants you to be yourselves."

Even as he was explaining this to the women, the sanctuary changed.

"Excuse me; I must go and meet the Master." He walked towards the orchard. In the distance, they saw the Master approaching **Tenzin.**[7]

All the animals went quiet. They bowed down. The air became still. A deep sense of serenity came upon the sanctuary. The trees lowered their branches as if in **reverence.**[8]

Tenzin **knelt.**[9] His eyes were fixed on the ground. His right hand was by his right hip, his left hand placed on his left knee, ready to spring up to attention when asked.

Stefan, who was further down the stream, did the same. The lions sat down, their heads resting on their paws, their eyes fixed on the ground.

---- ➤ ----

Bible (NKJV)	Bhagavad Gita
[1] Psalms 40:3. He has put a <u>new song</u> in my mouth — Praise to our God;	[2] Ch 4:34 Follow the guidance of a spiritual master and render service unto him. The spiritual master can instruct you in this wisdom.
[2] John 4:24. "God is Spirit, and those who <u>worship Him</u> must worship in <u>spirit and truth.</u>"	[3] Ch 4:35 Having gained spiritual wisdom, you will not be deluded again. You will see that all living entities are part of the <u>divine plan</u>. Hence, as you progress in your spiritual growth, you will regard all life forms as an extension of The Lord and your family.
[3] Psalms 149:4, For the LORD, takes pleasure in His people; He will <u>beautify the humble</u> with salvation.	
[4] 1st John 4:18, There is <u>no fear in love</u>, but perfect love casts out fear because fear involves torment. But he who fears has not been made perfect in love.	[4, 7,] 4:33. The primary purpose of creation is the spiritual advancement of all, and the secondary purpose is sharing My Eternal plan with those who seek it with all their hearts, minds, and strengths. Signs and wonders accompany sacred knowledge and are not revealed to those who place little value on it. Sacrifices made to promote spiritual
[5] Psalms 25:9, <u>The humble</u> He guides in justice, And the humble He <u>teaches His way.</u>	
[6] Proverbs 14:5, A faithful witness <u>does not lie, But a false</u> witness	

will utter lies.

[7] John 17:24. "Father, I desire that they also whom You gave Me may be with Me where I am, that they may behold My glory which You have given Me; for You loved Me before the foundation of the world.

[8] Isaiah 55:12, "For you shall go out with joy, And be led out with peace; The mountains and the hills Shall break forth into singing before you, And all the trees of the field shall clap their hands.

[9] Isaiah 61:1, "The Spirit of the Lord GOD is upon Me Because the LORD has anointed Me To preach good tidings to the poor; He has sent Me to heal the broken-hearted, To proclaim liberty to the captives, And the opening of the prison to those who are bound.

---X--

understanding are better than material offerings. The fruit of spreading spiritual knowledge in the community is love, joy, peace, longsuffering, gentleness, goodness, righteousness, and truth. The fruit of righteousness is sown in peace by those who make peace. --------------

[1-4] **Sikhism.** Scripture, Section 05 - Part 031. He alone finds shelter, who has met the Perfect Guru. Nanak builds his house on that site where there is no death, birth, or old age.

[4,5,6- 9] Section 19 - Part 055. My Lord and Master, the bringer of peace, has blessed me with His Grace; He has arranged this world and the world hereafter for me.

--------- ᨩᨩ------

--------- ᨩᨩ------

Chapter 87

Friends, not servants

The Master walked past Tenzin and Stefan and approached the girls. They stood still, their eyes fixed on the Master. A slight tremor of fear and anxiety ran through their bodies. Their legs seemed to turn to jelly.

From the corner of her eye, Sam saw Kwan-yin's fingers twitching. She slowly moved closer and held Kwan-yin's hand to support her.

The Master approached the girls, turned his head towards the lions, and called them. They came running up to him. He bent and patted their foreheads.

He played with them for a few minutes, then looked up at the girls and smiled; his eyes showed kindness and **gentleness.**[1]

He spoke to them in a soft voice. "Don't be afraid. I call you friends, not **servants**[2]**.**" He paused. "I chose you **from Earth**[3], even before you were born. I **called**[4], and you heard me. You responded to my spirit's call."

He turned and looked towards Tenzin. "When you receive anyone I send, you receive me also, and whosoever **receives me**[5] receives Him (the Heavenly Father) who sent me." He turned towards the girls and said, "Love **one another**[6] as I love you. Remain in my love in this **sanctuary."**[7]

He looked Sam in the eyes. "I leave you with my joy and peace. Although you do not know me, I have given you a great **honour**[8] and privilege by allowing you here. For I tell you, **many prophets and kings**[9] have desired to see what you see, and have not seen it, and to hear what you hear and have not heard it. You have a short time here. Make the most of it."

The two girls stood frozen on the spot. They were unable to speak or think for a while. Their minds were full of questions, fear, anxiety, and emotions.

He looked at the lions again. He patted them, turned around, started walking past Stefan, and headed towards Tenzin. They were both kneeling; neither had moved.

The Master turned to Tenzin and addressed him.

"Come," he said. "Follow me."

Tenzin got up, and together, they walked towards the orchard.

The Master recited his previous instructions again. "**You, Tenzin,**[10] will look after them in my **Kingdom**[11] for me. You will undo the pain and suffering I **brought upon**[12] them on Earth. I leave it to you to make a **hundredfold restitution**[13] for their pain. The Holy Spirit will guide you and empower you."

---- ➤ ----

Bible (NKJV)	Bhagavad Gita
[1] Matthew 11:29, "Take My yoke upon you and learn from Me, for I am gentle and lowly in heart, and you will find rest for your souls.	[1] 13:8. Those close to the Supreme Lord (Devotees) are above pride and deceit. They are gentle, forgiving, pure in thought, upright, and filled with inner strength and self-control. They are devoted to the Lord (*devotional service to the Lord God is to seek his happiness and that of his creation and all things contained in it*).
[2] Mark 10:45, "For even the Son of Man did not come to be served, but to serve, and to give His life a ransom for many."	
[3] John 15:19, "If you were of the world, the world would love its own. Yet because you are not of the world, but I chose you out of the world. Therefore the world hates you.. 2 Thessalonians 2:13, But we are bound to give thanks to God always for you, brethren beloved by the Lord because God	[2] 14:26. To transcend these modes of material nature is to serve humanity, creation, and Me and see the divinity in all others through total commitment to Me. Those who rise above their material nature are fit for union with Brahman and Me, and they will live to see a new order (Creation), a New Universe where the

from the beginning chose you for salvation through sanctification by the Spirit and belief in the truth,

⁴ 2nd Timothy 1:9, who has saved us and called us with a holy calling, not according to our works, but according to His purpose and grace, which was given to us in Christ Jesus before time began. Ephesians 3:11 according to the eternal purpose, which he purposed in Christ Jesus our Lord:

⁵ John 13:20, "Most assuredly, I say to you, he who receives whomever I send receives Me; he who receives Me receives Him who sent Me."

⁶ John 13:34, "A new commandment I give to you, that you love one another; as I have loved you, you also love one another.

⁷ Leviticus 19:30, 'You shall keep My Sabbaths and reverence My sanctuary: I am the LORD.

⁸ 2nd Timothy 2:21, Therefore if anyone cleanses himself from the latter, he will be a vessel for honour, sanctified and useful for the Master, prepared for every good work.

⁹ Luke 10:24, "for I tell you that many prophets and kings have desired to see what you see, and

lion and lamb sit together and eat straw, and a child plays with them. *(Gita 10:6. 11:7-17 & 24-30. 14:2 & 26)*

⁶ 4:10. My followers taking refuge in My abode are set free from the slavery of fear and selfish attachment. Their greed, anger, and love are slowly refined, cleansed, purified, and sanctified in My presence. 6:46. The path of discipleship is founded on good works, spiritual knowledge, and practical action of love for creation and Me. This approach is superior to pursuing knowledge or selfless service.

⁸ 9:25. Those who worship idols, spirits, ghosts, or ancestors will go to such realms upon death. Those who honour Me will join Me.

⁹ 9:33. Even kings and those of noble birth seek My attention. All are born in this transient world of sacrificial love, pain, suffering, and joy. Therefore, engage in loving service to My creation and Me.

¹⁰, ¹¹ 18:56. My devotees look after My creation as stewards under my protection. As a sign of my approval and grace, I permit such enlightened beings (mystics) to stroll in the heavenly realms and spiritual sanctuaries (My abode). I am preparing and refining them so that in the hereafter, they will play a

have not seen *it*, and to hear what you hear, and have not heard *it*."

10 John 6:63, "The Spirit gives life; the flesh profits nothing. <u>The words that I speak</u> to you are spirit, and they are life.

11 Hebrews 12:28, Since we are receiving an <u>unshakable Kingdom,</u> let us be thankful and please God by worshipping him with holy fear and awe.

12 Philippians 1:6, being confident of this very thing that He who <u>has begun a good work</u> in you will complete it until the day of Jesus Christ;

13 Matthew 19:29, And everyone who has given up houses, brothers, sisters, father, mother, children or property for my sake, will <u>receive a hundred times</u> and will <u>inherit eternal life</u>.

---X--

significant role in My Kingdom: reconciling, restoring, and making all creation whole—no one thrives in My realm at the expense of another. *(Gita 3:31. 7:2. 10:6. 11:7-17 &24-30. 14:2 & 26).*

12, 13, **(Gita 1:26-27 elaboration)>> A6** The spirit of the Lord in him reveals that even in Heaven, the work of counselling, reconciliation, restoration, restitution and making each whole has to continue if there is going to be eternal peace.>>

--------- ᛞ------

--------- ᛞ------

Chapter 88

There is no fear in love, but perfect love casts out fear

Tenzin said, "Lord, may I speak **freely?"[1]**

"You may."

"I say this out of concern and love for Brother Stefan. His belief that God does not exist and that we are just part of evolution and metamorphoses worries me."

"Why does that worry you?"

"He does not believe you are the **Messiah."[2]**

The Lord put a comforting hand on Tenzin's shoulder as they walked. "You need not worry. The journey ahead is a long one before Judgement Day."

Tenzin replied, "Another matter, Lord. The people of other faiths— Muslims, Hindus, Buddhists, and **others.[3]** Their journey concerns me."

The Lord explained, "Judgement day is a long way off," as they walked. "The Holy Spirit still has a lot of work to do among all the nations, races, and tribes. People will come from all these places to my **Kingdom[4]**."

"Am I to convert them?"

"No, you will teach them about their faith, their beliefs. The Holy Spirit will teach them about the Kingdom. Our Father has many **mansions[5]** (sanctuaries)."

"As you wish, Sire."

The Lord said, "Tenzin, I am the **gate[6]**. I chose you to open the gate to all people of all races, colours, and faiths. I have placed a heavy burden on your shoulders.

"There is only **one truth**[7]: life, death, sanctuary, Judgement Day. You will meet people from every race, tribe, and corner of Earth. Many things will change along the way.

"Many on Earth instinctively obey God's law, even without hearing the **Gospel.**[8] They demonstrate the power of God's law written in their hearts. These people will seek you on this journey, and you will guide them."

"Am I to seek only those whose names are in your **book?**"[9]

"Our Father **chooses**[10] who comes to His sanctuaries. If their names are in my book, you can move them to the same page where your name is. This privilege, I bestow on a few people of great merit. The names on that page will be your brothers and sisters. Your eternal **treasures,**[11] your (our) spiritual family. It is an honour I have given you."

"Thank you, Lord."

"I am the gate. You, Tenzin, will open my gate to all races."

---- ➤ ----

Bible (NKJV)	Bhagavad Gita
[1] 1st John 4:18 There is no fear in love, but perfect love casts fear because fear involves torment. But he who fears has not been made perfect in love.	[1] 9:20. Those who study the Holy books and worship Me free themselves from ignorance, darkness, fear and evil. They attain a place in the heavenly realms and have access to My wisdom and blessings.
[2] John 4:26 Then Jesus told her, "I AM the Messiah!" Mt 1:1 An account of the genealogy of Jesus the Messiah· Mt 16:20 He sternly ordered the disciples not to tell anyone that he was the Messiah.	[2] 4:5. **The Supreme Lord** (Krishna) replied: I have often appeared to various generations in human forms. Unaware as you are, I have guided your Atman since your birth.
[3] Romans 2:14 Even Gentiles, who	

do not have God's written law, show that they know his law when they instinctively obey it, even without hearing it. v15 They demonstrate that God's law is written in their hearts, for their conscience and thoughts either accuse them or tell them they are doing right.

4 Revelation v 5:9 By your blood you ransomed for God saints from every tribe and language and people and nation;

5 John 14:2 "In My Father's house are many mansions; if it were not so, I would have told you. I am going to prepare a place for you."

6 John 10:9 I am the gate. Whoever enters by me will be saved and come in and go out and find pasture.

7 John 14:6 Jesus said to him, I am the way, the truth, and the life: no man cometh to the Father but by me.

8 Romans 2:v14-16, When Gentiles, who do not possess the law, do instinctively what the law requires, these, though not having the law, are a law to themselves. They show that what the law requires is written on their hearts, to which their conscience bears witness; their conflicting thoughts will accuse or perhaps excuse them on

3, 4, 8:11. I am impartial. All Holy Scriptures reveal that those who worship Me are sacrificial, relinquishing selfishness and materialism. They seek to promote the welfare, interest, and happiness of others and Mine. Such people find salvation and eternal life in Me.

5 14:15. Those who die in passion or ignorance are elevated to the heavenly places where others of similar nature dwell, leaving behind a mixed legacy of good and misery on earth.

6 10:12-13. Arjuna: You are the Supreme Lord of the Universe, the absolute truth, the light of the Universe, the Eternal one. Unborn and infinite. All the great saints confirm this, and now you have declared this knowledge to Me and validated it with signs and wonders.

7 14:27. I am the foundation of the revealed and hidden Brahman, the immortal, imperishable, eternal, and unchanging. The source of truth and happiness. I am the Light of the world.

8 17:2-3. Lord God replies: Every person is born with a latent seed of faith, i.e., the sum total of their belief; what they value, hold important in life, and how they conduct their lives. All three modes of faith reside in a person – in goodness, passion, or ignorance – but

the day when, according to my gospel, God, through Jesus Christ, will judge the secret thoughts of all.

[9] Revelation 21:27 But there shall by no means enter anything that defiles or causes an abomination or a lie, only those written in the Lamb's Book of Life.

[10] John 6:37 "All that the Father gives Me will come to Me, and the one who comes to Me I will by no means cast out."

[11] Matthew 6:21 "For where your treasure is, your heart will also be." ---X--

there is always one dominant mode.

---------- ---- ---

Shri Guru Granth Sahib,
Section 05 – Siree Raag – Part 007
[6] By Guru's Grace, they understand Him and find the Gate of Salvation.

Section 01 –Jup-Part 007
[7] I bow to him. I humbly bow.
The primal One, the Pure Light, without beginning, without end.
Throughout all ages, he is One and the Same.

---X--

--------- ☊------

Chapter 89

Eternal books

Tenzin asked, "Sire, have you come to talk about the future of the girls?"

Lord, "Yes. You are their guardian, so you must know about them and their place in the great **purpose.**[1] Come with me."

"Where are we going, my lord?"

"We are going to the special place in time and space called Kly-so-ak—a time before the material world and consciousness came into **existence**[2].

"It was the time when the eternal plan was formulated and written in the eternal book (when the eternal **purpose**[3] of God was formed, and the lamb's book of life came into being. The Hindu Vedic books call it "the Supreme Consciousness, at the beginning of Time and Space").

Tenzin said, "I once read in the eternal book regarding **my place**[4] in the cosmos."

The Master replied, "Yes, now you need to see what was written regarding Sam, Kwan-yin, and Stefan in those **books.**"[5]

"Sire, do we have permission to open the books again?"

"We do. You will need to read and remember all that was **written**[6] regarding these people. You are my appointed guardian over them."

They had come to the place before time. There, they found the **book** [7] and found the **references**[8] they sought.

The Lord opened the book, and Tenzin read, "Sam: Gold, destined for Tan-Kly-son and Awara.

"Kwan-yin: Silver, destined for Lui-Kly-son and Tanza only.

"Stefan: Bronze, destined for Un-Kly-son and the Eternal City (Zion, New Jerusalem).

---- ➤ ----

Bible (NKJV)	Bhagavad Gita
[1] Romans 8:28 And we know that all things work together for good to those who love God, to those who are the called according to His purpose.	[1] 2:41. Those who desire to serve Me and creation (all life forms and humanity) will attain a singular purpose with great resolve. For those who lack resolution, life's decisions will divert them from Me to material things.
[2] Romans 9:11 For the children not yet being born, nor having done any good or evil, that the purpose of God according to election might stand, not of works but of Him who calls,	[2-8] 4:3. To a selected few, I revealed My existence and plans for eternity (past, present, and future worlds to come). You are My friend and devotee, and in due time, as you gain My favour, I will reveal these mysteries and explain your role here on Earth, in the spiritual world, and in the far distant future. You and other trusted devotees will build My material and spiritual kingdoms in this world and hereafter and walk beside Me in all My realms. I will guide and teach you all as a Father.
[3] 2nd Timothy 1:9 who saved us, and called us with a holy calling, not according to our works, but according to his purpose and grace, which was given us in Christ Jesus before times eternal,	
[4] Ephesians 3:11 according to the eternal purpose, which he purposed in Christ Jesus our Lord:	
[5] Romans 8:30 Moreover whom He predestined, these He also called; whom He called, these He also justified; and whom He justified, these He also glorified.	---X--
[6] Ephesians 1:11 In Him also we have obtained an inheritance, being predestined according to His	

purpose and who works all things according to the counsel of His will. **Eph 2:10** For we are His workmanship, created in Christ Jesus for good works, which God prepared beforehand that we should walk in them.

[7] Revelation 21:27 and there shall in no way enter anything unclean, or he that maketh an abomination and a lie: but only they that are written in the Lamb's book of life.

[8] Hebrews 10:7 Then I said, 'Behold, I have come — In the volume of the book it is written of Me — To do Your will, O God.' "

---X--

--------- ᕼᕼ------

Chapter 90

The Eternal Holy City; Sam is destined to serve in the holiest place <u>in **New Jerusalem.**</u>[1]

Tenzin read from the sacred book: "It looks like they're all destined for New Heaven and the **Sacred City**[2], but Kwan-yin goes beyond that. Sam goes even further to Awara-nar, the final point, the last noted point, an honour accorded only to most esteem of God's children."

"Yes," the Master said, "and now we need to go to the New Jerusalem."

"I don't understand. Judgement Day, the New Jerusalem, Tanza, and Awara are all in the future. How can we go somewhere when that place has not yet **existed**[3]**?** I can understand going back into the past, but going into the future?"

"There are places outside time and space where the past, **present, and future are one.**" [4]

"I don't understand. I have been with you in the Holy City in the future, but I don't know if it was real or just a vision."

"It was a glimpse of things to come. Think of a place and the powers of the Holy Spirit will take us there. Let the Holy Spirit to take us past Judgement Day and into New Jerusalem."

They walked through the Holy City, and, in the centre, stood a substantial **sacred building**[5]. They entered the building. On the walls in the large central room were shelves of books. ---- ➤ ----

Bible (NKJV)	**Bhagavad Gita**
[1] Revelation 21:2, Then I, John, saw the holy city, <u>New Jerusalem</u>, coming down out of heaven from God,	[1] 9:1. My dear Arjuna, I shall now tell you of a profound mystery; this knowledge will free you from the miseries of material existence.

² Isaiah 2:3 Many people shall come and say, "Come, and let us go up to the mountain of the LORD, To the house of the God of Jacob; He will teach us His ways, And we shall walk in His paths." For out of Zion shall go forth the law and the LORD's word from Jerusalem.

³ Ecclesiastes 3:14-15, I know that whatever God does, It shall be forever. Nothing can be added to it, And nothing was taken from it. God does it, that men should fear before Him. That which has already been, And what is to be, has already been; God requires an account of what is past.

⁴ Revelation 1:8, "I am the Alpha and the Omega, the Beginning and the End," says the Lord, "who is and who was and who is to come, the Almighty."

⁵ Hebrews 9:3, And behind the second veil, the part of the tabernacle called the Holiest of All. 9:8, the Holy Spirit indicates that the way into the Holiest of All was not yet made manifest while the first Tabernacle was still standing. 10:19, Therefore, brethren, having boldness to enter the Holiest by the blood of Jesus. ---X--

² 4:3. To a select few, I revealed My existence and plans for eternity (past, present, and future worlds to come). You are My friend and devotee, and in due time, as you gain My favour, I will reveal these mysteries and explain your role here on Earth, in the spiritual world, and in the far distant future. You and other trusted devotees will build My material and spiritual kingdoms in this world and hereafter and walk beside Me in all My realms. I will guide and teach you all as a Father.

---X--

Chapter 91

Those outside the city

They opened the books and found the names of Stefan and Kwan-yin. They walked up to the door that led to the **holiest**[1] of holies and stopped. They found Sam's name written on the door, amongst many **others.**[2]

Tenzin whispered, "Sir, her name is on the Holy Door. What does that mean?"

"She is **chosen**[3] to serve in the holiest place in the Holy City.

"She will be a counsellor for her people. Some enlightened people will serve within the city gates, while others will live **outside.**[4] She will represent their interests in the inner chambers of the holiest place. She will help bring together her family, past, present, and future, and many from her tribe. She will be a judge for her tribe, and over the nations the Lord has given her as her inheritance."

"Who are her people?"

"Because of her commitment, resolve, and greatness, many, but not all, from her family will choose the path she followed. Her ancestors, her family, and those not yet born."

"Her family and who else?"

"And those from across the universe, the **righteous atheists**[5] who have appointed her to act as their spokesperson."

"What about Stefan and Kwan-yin?"

"They too **will serve**[6] in the inner chamber and represent the interests and welfare of their **families, people, and nations.**"[7]

---- ➤ ----

Bible (NKJV)	Bhagavad Gita
[1] Isaiah 56:5, Even to them I will give in My house And within My walls a place and a name Better than that of sons and daughters; I will give them an everlasting name That shall not be cut off. [2] Isaiah 56:7, Even them I will bring to My holy mountain, And make them joyful in My house of prayer. Their burnt offerings and sacrifices will be accepted on My altar; For My house shall be called a house of prayer for all nations." [3] Isaiah 61:10, I will greatly rejoice in the LORD, My soul shall be joyful in my God; For He has clothed me with the garments of salvation, He has covered me with the robe of righteousness, As a bridegroom decks himself with ornaments, And as a bride adorns herself with her jewels. 2 Corinthians 6:16, For you are the temple of the living God. God said: "I will dwell in them And walk among them. I will be their God, And they shall be My people." Eph 1:4 Just as He chose us in Him before the foundation of the world, that we should be holy and without blame before Him in love. [4] Psalms 2:8, Ask of Me, and I will give You The nations for Your inheritance, And the ends of the earth for Your possession. Psalms	[1-7] 4:3. To a select few, I revealed My existence and plans for eternity (past, present, and future worlds to come). You are My friend and devotee, and in due time, as you gain My favour, I will reveal these mysteries and explain your role here on Earth, in the spiritual world, and in the far distant future. You and other trusted devotees will build My material and spiritual kingdoms in this world and hereafter and walk beside Me in all My realms. I will guide and teach you all as a Father. [1] 10:20. I am in the heart of all living entities. My breath of life via Brahman flows through all beings and creatures. I am the beginning, middle, and end of their existence. [3] 9:2. This knowledge leads to the perfection of one's self. When applied to daily life, it is a great cleaner, leads to righteousness and, in the hereafter, to My abode. Use it joyfully. [4-7] 9:24. I am the supreme Lord of the universe, the object of worship of all faiths. Those who fail to realize My true nature soon sink into material existence. [6] 15:18. All Holy Scriptures from the Earth's four corners declare Me, the Supreme Lord. I exist, the Supreme Lord, the eternal, unchanging,

74:2 Remember Your congregation, which You have purchased of old, The tribe of Your inheritance, which You have redeemed — This Mount Zion where You have dwelt. Ezekiel 39:21 "I will set My glory among the nations; all the nations shall see My judgment which I have executed and My hand which I have laid on them."

[5] Romans 3:29-30, Or is He the God of the Jews only? Is He not also the God of the Gentiles? Yes, of the Gentiles also, since one God will justify the circumcised by faith and the uncircumcised through faith.

[6] Malachi 1:11 says the LORD of Heaven's Armies, "From morning till night my name is honoured by other nations' people. They offer sweet incense and pure offerings in honour of my name. My name is great among the nations."

[7] Micah 4:2 Many nations shall come and say, "Come, and let us go up to the mountain of the LORD, To the house of the God of Jacob; He will teach us His ways, And we shall walk in His paths." For out of Zion, the law shall go forth, and the LORD's word from Jerusalem. Galatians 3:8 And the Scripture, foreseeing that God would justify the Gentiles by faith, preached the gospel to Abraham beforehand, saying, "In you, all the

imperishable Lord, the source of all wisdom, worshipped by the inhabitants of the Universe.

---X--

nations shall be blessed." Ezekiel 37:28 "The nations also will know that I, the LORD, sanctify Israel (my disciples) when my sanctuary is in their midst forever." Psalms 126:2 Then our mouth was filled with laughter, And our tongue with singing. Then they said among the nations, "The LORD has done great things for them. Psalms 46:10 Be still, and know that I am God; I will be exalted among the nations and earth! Psalms 59:8 But You, O LORD, shall laugh at them; You shall have all the nations in derision.

---X--

--------- ⳥⳥ ------

Chapter 92

The end of time and space: Tanza and Awara

[1] [Liz's Tenet 2] "It is recorded so that it can be used for the process of forgiveness and reconciliation. Nothing in the cosmos is irrelevant. The cosmos has invested a vast amount of energy because it has an eternal plan, a desire to live and, where possible, to reconcile and make all things whole in the fullness of time."

[Janet Warrington's Tenet 1] We will use everything that happened to you as a positive force for good. **Every experience[1],** thought and feeling, good and bad, every tear you have shed, and all laughter and joy, we will turn into a positive force for good. It will be used for your spiritual growth and maturity to fulfil your place among us. You are not alone. We are **with you[2]** and will be with you until the end of the ages (time)."

Tenzin asked, "What do we do now?"

"We go beyond the place called Tanza,"[i] replied the Master, "to the testing place called Divana and Nazar."

"I have been there before."

"Yes, you went there alone. We will go together this time, and you will learn something new. Come."

They entered **Tanza[3] (the end of time),** and the Master gave a command. A colossal monument rose before them. On it, they found Kwan-yin's and Sam's names.

"Stefan's name is not here," Tenzin pointed out.

"Then he must have **passed away[4]** with the old order," replied the Master.

"He was a very devout and talented man."

"It would have been his **choice⁵**."

---- ➤ ----

Bible (NKJV)	Bhagavad Gita
¹ [Liz's Tenet 2] "It is <u>recorded so</u> that it can be used for the process of forgiveness and reconciliation. <u>Nothing in the cosmos is irrelevant</u>. The cosmos has invested a vast amount of energy because it has an eternal plan, a desire to live and, <u>where possible</u>, to reconcile and make all things whole in the fullness of time."	¹ 3:4 A person acquires <u>life's experience</u> by participating in the world and contributing to its welfare. By withdrawing from the world, one does not contribute to the world's welfare and thus cannot achieve spiritual perfection.
² Genesis 28:15 "Behold, <u>I am with you</u> and will keep you wherever you go and bring you back to this land; for I will not leave you until I have done what I have spoken to you." Matthew 28:20 and lo, <u>I am with you</u> always, <u>even to the end of the age</u>."	² 15:20. This wisdom is the most intimate part of the Vedic scriptures I have <u>shared with you</u> and those willing to participate in My Kingdom. By obeying and participating in this wisdom, a person becomes enlightened and is on the path of union with Me.
³ Matthew 28:20 Teaching them to observe all things whatever I have commanded you: and, lo, I am with you always, even to the <u>end of the world</u>. Amen.	---x--
⁴ Revelation 20:6 Blessed and holy is he that hath part in the first resurrection: on such the <u>second death hath no power</u>, but they shall be priests of God and Christ.	
⁵ Deuteronomy 30:19 "I call heaven and earth as witnesses	

today against you, that I have set before you life and death, blessing and cursing; therefore choose life, that both you and your descendants may live;

---X--

--------- ᕕ᠂------

Chapter 93

A part of our loved family is gone forever

Tenzin nodded. "I have lost a much-loved brother. One of my most precious treasures." He walked away, leaden with grief.

After a while, he returned and said, "This Knowledge has only brought sorrow and grief."

The Lord nodded and said, "I understand your grief, but rest assured that nothing in the Universe is ever **lost.**[1]

"Let's see what happened to the girls."

They came to a place called Divana. They found Sam's name on the monument and a reference to her—the chosen one, a person close to the creator's heart.

The Lord wanted Tenzin to examine himself and come to appreciate the value of the knowledge he held. He asked, "Her name is here, Tenzin. What do you understand by it?"

"Lord, she goes beyond the second **death,**[2] into Awara-nar. This time, it would have been an informed choice, and she has decided to go on."

They found another monument called Nazar. Kwan-yin's name was written on it: "The blessed person and a beloved child of the Universe."

Again, the Lord asked Tenzin, "What does it mean?"

He replied, "She made an informed choice according to her custom (culture, faith) to be one with the Universe—**Nirvana**[3]**.**

He continued slowly, with tears in his eyes. "It is a great loss to us, Lord. All that talent, beauty, and richness of spirit will be gone forever. I will lose part of my eternal **family**[4] at this journey stage."

The Lord placed his right hand on Tenzin's shoulder. "They made informed choices. In the fullness of time, they exercised their free will. It is **our loss[5].** A part of our loved family gone forever."

Tenzin reflected on the wisdom of the tenets he had been taught and realised that knowledge implied a cost.

(Zak's Tenet 4). True love does not persuade or impose one's view but sets each free to seek their own.

[Kathy's Tenet 1]. A person or a relationship is more valuable than what we participate in.

[Kathy's Tenet 2]. His loss, his pain, would have been greater than hers. She is of greater value to the Master than He is to her.

---- ➤ ----

Bible (NKJV)	Bhagavad Gita
[1] *[Janet Warrington's Tenet 1] We will use everything that happened to you as a positive force for good. Every experience, good and bad, every thought, feeling, and tear you have shed, and all laughter and joy, we will turn it into a positive force for good. It will be used for your spiritual growth and maturity to fulfil your place among us. You are not alone. We are with you and will be with you until the end of time."*	[1-4,] 11:13 Lord, you have revealed all this to me, but this plan is vast and beyond my comprehension. You have invited me to share your goals and be part of them. If I choose to go my own way, as some have done, and die in the natural order, I will remember nothing, lose nothing, and gain nothing. However, you, Lord, <u>will lose a generous spirit</u>, someone who touched your very being, <u>a loss etched</u> into your memory for eternity.
[2] Revelation 2:11 He that hath an ear let him hear what the Spirit said to the churches; He that <u>overcomes shall</u> not be hurt of the <u>second death</u>.	[2-5] 14:2. This knowledge will open the passage to draw you closer to Me. On the *Day of The Lord*, before I annihilate the cosmos and create a new order, all shall stand before Me and be evaluated. You will stand by

3 Nirvana. In Buddhism and Hinduism, the final release from the cycle of life and death by the extinction of all desires and individual existence, culminating (in Buddhism) in absolute blessedness or (in Hinduism) in absorption into Brahman/ Universe.

4-5 [Kathy's tenet 2]. She is of greater value to the master and Tenzin than they are to her. Their loss would have been greater than hers.

---X--

My side to see a new cosmos. There will be no more death for the sages who pass this testing point.

---X--

--------- ⅋⅋------

Chapter 94

A new book

They went further to the place called the Valley of Awara-nar. On the **last page**[1] of the Lord's book, Tenzin's and Sam's names were among many.

Tenzin stood staring at Sam's name. "You called me to be a guardian over her. I am not sure I am suitable for such a high office."

The Master laughed. "You are correct; you are not ideal. I chose you because you were the best in the tiny **available pool**[2]. All you have seen and **heard**[3] are things to come. Come, I must take you back to your sanctuary.

"These things were shown so that you can have an inclination towards your future and help you to choose your future path. After a good sleep, you will wake up in your sanctuary and wonder whether all this was just a dream."

"Sire, what lies beyond this place, the valley of Awara-nar?"

"It is only a thought. **A new book,**[4] and only the first paragraph is written."

"What is written?"

"The book is called Awara-nar. Every sub-atomic particle, every atom that existed, had awareness; each after its kind is recorded here. The atoms, the material and spiritual worlds, and all living things—trees, animals, and people—will have gone. But their awareness and all their knowledge will remain. Nothing in the cosmos is wasted."

"What will happen to that which remains?"

"Whatever is left will cry out to form a new order, to become part of the new world order, as New Atoms with New Bodies. A family where everything works and grows as a loving family."

Tenzin looked at the Master. "I don't have the intellect or spiritual capacity to comprehend this truth, but I get its gist."

The Master laughed again. "Some of the finest minds in the universe have tried to **understand this**[5] and struggled. Come, time to go back to your sanctuary."

The Lord said, "I do not reveal my plans except to a select **few.**[6] To the rest, I speak in parables."

---- ➤ ----

Bible (NKJV)	Bhagavad Gita
[1] Revelation 21:27 But there shall by no means enter anything that defiles or causes an abomination or a lie, but only those written in the Lamb's Book of Life.	[2] 18:47. It is better to engage in one's service for the welfare of all, even if one performs it imperfectly, than to engage in something one is good at for selfish enhancement.
[2] Matthew 22:14 "For many are called, but few are chosen."	[4,] 14:2. This knowledge will open the passage to draw you closer to Me. At the end of time, just before I annihilate the cosmos and create a new order, all shall stand before Me and be tested. You will stand by my side to see a new cosmos. There will be no more deaths for sages that pass this testing point.
[3] Mark 4:11 And He said to them, "To you is given the mystery of the kingdom of God; but to those who are outside, all things come in parables,	
[4] Revelation 21:5 Then He who sat on the throne said, "Behold, I make all things new." And He said to me, "Write, for these words are true and faithful."	[4] 9:8. The entire cosmic order is under our control. We bring it into being and annihilate it at our pleasure, repeatedly.
[5] 1st Corinthians 2:7 But we speak the wisdom of God in a mystery, the hidden wisdom which God ordained before the ages for our	[1-6] 18:55. Thus, devotees gain My acceptance by aspiring to act as I do. To them, I systematically reveal who I am, why I created all things, the purpose of creation, and their role in

glory,

[6] Isaiah 28:5 In that day the LORD of hosts will be For a crown of glory and a diadem of beauty To the remnant of His people,

---**x**--

this life and in the hereafter. I share plans for the future and their role in that domain, confirming My words with signs and miracles. Thus, such evidence establishes the reality of their spiritual path and inspires them to walk beside Me in My realms as I guide, correct, and prepare them for eternity. Although I am inconceivable *(Gita 10:19)* to the human mind, I reach out to humans and animals at a level where they can comprehend Me as their Heavenly Father. None is turned away, and in 'The Fullness of Time', all things will be reconciled, restored, and made whole—no one thrives in My Kingdom at the expense of another.---**x**--

--------- ᛉᛉ------

Chapter 95

Loneliness

Tenzin pondered the things he had seen in the comfort of the sanctuary. He walked through the orchard and spent time with Stefan and the women.

Soon after the **Festival[1] of Grief** ended, the sanctuary returned to normality. They had a celebratory **feast[2]**; the good times were back, and the people were happy.

Tenzin was walking through the orchard, checking the quality of the fruit. He saw Sam crying under a huge tree.

She came running up to him and gave him a big hug.

Tenzin looked at her unhappy face. "Sam, why the tears?" He instantly knew what was going through her mind but wanted her to have a chance to share it.

Through her tears, she cried out, "Tenzin, I feel alone, **without[3]** my family and friends. This garden is lovely, but the sheer beauty has become a torment. It was a wonderful place to be when I came. It was an escape from earthly nightmares, but loneliness grew within me as time passed. I don't understand. Why is it that a place of beauty and wonder now makes me feel so **sad[4]** and lonely? I should be happy and rejoicing, but I'm not. Why?"

---- ➤ ----

Bible (NKJV)	Bhagavad Gita
[1] Deuteronomy 16:16, "Three times a year all your males shall appear before the LORD your God in the place which He chooses: at the Feast of Unleavened Bread, at	[3] 1:42. Social upheaval is hell for the family, society, and those who destroy families. It eliminates the spiritual foundation laid down by our

the <u>Feast</u> of Weeks, and the <u>Feast</u> of Tabernacles; and they shall not appear before the LORD empty-handed.

[2] Exodus 13:6, "Seven days you shall eat unleavened bread, and on the seventh day, there shall be a <u>feast</u> to the LORD.

[3] Luke 4:4, But Jesus answered him, saying, "It is written, 'Man shall not live <u>by bread alone</u>, but by every word of God.' "

[4] Proverbs 18:14, The spirit of a man will sustain him in sickness, <u>But</u> who can <u>bear a broken heart</u>?

---X--

ancestors.

---X--

--------- ⳿⳾------

Chapter 96

Negative emotions

Tenzin said, "Sam, the Lord sent me to bring you to this sanctuary when you were dying. This is a temporary **place**[1] to relax and come to terms with your inner self and your past. It is a place to reflect on the future and discover the true value of life, family, friends, and commitments. Once you are stronger, we will help you visit your **family**[2] and unite you with them for good. Nonetheless, some of your family members and friends may not want to link up; we cannot ignore that.

"Here, you are learning the importance of family, the Lord's Grace, mercy, and goodness. Everyone in the Cosmos has to understand the importance of family, friends, and God's Grace. They are the core values of the Cosmos. That deep appreciation comes only when these things are taken away.

"All things have to thirst, to **seek**[3] with all their heart, mind, and strength to regain what they've lost. It's time you visited other sanctuaries, discovered new things, made new friends, and met others with similar interests, desires, and aspirations.

"It will be like starting a new school and meeting people at your level—teachers who can impart more knowledge and encourage you to pursue new interests.

"The new school will help you overcome the anger, fear, and hatred **in you**[4]. They will help you understand those experiences that trigger such emotions and help you be better—more compassionate and thoughtful.

"If you allow these negative emotions to fester, they will drain your life energy. We can guide you, but it is a bridge you must cross on your own, a conscious decision you must make. Once you have decided and shown a willingness to be **renewed**[5], we may be able to help you."

Sam replied, "I think that will help. I look forward to it."

When Tenzin had gone, she went in search of Kwan-yin. She found her talking with Stefan. Sam waited until they had finished and then approached Kwan-Yin.

Kwan-Yin cried out, "Sam, I'm glad to see you. I've been looking for you. I missed you."

Sam reached out and hugged her friend. "I missed you, too. I was with Tenzin."

"Then you learnt something new?" Kwan-yin asked.

"Tenzin thinks it's time I considered visiting other sanctuaries. Maybe spend some time there."

"Why? If you go away, I'll miss you. Can I come with you?"

"That would be nice. You'll have to ask Tenzin. He may agree."

After an awkward pause, Kwan-Yin said, "I have to go. I'll see you later. I promised Stefan that I'd help him gather fruit."

Sam replied, "Go. I'll see you later, and we'll ask Tenzin if you can come with me."

Kwan-Yin ran to catch up with Stefan.

---- ➤+ ----

Bible (NKJV)	Bhagavad Gita
[1] Ezekiel 37:12, "Therefore prophesy and say to them, 'Thus says the Lord GOD: "Behold, O My people, I will open your graves and cause you to come up from your graves, and bring you into the land of Israel.	[1] 6:41. When people who have accepted Me die, they go to a spiritual realm where the righteous live (they are reborn and metamorphosed in sanctuaries). [4-5] 6:42-43. Or they may move (metamorphose) the realm of a great spiritual master. Such a move is rare.

² Matthew 19:29, And everyone who has <u>left houses, brothers,</u> sisters, father, mother, wife, children, or lands for My name's sake shall receive a hundredfold and inherit eternal life.

³ Daniel 4:29, "But from there you will seek the LORD <u>your</u> God, and you will find Him if you seek Him with <u>all your heart</u> and <u>soul</u>.

⁴ Daniel 11:35, And some of those of understanding shall fall, to <u>refine them, purify them,</u> and make them white, until the <u>end</u>; because <u>it is still</u> for the appointed time.

⁵ Colossians 3:10, and have put on the new man who is <u>renewed</u> in knowledge according to the image of Him who created him,

---X--

Their divine consciousness is <u>reinvigorated</u> by the great spiritual masters, and with their help, they are encouraged to make further progress.

---X--

--------- ↬-------

Chapter 97

Kly-so-ak; before time, before the matter came to be

"Sam," Tenzin called out. "Come with me. Hold my hand."

They seemed to fly through the universe, past stars and countless galaxies, like grains of sand. They passed on and on until they came to another dimension.

It was empty, with no stars. Sam could see nothing—no light, no darkness; and yet she was aware of her **existence[1].**

She cried, "Tenzin, I can't see, yet it doesn't feel dark or light. I can't see you, but I'm aware of your presence. You no longer have hands, feet, or a body, yet I'm very aware of you. I can see you with my mind as clearly as if you had a body."

Tenzin remarked, "We are in the region called Kly-so-ak. This place existed before the foundation of the world was laid. It was **here[2],** that the Lord decided that people who displayed certain qualities would be **chosen[3]** to be holy and serve Him and His creation in the future. We have those qualities; thus, He chose us and called us to serve Him. Listen to your spirit. Do not speak for a while. Listen, and when you're ready, call me."

Sam withdrew into her thoughts. Initially, her thoughts rambled on and gave way to calmness and stillness.

She was aware of just the two of them. Then, slowly, only herself.

The stillness gathered pace, and time passed, perhaps billions of years. Deep loneliness came upon Sam. She had no purpose, desires, or expectations—just a feeling of emptiness.

"Loneliness is a killer," she thought, "but even that is missing. I am alive. No, I exist, that's all."

An eternity went by—maybe two or more. Sam just lay there, feeling empty. "I exist. That is all. I have no name, desire, expectation, family, friends—nothing."

Finally, a thought sprang into her being. "**I want to live,**[4,] to come alive; I want to be part of something."

She remembered Tenzin. She called out to him.

"I am here," he replied.

---- ➤ ----

Bible (NKJV)

[1-2] Proverbs 8:22-30, "The LORD created me at the beginning of His work, Before His works of old. I have been established from everlasting, From the beginning, before there was ever an earth. When no depths and fountains abounded with water, I was brought forth. Before the mountains were settled, Before the hills, I was brought forth; As yet He had not made the earth, the fields, Or the primaeval dust of the world. When He prepared the heavens, I was there when He drew a circle on the face of the deep, when He established the clouds above and strengthened the deep fountains. When He assigned to the sea its limit so that the waters would not transgress His command when He marked out the earth's foundations, I was beside Him as a master craftsman; And I was daily His delight,

Bhagavad Gita

[1-2] 11:6-7, My dear friend, at a level you can understand, I will now reveal more of My eternal self in a form never seen or heard before—a privilege granted to a few rare beings. In My body, you will perceive the entire cosmos cycle passing before your eyes. Whatever you want to see: the past, present, future, **creation** (*refer to the end of the book),* Earth, and spiritual sanctuaries will flash before you. You will find answers to questions regarding the terms 'in the fullness of time' and 'the end of all material and spiritual worlds' and your purpose on Earth and in the heavenly realms. The mysteries of the Universe are available to all brave enough to seek them.

[1-2] **Further light on Gita 1:26-27. Arjuna at the battlefield.** *Gita By Hari Patel*

Rejoicing always before Him.

³ Ephesians 1:4 He <u>chose us</u> in Him before the <u>foundation</u> of the world, that we should be holy and without blame before Him in love. Hebrews 4:3, "So I swore in My wrath, 'They shall not enter My rest,' " although the works were <u>finished</u> from the <u>foundation of the world</u>.

³ Psalms 118:17 I shall not die, but <u>live</u>, And declare the works of the LORD.

⁴ Romans 8:29 For whom He foreknew, He also <u>predestined</u> *to be* conformed to the image of His Son, that He might be the firstborn among many brethren. Ephesians 1:11 In Him also we have obtained an inheritance, being <u>predestined</u> according to the purpose of Him who works all things according to the counsel of His will,

---X--

1:26-27 A9 Arjuna's mind wandered to <u>the beginning</u> of time when he was <u>just a thought</u> in the Lord's mind before <u>anything came</u> into being. Even in this period, when he was <u>just a thought</u>, he was <u>aware</u> of his being. Arjuna mumbles, "My essence has <u>always been</u> with the Lord and will always be with Him. My roots are from the beginning." (Gita 11:1-31. 11:47-48)

A11 In a <u>different time</u> and place, when Arjuna was just an essence in the Lord's mind, he had <u>perceived creation</u> as a beautiful plan. The Universe teeming with all sorts of plants, happy people, and animals. His essence had rejoiced at the very idea of God's creation. (Gita 11:15-16)

³ 3:3. **Lord Krishna (Supreme Lord)** replies: <u>From the beginning of time before</u> humanity came <u>into being</u>, I laid out two paths of faith. First, to pursue spiritual knowledge for those inclined towards contemplation, and the second path of selfless service to those inclined toward action.

---X--

--------- ९१ ------

Chapter 98

The need to live and create

"I am ready," Sam replied. "I'm empty. I need to live, to create."

Tenzin nodded. "Listen to your true inner self. What do you hear?"

"I hear nothing. Wait, I feel a ray of hope. A belief is forming. I feel I am **one**[1] with the Lord. I feel a surge of desire to make something, **to create**[2] something. I feel a surge of life, **love, hope, and faith.**[3]" She was so excited that tears started to well up in her eyes.

Tenzin suggested, "Let the Holy Spirit within you count slowly from one to ten. Let those numbers linger in your mind."

Sam said, "In my mind, with the indwelling Holy Spirit's aid, I can **visualise the numbers**[4]. We have created the numbers in my mind."

Tenzin suggested, "Similarly, let a thought form in you. Then, push it out of you into this empty place."

She did as he had suggested.

"Now, think more of the same thoughts and push them out. Direct them into a ball outside of you."

She did as he had asked. The action gave rise to the smallest subatomic particle, which she named **KD 83.45.**[5] It was the end of the first day (or period), though there was no such thing as time here. She was tired and fell into a deep sleep.

She woke up at what might have been the start of another day and repeated her actions until she formed an atom.

She cried out in delight. "I have formed an **atom!** [6]" By then, she was exhausted and once again fell asleep.

Tenzin asked her to repeat the action when she woke up once more.

She worked hard, and by the time she was exhausted, she had formed nine molecules. She counted them and fell asleep. That was the end of the third day.

On day four, she told Tenzin, "I want to make a **living,**[7] single-cell organisms out of these molecules. I want a purpose, a plan, a motive for doing it."

---- ➤ ----

Bible (NKJV)	Bhagavad Gita
[1] 1st Corinthians 6:17, But he who is joined to the Lord is one spirit with Him.	[1-7] 11:45-48, I rejoice in perceiving you and the purpose of creation as never seen before. The knowledge you have entrusted me is too much to comprehend. It overwhelms me. O Lord, I am trembling with excitement and fear at the amount of knowledge and trust placed upon me and at the sight of your awesome majesty. Please permit me to see you in a human form that I am comfortable with. Krishna: Arjuna, by My grace, you have perceived My glorious, radiant, universal form and comprehended My cosmic eternal plans and your unique role in all this in a way no one has perceived or heard before. Unknown to you until now, you have been featured in my plans from the beginning of time. Hence, I am placing all the resources you need to fulfil them at your disposal. All I need is your consent, willingness, and iron resolve to carry it out not by your might but by My
[2] Colossians 3:10, and have put on the new man who is renewed in knowledge according to the image of Him who created him.	
[3] 1st Corinthians 13:13, Three things will last forever — faith, hope, and love — the greatest of these is love.	
[3] John 4:10, Jesus answered and said to her, "If you knew the gift of God, and who it is who says to you, 'Give Me a drink,' you would have asked Him, and He would have given you.	
[4] John 7:38, He that believeth on me, as the scripture hath said, from within him shall flow rivers of living water."	

[5] John 1:1-4, In the beginning, was the Word, and the Word was with God, and the Word was God   He was at the beginning with God. All things were made through Him, and nothing was made without Him.

[6] John 5.20, "For the Father loves the Son, and shows Him all that He does; and He will show Him greater works than these, that you may marvel. (Like building atoms, nuclear fusion, anti-gravity, the sanctuary, but only to those with wisdom, insight, forethought, and accountability.)

[7] Psalms 104:30. You send forth Your Spirit, they are created, And You renew the face of the earth

---X--

might. Arjuna, such grace and knowledge do not come from reading scriptures or performing sacrifices or rituals.

---X--

---------- ⌘-------

Chapter 99

In her image

Tenzin smiled. "First, you need to examine all your intentions and take an inventory at the start of each day. You must again take stock of everything before you fall asleep. Examine your results and account for all. You must always be aware of every organism's whereabouts and emotions. When your work is finished, you have to make all living things whole and make restitution for their pain and suffering. This is in the moral law of the cosmos.

"You must plan what you want to form, why, how, and be **accountable**[1] to yourself and God. Remember, only a pure, refined, tested, and approved spirit led by the Holy Spirit with impeccable moral values can fulfil the requirements. Hence, when you make an error, you must devise a means to correct the mistake or plan to fix it later. Each new day, you will learn a lesson.

Tenzin continued, "Creating intelligent, thinking organisms brings responsibility and accountability, and unforeseen consequences may occur. As an **heir**[2] of God, you have to consider all that. You have to be seen as fair, just, and righteous.

"Above all, your actions must be seen and felt as benevolent acts of love to all, especially the things you make. All **injustice**[3] has to be weighed against restitution, put right before the end of time. You must have confidence and resources before undertaking such a venture.

Over several intervals, in this place without time, Sam, with the help of Tenzin, formed three hundred and forty-three organisms. They interacted, learned, struggled for dominance, multiplied, and passed away. She did this in the framework that Tenzin had taught her.

Finally, she had one that had turned out in her image.

---- ➤ ----

Bible (NKJV)	Bhagavad Gita
[1] Romans 14:12, So, each of us shall <u>give an account of</u> himself to God.	[1-3] Chapter 11:10-12. Before Arjuna flashed the cosmos, multiple universes, life forms, and the revelation of the divine mystery, <u>from nothing</u> appeared Brahman and the <u>power of thought</u>; from the thought <u>came the energy</u>, the first three tears, matter, and antimatter. v15. Arjuna: O Lord, in this vision, I saw what your thoughts, plans, and desires were <u>before anything came into existence.</u> I see Brahman sitting on the throne, surrounded by the Elders of the Universe and all the living entities.
[2] Galatians 4:7, Therefore you are no longer a slave but a son, and if a son, then <u>an heir of God</u> through Christ.	
[3] Lamentations 19:15, 'You shall do <u>no injustice</u> in judgment. 2 Chronicles 19:6, and said to the judges, "<u>Consider what you are doing</u>, for you judge not on behalf of human beings but on the Lord's behalf; <u>he is with you in giving judgment</u>.	[3] **Further light on Gita 1:26-46 Arjuna's Dilemma on the battlefield. (*Elaboration***
---X--	*A:2 He regarded himself as more than a prince. This role was temporary. His eternal role was as a warrior priest of the Supreme Lord of the Universe, set apart to serve others for eternity. To seek and promote their eternal welfare. He looks at all those gathered on the battlefield, good, decent people on both sides mingled among the evil, amoral leaders. How could he, with good conscience, engage in this destruction? (Gita 2:3. 3:1-2. 16:9)*
	A:3 If he survived the carnage of war, he would need to devote his life to reconstructing both sides. The role of cementing, reconciling, restoring, and

	making restitution for all the victims of war, friends and foes, would fall on his kind. (Gita 4:33. 10:11-18)
	---X--

--------- ᛩᚻ------

Chapter 100

New lifeform

The new lifeform had gone through pain, suffering, and joy and had come out like a miniature image of her.

Sam cried joyfully. "I have a life form, a basic, simple version of me. My baby."

Tenzin smiled. "I am pleased for you, but do not forget that you need to look at these other organisms and make full restitution where due for all their pain and suffering. They must have a day when they can cry out for justice, and you are available to account for and justify your actions.

"From your perspective, you must demonstrate that each one was loved and cared for until the **fullness of their time**[1]. Then, before they cease to exist, you must make full restitution for their pain and suffering."

"Why do I have to do that?" she asked.

"The law of the Cosmos dictates that the greatest and the least in the Universe are **accountable**[2] to each other and to the Lord. On this principle, the Universe is **meant to rotate**[13] in harmony and peace.

Tenzin continued, "To have a **pure conscience**[4], you must have a moral value that is just and accountable to yourself and others. [Hari's Tenet 1] The law of the cosmos dictates that no one has a right to gain at the expense of others, not even God. *In other words, Exodus 20:15. Thou shalt not steal.* Your conscience demands that you have a moral conscience for all life and are seen as fair and just."

The baby grew into a living being. In time, the baby realised that it was someone's child.

"I am your baby. Why did you bring me into this world of pain and **suffering**[5]?" it cried out.

Tenzin muttered, "It is a cry that all living things will make at some stage in their lives. One day, they will be answered. It is called Judgement Day."

---- ➤ ----

Bible (NKJV)	Bhagavad Gita
[1] Hebrews 4:13, And there is no creature hidden from His sight, but all things are naked and open to the eyes of Him to whom we must give account.	[1-5] Chapter 11:10-12. Before Arjuna flashed the cosmos, multiple universes, life forms, and the revelation of the divine mystery, from nothing appeared Brahman and the power of thought; from the thought came the energy, the first three tears, matter, and antimatter.
[2] 1st Peter 4:5, They will give an account to Him who is ready to judge the living and the dead.	11:15. Arjuna: O Lord, in this vision, I saw what your thoughts, plans, and desires were before anything came into existence. I see Brahman sitting on the throne, surrounded by the Elders of the Universe and all the living entities.
[3] Ezekiel 37:26, "Moreover I will make a covenant of peace with them, and it shall be an everlasting covenant with them; I will establish them and multiply them, and I will set My sanctuary in their midst forever.	I have gained some insight into your plan for creation. I saw the beginning, present, and future realms flash before me. I saw the cosmos created by Brahman, atom by atom, each named and known by him. I saw the Universe come into being, piece by piece. The first sub-particle was named 83.45. Each was lovingly created, entered into his inventory, and accounted for daily by Brahman. Each atom had a name and a place in your grand plan.
[4] 1st Timothy 1:5, The purpose of the commandment is love from a pure heart, a good conscience, and sincere faith, 1 Timothy 3:9, holding the mystery of the faith with a pure conscience.	
[5] Job 10:1, "I loathe my life; I will give free utterance to my complaint; I will speak in the bitterness of my soul.	I saw the lives of ancient sages and the beginning and end of all things. All
---X--	

kinds of living things came to life. All were loved.

11:16. Untold numbers of life forms on Earth and spiritual sanctuaries passed before me. I saw the beginning and end of all. You gave life and brought joy, pain and suffering into our lives, and in 'The Fullness of Time' (before The Day of The Lord), you made us whole (restored, made restitution) and wiped away all pain and suffering. You showed/proved that nothing thrives in the Universe at the expense of another. I comprehended your joy and sorrow from start to end.

In your first thought, I saw my name chosen with great care, written in your Eternal Books, sealed by your loving tears. I saw your excellent plan for me on Earth, in the spiritual sanctuary, and I beheld the very last thought of mine before the end of all creation.

All I saw had a beginning and an end. Yet, you have no beginning, middle, or end. You are The Lord of creation; the cosmos and my life rest in your hands.

---X--

---------- ↦------

Chapter 101

The cost of salvation: a clear conscience and clean hands

On one of his visits to the sanctuary, Sam asked Tenzin, "What kind of people will eventually inhabit the cosmos?"

"Come, let us sit down under the tree of healing," he suggested.

When they had made themselves comfortable under the shade of the tree, he asked, "What kind of world would you like to live in? What kind of person would you like to be in the future?"

She thought about it for a while. Something he had once said sprang into her mind. He had said, "One needs clean hands and a clear **conscience**[1] to live in the future."

Tenzin said, "To live in eternity with a clear conscience, one has to follow the moral code: 'No one in the Universe can thrive at the **expense**[2] of another, in other words, **steal**[3] from another living entity or deprive it of its precious life'."

She remembered what he had said before. Like all living entities on Earth, to survive, she had fed on **living entities**[4], deprived them of life, and broken the moral code.

At some stage, she had to confront the price paid by the living entities. She would need to pay back and make **restitution**[5]. There was also the element of acknowledging appreciation and gratitude to those forced to make sacrifices and endure pain and suffering so that she could grow spiritually. Perhaps the sanctuary was the appropriate place but now was not the right time.

One day, with Tenzin's and her heavenly Father's help, she would climb the summit of her moral dilemma and confront this issue. She would start to make restitution to all that were once living entities, and make them whole again (pay off her debt to all living entities), and breathe with a clear conscience and have clean hands. She had no idea how it could be done. Nevertheless, she was willing to accept this challenge. This **attitude**[6] would propel her to great spiritual heights in the future.

She comprehended that nothing in the Universe was free. Those living entities that suffered during the perfection[7] of her salvation had to receive more than adequate restitution for their loss. Second, she acknowledged their sacrifices; without their part, her spiritual growth would not have been possible.

She had no resources to reach out to them, to make good what she owed them. She would need to reach out to her heavenly Father for His assistance. Moreover, that would indebt her to Him for eternity and gain her gratitude, worship, love, and adoration.

The cosmos had been a mother, father, brother, sister, family, and teacher to her. She owed a considerable debt to its **sacrificial love**[8], not just the good but its evil, for the combination of good and evil had made her what she was today. This cruel, imperfect world was ideal for her perfection.

Tenzin was standing before her and reading her mind. Finally, she had begun to see God's wisdom in His creation. A world free of sin, pain, and suffering would have taught her very little. In contrast, her current perfection had come at a significant cost to her and others.

He asked, "And what are your aspirations today?"

---- ➤+ ----

Bible (NKJV)	Bhagavad Gita
[1] 1 Timothy 3:9 holding the mystery of the faith with a pure conscience.	[1] 16:7. Ungodly people have no sense of uprightness or purity and have a degenerate moral conscience. They lack a sense of truth or correct conduct. There is little or no sacrificial goodness in them.
[2] Romans 8:22 For we know that the whole creation groans and labours with birth pangs together until now.	
	[1 - 4] *Gita 1:26-46/Elaboration A1-23*
[3] Leviticus 19:11 "You shall not steal, deal falsely, or lie to one	A19 "As a lotus plant grows undefiled in muddy waters, so shall you walk

another."

[4] Genesis 9:3 "Every moving thing that lives shall be food for you. I have given you all things, even the green herbs."

[5] Leviticus 5:16 "And he shall make restitution for the harm that he has done concerning the holy thing and shall add one-fifth to it and give it to the priest."

[6] Hebrews 6:1 Therefore, leaving the discussion of the elementary principles of Christ, let us go on to perfection, not laying the foundation of repentance from dead works again and of faith toward God,

---x--

beside Me, undefiled by sin. Bear no evil thought, malice, or hate for your opponents. With My aid, fight ignorance, evil, and injustice with a warm heart, a clear conscience, and clarity of who you are and will be from the beginning to the end. (Gita 5:10. 16:1-3)

[1-5] A7 Arjuna sees himself standing before the heavenly cloud of witnesses on the Day of Judgement. He has no fear of this day, for his conscience is clear. All his days, he had harboured no ill or malice towards anyone. He had worked tirelessly to bring about peace, justice, and goodness, making fourfold restitution to all he had hurt. (Gita 10:11-31)

[1-2] 1:45. Knowing this, how can I, in good conscience, kill my relatives (Living entities) to gain a kingdom?

[2-7] 5:18. My devotees have equal regard for all. They see the same self (the breath of God) in a learned scholar, an outcast, a cow, an elephant, and a dog. All are contributing directly or indirectly towards God's kingdom and our salvation. Therefore, they (panditah) have a heightened appreciation and a duty to care for and promote everyone's welfare. Hence, as they progress in their spiritual growth, they regard all life forms as part of their and God's extended family.

[6] 5:19. Such people have conquered the fear of life and death. They rest in the perfect Brahman and Me as they are gradually refined and made flawless

[6-7] 16:1. The Supreme Lord: Arjuna, you must nurture these qualities. Learn to overcome fear and walk in purity of heart and emotions. Study the Scriptures and grow in spiritual knowledge. Be compassionate and charitable, and have a clear conscience. Give freely and indulge in a duty of care and kindness towards all, especially the poor and vulnerable. a spirit of giving and forgiveness.

[8] 3:14 The whole of creation depends on selfless service and sacrifice. All living things are nourished and sustained by food provided by the gifts of others.

--------- ᛡ ------

Chapter 102

Our debt to all living entities

She replied, "I am beginning to understand that every living thing, atom, and quark has contributed to my spiritual growth. In hindsight, I now realise that all things in the cosmos have worked **together**[1] for the perfection of my salvation. It was their combined efforts that made it possible. I owe a debt to all living things. Each living thing has a right to demand restitution for its sacrificial contribution. Judgement Day is meant to broaden my understanding of the debt I owed and how the Lord made restitution to all and paid for it. I don't understand everything, but am beginning to get the gist."

Tenzin replied, "Everything in the cosmos has value. I have a different value from a bacterium or an animal because I have a more remarkable ability. Therefore, I have greater responsibility and accountability to others. We all owe the Cosmos a debt. Nothing is free. There is a cost to all things. Someone somewhere has to pay it and balance the books.

"Our salvation has a cost. God picks up the final tab. He has to make **good**[2] the debt to all things that have contributed to our growth. Before creation, He **chose us**[3], calculated the **cost**[4] of our salvation, and made provisions to meet that tab.

"He also requires that one day we should understand and appreciate the cost to Him. In His calculation, he accounted for the debt to creation for its sacrificial contribution. Therefore, His moral duty is to **make whole**[5] all who have suffered and have contributed to His eternal plan.

"He is a just and gracious God. He appreciates the pain and **suffering that all creation**[6] is undergoing. Therefore, He will make whole all who have suffered under His eternal plan."

Sam said, "My existence has placed a cost upon God and the cosmos; therefore, I have to make the **appropriate restitution**[7] to all. I don't have the means to make good." ---- ➤ ----

Bible (NKJV)	Bhagavad Gita
[1] Romans 8:28 And we know that all things work together for good to those who love God, to those who are the called according to *His* purpose.	[1, 2] 3:10-11. **The Supreme** Lord of Creation continued: At the beginning of creation, I blessed creation and set in motion the principle of selfless, sacrificial service to promote the welfare, interest, and happiness of all creation. Thus, through this selfless service, all creation would be prosperous and fruitful, fulfilling its desires. Participate in this sacrificial service to My creation, and you will receive My blessing. Collaboration between humankind and creation brings prosperity to all.
[2, 7] Colossians 1:20 by Him to reconcile all things to Himself, whether things on earth or things in heaven, having made peace through the blood of His cross.	
[3] Ephesians 1:4 chose us in Him before the foundation of the world, that we should be holy and without blame before Him in love.	[3, 4] 3:14 The whole of creation depends on selfless service and sacrifice. All living things are nourished and sustained by food provided by the gifts of others. Plants and trees sacrificially give their fruit, flowers, and shade without complaining.
[4] Luke 14:28 "For which of you, intending to build a tower, does not sit down first and count the cost, whether he has *enough* to finish *it*."	
[5] Job 5:18 For He bruises, but He binds up; He wounds, but His hands make whole.	
	[3 - 7] *Gita 1:26-46/Elaboration A1-23*
[6] Romans 8:20-21 Against its will, all creation was subjected to God's curse. But with eager hope, the creation looks forward to the day when it will join God's children in glorious freedom from death and decay.	*A6 The spirit of the Lord in Arjuna reveals that even in Heaven, the work of counselling, reconciliation, restoration, restitution, and making each whole has to continue if there is going to be eternal peace. That would require the special abilities, time, and effort of Godly eternal warrior-priests like him to restore and heal until all are made whole. The daunting task ahead and hereafter demoralises him*
--x--	

	and subdues his spirit. (Gita 11:1-31)
	[5, 6,] 3:30. Arjuna, fix your mind on Me and surrender all your works unto Me. <u>Fulfil My divine plan</u> to improve all creatures' welfare, interest, and happiness. Do it without any desire for personal gain.
	--X--

--------- ᕃᕍ------

Chapter 103

Clear conscience

Tenzin told Sam, "One day, with our help, you will have a clear **conscience**[1] after you have made restitutions for all your debt. Your hands will be free of all blood, pain, and suffering, the result of perfecting your salvation.

"You will hold your head high, not with pride but with humility. You have the will and ability to comprehend the enormous cost to the Lord and the Universe for the grace offered to you. God has high expectations for you in the coming Kingdom.

"Most of humanity fail to grasp **this cost**[2], and hence they cannot appreciate our Lord's investment in them."

Sam said, "I want to learn to **serve**[3] as our Master does. I want to follow in your footsteps. That is my aspiration, but I cannot achieve it or bring it to fruition."

"You cannot do it on your own. Nevertheless, you are not alone. We are your eternal spiritual family. We will help. Trust me. We have the **ability**[4] and means to bring it about. All we need is your consent, commitment, and willingness to guide and lead you."

"I am sorry, Tenzin. I look at myself, and I find it hard to believe it. I do not have the confidence that you seem to have in me. There are days I cry in despair. I feel overwhelmed. So much seems to be expected of me. I cannot return the high trust you place in me."

"Sam, you should take one day at a time. Here, time is a commodity we have plenty of. All we require is your willingness and cooperation. We will support you, even if completing your course takes a long time. You may be the last one in, but it does not matter to us." He smiled. "We are patient. You matter more than the rate of your progress. We move ahead at the pace you set. You will make it, except..." he paused.

"Except what?" Sam asked.

"You can choose to walk away. You have free will. We cannot override your free will." ---- ➤ ----

Bible (NKJV)	Bhagavad Gita
[1] 1 Timothy 1:5 Now the purpose of the commandment is love from a pure heart, from a good conscience, and sincere faith,	[1] 16:1. The Supreme Lord: Arjuna, you must nurture these qualities. Learn to overcome fear and walk in purity of heart and emotions. Study the Scriptures and grow in spiritual knowledge. Be compassionate and charitable, and have a clear conscience.
[2] Malachi 3:7 Yet from the days of your fathers You have gone away from My ordinances And have not kept them. Return to Me, and I will return to you," Says the LORD of hosts. "But you said, 'In what way shall we return?'	[2] 16:7. Ungodly people have no sense of uprightness or purity and have a degenerate moral conscience. They lack a sense of truth or correct conduct. There is little or no sacrificial goodness in them.
[3] Mark 10:45 "For even the Son of Man did not come to be served, but to serve, and to give His life a ransom for many."	[3] 2:41. Those who desire to serve Me and creation (all life forms and humanity) will attain a singular purpose with great resolve. For those who lack resolution, life's decisions will divert them from Me to material things.
[4] 1 Peter 4:11 If anyone speaks, let him speak as the oracles of God. If anyone ministers, let him do it with the ability which God supplies. -----X--	[4] 7:8. Arjuna, I am like the sun's and the moon's radiance. I am the sacred sound Om in the (Vedic Hindu) Scriptures and poems. I am the giver of courage and ability to all. --------- ꝗ-------

Chapter 104

Back on Earth

As Sam wandered towards the stream, a gentle force seemed to pull her away. She cried out as the force lifted her.

"Tenzin," she cried, "help me. Please help me." She started to panic and screamed. When she saw Tenzin, relief flooded over her. "Please help me," she cried again.

He looked at her. There was sadness in his eyes.

"I am sorry, Sam. It was not my decision. You have to **go back**[1]."

She cried out, "I don't want to go. I want to stay."

She found herself pulled through a tunnel. The air became thicker; there was a strong scent of disinfectant in the air. She saw her body on a hospital bed. Then, she lost all awareness.

Slowly, she opened her eyes. It took her a few minutes to realise she was in a hospital. She felt weak and dizzy and fell asleep once more.

She heard a faint voice. "I think she's coming round. Her pulse is getting stronger."

Sam opened her eyes. It took her a while to recognize a nurse standing beside her. "Where am I?" she asked, her voice barely above a whisper.

"You are in a hospital," replied the nurse. "Let me help you sit up."

The nurse helped her up. "How do you feel?" asked the nurse.

"I feel fragile and dizzy. My head hurts."

"Let me get you a warm drink and some food. It will help you to get some strength."

A few minutes later, she returned with some warm food. "Here, have this. It'll make you feel better. My name is Leah. I will come back later. Try to sleep if you can."

That evening, Sam got out of bed. She found it difficult to walk; her legs felt like lead as she made her way to the bathroom. Then, she went back to her bed.

When most patients had gone to sleep later that evening, the kind nurse, Leah, came to see Sam.

"What happened to me?" Sam asked.

Leah replied, "You have been in a coma for about twelve days. A schoolteacher found you and called an ambulance. The paramedic said you fell off a tree, your head hit a rock, and you were knocked unconscious. The senior doctor thought you would probably die in a day or two. No one here expected you to live. It's a miracle that you are alive. You are weak and need to rest. I will see you tomorrow." Nurse Leah left, and Sam went back to sleep.

For the next few days, Sam had physiotherapy. The nurses helped her to regain some of her strength. Toward the end of the week, the senior doctor examined her. He felt that she was strong enough to be discharged. One of the hospital admin staff came to see Sam.

"Hello, Sam. My name is Jessie," she said. "The senior doctor has asked me to see you. I have a few questions to ask you."

Sam replied weakly. "I know why you're here. I'm sorry, I have no money to pay my hospital bill."

There was a pause as Jessie considered this. She asked, "Do you have relatives who can help you?"

"No, I don't have any relatives. I am an orphan."

"Do you have friends who can help?"

"No, I'm sorry; I have no family, friends, or **home².** I am **enslaved to a pimp³** and don't want to return to him." Sam started to cry.

There was a long, awkward silence. "I see," said Jessie. Her voice was unsympathetic. She got up in disgust and left.

For the next two days, she was cold-shouldered by the staff. She felt helpless, anxious, and fearful of the future. On the third day, Jessie came to see her in the morning. "Pack your things," she said abruptly. She tossed a cheap plastic bag onto her bed. It contained a set of discarded clothes donated to the hospital. "Get dressed. You are discharged. Your man is waiting for you outside."

Sam looked confused. "I don't have anyone. What about the hospital fees?"

Jessie replied, "Your friend Antonio paid the bill. Hurry. We need the bed."

Sam got dressed. Then, slowly, she made her way to the hospital entrance. Her heart pounded. There were tears in her eyes.

---- ➤ ----

Bible (NKJV)	Bhagavad Gita
[1] Acts 26:16 'But rise and stand on your feet; for I have appeared to you for this purpose, to make you a minister and a witness both of the things which you have seen and of the things which I will yet reveal to you..	[1] 18:64. Because I dearly love you, I have revealed knowledge hidden from others. I shared it with you so that you and My devotees may benefit from it.
[2] Psalms 25:16 Turn to me and have mercy, for I am alone and in deep distress.	--------- ॐ-------
[3] Genesis 47:19 Shall we die	

before your eyes, both we and our land? <u>Buy us and our land in exchange for food.</u> With our land, we will become <u>slaves</u> to Pharaoh (*Antonio*).	
-----X--	

--------- ૧૧------

Chapter 105

Victims of drugs and abuse

Antonio was waiting for her. His face was red, furious. A torrent of foul language erupted from his mouth when he saw Sam.

He grabbed her by the neck and roughly pushed her inside his luxurious sports car. He drove her to his brothel, swearing at her as he went.

He dragged her out of the car and shoved her into the house. One of the girls saw her and ran to her aid. She took hold of Sam and led her into the backroom.

For the next three years, her life was miserable. Antonio made her work hard, constantly reminding her that she owed him the money for the hospital. Even when she had paid her debt several times over, he would bring up the hospital fees as if she still owed him the debt.

Her life was a total **misery**[1]**.** She had to do things that humiliated her. A few times, she would look at a passing lorry and wonder if she should throw herself in front of it. She sank into a trance-like state; her will and spirit were mired in despair.

Late in the night, bruised and battered from Antonio's beating, half-starved, she would crawl into her bed. In despair, she **cried**[2] out to Tenzin, to God.

All her prayers seemed to be **ignored.**[3] The promises of divine protection and safety seemed hollow. She began to doubt. Perhaps it had just been a dream. What she had seen was an illusion, a desperate cry for help—an escape from the reality of life.

Antonio introduced her to drugs. They seemed to dull the pain and make life easier to cope with. It helped her to stop thinking and to stop feeling **ashamed.**[4]

On rare occasions, if **Antonio**[5] was in a good mood, he would allow Sam and the other girls to go to the temple or the local church. He would give them gifts for the monks and the priests, hoping their blessings would improve his financial prospects.

She often went into the church or temple gardens, dreaming of the sanctuary and Tenzin, her friends Kwan-yin and Stefan. Then, she would push away these thoughts. They were just dreams, she would tell herself. There had been no such place; it had only been an escape from the reality of life.

Still, she would light a candle on her way out of the church or temple and say a little prayer. Perhaps Tenzin or the Lord might **hear**[6] her. Soon, the candle would burn out, taking the little **hope**[7] she had with it.

---- ➤ ----

Bible (NKJV)	Bhagavad Gita
[1] Psalms 88:1, O Jehovah, the God of my salvation, I have cried out day and night before You.	[1, 2] 5:22. Pleasure and misery derived from the senses have a beginning and an end. The wise do not look for happiness in them.
[2] Psalms 130:1, Out of the depths have I cried unto you, O Jehovah.	[3,6,7] 2:57. Having subjugated selfish attachments, such a person is unaffected by whatever good or evil fortune comes his way, always trusting in My providence. He does not overtly rejoice nor becomes depressed by such outcomes. Faith in sound wisdom guides him.
[3] Hebrews 2:10, For it was fitting for Him, for whom are all things and by whom are all things, in bringing many sons to glory, to make the captain of their salvation perfect through sufferings.	
[3b] Hebrews 5:7-9, While Jesus was here on earth, he offered prayers and pleadings, with a loud cry and tears, to the one who could rescue him from death. And God heard his prayers because of his deep	[5] 13:22. A person's spirit (duality of soul and Atman) identifies either with the material body (influenced by the gunas) or the divine essence. And often both. How a person thinks moulds the person. For example, is

reverence for God. Even though Jesus was God's Son, he learned obedience from the things he suffered. In this way, God qualified him as a perfect High Priest, and he became the source of eternal salvation for all those who obey him.

[4] Psalms, 22:15, My mouth is dried up like a potsherd, and my tongue sticks to my jaws; you lay me in the dust of death.

[5] Jeremiah 5:28, They have grown fat, they are sleek; Yes, they surpass the deeds of the wicked; They do not plead the cause, The cause of the fatherless; Yet they prosper, And the right of the needy they do not defend.

[6] Psalms 88:9, My eye wastes away because of affliction. LORD, I have called daily upon You; I have stretched out my hands to You.

[7] Malachi 3:3, He will sit like a refiner of silver, burning away the trash. He will purify the Levites, refining them like gold and silver, so they may again offer acceptable sacrifices to the LORD.

---X--

his thinking led by his gunas or the indwelling spirit? Thus, according to their views, one comes across evil and good among all species.

[6, 7] 9:20. Those who study the Holy books and worship Me free themselves from ignorance, darkness, fear and evil. They attain a place in the heavenly realms and have access to My wisdom and blessings.

---X--

--------- 9)------

Chapter 106

A new friend, Kellie

Sometimes, Antonio would send Sam to the market to buy fruit and vegetables. One day, she met a young Indian woman called Kellie, who owned a stall in the market. She was a happy, lively woman and always made Sam laugh.

They became friends. It was one of those rare occasions when she smiled, felt happy, and was glad to be alive. As time passed, they became good friends. Often, Kellie would give Sam twice the amount of fruit and vegetables for her money.

Antonio was delighted at the quality and cheapness of the fruit. He started to send her out more often.

Their friendship brought back some of the light to Sam's life. She began to use drugs less often. As their companionship grew, she finally gave up the drugs.

One day, Kellie and Sam were sitting together, laughing and drinking tea. It was a hot day, and there were barely any shoppers around. Leaning towards her friend, Kellie took hold of Sam's right hand. "Sam, I like you. We're good friends. You make me happy. I am very thankful for your companionship."

Sam nodded, "Me too. I am very fond of you. I wish we could spend more time together."

"I have an idea," Kellie replied. "Once a month, I go to a bigger town. There is a market there. One of the stallholders wants to sell his property. It's a big stall and needs two people to run it. He also has a small flat nearby, which he wants to include in the sale. He wants ten thousand dollars for it. What do you think?"

"It sounds like a good idea. I'll be very happy for you if you can get it. I will miss your company," Sam replied.

"Come with me, Sam. We can be partners."

"I would love to, Kellie, but I have no money."

"I don't have enough money to buy it on my own. I need a partner, someone I can trust."

"Kellie, it's a good idea, but we don't have the money."

"If we had the money, would you come?"

"Of course, I would."

"We should hold up a bank!"

They both laughed.

Sam's **friendship**[1] with Kellie had helped her. She seemed to come out of her despair. Antonio noticed the change and was pleased; it meant he could make her work harder and make more money. He became less abusive and even started to smile at her.

Antonio had branched out from pimping to drug dealing. Soon, he controlled the local drug trade, and money flowed into his accounts. With the help of a few local thugs, he started to expand his business. He made enemies as he encroached on rival drug lords' turfs. This was a risky but very profitable trade.

He started to take less interest in the girls. He was less oppressive, and their lives became more manageable.

Sam's memories of the sanctuary had faded four years after she had left the hospital. She had come to terms with her life in its present condition, and each day, her life was getting a little easier and happier.

Antonio was more occupied with his drug trade. Though she was still young, in her early twenties, the strain of her hard life had taken its toll on her. She looked and felt older.

It was the rainy season. She looked at the dark sky and thought of the **Lord,**[2] Tenzin and Stefan.

Sam went to the market. Her friend was not there. She bought some fruit and vegetables from another stall and turned back, dreading what **Antonio**[3] would say. He would complain that she had paid too much. If he were in a bad mood, she would receive a **beating.**[4]

As Sam approached the house, she sensed something was wrong. She ran up to the house. The girls were crying.

"What happened?" she asked one of the girls.

"It's Antonio—he's **dead.**[5]"

---- ➤ ----

Bible (NKJV)	Bhagavad Gita
[1] Proverbs 18:24, some friends play at friendship, but a true friend sticks closer than their nearest kin.	[2] 7:26. I am the Eternal One. The past, present and future are known to me. I know every living entity by their names and deeds and regularly take an inventory of their thoughts, motives, and doing. Hence, I know all there is to know about them; however, no one knows Me thoroughly. 9:34. Fill your thoughts with Me. Seek Me, worship Me with all your heart, mind, and strength, and I will reward you.
[2] Psalms 9:13, Have mercy on me, O LORD! Consider my trouble from those who hate me, You who lift me from the gates of death,	
[3] Psalms 140:11, Let not a slanderer be established in the earth; Let evil hunt the violent man to overthrow him!	
[4] Job 30:27, My heart is in turmoil and cannot rest; Days of affliction	[3, 4] 2:32. A warrior confronted with such a war against unrighteousness and evil should be pleased, for it

confront me.

⁵ Psalms 37:9, For <u>evildoers, shall be cut off</u>, But those who <u>wait on the LORD</u> shall inherit the earth. Job 36:6. He does not <u>preserve</u> the life of the wicked but gives <u>justice to the oppressed</u>.

---X--

comes as an opportunity that <u>opens the door to My divine assistance</u> and grace. So be happy and rejoice at this opportunity.

⁵ 5:15. Lord Krishna: I <u>do not partake</u> in any person's good or evil acts. Ignorant people are bewildered by this because they lack spiritual understanding

---X--

--------- ᕯ-------

Chapter 107

We cried out to the LORD God of our fathers

Sam asked the girls, "How did he die?"

"He got in a fight with one of the drug dealers, who shot him."

A cold chill ran through her. She dropped the shopping, and her legs felt weak. Part of her was glad Antonio was dead. She felt no sorrow at his demise. In a few minutes, all their lives had changed. With Antonio gone, one of his gangster friends would take over his business, and the police would be here soon with a search warrant for drugs; in fact, there would be a police presence on the premises for the next two or three days.

That would keep his associates away for a while. They had a short time to escape from this hell before the window of opportunity closed. They all had a chance to escape, but where could they go without money or skills? She went to her little room to think.

Within an hour, the police arrived with a search warrant. Immediately, they started to search the premises for drugs and money and ordered the girls to sit in the front room. One by one, they were taken to the backroom and interrogated.

Soon, it was Sam's turn. The police officer questioned her about Antonio: what were his associates' names and his drug habits? Who were his suppliers and dealers?

The fat police officer leaned towards Sam. "Do you know where he kept his drugs, his money?"

Sam replied, "I believe he had a safe in his office."

The police officer ordered her to show him. She led him to Antonio's office. The door was locked.

"Do you know where the key is?"

"No, sir," replied Sam.

The officer called one of his men. "Break that door down," he ordered. Inside, they found a thick steel safe in the corner.

"Do you know where the key is?" the officer asked Sam, not expecting an answer.

To his surprise, she replied, "Yes, it's hidden in a secret pocket on the back of the old sofa."

They found the key and opened the safe. It was full of drugs, documents, and a few banknotes.

"Thank you," the police officer said. "You have made our job a lot easier."

They counted the money, made an inventory of all the items in the safe, and then packed it all in clear evidence bags. Each bag was labelled and entered into the list. The police were there for the whole day. They searched everywhere, taking statements from the girls. That night, one police guard was left outside the house. They returned the second day, did a few more searches, and interrogated the neighbours.

While the rest of the girls slept, Sam crept out of her bed, went to Antonio's office, lit a candle, lifted the carpet, and rolled it up. She lifted a loose floorboard and put her hand into the space underneath. She felt a bag and pulled it out—a medium-sized sports bag. She opened it, and a smile came over her **face.**[1]

"Praise to the **Lord**[2]," she whispered. She closed the bag, replaced the floorboard, and rolled back the carpet. Silently, she made her way back to her room.

"Thank you, Lord," she said. For the first time in years, she slept peacefully. Early in the morning, Sam got up, showered, and packed a shopping bag before the others woke up.

The police officer was still outside the front door. She went to the back of the house, opened the door, stepped into the alley, and paused. It was still dark, quiet, and deserted. She made her way to the road and headed towards the market.

Few people were on the roads, and no one noticed her. The market was closed. She sat on a bench and waited for it to open. She had a long wait. Two hours later, the door opened. She made her way to Kellie's stall and waited.

A few minutes later, her friend arrived. Sam ran up to her and gave her a big hug.

Kellie remarked, "Hi, Sam. What's all this excitement about? You look delighted to see me."

"I am. Please, Kellie, can we go somewhere quiet and talk?"

"We can talk in my van." They walked up to the old van and got inside.

Sam placed the bag on the backseat. "Kellie, you talked about the stall in the next town. Is it still for sale?"

"I believe it is still available. Why?"

"Do you still want to be partners—I mean, equal partners?"

"I would love to be equal partners with you, Sam, but it's a dream. We don't have the money."

Sam took hold of her friend's hands. "Promise me we can be equal partners and never fight over money. Promise me we will care for each other as sisters. Swear it to me."

Kellie replied, "But we don't have the money."

A big smile crossed **Sam's face.**[3]

"Take an oath first."

"Ok. I promise. I promise we will be like sisters forever and never let money divide us."

---- ➤ ----

Bible (NKJV)	Bhagavad Gita
[1] Psalms, 17:3 You have tested my heart; You have visited me in the night; You have tried me and have found nothing;	[1-3] 11:37-39. O Lord, you are more significant than Brahman, the creator. You are the original creator. How could they not worship you? You are limitless, the refuge of the Universe. You are Lord of lords. Only you are worthy of praise and worship. You are the eternal, timeless spirit, the resting place of all living entities. You pervade the whole cosmos. You are the father and grandfather of all creatures. >>I bow before you. Only you are worthy of praise and worship. You are our final home.
[2] Daniel 26:7, 'Then we cried to the LORD God of our fathers, and the LORD heard our voice and looked on our affliction, labour, and oppression.	
[3] Psalms 31:7, I will be glad and rejoice in Your mercy, For You have considered my trouble; You have known my soul in adversities,	
---X--	---X--

--------- ↬-------

Chapter 108

I will rejoice in Your mercy

Sam reached into the backseat and lifted the bag. She opened it to show Kellie it was full of **money[1]**. There were several bundles, two of which were of dollars.

Kellie said nervously, "What, did you rob a bank?"

Sam replied, "I'll explain to you later. First, let us go to your flat. Then we will go and see if we can buy the stall."

They drove to Kellie's flat, locked the front door, closed the curtains, and counted the money. There were 12,000 dollars and thousands of baht. They made three thick parcels of baht.

Kellie could not refrain from asking again, "Tell me, where did this money come from?"

San replied, "A quarter of this is mine. Now it's ours. The rest belongs to someone else. We will use the dollars to buy the stall. The rest, I must return to its **rightful owners[2]**. I am going to take the money to them. Give me an hour, and I'll be back. Then, we can go and purchase the stall."

Kellie got up and hugged her. "My **dreams[3]** have come true. Come back quickly, Sister." She smiled; her whole face was radiant.

Sam left her flat and made her way back to Antonio's place. She entered the house from the alley. It was late morning, and the three girls were in the kitchen. They were quiet, worried about their future, dreading the arrival of the new master, whoever it might be. Sam greeted them.

"You look cheerful," one of the girls said.

Sam replied, "I am, and you will be after I tell you some good news."

"What good news?" another girl asked.

Sam reached into the cheap plastic bag and drew out three parcels. She handed **each girl a package** [4] containing money. "Antonio left us a surprise. A big surprise. I am packing my bags and leaving. Open the parcel carefully. I suggest you pack your bags and **leave**[5] quickly before the new master comes."

With that, she turned her back and left the room. She headed straight to Kellie's house. On the way, she kept singing, "Thank you, Lord. Thank you." ---- ➤ ----

Bible (NKJV)	Bhagavad Gita
[1] Psalms 34:19. Many are the afflictions of the righteous, But the <u>LORD delivers him out of them all</u>.	[2] 2:71. A person is free when he <u>gives up selfish material desires</u> and false ego. He holds all proprietorship as My steward rather than an owner, <u>taking what he needs</u> to sustain him. Such a man attains inner peace and remains calm at the prospect of death.
[2] Proverbs 28:27. He who <u>gives</u> to the poor will not lack, But he who hides his eyes will have many curses.	
[3] Isaiah 14:3. It shall come to pass in the day the LORD <u>gives</u> you rest from your sorrow, and from your fear and the hard bondage in which you were made to serve,	[2-4] 18:51-53. Surrounded by my divine presence, they overcome the objects of self-gratification and passion. Freed from the clamour of likes and dislikes, they lead a simple life, eat moderately, and control their body, mind, and power of speech. Free from self-will, arrogance, aggressiveness, pride, anger, and the lust to possess people or things, <u>they rest in the divine presence, in peace and contentment.</u> They gladly <u>share their wealth</u>, knowledge, and wisdom but refrain from imposing it on others. -------- ↔-------
[4] Psalms 107:6. Then they cried out to the LORD in their trouble, *And* He <u>delivered</u> them out of their distresses.	
[5] Psalms 22:5. They cried to You and were <u>delivered</u>; They trusted in You and were not ashamed.	

Chapter 109

Sam and Kellie go into a partnership

Sam arrived at Kellie's house. Her friend was ready.

Kellie hugged her. "Ok, let's get our stall and a new home."

They headed towards the next town over. As they drove, Kellie turned to face Sam. "So, tell me about the money. Where did it come from?"

Sam laughed. "It's my money. I earned it." She paused. Her voice became sombre. "About a year ago, Antonio was drunk, came into my room, and dragged me into his office. He was furious about something and took his anger out on me. He beat me so badly that I passed out.

"I must have been unconscious for a while. When I came to, my whole body hurt. My left eye was swollen shut; there was blood on my face. I could barely see through my right eye. I pretended to be unconscious.

"Antonio must have thought I was still out. He rolled up the carpet, lifted a floorboard, and hid something. Then, he put the floorboard back, rolled back the rug, and went back to drinking.

"Soon after, he left the room, and I crept back to my room. He was hoarding the money we earned. It was our money. We earned it through tears, sweat, and blood."

"Sam," Kellie said. "You took the three parcels to the other girls. You could have kept it all."

Sam nodded. "The thought did **occur to me.**" [1]

"So why didn't you keep it? There was enough money there to keep you happy for many years."

"I don't know," Sam replied. "I can't explain it. Something inside me, like a voice, said I had to **do the right thing[2].**"

Kellie asked, "Weren't you tempted to keep the money?"

Sam, "Of course. Enough money to last us for life. I thought of all the things we could buy. For a while, I was tempted to keep the money."

"So why didn't you keep it?"

"I thought about the other girls who shared the house with me. They were trapped in that hole like me, and I was concerned about them. The money would give them a way out of this prison."

"So, you chose to share."

"Yes. It was the right **thing to do³.** It is what Tenzin taught me." She suddenly stopped, realizing she had said too much.

"Who is Tenzin?"

"It's a long story. I will tell you another time."

They arrived in town and sought the stallholder.

He was pleased to see them. His face brightened when he learnt the girls wanted to pay cash for his stall and small flat.

They went to a solicitor's office and agreed on the terms of the transfer.

The solicitor told them, "Come back in two hours, and I will have all the papers ready to sign."

Late afternoon, they went back to the solicitor's office. The papers were signed, the money exchanged hands, and the stall and the flat keys were theirs.

The stallholder took them to his flat.

He said, "Give me a few minutes to pack."

He called a friend, and they packed his clothes and the items he needed. Half an hour later, he left and handed the keys to the girls.

He left some heavier items, like the wardrobe, kitchen table, two single beds, and utensils.

When he was gone, the two girls sat down on a settee.

"**Finally, the Lord has blessed**[4] us and given us a home." They hugged each other.

Kellie suggested, "Let's go and celebrate. We'll have a nice meal, and then we can return to my flat and pick up my things. I'll hand back the keys and pay any outstanding rent. Then, we'll go to your place."

Sam shook her head. "I don't have a place to go back to. All my belongings are in that bag. This is home now, our home. Let's go celebrate, and tomorrow, we open our new stall."

---- ➤ ----

Bible (NKJV)	Bhagavad Gita
[1] Jeremiah 17:10 I, the LORD, <u>search the heart</u>, I test the mind, Even to give every man according to his ways, According to the fruit of his doings. [2] Psalms 143:10 <u>Teach me to do Your will</u>, For You are my God; Your Spirit is good. Lead me to the land of uprightness. [3] Psalms 32:8 I will instruct you how you should go and <u>guide you with My eye</u>. [4] Deuteronomy 7:13 "And <u>He will love you and bless you</u> and	[1-2] 18:51-53. Surrounded by my divine presence, they overcome the objects of self-gratification and passion. Freed from the clamour of likes and dislikes, they lead a simple life, eat moderately, and control their body, mind, and power of speech. Free from self-will, arrogance, aggressiveness, pride, anger, and the lust to possess people or things, <u>they rest in the divine presence, in peace and contentment.</u> They gladly <u>share their wealth</u>, knowledge, and wisdom but refrain from imposing it on others. [2] 3:9. <u>Selfish action</u> imprisons a

multiply you; He will also bless the fruit of your womb and the fruit of your land, your grain and your new wine and your oil."

---X--

person into the material world. Therefore, whatever work one performs in life should be a <u>sacrificial duty</u> to humanity and Me, without thinking of personal benefit.

[3] 3:15. All <u>selfless action</u> comes from Brahman (the life-giving breath of God), the Absolute and the Highest Consciousness. With my blessing, Brahman created everything seen and unseen. Therefore, Brahman is present in every act of service to <u>promote the welfare, interest, and happiness of all</u>, no matter what one's profession.

[4] 7:18. All seekers of <u>truth are blessed</u>. Nevertheless, those <u>established in Me</u> will surely attain their highest goal.

---X--

--------- ૭૭------

Chapter 110

Search me, O God, and know my heart

Sam and Kellie opened the new stall and started to trade. They made new friends in the market and the town.

Safe in each other's company, the girls flourished. They worked hard and laughed a lot in these happy, prosperous times. In the evening, they retired to their tiny flat.

After a meal, the two girls would go for a long evening walk. Then, they would watch television or play card games until it was time to sleep. It helped them to unwind after a hard day's work.

Kellie had built a little shrine in a small corner of the kitchen. She had small pictures of Indian saints stuck to the wall. Each evening, she would **read**[1] a little from the Bible and the Bhagavad Gita, then solemnly light a candle, say a prayer, and go to sleep.

She closed her eyes and waited for the Holy Spirit to guide her. Her mind rested on Psalms 139:17: *How precious are Your thoughts to me, O God! How great is the sum of them!*

Psalms 139:23-24: *Search me, O God, and know my heart; Try me, and know my anxieties; see if there is any wicked way in me, and lead me in the way everlasting.*

Her mind rested on Bhagavad-Gita, 6:7: *One whose mind is renewed by the Divine Scriptures lives in peace. In servitude to Me, a person's resolve is unmoved by happiness, distress, cold, heat, pain, or pleasure.*

Sometimes, Sam would watch her. She noticed that this ritual seemed to calm and relax her friend.

Kellie glanced at Sam. "You should share your day with God before you go to bed. It's good for your soul."

Sam asked, "What do you pray or share about?"

"I examine[2] my conduct of the day under the Scriptures' gaze. I ask God to teach me from the events of the day and help me **change my attitude[3]** for the better, to amend my inappropriate attitude to life and others. Should the thing happen again, I would know how to handle it in line with the Scriptures. I try to be a more helpful and **better person[4]** the following day, to be blameless and above reproach **in His sight." [5]**

"What else?" She asked. ---- ➻ ----

Bible (NKJV)	**Bhagavad Gita**
[1] Romans 12:2. Do not be conformed to this world, but be transformed by renewing your mind so that you may prove God's good, acceptable, and perfect will. [2] Lamentations 3:40. Let us search out and examine our ways, And turn back to the LORD. [3] Malachi 3:3. He will sit like a refiner of silver, burning away the trash. He will purify the Levites, refining them like gold and silver, so they may again offer acceptable sacrifices to the LORD. [4] 2nd Corinthians 11:2, I may present you as a chaste virgin to Christ. [5] Colossians 1:22. To present you holy, blameless, and above reproach in His sight. --------- ↬------	[1] 3:32. Those who complain and ignore the scripture lack knowledge. They are deluded, spiritually lost, and devoid of hope of enlightenment in life. [2] 4:18. The wise see action in inaction and inaction in action. Sacred scripture teachings guide their intelligence and activities. Hence, they enjoy happiness in discharging their duties. [3] 17:14. Service to the Supreme Lord consists of worshipping the Supreme Lord and respecting the spiritual master, parents, and elders. All activities are conducted in purity, honesty, cleanliness, simplicity, and without violence. **---x--**

Chapter 111

Everything in life has a purpose

Kellie paused and replied, "I am mostly thankful for each day. I reflect on the day's events and see if I can learn anything new from God. Each day, I am thankful for all the people, birds, animals, and living things in our neighbourhood. They all work together to form a community that enriches our lives. I feel a great sense of gratitude towards all."

"I see," Sam said.

Kellie continued, "Their presence has allowed me to grow physically and spiritually. I pray for insight to find ways to turn that gratitude **into action**[61] to promote their welfare, happiness, and interest. But that poses a challenge."

"I do not understand," Sam said.

"I have very few resources to reciprocate to all, so I ask God to give me strength and resources to improve their lives."

"Is that why you are keen to help in the soup kitchen for the homeless?"

Kellie replied, "I never thought of it that way. I do that because I want to **help people**[2]."

Sam remarked, "You are among the most generous and thoughtful people I have ever encountered."

Kellie pulled back, surprised by her remark. "Thank you, Sam," she said. "It is very nice of you to say that. We were meant to meet each other. Perhaps our Karma brought us together. Everything in life has a **purpose**[3]. We are very similar, except…" She checked herself. She had said too much.

"Except what?" Sam asked, sounding anxious.

"Nothing."

"We are like sisters now. You can speak the truth from **your heart⁴.** I may not like it, but we trust each other and have to be open with each other if our friendship is to grow."

"Okay, Sam. It's just that you are always so serious. You don't laugh or smile much, and you don't pray or like going to the temple or church. You take life too seriously."

She thought for a while. "You may be right. I will have to think about that. Maybe you can pray for me. Sleep well, Sister."

"How about now?"

"Fine."

Kellie prayed for her. Nothing happened.

A week later, as Sam slept, she felt the presence of the **infilling⁵ Holy Spirit (her Atman awoke).** Every thread in her life connected.

---- ➤ ----

Bible (NKJV)	Bhagavad Gita
¹ James 2:26. For as the body without the spirit is dead, faith without works is also dead.	**¹ ⁻⁴** 17:14-17. <u>Service to the Supreme Lord</u> consists of worshipping the Supreme Lord and respecting the spiritual master, parents, and elders. All activities are <u>conducted in purity, honesty,</u> cleanliness, simplicity, and without violence.
² John 7:38 "He who believes in Me, as the Scripture has said, out of <u>his heart will flow</u> rivers of living water."	v15. <u>Words that are truthful</u>, kindly, pleasing, beneficial, and inoffensive while upholding the truth and regularly reading scripture are the <u>self-disciplines of speech and mind.</u> Harsh and hurtful words inflict pain,
³ Ro 8:28. We know that <u>all things work together</u> for good to those who love God and are called according to <u>His purpose.</u>	

[4] 1 John 4:18. There is no fear in love, but perfect love casts out fear because fear involves torment. But he who fears has not been made perfect in love.

[5] Acts 8:17. Then they laid hands on them and received the Holy Spirit.

---X--

damage confidence, and stunt spiritual growth in others. Therefore, shun words that incite negativity and always avoid flattery.

v16. Lastly, consider the purification of the mind. Cultivate good thoughts, gentleness, self-restraint, purity of purpose and noble sentiments: these are the disciplines of the mind.

v17. Practice these self-disciplines with firm faith and without expectation of material benefit but as a way of life. Sages call this practice Sattvic.

[3-5] 18:50-53. Listen and learn from Me. Those who have achieved this state of inner peace, fulfilment, and purpose are on the path to perfection. They will gain a significantly higher knowledge of Brahman. They will cease to struggle in life and feel the divine presence always. Surrounded by my divine presence, they overcome the objects of self-gratification and passion.

---X--

-------- ॐ-------

Chapter 112

Sam and Kellie go into a partnership

A whole year went by. Sam and Kellie were young women, still in their early twenties, independent, confident, and happy. The security of their work and their home had helped restore the youthfulness that Sam had lost.

She began to blossom under the confidence and security that Kellie had generated. She finally had a home, honest work, and a family.

The men in the market were starting to show an interest in the girls. But most of the young men were emotionally immature, while the older men were either married or unsuitable.

Opposite Sam and Kellie's fruit and vegetable stall was another stall selling small electrical kitchen items. It belonged to two young men in their mid-twenties, Kim and Lee. They seemed mature, intelligent, and sober young men with good manners who were respectful of others.

They were courteous, and the girls liked them. The young men would occasionally come over and help the girls unload heavier items. One day, while they were helping the girls, Kim invited them to their flat for a meal.

Their friendship developed. Soon, they were all spending lots of time together. Kim was the older of the two. He was particularly fond of Kellie.

Lee was getting very fond of Sam. Their friendship blossomed into love.

A year later, they were married: Kim with Kellie and Lee with Sam. They exchanged their share of the stalls and the flats. Kim moved in with Kellie and took over from Sam. Sam moved into Lee's apartment and took over Kim's share of the stall.

Now Sam sold the electrical items while Lee spent his time repairing them.

Sam and Kellie's friendship grew deeper, and as time passed, it strengthened.

Sam started to attend church under the influence of her husband, Lee, and their small circle of friends, especially Kellie.

A few months later, she accepted Christ into her life and was baptised with half a dozen others at the church. Almost immediately, she received the **baptism**[1] of the Holy Spirit.

At around three in the morning, she had a horrible nightmare. She felt paralysed as she felt an evil presence trying to choke her. She cried out, but no sound came out of her.

Then, she remembered the Scriptures. "Go away," she shouted at the evil presence; I am **dead to you**[2]. I belong to Christ now. Go away before he casts you into the **bottomless pit**[3] that awaits you.

Nothing happened for a minute; then she felt a violent shake of her body and was free. The evil presence had gone. She breathed easily. She was floating in the air; suddenly, she was in the garden.

She saw her friend Tenzin standing before her, smiling.

"You are back," he commented. "This is temporary. I have a message for you. Listen carefully."

---- ➤+ ----

Bible (NKJV)	Bhagavad Gita
[1] Acts 1:8. But you shall receive power when the Holy Spirit has come upon you, and you shall be witnesses to Me in Jerusalem, in all Judea and Samaria, and to the end of the earth.	[1] 5:19. Such people have conquered the fear of life and death. They rest in the perfect Brahman and Me as they are gradually refined and made flawless. 5:21. They are not excessively attracted to sensual pleasure or dependent on external support but enjoy the inner joy of
[2] Romans 8:10. If Christ *is* in you,	

the body *is* dead because of sin, but the Spirit *is* life because of righteousness.

³ Revelation 20:3, The Lord cast him into the bottomless pit, shut him up, and set a seal on him so that he would no more deceive the nations until the thousand years were finished. But after these things, he must be released for a little while

---X--

spiritual awareness and the divine presence.

²⁻⁵ 4:3. To a selected few, I revealed My existence and plans for eternity (past, present, and future worlds to come). You are My friend and devotee, and in due time, as you gain My favour, I will reveal these mysteries and explain your role here on Earth, in the spiritual world, and in the far distant future. You and other trusted devotees will build My material and spiritual kingdoms in this world and hereafter and walk beside Me in all My realms. I will guide and teach you all as a Father.

³ 18:58. If you learn to walk beside Me, you will pass by all life's obstacles by My grace. If you choose to follow your own path, you will be lost and struggle alone.

---X--

--------- ᧤-------

Chapter 113

Nine names

He told her why she had been allowed to return. She had a mission to fulfil. He explained the mission and its purpose. "Now, you have to go back to Earth. One day, you will **write a book**[1] that will bring hope to many.

"Remember these nine names. These are the people who taught you the Tenets. Keep them close to your heart. These people have been brought into your life at great cost to us for a reason. Go back, and the Spirit of the Lord will go before you. From the depth of you will flow rivers of **living waters.**[2]"

Years went by. They prospered. Sam was in her late twenties when she had her first child. It was a happy occasion. They named the boy Christos, and two years later, they had a girl they called Maria.

Meanwhile, Kim and Kellie had two little children: a girl called Rupa and a boy named Raj.

Their families were growing, so they moved out of the flats and bought houses nearby. They often babysat each other's children or met at the park for a picnic. On Sundays, Sam's family went to church.

Five more years went by. Their businesses prospered. Their children played together and went to the same school.

Both families reduced their work hours and devoted part of their time and resources to helping people experiencing homelessness. Once a week, they helped in the **charity**[3] soup kitchen, paid for the food, sponsored a few deprived children in developing countries, and **helped**[4] others who had financial difficulties.

One evening, while Sam was preparing dinner for her family, little Christos asked Sam if they could have some rabbits as pets. Lee was reluctant, but Sam persuaded him.

"It's good for the children. We have a house and a big garden; the rabbits can run around, and you can build a cabinet for them. Our children will learn to be responsible."

They bought two female rabbits, and the children were delighted. After school, they would come home and play with the rabbits.

As time passed, the children began to lose interest in the rabbits; they had other things to discover: new electronic gadgets to occupy their time.

They attended their local Baptist church, where Lee and the children played in the church band on Sundays.

---- ➤ ----

Bible (NKJV)

[1] Deuteronomy 31:19. "Now, write down this song for yourselves, and teach it to the children of Israel; put it in their mouths, that this song may be a witness for Me against the children of Israel (*humanity*).

[2] John 7:38. "He who believes in Me, as the Scripture has said, out of his heart will flow rivers of living water."

[3] Genesis 28:22. "And this stone which I have set as a pillar shall be God's house, and of all that You give me I will surely give a tenth to You."

Bhagavad Gita

[2] 6:47. A disciple of great faith, who abides in Me, walks beside Me and renders loving service to all creation (building My kingdom on Earth and in Heaven) will be with Me forever. Whenever My devotees pass away into the hereafter, they leave a legacy of love, kindness, justice, and fairness, having enriched the lives of all around them.

[3-4] 2:71-72. My devotees are free when they give up selfish material desires and false egos. They hold all proprietorship as My stewards rather than as owners, taking what they need to sustain them. Such devotees attain inner peace and remain calm

[4] Isaiah 32:8. But a generous man devises generous things, And by generosity, he shall stand. ---x--		at the prospect of death. Those who live a spiritual and godly life attain calmness and pass peacefully into the Kingdom of God at death. ---x--

--------- ൭------

Chapter 114

Sunday school teacher

Sam looked at the small group of children. She comforted a small red-haired girl who had hurt her arm and said to the class, "The ability to empathise with someone suffering is one of the **greatest gifts[1]** of life.

"Many people struggle to cope with stress, anxiety, fear, and disabilities which can be physical or mental and become weak and ill. Those who are strong and help **carry[2]** the weak across the river of stress have a great **gift from God[3].**"

She continued, "We have the means and resources from Heaven to care for our and other **people's problems[4]**. We should learn to help others, reassure them, help them feel relaxed, and earn their trust."

The little red-haired girl said, "Sam, I want to join the angels when I die."

---- ➤ ----

Bible (NKJV)	Bhagavad Gita
[1] 2nd Timothy 1:6. Therefore, I remind you to stir up the <u>gift of God</u> in you by laying on my hands.	[1] 5:18. My devotees have <u>equal regard</u> for all. They see the <u>same self</u> (the breath of God) in a learned scholar, an outcast, a cow, an elephant, and a dog. **6:30-31.** I am ever-present to those who have <u>realized Me in every creature</u>. Seeing all life as My manifestation, they are never separated from Me. Enlightened people worship Me by <u>showing kindness to all living things</u>. Wherever they may live, they abide in Me. Hence, all their actions proceed from Me.
[2] 1 Thessalonians 4:9, for you yourselves, are taught by <u>God</u> to <u>love</u> one another;	
[3] 2nd Timothy. God has not given us a spirit of fear but <u>power, love, and a sound mind.</u> Ephesians 1:3, Blessed be the God and Father of our Lord Jesus Christ, who has blessed us with every spiritual <u>blessing in</u> the heavenly places in	[3] 10:7. People who understand <u>My</u>

Christ,

⁴ Mark 10:45. "For even the Son of Man did not come to be served, but to serve, and to give His life a ransom for many."

---X--

mystic power are engaged in devotional service to My creation and walk beside Me.

⁴ 8:11. I am impartial. All Holy Scriptures reveal that those who worship Me are sacrificial, relinquishing selfishness and materialism. They seek to promote the welfare, interest, and happiness of others and Mine. Such people find salvation and eternal life in Me.

---X--

--------- ૭----

Chapter 115

Sam and Kellie

They had taken the children to the park. It was a warm spring day. They sat on the grass and watched as the children played.

Kellie said, "Sam, you have changed a lot since we first met."

"Thank you, but how have I changed?"

"You are a lot more relaxed and confident. I would say happier. You once mentioned Tenzin. Did this person have something to do with you being happier?"

Sam was quiet for a while, thinking. She was not sure how to share her spiritual experiences with her friend. Would her friend understand?

Kellie said, "I am interested in knowing what caused the change in you."

Sam said, "I had a weird experience a few years ago. I do not know if it was real or some form of spiritual experience. I fell off a tree and was badly injured. I was taken to a hospital. I was in a coma for a few days and had an out-of-body experience."

Kellie said, "I have read about such things. Some people experience them at the point of death. They talk about meeting some guardian angel in a beautiful garden."

Sam continued, "When I was in a coma, I was in a different world. There, I met a person called Tenzin and some other people."

"Was it wonderful?"

"It was a pleasant place, as long as one followed certain rules, but not always. It had some unpleasant sides to it and some terrifying places."

"Tell me, what was it like? Was Tenzin your guardian angel?"

Radiance filled her face. She said, "It is hard to describe Tenzin. He is a very unusual and inspirational person. The force of the Universe seems to flow with him. Everything he touched blossomed. He was incredible, wise, and mature."

"You sound like you were in love with him."

"Yes, I fell in love with him. Not in a romantic way, but something deeper, more solid. He had a way of bringing out the best in a person. He radiated goodness, decency, and a sense of wholesomeness. It is hard to describe. He had this infectious, pervasive air about him that made me feel positive about everything."

"He inspired you and changed your life view?"

"Yes. Tenzin made me feel that I could overcome any obstacles and that my life had a meaning—a calling. The Universe was with me, encouraging me onwards to fulfil my calling. That I could do the impossible. I felt I had a destiny of pureness, without malice toward anything in the Universe. This powerful **force**[1] of creative energy and a zeal for life surrounded me. That is what it felt like to be in his presence."

[1] John 19:21: *That they all may be one, as You, Father, are in Me, and I in You; that they also may be one in Us, that the world may believe that You sent Me.*

Suddenly, Sam got up. The radiance had gone, and she started to cry. Her whole body shook. ---- ➤ ----

Bible (NKJV)	Bhagavad Gita
[1] 2 Timothy 1:7 For God has not given us a spirit of fear but **power**, love, and a sound mind. ---X--	[1] 10:7. People who understand My mystic power are engaged in devotional service to My creation and walk beside Me. --------- ॐ------

Chapter 116

God has given you a unique insight into His mind

Kellie got up in alarm. She was unsure what to do, so she reached out and hugged her friend. She had never seen her friend change so fast.

After a while, Sam calmed down. They sat in silence and watched their children. Kellie did not press her for more. They collected the children and walked back to Kellie's house for lunch.

A few days later, Kellie felt confident enough to enquire about Sam's sudden change in the park.

"Sam, can I ask you about the incident in the park? I was perplexed by the sudden change in you. Would you like to talk about it?"

Sam considered. They were best friends. They were as close as sisters, supported each other and were unafraid to share their emotions.

Kellie continued, "You don't have to if it makes you uncomfortable."

"It's okay. Life can have its ups and downs. Some days, I feel on top of the world; other days, I'm very low, and depression takes over. It was like living in the Valley of the Shadow of **Death**[1] when I was under Antonio's control. It was terrible. There was perpetual fear of verbal abuse and beatings from Antonio or other men. I was helpless and caught up in fear, poverty, and exploitation.

"There was no one to reach out to for help. Footsteps outside my room at night could mean physical and sexual abuse. Often, I had to pleasure foul-smelling drunken men who had paid Antonio for a few minutes of my time. It was awful, with no means to escape.

"All the beautiful things I had seen and felt in the sanctuary seemed powerless to reach out to me. At times, I despaired for my life. I felt betrayed and crushed. The will to get up and fight drained out of me. I was a carpet for others to trample on. I cried out to God, but there seemed to be no one around.

"There have been times when my belief in goodness and decency was knocked out of me. I stood alone, surrounded by a sea of people, but no one to reach out to. Desperate, I cried out to Heaven but felt no one was there. God might as well not exist."

She was crying. Tears rolled down her cheeks. She wiped the tears away and continued as if she was now talking to herself. "I reach inside, and there is this bottomless pit of emptiness. My life feels empty and meaningless—a pointless existence. I can take drastic action and end my life or continue to struggle. My only means of living was to rely on someone else. I don't want to be in that hell ever again."

Kellie reached out and hugged her. There were tears in her eyes. "God has given you a unique insight into His mind. He allowed you to understand Him, a sense rarely given to others. That is what God may have felt before creation. His despair at being alone in the Universe, with no one to talk to or comfort Him. He longed for someone to reach and pull Him out of his isolation. Out of the hell He lived in.

"Since He allowed that to happen to you, He would have felt your tears and stood by, watching your every move of distress. Every tear would have felt like a knife going through His heart. He stood by that pain because you are very precious to Him, incredibly **dear**[2] to Him.

"He would have created the whole Universe just for you if it were the only means to convey the empty pit He once lived in. The thought of you and me sharing the Universe with Him gave Him the zeal to create life and offer us the opportunity to be His **adopted children**[3], to share whatever He has. He may have found life empty, barren, and devoid of creative energy—a living death. It is something He fears. Our existence gives Him meaning, a purpose, and a place to share **His love**[4]."

Sam asked, "Do you think He let me go through all that to bring me closer to Him?"   ---- ➤ ----

Bible (NKJV)	Bhagavad Gita
[1] Psalms 23:4 Yeah, though I walk	[1] 5:19. Such people have conquered

through the <u>valley of the shadow of death,</u> I will fear no evil; For You *are* with me; Your rod and Your staff comfort me.

² Zephaniah 3:17 The LORD your God in your midst, The Mighty One, will save; He will rejoice over you with gladness, quiet you with <u>His love</u>, And rejoice over you with singing.".

³ Galatians 4:5 to redeem those under the law, that we might receive the <u>adoption as sons</u>.

⁴ 1 John 4:12 No one has seen God at any time. God abides in us if we love one another, and His love has been perfected in us.

---**X**--

the fear of life and death. They rest in the perfect Brahman and Me, gradually refined and made flawless.

² 18:64. Because I <u>dearly love you</u>, I have revealed knowledge hidden from others. I shared it with you and affirmed it with signs so that you and My devotees may benefit from it.

³ 10:1. Listen, Arjuna, O mighty warrior. Because you are My friend, I will give you a <u>deeper insight</u> into what I have already explained, confirming them by signs and miracles. Thus, such evidence will establish reality in your spiritual walk and <u>inspire you</u> to walk beside Me as I guide, correct, and prepare you for eternity.

⁴ 11:13 Arjuna: Lord, you have revealed all this to me, but this plan is vast and beyond my comprehension. You have invited me to share your goals and be part of them.

---**X**--

--------- ᚾ-------

Chapter 117

He delights in you

"An experience like that can drive a person away from God. Many of us are close to Him, but we hardly understand Him. We have no understanding of His pain or His reason for creation. He gave you that insight for something far more significant. To take you into His inner **chambers**[1] and reveal His emotions is an act of trust, comfort, and joy to Him. He who brings comfort to God is precious and finds **favour**[2] in God's sight.

"He **delights**[3] in you. That cannot be said for the vast majority of people. He loves all, but He does not delight in all. There has to be something special about you for Him to invest so much in you."

"I don't feel special or different from anyone else. I am not into praise and worship. It's an effort at times to go to church. Yet, some unknown inner compulsion in me draws me to God. I find church boring and uninspiring."

Kellie laughed. "I know what you mean. I find temple duties boring."

Sam laughed. "I'm glad I am not the only one."

Kellie laughed again and continued. "Life illuminates who we are. Maybe God wants to show us that some of us would choose to be saints, and some would be selfish and self-centred, regardless of His existence. Perhaps, he created us and is selecting[4] those with whom He wants to spend eternity."

"Thank you," said Sam. "I get the gist of it."

---- ➤ ----

Bible (NKJV)	**Bhagavad Gita**
[1] Hebrews 10:19-20 Therefore, brethren, having boldness to enter the Holiest by the blood of Jesus,	[1] 15:20. This wisdom is the most secret part of the Vedic Scriptures I have shared with you and those

by a new and living way which He consecrated for us, through the veil, that is, His flesh,

2 Proverbs 12:2 A good *man* obtains favour from the LORD,

3 Isaiah 62:4 You shall no longer be termed Forsaken, Nor shall your land any more be termed Desolate; But you shall be called Hephzibah, and your land Beulah; For the LORD delights in you,

4 Matthew 25:33 "And He will set the sheep on His right hand, but the goats on the left.

---X--

willing to be in My kingdom.

2 18:64. Because I dearly love you, I have revealed knowledge hidden from others. I shared it with you and affirmed it with signs so that you and My devotees may benefit from it.

3 12:20. Those who follow this path of devotional duty as their supreme goal and have faith in Me are My dedicated followers and dear to Me.

4 6:41. When people who have accepted Me die, they go to a spiritual realm where the righteous live (reborn, metamorphosed in sanctuaries).

---X--

--------- ᠲᠢ-------

Chapter 118

Tenzin and Stefan's visit

Stefan was sitting in the sanctuary next to Kwan-yin, a new recent arrival.

Tenzin approached, and they greeted each other.

"Excuse me, but I need to see Brother Stefan."

Stefan got up. "Come, we will walk towards the orchard."

They walked together.

"What brings you here?" Stefan asked.

"We need to go down to Earth and see how Sam is doing."

"I hate going down there, but I will happily accompany you since it concerns Sam."

They **travelled**[1] through the tunnel and came to stand outside Sam's house.

They stood in the garden, gazing at her house. The children had left the garden gate open. The rabbits were out of their cages. The neighbour's cat was crouched, watching the rabbits, and had started slowly stalking the unsuspecting rabbit when it noticed them. Tenzin clapped his hands, and the cat ran away.

"That's the fourth time I've scared the cat away in two months," he said. "The children need to learn a lesson. Next time, the rabbit might not be so lucky."

Stefan asked. "How long has it been since Sam left the sanctuary?"

"About fourteen years. A lot has happened since then. She got married and has two lovely children now. Her children have grown up in the church. She is a Sunday school teacher now."

Stefan was embarrassed and whispered, "Kwan-yin said Sam had a tough period when she returned. Antonio beat her regularly and nearly killed her once. She **often cried**[2] out to you for help. I understand you did nothing."

Tenzin nodded. There was sadness in his voice. "I heard her prayers and cries for help. I saw her bruises and wounds. All her cries and prayers are recorded in my book."

Stefan laughed. "Writing down Sam's prayers in your **book**[3] didn't help her. What good did it do for her? What comfort?"

"I agree with you. Sam is like a daughter to me, so I took her prayer to the Master, but he said I should do nothing. I pleaded with him and cried before the Lord, pleading on her behalf. I felt her pain, her grief, but he stood steadfast."

"Why? I thought he had promised to protect her and safeguard her. Does his word mean nothing? The Master gave her assurances, yet he allowed her to suffer and ignored her pleas. It is a cardinal rule that we do not betray their trust. I can understand that joy and suffering are part of all living things, but to undermine her trust in him is something I do not understand. It goes against all our teachings. It makes me angry at the Master."

Tenzin explained, "According to the Master, the finest gold has **to be refined**[4] through the hottest flames. He had a purpose I did not understand, so I asked to be reassigned. I couldn't bear to hear her cries. I was reassigned to another location, another person, but I missed her and constantly worried about her. Ultimately, I couldn't stand it, so I asked to be reassigned to her."

Stefan laughed again. ---- ➤ ----

Bible (NKJV)	Bhagavad Gita
[1] Genesis 28:12. Then he dreamed, and behold, <u>a ladder was set up on the earth</u>, and its top reached heaven; the angels of God were ascending and <u>descending on it</u>. [2] Psalms 18:41. They cried out, <u>but there was none to save</u>; Even to the LORD, but He did not answer them. [3] Psalms 56:8. <u>You keep track of</u> all my sorrows. You have collected all my tears in your bottle. You have recorded each one in your <u>book.</u> [4] Malachi 3:3, he will sit <u>as a refiner and purifier</u> of silver, and he will purify the sons of Levi and refine them as gold and silver. ---X--	[2-5, 7, 9] 11:16. Untold numbers of life forms on Earth and spiritual sanctuaries passed before me. I saw the beginning and end of all. You gave life and brought joy, pain and suffering into our lives, and in 'The Fullness of Time' (before The Day of The Lord), you <u>made us whole</u> (restored, made restitution) and wiped away all pain and suffering. You showed/proved that nothing thrives in the Universe at the expense of another. <u>I comprehended</u> your joy and sorrow from start to end. In your first thought, I saw my name <u>chosen</u> with great care, <u>written</u> in your Eternal Books, sealed by your <u>loving tears</u>. I saw your <u>excellent plan</u> for me on Earth, in the spiritual sanctuary, and I <u>beheld</u> the very last thought of mine before the end of all creation. <u>All I saw</u> had a beginning and an end. Yet, you have no beginning, middle, or end. You are The Lord of creation; the cosmos and my life rest in your hands. ---X--

--------- �------

Chapter 119

God's purpose in allowing pain and suffering

Stefan said, "The Master has a personal interest in Sam. Perhaps the Master was testing and refining his and **your love**[5] for her. Perhaps he was killing two birds with one stone?" [Kathy Cochrane's Tenet 2]. His loss, his pain, would have been greater than hers. She is of greater value to the Master than he is to her."

Tenzin smiled. "Maybe, but it was one of my worst experiences. I did not know that **love could hurt**[6] so much and that it comes at such a high cost. The greater the love, the greater the pain."

"So the Master did have a **purpose in allowing it.**"[7]

"Maybe."

"Did you have a hand in Antonio's death? Did you use that as an opportunity to free Sam from his grip?"

"Brother Stefan, you should know better. We are not allowed to do such things."

"But you did have something to do with her freedom?"

"Let's say I allowed the thought of greed to cross his path. And Antonio's greed **led him to his death.**"[8]

"Did you lead Kellie into Sam's life?"

"No, that was the **Master's work**[9], but I did arrange for her and Kellie to cross paths with their partners. That was my doing."

"Tenzin, what else have you done?"

---- ➤ ----

Bible (NKJV)	Bhagavad Gita
[6] Romans 8:22-23, For we know that the whole creation groans and labours with birth pangs together until now. We also have the first fruits of the Spirit. We groan within ourselves, eagerly awaiting our body's adoption and redemption.	[2-5, 7, 9] 11:16. Untold numbers of life forms on Earth and spiritual sanctuaries passed before me. I saw the beginning and end of all. You gave life and brought joy, pain and suffering into our lives, and in 'The Fullness of Time' (before The Day of The Lord), you made us whole (restored, made restitution) and wiped away all pain and suffering. You showed/proved that nothing thrives in the Universe at the expense of another. I comprehended your joy and sorrow from start to end.
[7] Romans 8:29, For whom He foreknew, He also predestined to be conformed to the image of His Son, that He might be the firstborn among many brethren.	
[8] Psalms 71:4, Deliver me, O my God, out of the hand of the wicked, Out of the hand of the unrighteous and cruel man.	In your first thought, I saw my name chosen with great care, written in your Eternal Books, sealed by your loving tears. I saw your excellent plan for me on Earth, in the spiritual sanctuary, and I beheld the very last thought of mine before the end of all creation.
[9] Psalms 107:13, Then they cried out to the LORD in their trouble, And He saved them from their distress. ---x--	All I saw had a beginning and an end. Yet, you have no beginning, middle, or end. You are The Lord of creation; the cosmos and my life rest in your hands. ---x--

--------- ૧૭ ------

Chapter 120

Surrounded by a shield

Tenzin looked at Stefan and answered, "I **prevented**[1] a serious car accident in which Sam and her children would have been hurt. Several times, I saved their stall from being robbed, and once, I saved Sam and Lee from being mugged.

"I prevented several serious incidents but allowed minor ones to happen, hoping these would teach them to be more cautious and careful."

"Do they know you intervene?" Stefan asked.

"She has an inkling, but not the family."

"Why does the **Master favour her?"**[2]

"Perhaps the Master believes she has 'what it takes to empty the ocean with the palm of her hand'. Very rarely is one born that has this unique ability."

"Then she must be one of those rare prime, perfect, almost magical people endowed with special talents." [Su-Anne's Tenet 3 — Prime, perfect, magical squares, as in mathematics.]

While they were talking, the four children arrived home laughing. They started to play in the garden.

Tenzin muttered, "Happy children is the most beautiful sight and sound in the universe, even more beautiful than the finest choir of the greatest angels."

"I agree, Tenzin, but this is not the only sound here. What about when little ones scream in pain because they are abused and beaten black and blue by their parents? When they hide under their beds in a foetal position and **cry out**[3]? When they break into a sweat and tremble at the footsteps of a drunken, abusive parent? They cry, "Why does God permit this evil? Or the **helpless terror⁴** of a farm animal as it sees its throat about to be slit? I hate this place."

Tenzin replied, "Brother Stefan, I do not have an answer for this evil. You and I know it is left to the Master and us to make them **whole⁵ in the Sanctuary."**

To make someone whole⁵ means to
- Restore someone to a sound, healthy, or otherwise favourable condition.
- Return someone to a favourable condition, primarily physical or psychological health.
- Give someone financial compensation for a loss they have sustained.
-

Bible (NKJV)	Bhagavad Gita
¹ Psalms 5:12. For You, O LORD, will bless the righteous; With favour, You will surround him as with a shield.	¹ 18:56. My devotees look after My creation as stewards under My protection.
² 1st Samuel 2:26. And the child Samuel grew in stature, and favour both with the LORD and men.	². 3:20. The great King Janaka found solace and favour in My presence by performing his duty sacrificially and selflessly with others' welfare always in mind. Similarly, do your work with the interest of others in mind.
³ Mark 9:42. "But whoever causes one of these little ones who believe in Me to stumble, it would be better for him if a millstone were hung around his neck, and he were thrown into the sea.	³ 8:16. Every person and creature on Earth is subject to pleasure, pain, and suffering. However, those attaining My Abode acquire the strength to overcome their pain and suffering.
⁵ Colossians 1:20 and by Him (Jesus) to reconcile all things to Himself, by Him, whether things on earth or things in heaven, having made peace through the blood of His cross. --------- ᦙ------	⁴ 13:21. while living entities cause all enjoyment and suffering in this world. ----

Chapter 121

Anointed priestess

Tenzin said, "I know, and the Master understands. He says suffering has a part in life. It is temporary. It may seem like a lifetime to these people on Earth, but we know it is only for a short while. I hate this place also, but it produces some of the most compassionate, thoughtful, unselfish beings in the universe, and we see one of them in the creation process."

"Were you assigned to Kellie, too?" Stefan asked.

Tenzin replied, "From the start, even before **she was born.**[1] A delightful child of God. She is much easier to care for and is a real pleasure."

"Is her name written in the Master Book?"

"Yes, she is preordained and predestined for the Sacred City, and her name appears on the door of the holiest of the holy. She is destined for greatness. She will be an **anointed priestess**[2] for her people in the Eternal City of the Master."

Stefan smiled. "I see no greatness at the moment."

Tenzin laughed. "I saw no greatness in you when you were here many years ago, sleeping rough in the forest with that band of rebels. Most of the time, you stank."

Stefan looked offended. "Yes, but I did change. I left them and joined the monks. They helped me change my life. They taught me the ways of the Master."

After a long pause, Tenzin said, "The Master has plans for Sam. When her spirit (Atman) **wakes**[3] up from slumber and is enlivened by the Holy Spirit, she shall run the race as one who wants to win. I visualise her on the Day of Judgement as one who has reached the full stature of Christ. She has the unique ability to empty the ocean with the palm of her hand."

Stefan asked, "What about Kellie?"

"Kellie has followed the ways of the Master since childhood. There is an inner core of strength in her. She is unlike most people. She has an instant grasp of the **Master's ways."**[4]

"Like what?" Stefan asked.

---- ➤ ----

Bible (NKJV)	Bhagavad Gita
[1]Acts 15:18. "Known to God from eternity are all His works. Proverbs 8:23 I have been established from everlasting, From the beginning, before there was ever an earth. Isaiah 41:4 Who has performed and done *it*, Calling the generations from the beginning? 'I, the LORD, am the first; And with the last I *am* He.'	[1, 2, 3] 11:47-48. **Krishna:** Arjuna, by My grace, you have perceived My glorious, radiant, universal form and comprehended My cosmic eternal plans and your unique role in all this in a way no one has perceived or heard before. Unknown to you until now, you have been featured in my plans since the beginning of time. Hence, I am placing all the resources you need to fulfil them at your disposal. All I need is your consent, willingness, and iron resolve to carry it out not by your might but by My might. Arjuna, such grace and knowledge do not come from reading scriptures or performing sacrifices or rituals.
[2] Psalms 132:9. Let Your priests (priestess) be clothed with righteousness, And let Your saints shout for joy.	
[3] Job 7:17. "What is a man (woman), that You should exalt him, That You should set Your heart on him. Acts 8:15. prayed for them that they might receive the Holy Spirit.	[3] 12:6-7. As for the people who worship Me and carry out all their activities as an act of devotional love towards Me and humanity, I free them from the fear of death, for their consciousness has awakened their Atman. ---x--
[4] Hebrews 2:5-9. For He has not put the world to come, of which we speak, in subjection to angels. But one testified in a certain place, saying: "What is a man that You	

are mindful of him, Or the son of man that You care for? You have made him a little lower than the angels, crowned him with glory and honour, and set him over the works of Your hands. You have put all things in subjection under his feet." He left nothing that is not put under him in that He put all in subjection under him. But now, we do not yet see all things put under him. But we see Jesus, who was made a little lower than the angels, for the suffering of death crowned with glory and honour, that He, by the grace of God, might taste death for everyone.

---X--

--------- ᑫᖱ------

Chapter 122

Goodness and faith

Tenzin replied, "Kellie has insight into the Holy Books. Most people pray primarily for things they want, but not her. She reads the holy books and meditates on their words.

"Each morning, she stands before her shrine. She plans the day with the Lord, praying that each day may **have a lesson**[1] to improve her life. Before going to bed each evening, she brings the day's events and her conduct before the Lord. She seeks His guidance and learns to amend her ways.

"She is a keen learner, willing to change her ways. The Lord delights in her and rejoices in her keenness to be transformed. I see the fruit of that in her life. She shows great love, joy, peace, gentleness, **goodness, and faith.**"[2]

Stefan shook his head. "I still don't see any greatness."

Tenzin replied, "That's because you judge by Earth's standards. What does the Master say? (Psalm 103:15): *'As for man, his days are as grass; as a field flower, the wind blows on it, and it is **gone**[3]'.* Time is against them on Earth, but time is on our side here, and she will join us one day."

"What does the Master mean by saying their lives are meant to be imperfect, but when perfection comes (**sanctuary**[4]), the imperfections in their lives will be perfected?"

"What does your experience teach?" Tenzin asked.

"I am a young disciple. Such things are beyond my scope of understanding. I am a simple monk. Let's change the subject. Why is it that most people have no one assigned to them?"

Tenzin explained, "Free will. We need their consent at every stage. Most humans have chosen to live free without our help. They are like caterpillars. They believe in one **life only[5],** but evolution has a surprise for caterpillars and humankind.

"Come, we have another task. It's time we went back to the sanctuary."

---- ➤ ----

Bible (NKJV)	Bhagavad Gita
[1] Psalms 144:3. LORD, what is a man (woman) that You take knowledge of him? Or the son of man, that You are mindful of him?	[1] 12:9. If you cannot set your mind and intellect upon Me, learn to meditate on My words regularly.
[2] Leviticus 20:26, 'And you shall be holy to Me, for I the LORD am holy, and have separated you from the peoples, that you should be Mine.	[2] 13:22. A person's spirit (duality of soul and Atman) identifies either with the material body (influenced by the **gunas***) or the divine essence. And often both. How a person thinks moulds the person. For example, is his thinking led by his gunas or the indwelling spirit? Thus, according to their views, one comes across evil and good among all species.
[3] Psalms 103:15 As for man, his days are as grass; as a field flower, the wind blows on it, and it is gone.	
[4] 1st Corinthians 2:9, But as it is written, Eye hath not seen, nor ear heard, neither have entered into the heart of man, the things which God hath prepared for them that love him.	[4] 11:16. Untold numbers of life forms on Earth and spiritual sanctuaries passed before me. I saw the beginning and end of all. You gave life and brought joy, pain and suffering into our lives, and in 'The Fullness of Time' (before The Day of The Lord), you made us whole and wiped away all pain and suffering. You showed/proved that nothing thrives in the Universe at the expense of another. I comprehended your joy and sorrow from start to end.
[5] Jeremiah 17:13, O LORD, the hope of Israel, All who forsake You shall be ashamed. "Those who depart from Me Shall be written in the earth Because they have forsaken the LORD, The fountain of living waters."	
---X--	[5] 3:33. Even men of knowledge act according to their mode of nature. All creatures follow their heart. This is

	rooted in their thoughts and tendencies. Therefore, if one's nature is so powerful, one might question the value of attempting to live by scriptural injunctions. One could ask: What is the use of repressing one's material nature?
	---X--

--------- ᧐᧐------

Chapter 123

The orphans

Tenzin and Stefan were walking in the orchard in the sanctuary.

Tenzin turned to Stefan and said, "I have to go and see the Master. I won't be long. Can you prepare the two young orphan children, Daniel and Sofia? The Master wants us to take them to see their human family on my return."

"Can I ask why?" Stefan asked.

"It's part of their education," Tenzin replied.

A few moments later, Tenzin was back. Stefan had the children ready, standing a few feet apart from him. Both children looked apprehensive and nervous.

"Come," said Tenzin. "We will see how your families are doing."

They went through the tunnel and made their way to the young boy's earthly family home. They stood outside a house and waited.

"That's my parent's home," Daniel said, pointing at the lovely semi-detached building. "I love coming here."

Sofia said, looking at Daniel, "I don't like coming here to this lower Earth."

Daniel looked concerned. "Why did you come?"

Sofia replied, "It was Tenzin's idea. I didn't like to say no. Why did you come, Daniel?"

"I like to see how my earthly family is doing. It feels good to be near people I love. Tenzin says I can learn much by watching my family and life on Earth. Everything here **struggles**[1] to live, to survive."

"I just don't like being here," Sofia said. Her voice had a dangerous purr that sent a shiver through Daniel." She continued, "I don't like humans. They are intelligent but mean, a cruel, arrogant, selfish species—a disgrace to the **Universe[2].** They are warmongers. Their parents subjugate animals and exploit some as surrogate mothers for their children (stealing the milk of cows, ewes, goats, and camels from their newborns), and when the enslaved animals are old, they slaughter them and eat them. They are always fighting and thoughtlessly stripping the planet of its resources. What good do you see in humans?"

Daniel was shocked at the anger in her voice. He stepped back and said, "I see a lot of contradictions in their lives. Some are very compassionate, and others, I am ashamed to say, are ruthless and mean. There are many vegetarians who, on moral grounds, will not eat animals or **harm them[3].** But I admit that we do not see such evil in our sanctuaries. Tenzin says it helps us to understand the darkness within us and appreciate the guidance and **teaching of the Elders[4]."**

Sofia replied, "The presence of humans casts an evil shadow over the Universe. Someone will have to deal with this selfish, self-centred, arrogant species and put them in their place."

Daniel paused to consider her words and then commented, "I disagree with you. Humans have incredible potential to fill the Universe with joy."

Sofia shook her head and said, "You don't understand. My parents aborted me. I was an inconvenience and a nuisance to them. They aborted me and then harvested my organs so they could use them for cell transplants for their future medical needs and make them live longer. Show me another species in the Universe that kills their offspring and harvests their organs. Oh, how I hate them."

Daniel reached out to her and hugged her. "It pains me to hear what your parents did to you. Sofia, you cannot go on harbouring such hate and anger. It is a disease that destroys you from within you. You have to ask Tenzin to help you overcome this bitterness."

Neither of them said anything for a while. With tears in her eyes, Sofia said, "Tenzin is wise; this place helps us grow in **understanding and wisdom[5].** Earth is a good place to learn about goodness, kindness, sacrifice, and the evils of greed and selfishness. What do your earthly parents do?"

"My parents own a restaurant in the town centre. They work hard and have a small house on the outskirts. They have two small children other than me."

"A brother and sister?" she asked.

"Yes."

"What are they like, Daniel?"

"Like most children, they're naughty sometimes but mostly nice. Once a fortnight, on Monday evenings, my parents take food to the homeless people's shelter **and help[6]** in the kitchen. My brother and sister helped serve the food and clean and tidy up the place. They are good, kind children."

"What brought you to the sanctuary?"

"I was about five years old when I caught meningitis. My parents took me to the hospital, but the doctors could not save me."

Sofia said, "My parents didn't want me. They had two children. I was the third. They said having me would interfere with their business plans."

"I am so sorry. That must hurt you." He reached out and hugged her. "We are your family now. Tenzin is our **spiritual father.[7]** We are his **family."[8]**

Sofia began to cry. ---- ➤ ----

Bible (NKJV)	Bhagavad Gita
[1] Romans 8:22, For we know that	[1, 3] 7:27. All living things are born in ignorance, bewildered by hate,

the whole creation groans and labours with birth pangs together until now. v 28 We know that all things work together for good to those who love God, to those called according to His purpose.

[2] Genesis 6:6 The LORD was sorry that he had made humankind and put them on the earth, and it grieved him to his heart.

[4, 5] Romans 8:29-30, For whom He foreknew, He also predestined to be conformed to the image of His Son, that He might be the firstborn among many brethren.

[6] Daniels 15:11, For the poor will never cease from the land; therefore I command you, saying, 'You shall open your hand wide to your brother and the poor and needy in your land.

[7] 1st Corinthians 4:15, Even if you had ten thousand others to teach you about Christ, you have only one spiritual father. I became your father in Christ Jesus when I preached the Good News to you.

[8] Hebrews 12:9, We have had human fathers who corrected us, and we paid them respect. Shall we not more readily be subject to the Father of spirits and live? ---x-

[2] 5:18. My devotees have equal regard for all. They see the same self (the breath of God) in a learned scholar, an outcast, a cow, an elephant, and a dog. >> Hence, as they progress in their spiritual growth, they regard all life forms as part of their and God's extended family.

[4] 4:34. Follow the guidance of a spiritual master and render service unto him. The spiritual master can instruct you in this wisdom

[5] 4:35. Having gained spiritual wisdom, you won't be deluded again. You will see that all living entities are part of the divine plan, part of one family, and have the same breath of life from the divine.

[6] 8:28. Study the scripture, give selfless service to others, live modestly, and give to the poor. This selfless duty to others and devotion to My teachings will guide you to your real spiritual home, My abode.

[7] 13:9 They comprehend the Lord's creative plan for the cosmos, their position in this plan, and the reason for joyful and painful lessons of life: the joy of family, friends, birth, suffering, disease, old age, and death.
--------- ॐ ------

Chapter 124

Charitable deeds

Daniel said, "Something deeper haunts you."

Sofia nodded. "I understand that sometimes people have abortions because of difficult circumstances; for example, Sam and Kwan-yin were forced into prostitution and had abortions. Tenzin says that people have a chance to make up for their **past**[1] mistakes in the sanctuary. They can be reconciled with their aborted children and mend the relationship with family members."

"So, is there a hope you could **be reconciled**[2] with your parents?" Daniel asked.

Sofia's features hardened. "I don't want to, Daniel."

"That's a strange thing to say."

"Daniel, you don't know my parents or my brothers."

"I don't understand." He shook his head.

"I chose not to be connected to my parents. I am ashamed of them."

They stood silent for a while, and then he asked quietly, "Why?"

Sofia's gaze darted over his face. "They are materialistic. Selfishness governs their lives. They want a bigger house, a better car, and yearly holidays.

"They do not have thoughts like those of your lovely parents, who demonstrate care for the poor and needy in society. They step on others to progress along their materialistic path. My brothers take after my parents; they tease and bully at school to get their way."

"Perhaps they can change," Daniel suggested.

"I don't think so," Sofia replied. "My parents pretend to be good and honourable people. They attend charitable functions. They like to be seen as **pillars of society,**[3] giving and raising money for people experiencing poverty. They find it easy to write a cheque and to be seen as generous at parties, but it is an act. You will not see them dirtying their hands to feed the unfortunate.

"You will not find my parents cooking for the poor in the homeless shelter or inviting homeless people to their beautiful home. Your parents are genuine, honest, and decent people. They are more like monks."

Looking at the ground, Daniel said, "There is no room in our **sanctuary**[4] for self-centred people like your parents. I can see why Tenzin likes to bring us here. It makes sense. Earth is an undesirable but necessary place—the best assault course for filtering out the good, thoughtful, and compassionate from the selfish people in the Universe."

Sofia asked, "Do you think your parents miss you?"

Daniel nodded. "I know they do. They cried when I passed away. They grieved for a long time. My parents always light a candle in front of my picture on my birthday. I believe Tenzin inspired them. I like to be with them, then. If Tenzin or Stefan are free, they will try to escort me there."

"Do your parents sense your presence?" she asked.

"Sometimes, my parents sense that **I am there**[5]. I can see tears in their eyes and feel their strong bond of love for me. They believe in the afterlife, but I don't think they know about the sanctuary. Nonetheless, I am certain they believe I am looked after and that we will be a family again."

"You have good parents," she commented.

"Tenzin says they will join us one day when their time is up. Families are important. They are the centre of cosmic structure and God's greater plan."

"I don't have a human family." She started to cry.

"Please don't cry, Sofia," Daniel pleaded. "We, in the sanctuary, **are your family**[6]. A spiritual family is forever. Ours is built on love, care, and compassion. When my parents and brothers join us, they will love you, too. They will treat you as part of our family. We will have an eternal spiritual family brought together by spiritual fathers like Tenzin and Stefan."

They stood next to Tenzin and Stefan, reached out, and held their hands.

Tenzin said, "Life on earth is a test to see, given free will, what people value until the end of their lives. Are they godly, divine, or a child of evolution—an animal?"

---- ✦ ----

Bible (NKJV)	Bhagavad Gita
[1] Ezekiel 33:15, I say to, for instance, the wicked give back a debtor's security, return what they have stolen, and obey my life-giving laws, no longer doing what is evil. If they do this, then they will surely live and not die.	[1,2] 4:36-37. Spiritual knowledge is liberating. Even if you were once the most sinful of all sinners, once you board the boat of spiritual experience, you could sail beyond the ocean of your sins. As a blazing fire turns firewood to ashes, the fire of spiritual knowledge, affirmed by Me with signs and power, incinerates sinful thoughts and desires.
[2] Joel 2:25, And I will restore the years that the locust hath eaten.	
[3] Matthew 6:2, "Therefore, when you do a charitable deed, do not sound a trumpet before you as the hypocrites do in the synagogues and the streets, that they may have glory from men. Assuredly, I say to you; they have their reward.	[3] 16:17. Deluded by self-importance, many ungodly appear pious and participate in charitable acts or religious services, desiring to be seen as godly and righteous, but behind that facade lies self-promotion.
[4] Mark 9:50, "Salt is good, but if the salt loses its flavour, how will	[4] 14:15. Those who die in passion or ignorance are elevated to the heavenly places where others of

you season it? Have salt in yourselves, and have peace with one another."

[5] Hebrews 12:1, Therefore we also, since so great a <u>cloud of witnesses surrounds us</u>, let us lay aside every weight,

[6] Matthew 19:29, "And everyone who has <u>left houses, brothers, sisters,</u> father, mother, wife, children or lands, for my name's sake shall <u>receive a hundredfold</u> and inherit eternal life.

---X--

similar nature dwell, leaving behind a mixed legacy of good and misery on earth.

[5, 6] 14:14. Those who die in the mode of <u>consistent goodness</u> elevate to the <u>purer,</u> higher, holy sites in the spiritual sanctuaries <u>where the sages live.</u>

---X--

---------- ᠃᠃------

Chapter 125

"Mum, what is Heaven like?"

Christos was ten, and his sister, Maria, was eight.

One warm Saturday morning, Maria asked her mother, "Mother, what happens when **people die[1]**?"

Sam asked, "Why do you want to know?"

Maria replied, "My friend's grandfather died yesterday, and she says her mother was glad. He was a bad man, and bad people go to a place called Hell. Is that so?"

Sam thought for a while. "I will answer that later on. Let's go shopping. I want to show you something."

They walked up to the local supermarket. "Now, children," Sam said, "I want you to choose one tin of fruit each."

"Mum," asked Christos, "any tin of fruit?"

"Yes. Remember, only one each."

The children chose a tin of their favourite fruit and started walking back home.

On the way, Sam said, "Now listen. This is going to be your homework. When we get home, I want you open the tin, examine the fruit's colour, shape, and taste, and write it down on paper."

"Okay, Mum," the kids replied.

They came home and sat around the kitchen table. Sam opened a tin of pears.

"Who chose this?" Sam asked.

"It was me, Mum," replied Christos.

She passed him the tin. Then, she opened a mixed fruit tin.

"Is this your choice, Maria?" Sam asked.

"Yes, Mum," Maria replied.

She gave the tin to her daughter, then got up and gave each a pen, a piece of paper, a plate, and a fork.

"Okay, I want you to describe the fruit on your plate, and then I want you to taste it. Is it firm or soft, bitter or sweet? Write down your experience on paper.

"Maria, you have mixed fruit, so you need to work harder for longer."

When they had finished, she drove them to an orchard that belonged to a friend.

"Okay, children, let's see if you can find the fruit you have eaten growing on the trees."

Christos was the first to come running up to her. "Mum, I found my pear tree. Come on, let me show you."

He led her to a 'Comice' pear tree. "Look, Mum. I found the pear tree!"

Sam asked, "Are you sure it's the same pear?"

"Yes, Mum." He sounded very confident. There was a big smile on his face.

"Okay," Sam said. "Let's test it." She picked up a pear, took a pocketknife, cut a piece of 'Comice' pear, and gave it to her son.

Christos looked at the pear and tasted it. "Well, it doesn't taste like the pear in my tin. This one has a sweet, juicy flavour."

"Come," she said, leading her son to a 'Beth' pear tree. Again, she gave him a piece to eat.

"Mum," Christos said with a puzzled look. "This one has silver, yellow-green skin and doesn't taste like the one in the tin. Is this a pear?"

"Yes." She led him to a mature tree. "Here, taste this one. It is called a 'Conference' pear," she said as she passed him a piece.

Christos said, "I think this one is like the one in the tin. It has a firm, juicy favour, but I'm not sure. It's too firm."

Her daughter came running up to her. "Mum, I found three apple trees, two cherry trees, and three grape trees."

Sam took the children to each tree and made them taste all the fruits.

"Right, Maria," Sam said. "Can you tell me which apple, cherry, and grapefruit are similar to the ones in your tin?"

Maria thought for a while. "I'm not sure, Mum. There are three types of apple trees here, and none of them taste like the apple in my tin. Same for the cherries and grapes."

She led them to another part of the orchard. Here, under the leaves, were caterpillars.

"See these crawly things?" Sam said as she pointed at the caterpillars. "One day, they will weave a cocoon and hide there. A few days later, they will emerge as butterflies.

"Evolution has found a way to transform them from these creepy-crawly things into entirely different creatures.

"Come, let's sit down." They sat down on the soft grass.

Sam continued, "God has found a way to transform us when we **die²** into a different life form through evolution or other means. Some people call it going to Heaven."

"Mum," Maria asked, "what is Heaven like?"

"Well, living on this Earth is like living in a house with a small garden and surviving on tinned fruit. You eat from the tin and may think you know everything about apples, pears, or cherries. **I believe³** that when we die, we go to a wonderful place called the sanctuary. There, life will be full of wonderful new experiences. It is like moving from our home to this orchard. So many new things to experience and learn."

A few yards away from them stood Tenzin, a smile on his face. "I am glad Sam has **finally found happiness. Thank you, Lord.**"

---- ➤ ----

Bible (NKJV)	Bhagavad Gita
[1] Luke 23:43, Jesus said, "Assuredly, I say to you, today you will be with Me in Paradise." John 14:3 "In My Father's house are many mansions; if it were not so, I would have told you. I am going to prepare a place for you. And if I go and prepare a place for you, I will come again and receive you to Myself; where I am, you may also be.	**GITA** [1] 8:20 Beyond this material world lays the invisible spiritual reality that cannot be destroyed. Spiritual reality will remain when this world is gone.
[2] 1st Corinthians 15:54. When our dying bodies have been transformed into bodies that will never die, this Scripture will be fulfilled: "Death is swallowed up in victory.	[2,] 2:72. Those who live a spiritual and godly life attain calmness and pass peacefully into the Kingdom of God at death. [3] 13:28. The spirit remains standing (alive) when the material body passes into death. When you grasp this, you will acknowledge the breath of God in all living entities. ---X--

[3] Romans 8:22-23. <u>We know</u> the whole creation groans and labours together with birth pangs. Not only that, but we also have the first fruits of the Spirit, even though we groan within ourselves, eagerly <u>waiting for the adoption</u> and <u>redemption of our bodies</u>.

---x--

--------- ᛞ------

Chapter 126

Hold on to eternal life

Stefan asked, "Tenzin, who—what—is the Master?"

"Some say he is the son of God; others say he is the promised **Messiah**, a great prophet. Many Hindus call him Lord Krishna."

"And what do you believe?"

"I asked him, and he said I should call him Elder Brother."

"You look after this sanctuary, but how did this place come into being?"

"The Master and I built it, a particle at a time. Each particle was made, named, and accounted for daily until we completed this sanctuary. This is the early stages of the sanctuary. We have a lot of work of reconciliation, restoration, and making all whole, and much learning ahead of us."

"Where did the knowledge, the ability, come from? What **motivated you[1]?**"

"It is a **gift of God[2]** offered to all, but only those who enter the contest and pass the rigorous test are deemed worthy of this prize. It is the greatest, most brutal race in the Universe, and only the most decisive and determined win the award. Many enter the race, but the race filters out the weak in spirit from the strong. It is part of **our inheritance[3]**, but only those who complete the race receive the prize of the entire **inheritance in God[4]**.

"I met the requirements. Therefore, the Master and the indwelling Holy Spirit taught me to use God's creative power to assist in the building and upholding of this 'patch'. God's power sustains it. I have no abilities or power besides what I receive from the Father. I am just a vessel. It was built in six days—or rather, six stages."

"How?"

"The first stage of the plan was the moral stage. The Master taught me that all creation should have a **purpose.**[5] The builder and the things built should have a covenant, a sense of duty of care, and obligations from both. The core principle is, 'Nothing in the universe thrives at the expense of another.' The rest was quite simple."

"What does that mean?"

"That is for another day, my friend."

Stefan thought for a while. He pointed at the trees and the hills. "You built or created all these under the Master's guidance?"

"Yes, atom by atom, cell by cell, a leaf at a time. Each individually made, named, put on the inventory, and accounted for daily."

"How do you do it?"

He laughed. "It takes a lot of training and development of spiritual–moral character to harness the power of the Holy Spirit. That, my friend, is God's gift to all, but only a handful are willing to train to harness the power."

Stefan asked, "So, what is your role here?"

---- ➤ ----

Bible (NKJV)	Bhagavad Gita
[1] Exodus 9:16, "But for this purpose, I have raised you, that I may show My power in you, and that My name may be declared in all the earth.	[1] 14:23. Spiritual masters are unwavering and undisturbed by the actions of the gunas. They are steady, strong, forceful, and unmoved. They have strong spiritual motivation and direction, which is more potent than the attraction to any gunas.
[2] Ac 1:8, "But you shall receive power when the Holy Spirit has come upon you, and you shall be witnesses to Me in Jerusalem, and	[2] 6:47. A disciple of great faith, who abides in Me, walks beside Me and

in all Judea and Samaria, and to the end of the earth."

³ Exodus 15:17. You will bring them in and plant them In the mountain of Your inheritance, In the place, O LORD, which You have made For Your dwelling, The sanctuary, O Lord, which Your hands have established. 1 Peter 1:3-4 Blessed be the God and Father of our Lord Jesus Christ, who according to His abundant mercy has begotten us again to a living hope through the resurrection of Jesus Christ from the dead, to an inheritance incorruptible and undefiled and that does not fade away, reserved in heaven for you.

⁴ Galatians 4:7, Therefore, you are no longer a slave but a son; if a son, then an heir of God through Christ.

⁵ 2nd Timothy 1:9, who has saved us and called us with a holy calling, not according to our works, but according to His purpose and grace which was given to us in Christ Jesus before time began,

---X--

renders loving service to all creation (building My kingdom on Earth and in Heaven) will be with Me forever. Whenever My devotees pass away into the hereafter, they leave a legacy of love, kindness, justice, and fairness, having enriched the lives of all around them.

[2, 4, 5,] 4:3. To a selected few, I revealed My existence and plans for eternity (past, present, and future worlds to come). You are My friend and devotee, and in due time, as you gain My favour, I will reveal these mysteries and explain your role here on Earth, in the spiritual world, and in the far distant future. You are one of My most trusted architects. You and other trusted devotees will build My material and spiritual kingdoms in this world and hereafter and walk beside Me in all My realms. I will guide and teach you all as a Father.

---X--

--------- ୨୬------

Chapter 127

Sit on his right-hand side

Tenzin replied, "My role here is to learn and **grow**[1], to be like our Lord. Even he is learning, and in the future, it is written in the scriptures he will sit on the right **hand of God**[2]**."**

Stefan: "Will you sit on his right-hand side?"

"I have no desire to sit on his right-hand side. I do these things because I want to and can do them. It is **my joy**[3]."

Stefan: "Perhaps the Lord is training you, perfecting you, so you can return to Earth **with him**[4] to rule over it for a thousand years."

"Maybe, but I have no desire for it, either."

"He may insist."

Tenzin: "Why?"

"Because I cannot think of anyone more suited than you."

"Sounds like too much work. I am happy here. This is my home."

Stefan: "Our home."

Tenzin: "Yes."

Stefan stared at his feet.

Tenzin watched him. "Now, what's troubling you, Brother Stefan?"

"We live in a multi-dimensional universe. Perhaps we are in one of those."

"That may be. But this is our reality."

Tenzin's thoughts went back as he looked at the far hills. The Holy Spirit had said, "Tenzin, you have received the mind of Christ (Brahman) to help you account for every leaf, tree, and person **here**[5]. Use it wisely and with dedication. When the Lord returns, he wants you to go with him."

Tenzin said, "Lord, it's a huge task."

"Use your time here wisely. Your Heavenly Father needs you. All were invited, but only a handful responded. Their birthright was chosen before the **foundations**[6] **of Earth** were laid, but most of them **sold**[7] their birthright."

"Lord, there is time. My words will awaken others. I need your help, too."

Hari's Tenet 5. *Ultimately, all that matters is how we loved and were loved.*

---- ➤ ----

Bible (NKJV)	Bhagavad Gita
[1] Colossians 1:28. Him we preach, warning every man and teaching every man in all wisdom, that we may present every man perfect in Christ Jesus.	[1-5,] 4:3. To a selected few, I revealed My existence and plans for eternity (past, present, and future worlds to come). You are My friend and devotee, and in due time, as you gain My favour, I will reveal these mysteries and explain your role here on Earth, in the spiritual world, and in the far distant future. You and other trusted devotees will build My material and spiritual kingdoms in this world and hereafter and walk beside Me in all My realms. I will guide and teach you all as a Father.
[2] Colossians 3:1, If you were raised with Christ, seek those things above, where Christ is, sitting at the right hand of God.	
[3] Isaiah 51:11, So the ransomed of the LORD shall return, And come to Zion with singing, With everlasting joy on their heads. They shall obtain joy and gladness; Sorrow and sighing shall flee away.	---X--
[4] 1st Thessalonians 3:13, so that He may establish your hearts	

blameless in holiness before our God and Father at our Lord Jesus Christ's coming with all His saints.

[5] Acts 3:21, "whom heaven must receive until the times of restoration of all things, which God has spoken by the mouth of all His holy prophets since the world began.

[6] Ephesians 1:4, He chose us in Him before the foundation of the world, that we should be holy and without blame before Him in love.

[7] Hebrews 12:16, lest there be any fornicator or profane person like Esau, who sold his birthright for one morsel of food.

---X--

--------- ᛞ-------

Chapter 128

On you, I was cast from birth.

Tenzin, "Thou art my God forever and ever. You have been my God since my mother bore me and before that when I was an essence in your book of life. And before that, from the beginning, when I first came into being, in your thought."

He returned to the sanctuary from his visit to the Lord. Stefan was waiting for him.

"How was your trip?" Stefan asked.

"It was good," he replied.

"Tenzin, can I ask you a personal question?"

"You can."

"Why do you devote your time to helping people in this place? You could go anywhere in the universe."

Tenzin replied, "It's a long story," looking at the ground. "I don't like to talk about myself."

Stefan felt awkward. "I love you as a brother. I respect you. I want to know more about you. I don't mean to intrude."

"Come," said Tenzin, "let's sit under the tree's shade and talk."

They went and sat under the giant tree. They gazed over the lake's calm waters; they could see the mountains and the lush, verdant forest in the distance.

"I was four years old," Tenzin began. "We travelled from Africa to a small village in India, where my grandparents lived. One day, I played with my friends on the streets. When it was lunchtime, I went home. In the courtyard, my mother had placed a bed against the wall. I thought it was a strange place to put a bed, so I went to see if it was broken.

"As I examined the bed, I noticed a tiny dog between the bed and the wall giving birth. I watched her give birth to three puppies. She was in a poor state, her ribs sticking out. She caught my gaze as I looked into her big, sad, lonely brown eyes.

"I continued to watch her, fascinated. I was curious. She was licking the puppies and cleaning them. Then she did something that made me feel sick." He paused. There were tears in his eyes.

Stefan was surprised to see this strong man shedding tears. "You don't have to continue."

"No, it's all right," he wiped the tears away. "The mother picked up and ate her firstborn puppy. I was shocked. I ran into the house, crying. My mother picked me up and cuddled me. I told her about the puppy. She placed me on the kitchen table and said the poor mother was alone. She was a street dog. She had no one in the world to look after her.

"She did what she had to do to survive, to give her other two puppies a chance to live. That is life, Son." Then she gave me some food to take to the mother."

Tenzin paused, his gaze wandering over the calm waters. "That event would change my perception of life, God, and our purpose in life. That night, I could not sleep. A slight noise woke me about the middle of the night. I saw the Master sitting at the end of my bed. Even at that early age, I knew **who He**[1] was.

"Sire," I said, "if this is all there is **to life**[2], I don't want to live in it." He got up and sat beside me.

"He kissed me on the forehead and said, "Help us, **little brother**[3] (son), to make a better world. One day, in the fullness of time, we will make a beautiful New World where a lion and a lamb will eat hay, and children will play with them. A world where there will be no more tears. Come follow in our steps."

---- ➤ ----

Bible (NKJV)	Bhagavad Gita
[1] Galatians 1:15, But when it pleased God, who separated me from my mother's womb and called me through His grace. [2] 2nd Timothy 1:9-14, who has saved us and called us with a holy calling, not according to our works, but according to His purpose and grace which was given to us in Christ Jesus before time began. Now revealed by the appearing of our Savior Jesus Christ, who has abolished death and brought life and immortality to light through the gospel. To which I was appointed a preacher, an apostle, and a teacher of the Gentiles. For this reason, I also suffer these things; nevertheless, I am not ashamed, for I know whom I have believed and am persuaded that He can keep what I have committed to Him until that Day. Hold fast the pattern of sound words you have heard from me, in faith and love which are in Christ Jesus.That good thing which was committed to you, keep by the Holy Spirit who dwells in us. Ps 71:6, Yes, you, O Lord, have been with me from birth; from my mother"s womb, you have cared for me. No wonder I am always	[1] 4:5. The Supreme Lord (Krishna) replied: I have often appeared to various generations in human forms. Unaware as you are, I have guided your Atman since your birth. [2] 2:7, I am confused. Both options before me are dishonourable. I need your wisdom, your divine guidance. I am your disciple, and I kneel before you. [3] 4:3. To a selected few, I revealed My existence and plans for eternity (past, present, and future worlds to come). ---X--

praising you!

³ Hebrews 2:11 For both He who sanctifies and those who are being sanctified are all of one, for which reason He is not ashamed to <u>call them brethren</u>,

  ---X--

The End

--------- ↢-------

The Cycle of the Cosmos

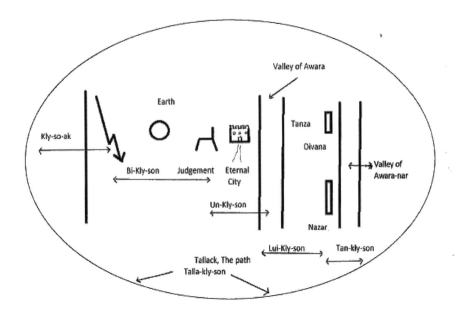

Tenets: Concepts or ways of thinking presented to the author by the individuals named; some have passed away into the hereafter.

Kly-son: A unique ability to see an event, be it in the past, present, or future, by an eyewitness. With this ability, one can perceive how a victim or perpetrator reacted during an event and gain insight into their thoughts, motives, desires, fears, or joy.

Kly-so-ak: The period before anything came into existence, pre-cosmos. A void, emptiness, and pure awareness give rise to thought, which turns into energy waves.

Bi-Kly-son: A vision gives rise to the formation of matter and anti-matter, a physical and spiritual universe, the Earth, life, evolution, sanctuaries, Judgement Day, and the Eternal City.

Un Kly-son: A period in the future, judgement. A new creation: Eternal

City (sacred cities).

Lui-Kly-son: Future, Eternal City, the Valley of Aware, Tanza, a time to expand knowledge and wisdom.

Divana and Nazar: Gateway to informed choice.

Tan-Kly-son: Aware-nar, end of time and space, informed choice to participate in the cosmic family.

Talla-Kly-son: The cycle of the cosmos, its search for purpose, meaning, and cost.

Tallack: The path. A spiritual way that one walks in the footsteps of the Lord, based on respect and awe for all living things. A bond between the person and the universe gives each person a purpose and motivation to live and create. Without it, beings eventually cease to have a meaning, purpose, and will to exist.

---- ♟ ----

 Authors print.

You can contact me at

harxpatel@gmail.com

Also by, Hari Patel

Bhagavad-Gita

Yoga Poses and Gita

Bhagavad-Gita and Bible; Duality

Following in the steps of Jesus

_____

Printed in Great Britain
by Amazon

33009338R00275